CITY OF SCREENS

CITY OF

SCREENS

IMAGINING AUDIENCES IN MANILA'S
ALTERNATIVE FILM CULTURE

JASMINE NADUA TRICE

DUKE UNIVERSITY PRESS   DURHAM AND LONDON   2021

© 2021 Duke University Press
All rights reserved

Cover designed by Drew Sisk
Text designed by Amy Ruth Buchanan
Typeset in Chaparral by Westchester Publishing Services

Library of Congress Cataloging-in-Publication Data
Names: Trice, Jasmine Nadua, [date] author.
Title: City of screens : imagining audiences in Manila's alternative film culture / Jasmine Nadua Trice.
Description: Durham : Duke University Press, 2021. | Includes bibliographical references and index.
Identifiers: LCCN 2020021680 (print)
LCCN 2020021681 (ebook)
ISBN 9781478010586 (hardcover)
ISBN 9781478011699 (paperback)
ISBN 9781478021254 (ebook)
Subjects: LCSH: Motion pictures—Philippines—Manila—Distribution. | Motion picture theaters—Philippines—Manila. | Independent films—Philippines—Manila. | Motion picture industry—Philippines—Manila.
Classification: LCC PN1993.5.P6 T753 2021 (print) | LCC PN1993.5.P6 (ebook) | DDC 791.4309599/16—dc23
LC record available at https://lccn.loc.gov/2020021680
LC ebook record available at https://lccn.loc.gov/2020021681

Cover art: Map of Metro Manila, Philippines, adapted from the author's website, cityofscreens.space. The interactive map charts film institutions, screening spaces, and film locations.

For my mom,

NANCY NADUA TRICE

CONTENTS

ACKNOWLEDGMENTS ix

INTRODUCTION 1

ONE. Revanchist Cinemas 39
and Bad Audiences, Multiplex
Fiestas and Ideal Publics

TWO. The Quiapo Cinematheque and 79
Urban-Cinematic Authenticity

THREE. Alternative Exhibition and 113
the Rhythms of the City

FOUR. "Not for Public Exhibition": 153
Cinema Regulation, Alternative
Cinema, and a Rational Body Politic

FIVE. "Hollywood Is Not Us": 189
National Circulation and
the Speculative State

EPILOGUE 230

NOTES 241

BIBLIOGRAPHY 281

INDEX 299

ACKNOWLEDGMENTS

This book was a collaborative project in many ways, and I am indebted to numerous readers and friends for their comments and advice. I would like to thank my cousins in Las Piñas, Metro Manila, especially RJ Vekka Nadua, for contacting me when I was a graduate student in Bloomington, Indiana, and spurring my interest in returning to the Philippines. When I arrived, I benefited from the care of the entire Nadua clan—Tito Bobie and Tita Estelle, Tito Butch and Tita Riza, and all the cousins: Toni, Frances, Patrick, Carlo, and Joan. As I settled into Quezon City, Aida Santos, Diego Maranan, and Kharen Surita made me feel like I had a family away from home. Aida's and Diego's generosity and commitments to both art and activism were a constant source of inspiration. Ed Maranan generously shared his insights when he was a member of the Film Development Council, and like many others, I was deeply saddened by his passing.

I owe much gratitude to my professional home in Manila, Isis International (now Io International). Isis had welcomed feminists from around the world for over two decades when I arrived, and I learned a great deal about feminist media activism in my time there. In particular, I'm grateful for the support of my friends and colleagues Danicar Mariano, Tesa De Vela, and Mira Ofreneo, who welcomed me into the People's Communications for Development project.

This book would not have happened if I hadn't met the pioneering film critic Alexis Tioseco early in my time in Manila. His enthusiasm for Philippine cinema was infectious, and film scenes around the region still feel the loss of him and his partner, Nika Bohinc.

My graduate school mentors, particularly Barbara Klinger, Greg Waller, and Joan Hawkins, were a crucial part of this project's early stages. My colleagues at the National University of Singapore, Paul Nerney, Bea Lorente, Anu Ramanujan, and Patrick Wade, offered feedback and support at a critical time. At UCLA, my students and colleagues have been an indispensable part of the project's growth—I am especially indebted to Victor Bascara, Karrmen Crey, Stephen Mamber, Purnima Mankekar, Kathleen McHugh, Chon Noriega, and Mila Zuo, who offered feedback on the manuscript in its early stages. I'm also very thankful that I get to work in the Cinema and Media Studies program alongside Ellen Scott, Steve Anderson, Shelleen Greene, Denise Mann, Veronica Paredes, and John Caldwell. It's my extreme good fortune that I have such inspiring colleagues. Roland Tolentino, José B. Capino, Mette Hjort, Virginia Crisp, and Bliss Cua Lim generously read the manuscript in progress, and their insights are a critical aspect of this work. At Duke, Elizabeth Ault's editorial insights have expertly guided this project down a long and winding road toward publication. I am also tremendously indebted to the four reviewers, whose perspectives have strengthened the work.

This project has also benefited from feedback provided at various presentations throughout its development. Participants at the Association for Southeast Asian Cinemas conferences have offered incisive commentary on different chapters over the years, especially Gaik Cheng Khoo and Mariam Lam. I have been grateful for invitations to present different aspects of this work at various venues, including the Film and Media Studies Department at the University of California, Santa Barbara; the East Asia Center at the University of Virginia; the Center for Southeast Asian Studies at the University of California, Berkeley; the Asian Film and Media Initiative at New York University; the University of the Philippines Film Institute; the Department of Communication Arts at De La Salle University; and the Kritika Kultura Lecture Series at Ateneo de Manila University. The commentary at these events has helped me see the work in new ways. Funding from the Asian Cultural Council, the Association for University Women, the UCLA Faculty Career

Development Award, a Hellman Fellowship, and the TFT Dean's Vision Fund Award have been an indispensable part of this project.

For their support throughout all aspects of my life, I am thankful for my friends and family. Sarah Sinwell and Natasha Ritsma have been essential readers and sounding boards. Christina Davis has helped L.A. feel like home. I'm thankful to Harmon and Libbi Brown for their ongoing encouragement. My parents, Nancy and David Trice, and my brother, sister-in-law, and niece—Chris, Pamela, and Emmy Trice—are a constant source of laughter and well-being. And finally, I am continually grateful for my partner in all things, David Brown.

INTRODUCTION

In 2008, the young, Manila-based critic Alexis Tioseco published a list titled "Wishful Thinking for Philippine Cinema" on his widely read blog. Tioseco's blog and his online magazine of Southeast Asian film criticism, *Criticine*, had become hubs of speculative discourse for the new Philippine film scene that had taken shape over the past several years. Since the turn of the millennium, the rise of digital production technologies and informal DVD and VCD circulation had led to a resurgence of films produced outside the domestic media conglomerates that had long been the primary source of mass entertainment. These films played primarily in international festival circuits, and Tioseco's wish list for this burgeoning scene focused on ways to bring them home. It included a "pure film studies" course, audience education, calls for more criticism of local cinema, a journal, more support for "regional" filmmakers outside the capital city, government-sponsored DVD releases of classical Philippine films, and a film library.¹ Describing the state's Film Development Council, Tioseco wrote, "They support filmmakers with finished films to go abroad to festivals for the pride they bring their country—I wish instead they would support their films locally, and help them get seen by a larger Filipino audience."² A commenter based in the Philippines but outside the capital replied, "Add one more: I wish the films of Martin, Diaz, de la Cruz, Torres, and all the others had at least a minimal distribution network, so that those of us that are not located in Manila can actually see the works you mention."[3] In this wishful vision, local makers produce films, local channels circulate them, discerning audiences see them, and thoughtful viewers write about them. This projected Philippine film culture would, ostensibly, require audiences *in* the Philippines.

When I moved to Manila in 2006, Philippine films were just beginning to make their mark on the international festival circuit. As a newcomer, the suggestions I received most frequently were those that marked the profound cultural and technological shifts in the city's cinema cultures. The two I heard most had to do with sites of film circulation. The first recommendation was that I look at Alexis's online magazine, *Criticine*.[4] The second was that I visit Quiapo, where I would find one of the city's oldest Catholic cathedrals and its biggest Muslim mosque, surrounded by a thriving maze of street vendors selling pirated DVDs. My initial research intentions focused on the city's mall multiplexes, but as I encountered the range of alternative film exhibition and distribution sites sprouting across the cityscape, they eventually became quite different. I can trace their transformation to these two foundational suggestions. Alexis generously familiarized me with the growing independent film scene that had taken shape over the previous couple of years. He screened films at his Quezon City home, due to a scarcity of independent screening spaces in the city, and he introduced me to filmmakers. Meanwhile, visiting Quiapo illuminated how the culture of piracy itself was becoming a valued aspect of Philippine cinemagoing, feeding nationalist narratives of local ingenuity and greater access to world cinema. Each in their own ways, these two recommendations were informal compensation for infrastructural shortcomings, and they captured the transformations of Manilenyo film culture in the early 2000s. The young cinephile's work and the informal DVD district were both hubs of the city's cinema circulation. They introduced me to a dynamic film culture undergoing major transformations.

But the wish for domestic audiences reflected in Alexis's list was not an easy matter.[5] Upon their return home from their festival runs, the films that had been so quickly welcomed into the annals of "world cinema" would have much more difficulty becoming a "national cinema" in anything other than prescriptive, top-down terms.[6] The city's ubiquitous mall multiplexes had little commercial incentive to play these films, regardless of whatever international distinction they had accrued. In the early-aughts moment of Philippine cinema's revival, other exhibition possibilities were scarce. Filmmaker Redd Ochoa spoke to a Philippine newspaper from the 2007 Montreal World Film Festival, where his feature, *Baliw* (Insane), screened in the festival's "Focus on World Cinema" section alongside two other Filipino films, Brillante Mendoza's *Foster Child* and Neal Tan's *Ataul* (*Casket for Rent*).[7] Ochoa noted that local circulation had proven to be a more difficult issue: "Only a handful of movie theaters in the Philippines show independent films. . . . Finding a venue to play a low-budget film in Manila is like looking for a needle in a haystack."[8] This was an aspiring national cinema without a national audience.

Perhaps no aspect of film culture is more common than an internationally lauded art cinema's absent national audience.[9] But despite, or perhaps because of this ordinariness, this absence has not generated a great deal of academic analysis. Methodologically, both art and independent cinemas are most often approached through examining texts or institutions of production rather than the vagaries of circulation and collective reception. But these matters of circulation and its limits define particular film cultures, often in inconspicuous ways. Similar rhetorics, spaces, and practices of circulation and reception gather art, independent, and other marginal cinemas under the broader rubric of alternative film culture. Urban networks comprise such film cultures, shaped by shared values and formed through the production and consumption of both films and film discourse. Shared values include distance from the mainstream film industry (a rhetorical touchstone constituted through its positioning within the local industrial structure and discourse) and an aspirational approach to cinema's place in public culture. I use the term "aspirational" because many of the works associated with such film cultures hold an uncertain place in relation to national and local distribution and exhibition channels. There has been fascinating work on the politics of *trans*national circulation and the kinds of global south films that festivals produce and exhibit.[10] As scholars have observed, these films often mediate social problems through a focus on representations of working-class, poor, or rural communities.[11] Debates around these films point to a combination of representational excess and domestic absence—these were films whose publics existed primarily outside national borders. Emerging largely from the growing body of research in film festival studies, scholarship in this area has focused on the transnational infrastructures that have brought these films into being.[12]

Focusing on problems of exhibition and distribution, I train my critical lens on what happens when films and their makers return home. Rather than seeing national and transnational cinemas in opposition to one another, I view them as mutually defining concepts that map onto localized debates about taste, class, and culture.[13] Often, these debates take shape in the urban, metropolitan centers that act as national gateways for transnational cultural goods, where dominant versions of national culture are shaped and disseminated. The chapters track practices of film circulation as they take shape within a specific space and time in Metro Manila, Philippines, from 2005 to 2012. I emphasize these years because they are rich with speculative discourse about what this nascent, urban film culture might become. The year 2005 saw the founding of two key funding and festival institutions, Cinemalaya and Cinema One Originals. The book ends in 2012, with the rise of the term "maindie," a portmanteau of "mainstream" and "independent."

I refer to this seven-year window as the "transition period" to indicate its specificity as a moment of technological, institutional, and cultural transformation within the film scene. Digital forms of production and dissemination were novel, their low cost providing new opportunities for alternative filmmaking. In later years, streaming, social media, and smartphones became ubiquitous among the city's middle class, and media texts were less moored to the physical object of circulation (VCDs and DVDs). In contrast, these early-aughts digital tools were anchored within material forms, thereby locating them within urban space. The era marks a precise, transitional moment for considering media circulation and the cultivation of a film culture through urban networks, public spaces, and discourse.

The chapters examine film circulation projects and initiatives, analyzing the discourses that surround their founding, operations, and, frequently, their closures. These initiatives often lived short lives, and new ones emerged to take their place. This ongoing cycle became a constitutive part of Manila's alternative film culture, an ephemeral counterpoint to the endurance of neoliberalism in the megacity where these projects struggled to take root. I analyze these initiatives' empirical operations, as well as the speculative rhetorics that surrounded them. Often, these speculative rhetorics envisioned these spaces of distribution and exhibition as sites for cultivating ideal film publics.

This distance between a prospective, ideal public and its actualized historical operations offers a productive point of engagement for one of the key tensions underpinning alternative cinema. Like other cultural forms, film is rooted in taste cultures, working as part of a system of social reproduction.[14] Alternative films' circulation is limited, conferring status on a rarefied viewership; at the same time, such films are often radical in their form and modes of production. Scholars of independent and art cinemas have long pointed to the contradiction between the putative oppositionality of formal experimentation and "artisanal" production, versus the tendencies for these kinds of works to circulate within a narrow social stratum.[15] This impasse is the foundation of any alternative film culture located in class-divided social settings. In the global south, the ways that domestic social divisions align with transnational cultural flows are especially charged. Rather than avoiding these contradictions, *City of Screens* aims to advance a critical framework for alternative cinema cultures that encompasses these paradoxes. Through analyzing a range of film circulation projects, this book confronts that contradiction, viewing this lack of consensus about alternative films' social status as a constitutive aspect of alternative film cultures. My hope is that acknowledging and animating these contradictions will frame them not as shortcomings but as signals of alternative film culture's vitality. I do not wish to simply affirm that cinemas of varying formal and aesthetic traditions circulate within different industrial and institutional channels to address publics of various kinds. Rather, I am interested in the conceptual possibilities offered through the frictions among these discourses and in how these contradictions evolved in the moment of a particular cinema's emergence, framing film circulation as a critical problem.

To understand how this contradiction between alternative films' radicalism and elitism might operate within Manila and perhaps also in other, similar urban centers, I find revisionist critiques of modernity and the public sphere useful for the ways that they have dealt with the contradictory incompleteness of publicity. As Bruce Robbins argues in his concept of the "phantom public sphere," publics are both necessary and impossible.[16] This phenomenon is especially conspicuous in the global south, where scholars have discussed publics as fractured along class and ethnic lines. Working from the premise of publics' necessary impossibility, I am interested in cinemagoing as both material and ideal—both a phenomenological experience and an ideal aspiration, constructed through projects and spaces of film circulation as well as the rhetorics surrounding them.

The chapters that follow offer a temporally bounded, spatial archive of alternative film culture in early-2000s Manila. They map a wide range of spaces that acted as outposts for alternative film circulation during that historical moment, including multiplex theaters, the informal DVD market, microcinemas, a university film institute, and state-owned national cinematheques. The rhetorics surrounding each site's establishment, operations, and eventual dissolution raise questions about the commerce of alternative cinemas, the values ascribed to them, and the potential audiences that they might reach, project, or exclude. Taken together, these sites form a shifting constellation of alternative cinema networks and publics, both realized and prospective, mapped across an unevenly developed city. Through this cartography, this book offers a model for understanding alternative film cultures in the Philippines' postmillennial transition period, a model whose underpinning propositions may apply in other settings with homologous levels of socioeconomic division and similarly complex relationships to transnational culture. It proposes that alternative cinema's publics are speculative. Their speculative, ideal form is a product of this cinema's inherent contradictions. Hence, alternative film culture is ultimately asymptotic: it is an ongoing trajectory, moving toward an ever-advancing horizon. Film circulation becomes the engine of this trajectory, as organizers seek to expand their domestic audiences.

These audiences had not always been so elusive. From the rise of the midcentury studio system to the 1970s, film was the most popular form of mass entertainment in the Philippines, which led to the colloquial idea of cinema as the "national pastime."[17] The art-house films that drew international accolades during the martial law period of the 1970s and 1980s included films that resonated with local audiences, such as *City after Dark* (dir. Ishmael Bernal, 1980) and *Himala* (dir. Ishmael Bernal, 1982).[18] But by the post-martial-law period of the 1990s, the film industry had declined due to numerous infrastructural problems.[19] By 1996, production levels plummeted following a government-instated 10 percent value-added tax on gross receipts, added to the 23 percent municipal amusement tax, which many in the film industry blamed for causing financial strain.[20] In 1998, the Philippine Motion Picture Producers Association (PMPPA) and the Movie Producers Distributors Association of the Philippines (MPDAP) released a statement addressing the "precarious state" of the local industry, pointing to several factors: exorbitant taxes, escalating production costs, competition from foreign films, censorship, piracy, high-cost star salaries, and cable television.[21] Due to rising taxes and production costs, it became cheaper to import Hollywood films than to make local ones. While numerous bills were introduced to curb the import of foreign films, none became law.[22] As the local industry declined, the Hollywood distribution system strengthened, and new releases began opening contemporaneously across such film capitals as Los Angeles, Tokyo, and Sydney.[23] Not incidentally, the 1990s also saw the Philippines' accelerated integration into the global economy through the Ramos administration's "neoliberal revolution."[24] The exhibition sector began to change as malls remade Philippine cityscapes, eventually becoming the primary film exhibitors.

Exhibition played a critical factor in the changing industry, pointing to the significance of film circulation and prospective film consumption in Philippine cinema imaginaries. Exhibitors began to play a part in the kinds of films being produced and the audiences associated with them. Here, a particular kind of industrial ethnicizing became clear, demarcating the lines between mass audiences and mainstream film producers. The Metro Manila Theater Association (MMTA) and the Greater Manila Theaters Association controlled the majority of film distribution. In his overview of cinema in the 1990s, Nicanor Tiongson describes the "mafia-type control of movie distribution by the two groups of Chinese businessmen," who instated a booking system that some critics viewed as a reason for the decline in production.[25] The two organizations controlled Metro Manila's two hundred movie theaters by 1996, deciding which films would be exhibited; whether they would play in first-, second-, or third-class cinemas; and which would be pulled before their booking ended.[26] Theater owners increased their share of profits, taking over a third of a film's total earnings.[27] They also invested in movie production to ensure a return on investment, creating a self-sustaining feedback loop between production and exhibition.[28] As Tiongson writes in 1994, "Unfortunately, producers continue to use the audience as an excuse for making only popular films. They say that they only give what the audience wants. Moviegoers' tastes and preferences are identified for them by bookers and owners of big theater chains who continually analyze the market for Filipino films. . . . These considerations become paramount when profit-oriented producers make their movies."²⁹ The assessments of "Chinese businessmen" as risk averse and profit minded evoke long-standing stereotypes that associate the Philippines' Chinese community with capital and commerce.³⁰ Such images shifted in tone and scope from the twentieth to the twenty-first centuries, from "pariah capitalist" to liberal "middle-classes" and "entrepreneur."³¹ Nonetheless, the maligned configuration of Filipino masses, mainstream foreign or domestic films, and Chinese businessmen persists in ethnicized imaginaries of the industry.³²

As this history suggests, concepts of "Philippine cinema" include visions of its audience—the speculative publics that emerge in public discourse within specific historical moments, mediating cinema's relationship to class, ethnicity, and ideas of locality. Controlled largely by national conglomerates, exhibition and distribution became a critical aspect of this construction. The mainstream industry's gradual decline reached a head in the early 2000s, falling from the usual two hundred to about fifty films produced per year in 2004.³³ An opportunity to restructure the Philippine cinema opened, made possible in part through the advent of low-cost, digital technologies for production and distribution outside the studio system, often vis-à-vis international festival circuits hungry for fresh content.

Dubbed "independents" in popular press coverage, the proportion of these films increased steadily during this period, going from 24 percent of locally produced films in 2005 to 34 percent by 2011.³⁴ As scholars and critics pointed out, these films' independence was nominal, as much of this initial output flowed from two festivals with ties to corporate media conglomerates: Cinemalaya and Cinema One. Founded in 2005, Cinemalaya—a festival, foundation, and conference—provides yearly "seed investments" to filmmakers (PHP 500,000, or approximately $10,000), based on script submissions.³⁵ The films debut at the state Cultural Center of the Philippines, a modernist, waterfront venue developed as a project of Imelda Marcos.³⁶ Until 2014, Cinemalaya's funding came largely from the media tycoon Antonio "Tonyboy" Cojuangco, who initially intended to use the films as programming for his video-on-demand channel.³⁷ Meanwhile, the Cinema One Originals festival began the same year. Involving a similar script-submission process, the festival is produced through the Filipino cable network Cinema One, owned by ABS-CBN. Nonetheless, the films it produces are sometimes far from conventional. For example, Sherad Anthony Sanchez's digital work, *Imburnal* (Sewer), tells a story of coming of age amid violence and poverty in a four-hour, "slow cinema" format. As one *Hollywood Reporter* review from the Hong Kong Film Festival described, "Asian, human rights, and avant-garde focused festivals are sure bets, but theatrical release is almost out of the question, even at home. . . . [The] film isn't without merit, but ultimately [it] alienates viewers."[38] The parameters of this new cinema were heterogeneous and contradictory, existing at the edges of the commercial media infrastructure. For this reason, I use the term "alternative" to describe the films under discussion in this book. The term points to the relational quality of the designation, while forgoing claims of autonomy from other media infrastructures.

Although the share of alternative films rose during this initial period, the financial feasibility of the film industry as a whole remained unstable. A Philippine Statistics Authority study released in 2012 stated that only two of the top ten highest-grossing films of all time were Philippine produced (*The Unkabogable Praybeyt Benjamin* [*The Unbeatable Private Benjamin*], dir. Wenn Deramas, 2011; *No Other Woman*, dir. Ruel S. Bayani, 2011).[39] Both were from the studio Star Cinema—the others were Hollywood blockbusters. While, certainly, alternative films might prioritize a different kind of economy, the idea of the domestic audience remained an implicit part of many of these works. The concern with audience and viewership became particularly evident when investigating the spaces and events developed to exhibit and distribute them. Sites of exhibition, distribution, and consumption became primary sites for envisioning circulation and the publics that these paths might imply. These visions offered speculative images of Philippine film culture in the early-aughts transition period, a moment when many exhibition and distribution initiatives hoped to overcome alternative cinema's inherent contradictions.

Speculative Publics and Alternative Film Cultures

Speculative publics are the visions of audience that promised to overcome these contradictions between radical texts and rarefied audiences. Evoking speculative fiction, the term suggests the fantastic, prospective dimensions of alternative cinema enterprises. In literary studies, speculative fiction contends with the "moral and ethical demands of worlds to come."[40] But the term "speculation" also has a history in finance, locating the concept of speculative publics within the recent history of neoliberalism. Theorists have responded to the concept's economic variation with their own treatises. For example, the Uncertain

Commons group published a 2013 manifesto, arguing, "More and more, it seems, the future is imported into the present, bundled up, sold off, instrumentalized. Some eagerly buy into these futures markets, placing their bets; others imagine things differently. All in all, nothing more than speculation and nothing less."[41] It may seem far afield to apply this mode of speculation to the small-scale art scenes under discussion here. But the term is not just economic; it is also cognitive and affective. While its economic application refers to the structures of late capitalism, speculation can also mean "to contemplate, to ponder, and hence to form conjectures, to make estimations and projections, to look into the future so as to hypothesize."[42] The current preoccupation with how to predict and fix the future is a specifically modern form of speculation that pathologizes uncertainty; as an antidote, the authors of the manifesto offer the term "affirmative speculation," a practice that "embraces uncertainty and, in so doing, remains responsive to difference, to unanticipated contingencies."[43] Roughly put, speculation describes both a structure and a form of agency, referencing the dialectic between infrastructural crisis and possible alternatives to the upheaval it wreaks.

I find the polysemy of the term "speculation" fitting. Its more dystopian connotations describe the environment in which alternative film movements emerged across Southeast Asia: the 1997 financial crisis caused by the speculative property market. These film movements arose in urban metro areas that neoliberalism had transformed with the construction of malls, office towers, and luxury condominium high-rises.[44] In the Philippines, this crisis was the culmination of a longer history that began with post–World War II economic policy, continued with the structural-adjustment programs imposed by the World Bank in the 1980s, and was consolidated under the Ramos administration in the 1990s.[45] Rooted in economic policy endorsed by the International Monetary Fund (IMF), the crisis spread across the region, marking the end of the "East Asian regime" of accumulation enabled through "developmental states."[46] Currency devaluation, unemployment, and bank closures followed, pushing millions into poverty across the region; the crisis was a devastating product of the chaos created through neoliberal policy.[47]

As Wendy Brown argues in her analysis of neoliberalism, this kind of chaos indicates a turn from calculation to speculation: "Financialization changes markets from predictable reactions to supply, demand, and price into markets where speculation is the driving dynamic— from interest to gambling, from stability to instability, from following the crowd to shorting it. . . . And it is very easy to crash."[48] The Southeast Asian independent film scenes unfolded in an environment characterized by instability and possibility. The term speculation points to these two kinds of potential, offered in both fictional aspirations and in the chaotic quest for profit.

If one side of speculation points to the possibilities of alternative film culture, the other points to its open-ended structure, arguing that alternative film culture's ever-receding end point is the ability to overcome its inherent paradoxes. The impossibility of overcoming these contradictions should not be seen as failure but as a constitutive part of alternative film culture's speculative structure. In this way, alternative film cultures are an asymptotic process; their speculative publics are an aspiration they cannot meet. Their circuitous movement toward this infinitely receding horizon shapes and defines them. In using the term "asymptotic," I adapt and revise a mathematical model, in which an asymptote is "a line which approaches nearer and nearer to a given curve, but does not meet it within a finite distance."[49] The model reflects both utopian and dystopian possibilities. In a more utopic view, it works as a microcosmic parallel to theories of radical democracy that posit democracy as always yet to come, never to be achieved but vital to seek.[50] Idealistic filmmakers and activists work to build institutions that will support the production and dissemination of films, creating a subjunctive, "would-be" projection of an alternative film culture. Within this projection, that film culture is economically sustainable and widely accessible. From another perspective, this ever-receding horizon mirrors the progressivist discourse of modernity—it offers a view of modernity's universalizing drive, positioning the possible publics of alternative film culture in a pedagogical relation to the agents of cultural production.

In the Philippines, mass audiences' crucial roles in political history connect screen media to broader questions about the possibilities of social transformation. If, as Chantal Mouffe contends, the political is predicated on "the always-to-be-achieved construction of a bounded yet heterogeneous, unstable and necessarily antagonistic 'we,'" grappling with how paradoxical alternative film cultures articulate various versions of this "we" reveals the problem of circulation—distribution, exhibition, and the dissemination of discourse—as a critical aspect of alternative cinemas.[51] This approach opens a useful arsenal of analytic tools. It enables me to engage frameworks that are well trodden in cinema and media studies, such those used in relation to national, transnational, art, and independent cinemas, and to combine them with a range of critical perspectives located in other fields, such as rhetoric, urban studies, geography, and anthropology. Through this interdisciplinary attention to cinema's social life, I aim to better understand the impasse of alternative cinema's limited circulation. Oscillating between material practices and speculation, cinema circulation initiatives offer a productive window onto this largely unacknowledged dimension of film cultures.

Asymptotic film cultures and speculative publics are not normative categories. Rather, the concepts offer a critical framework for theorizing the contradictions of alternative cinema in the global south, taking the heightened contentions around the absent mass audience as their premise. These contentions underscore the importance of film circulation as an aspect of such settings' diverse modernities. As Brian Larkin observes in his work on cinema in Nigeria, since the late nineties, Frankfurt-school-influenced cinema studies research has defined its object in terms of time ("early cinema," "new media"); however, it is also important to consider the medium across spatial and temporal difference.[52] A few works have taken on this project, including Bhaskar Sarkar and Joshua Neves in their groundbreaking anthology *Asian Video Cultures*, which theorizes Asian video practices as "penumbral," underscoring "the indelible presence of local cosmologies and practices in the mediation of globalities—distinctively local aspects that can never be fully subsumed within any universal imagination."[53] Focusing on peripheral video practices conducted in the vein of "making do" rather than vanguardist interventions into media culture, they observe, "Some of the most exhilarating instances of creativity appear when the fetish of creativity is abandoned in the throes of quotidian life."[54] *Asian Video Cultures* sits alongside other recent works in media studies (e.g., Brian Larkin's *Signal and Noise*, Ravi Sundaram's *Pirate Modernity*, Jeff Himpele's *Circuits of Culture*) whose theories of film and video cultures in sites such as Nigeria, India, and Bolivia offer compelling challenges to modernity's dominant ideologies of teleology, development, progress, and creative authorship. Instead, each of these works is grounded in the structures of media circulation, situating media forms within larger, localized urban networks. Unlike these works, however, *City of Screens* focuses primarily on the kinds of films and urban art scenes that modernist visions of culture would deem legitimate. This focus is not meant to privilege these works as worthier of study than their more commercial, mainstream variations. Rather, it is meant to demystify alternative cinemas by positioning them as components of larger sociocultural and institutional structures.

City of Screens maps cinema onto larger discussions about the incompleteness of modernities in the global south, offering the Philippines as a case study. It is important to note, however, that while modernity's incompleteness is more debated and perhaps more visible in the global south, it is an inherent aspect of modernities everywhere. In an argument that evokes the impasse of alternative cinemas, Susan Buck-Morss contends that the globalized public sphere gave rise to several paradoxes, among them a paradox between democratic egalitarianism and political elitism. As she writes, a "contradiction that needs to be considered in regard to the unfinished modern project is the tension between democracy in its radically egalitarian form and social hierarchies that exclude democratic participation."[55] Undoubtedly, her argument addresses a much larger scale. But it also applies to the cultural forms that refract larger political and social structures. While this impasse exists in any social setting, its cultural and political significance rises in conjunction with levels of social inequality. In Manila, these hierarchies are spatialized. As Rolando Tolentino argues, Metro Manila's overdevelopment, especially through the malls that house the majority of the city's cinemas, involves "the construction of an ideal transnational space housing everything within one roof; the franchisement of middle class entertainment and culture . . . and a trope for discussing gentrification in a social formation where seventy percent of the people live below the poverty level."[56] As Tolentino and others have written, Manila's urban space reflects and creates the city's social divisions. In contexts where a minority of middle-class intellectuals carries the bulk of the cultural power, the question of the mass audience is especially charged. Here, that audience holds a different political and cultural place than it does in societies where media availability and mass consumption are more easily equated with the loss of artistic authenticity and integrity.[57]

Circulation and (Inter)national Cinema

To understand how the frictions between absent/aspirational audiences and putatively national cinemas might work in settings like Manila, it is useful to look at how the figure of the mass audience fits into discussions of Philippine public culture. In its early years, the works variously called the Philippine New Wave, New Filipino Cinema, and

Philippine indie cinema circulated largely within a transnational institutional infrastructure, joining other Southeast Asian cinemas that flourished with the rise of digital production.[58] Film festival funding, distribution, and awards welcomed these films into an ostensibly decentered web of world cinema flows.[59] Because of these cosmopolitan trajectories, the politics of location became crucial to establishing these films' meanings within local settings, as critics and makers in the Philippines debated the stakes of domestic audiences. Rosalind Galt and Karl Schoonover observe that "global art cinema" maintains an "ambivalent relationship to location."[60] As they describe, art cinema is a "resolutely international category," defined through institutional context rather than text; even films considered popular cinema domestically sometimes become "art cinema" when circulated abroad.[61] This locational ambivalence also works domestically. Films considered "national cinema" abroad become "foreign art cinema" at home, despite the location of their production or the biographies of their makers. In this way, circulation becomes a controversial aspect of these works' definition; the question of which audiences films reach shapes how various publics understand them. In an often-cited 2006 essay that works to define world cinema in ways that go beyond "not Hollywood," Lúcia Nagib concludes that world cinema "has no centre. It is not the other, but it is us. It has no beginning and no end, but is a global process. World cinema, as the world itself, is circulation."[62] Written at the height of critical reassessments of the national cinema framework, the essay is a compelling call for flexible geographies that cut across films and movements. But this macroperspective's utopian view of a world cinema "us" can also be exclusionary, an unscalable model of cinema circulation that has limited reach. Examining domestic patterns of circulation and obstruction provides another view of world cinema's operations, one that is not always visible from large-scale perspectives.

As Philippine independent films crossed national borders to be feted by an international elite, they became tidily Filipino, aligning with the national identity ascribed to them. When they returned home, matters of class, taste, and culture refracted any easy labels. In a show-business magazine, the entertainment journalist Edgar O. Cruz wrote of the three Filipino films playing in the 2009 Cannes festival, critiquing their transnationalism, "Are the three films in the newly opened Cannes International Film Festival to be held in Cannes, France from May 13 to 24 a triumph for Pinoy movies? Perhaps to Pinoy moviemakers who are hanged up on the Gallic ambition. It looks to this writer as more like a French triumph than a Pinoy victory."[63] Cruz claimed that international programmers were inclined to screen the three films because of the works' histories of European funding and crew members.[64] Raya Martin's *Independencia* was selected for the Un Certain Regard section, while *Maynila*—a tribute to second-golden-age directors Lino Brocka and Ishmael Bernal that Martin codirected with Adolf Alix—screened out of competition. Brillante Mendoza's *Kinatay* screened in competition, going on to win Mendoza the festival's award for best director. Martin himself seemed aware of the kind of critique leveled by Cruz. Comparing their comments reveals competing discourses of cinema and nation. In a 2010 interview, Martin aligned national identity not with location but with his own authorship as director:

> When making my films, I don't necessarily ask myself whether this is Pinoy enough, or how this will impact the Philippines. My films are like mirrors I portray parts of myself on. As much as possible, I try my best to portray those parts of myself accurately and honestly. I'm Filipino. That's what makes my films Filipino. Not the wardrobe, not where I shot it. You can shoot a film in fucking Cavite [a province south of Manila] but if its ideology and sensibility is Western, then it isn't a Filipino film. But Lav Diaz can shoot a film in New Jersey and it will still be very, very Filipino.[65]

Martin asserts a deterritorialized version of cinema's cultural identity, based on adherence to a personal "ideology and sensibility"; it is an authorship-driven, textually based model. Meanwhile, Cruz's charges of cultural inauthenticity are based largely on contextual matters, constructing a vision of nationally produced images he sees as "contaminated" by transnational labor, finance, and reception. Martin's cinematographer for *Independencia* was Jeanne Lapoirie, a French director of photography known for working on such art-house films as François Ozon's *8 Women* (2002). Martin received €120,000 through the French Ministry of Foreign and European Affairs' Fonds Sud Cinema grant, which focuses on "supporting cultural diversity in world cinema" by funding filmmakers from the global south.[66] Meanwhile, Mendoza's work was funded by the producer Didier Costet's Paris-based Swift Productions. Such trajectories of finance and personnel are essential for filmmakers working in contexts where there is relatively little domestic support for the arts. But because these transnational collaborations involve distribution and exhibition as well as production, local critics sometimes see them as suspect, regardless of how necessary such border-crossing partnerships are.

Following the article's release, Cruz published praise for his self-described "exposé" online, though the extent to which this positive reception is representative is unclear. One director who offered kudos for Cruz's assessment of the Cannes films was Redd Ochoa. Maintaining that his remarks were not based on suspicion of other filmmakers' achievements, Ochoa commented, "I believe that it's not until we find success in our own soil that we'll be able to win the rat race that's brought forth to us by these competitions."[67] This comment highlights the contradictions that structure alternative cinema's role within public culture. Moreover, to a certain degree, these debates position filmmakers against audiences, a highly charged prospect in a context where the stakes of the mass audience connect to histories of political struggle.

As the debates involving Cruz and Martin suggest, the question of the mass audience is intensified within settings in the global south, where it is often seen as the locus of cultural authenticity and national possibility. While visions of mass audiences abound in many settings, in the Philippines such visions have long histories, connected to the ongoing process of nation building. A few years before the rebirth of alternative filmmaking was in full swing, a 2001 review by scholar Charlie Samuya Veric, published in the *Philippine Star* newspaper, put forward a notion of viewership, nation, and alternative film that laments an absent mass audience. Writing about Kidlat Tahimik's watershed 1977 experimental film, *Perfumed Nightmare*, Veric argues that problems of circulation undercut the film's revolutionary potential. Critics in the Philippines and beyond view the film as a landmark of Third Cinema. But Veric observes that its points of transmission are clandestine and cloistered; even when it reaches that most "mass" medium—the television—critics use opaque language to discuss it. The resulting image is one of a film culture fractured along class lines:

> How can a film be so revolutionary when only a small circle of well-perfumed aesthetes and pompous academicians have watched the film and talked about it among themselves? [The scholar E.] San Juan [Jr.] correctly remarks that Tahimik's films are "mainly viewed and appreciated by a Western metropolitan audience." As far as I can remember, the last time *Perfumed Nightmare* was shown on popular

TV programming was years ago in celebration of cinema's 100 years. (Was it at 11 p.m. when half of the viewers were already snoring?) This is the sadness of our cinema: the best of our movies are seen by the least of our people. Such isolation is made even more pronounced by critics whose discussion of a popular film is mediated by a language that a populace may find totally ungraspable, if not impossible. How can a revolution happen in a secret movie theater frequented by a coterie of critics speaking the most mysterious language?[68]

Veric's assessment is a common one. Philippine cinema's "sadness" is its stalled circulation, its struggle to reach broader publics within the nation rather than the "Western metropolitan audience."[69] As several critics and filmmakers have noted, the question of the mass audience remains critical within Philippine film culture. Like Veric, many filmmakers have used historically resonant terms such as "revolution" to describe the transition to digital technology; similarly, the term "feudal" has been a reference to the mainstream film industry.[70] While new digital technologies suggested new freedom for film*makers*, the revolution of film *audiences* remained prospective, as Veric notes. Read within the context of Philippine history, these debates around revolution and the cinema's potential role within it suggest the asymptotic nature of alternative film cultures, mapping the role of cinema within incomplete, always-impending modernities.

Mass Audiences

As these debates suggest, the mass audience holds a critical place in discussions of Philippine alternative cinemas, one that differs from its place in contexts such as the United States and United Kingdom. As scholars in those settings have recognized, the paradox of alternative cinemas lies in the disparity between the radicalism of the text and the narrowness of those texts' patterns of distribution, exhibition, and reception. This perspective pivots on notions of the audience as market, circulation as commerce, and commerce as corruption. But as the discussions above imply, this paradox works differently in the Philippines, where the mass audience is not as easily aligned with a loss of artistic integrity. The accounts above suggest connections between mass audiences and histories of revolutionary nationalism, which makes them difficult to dismiss as simple populism.

This notion of national collectivity has a complex history in studies of Filipino society; as in many other settings, it is an incomplete, perhaps impossible project. I aim to reorient the parameters of discussion a bit, to move away from the idea that a lack of collectivity at the national scale is necessarily preferable to more small-scale, short-term forms of communal association. I see the asymptotic model as an imperfect means of theorizing how film organizing might work, given the histories of colonization and more recent conditions of neoliberalism that have structured much of Philippine society. Many have written about the complexity of "imagining community" across the diverse classed, ethnic, and linguistic cultures constituting the Philippine archipelago. The sociologist Randy David links this problematic to the legacy of colonization, arguing that despite the Philippines' status as "the first modern republic in Asia," the country has not yet established a functioning democracy, and the state has failed to win the people's trust. David questions the idea of national collective identity.[71] He and other scholars argue that moral identities draw from family and broad kinship structures rather than externally imposed institutions.[72]

It may be useful to view these debates on the supposed failure of national community in light of theories that view failure as an inevitable outcome of capitalism and neoliberalism.[73] As Jack Halberstam notes, the market economy necessitates winners and losers, gambles and risks.[74] Within this context, failure is inevitable; but for marginalized communities, it can become a means of rejecting pragmatism and refusing to submit to dominant models of power.[75] Those with limited resources can exploit failure to work against disciplinary logics, using it to avoid institutional legibility.[76] This work finds some parallels in research on Philippine societies. The anthropologist Charles J-H Macdonald, for instance, argues that common understandings of Philippine society's personalistic values, lack of public consciousness, and randomness, ordinarily understood as its "uncrystallized" nature, are actually instances of the "anarchic harmony" common to many indigenous peoples of Southeast Asia.[77] Offering vastly diverse accounts of failure (urban/rural, Anglo-European / Southeast Asian), these theories map certain kinds of absence within a broader narrative of life within a capitalist social order. A lack of national community, an absent national audience—these supposed failures are inexorable within the conditions of late modernity, not just in the Philippines but in many settings. The idea of an asymptotic film culture is meant to acknowledge the inevitability of these absences. Within this context, the aim of a national audience for alternative cinema may likely fall short, but it will continue to cultivate collective aspirations, raising productive debates about culture, identities, and audiences. While I have reservations about ascribing deliberate "resistance" to the volatility of local film scenes, I appreciate how theories of failure frame this volatility as the outcome of broader political-economic conditions. As suggested in writings on the nature of national community in the Philippines, the issue of collective unity has initiated much debate in studies of Philippine culture, as a key dilemma connected to the instability of the nation-state and the legacy of colonization. The idea of extrafamilial collectivity within Filipino culture is a controversial topic, linked to the question of whether a broad "Filipino culture" as such can exist in a normative way.[78] Obviously, my work here addresses much smaller-scale, urban art enclaves. But when filmmakers lament their work's inaccessibility to larger audiences, their comments evoke these histories.

Discourses on the mass audience reflect these long-standing debates about nation building, and the problem of circulation becomes similarly critical. In her rejection of the bourgeois, hegemonic "imagined community," Neferti Tadiar argues for a revolutionary, antagonistic form of nationalism, distinguishing between ideas of "the people," which includes the exploitative classes, and "the masses," which jettisons these classes in a fight against imperialism and feudalism.[79] If Tadiar's focus is on the discordant possibilities of a revolutionary, national imagination, historian Caroline Hau's is on its more unifying dimensions. For Hau, culture is vital within middle-class, nationalist debate in midcentury, postindependence Philippines, where Filipino culture is seen as being contaminated by interaction with foreigners, especially colonizers, rendering it absent or damaged.[80] Nonetheless, Hau argues that the ability of this culture, however sullied, *to be shared by a large number of Filipinos* becomes a "theoretical and emotive binding agent invested with the symbolic power of suturing the social divisions that wound the Philippine social body."[81] What is implicit in Hau's reading is that while Filipino culture's *content* might be "impure," it becomes "national" in part through its patterns of circulation, which become the key to integrating a wider public. Culture becomes a means of "healing the rift between social classes."[82]

Tadiar's and Hau's views represent two ends of a widely varying spectrum between liberationist and unifying versions of the national imagination. Hau's model foregrounds the significance of circulation itself as an end goal for unifying diverse publics at the national scale. It highlights the affective dimensions of circulation as an object of national desire, one with emotional, "healing" potential. Bridging class antagonisms, this circulatory matrix becomes as critical as the texts themselves. But as Tadiar's critique suggests, others feel that these visions of national unity compromise revolutionary aims. Grappling with who the national "we" comprises, these debates evince the complexity of the Philippine cinema public, a scenario paralleled elsewhere in the global south. Alternative cinema's impasse maps onto these long-running arguments about the nature of cultural circulation, and this connection intensifies its political-cultural stakes.

Circulation and the Possibility of Cinema Publics

As this history suggests, the idea of publics holds a crucial place in discussions of the Philippine nation, a place that hinges on problems of circulation. The public sphere has existed at the interstices between the material and ideal since its inception. While Jürgen Habermas developed the model to discuss an imagined, nineteenth-century space of rational debate that existed outside the purview of the state or the marketplace, critics have pointed to the limitations of a democratic vision based solely on rational communication and the exclusion of nondominant groups.[83] What I find useful for considerations of alternative cinema is the public sphere's implicit, subjunctive temporality. For revisionist scholars who have salvaged its more progressive possibilities, the model functions as an affective, wished-for object of collective desire. Moreover, the divide between its less-than-ideal present and its hoped-for future is not static but activated and dramatized through public discourse, as the passages above suggest. In contrast to audiences, which are finite and complete, publics are a possibility in process.

In early-aughts Manila, much of this public discourse focused on problems of circulation and audiences. As such, *City of Screens* focuses on the heightened cultural significance of film distribution and exhibition. Cinema and media studies has recently seen an increase in rich studies of exhibition and distribution, much of it organized around industrial practices of film dissemination.[84] The cases under study here overlap with this work, but I am interested in focusing on a slightly different dimension. The chapters that follow examine how the constellation of networks and spaces linking texts to audiences take on *cultural* significance within a particular space and time. Due to the long history of intense debates about mass audiences, the film circulation initiatives that would ostensibly capture those audiences function in multiple ways: as institutional plans and practices, as objects of public imagination, and as formal, semiformal, and ad hoc systems.

Alternative cinemas provide a useful means of examining how circulation initiatives construct speculative publics. Existing at the peripheries of public culture, such cinemas are often seen as indifferent or antipathetic toward ideas of audience. But attention to domestic distribution and exhibition complicates this perception, constructing a notion of alternative cinema's *prospective, speculative publics*. To claim that alternative film cultures are speculative and asymptotic is not to view them as mere idealism, but to trace the ongoing negotiation between the empirical and the ideal that shapes these film cultures' public meaning. Circulation initiatives become a primary site of this negotiation. On the one hand, such initiatives encompass a range of material practices: hosting workshops and screening events; generating and circulating mission statements, plans, and promotional materials; becoming objects of popular discussion in journalism and online; acting as venues for film pedagogy and production. On the other, circulation initiatives are also premised on the idea of not-yet-realized potential: purely by their existence, they have the *capacity* to call publics into being. This is a complicated proposition, as scholars of publicity have pointed out. Access does not necessarily translate into structural change. As Nancy Fraser argues, to work toward a postbourgeois, postpatriarchal public sphere means seeking not only equal access to public discourse for subordinated groups but also equal power to determine the conventions, set agendas, and influence the procedures of communication.[85] Fraser points to how the fantasy of accessibility can function as a marker of distinction. Models of public formation that privilege dissemination alone fail to capture various groups' uneven levels of power to change the mechanisms of dissemination themselves. With limited financial and infrastructural resources, many of the initiatives that emerged in early-2000s Manila capture these dynamics.

These tensions have long been a point of discussion in theories of publicity, and they shed light on the notion of the mass audience as the structuring absence of alternative cinema. As the previous section established, the political potency of the mass audience heightens alternative cinema's underlying paradox. I am curious about how theories of publics might provide useful context for this dynamic, tying film circulation's temporality to larger discourses about incomplete modernities. As Michael Warner has argued, the concept of publics is itself paradoxical. Publics are both notional and empirical, internal and external to discourse: they are the imagined end point of discourse, but at the same time, they preexist it.[86] For Warner, publics are both known (an *entity* out there, to be targeted) and unknown (a *possibility* created through the circulation of texts). In this way, they are speculative: both imagined and empirical, an object of contemplation and anticipation. In a context where mass audiences evoke histories of political revolution, this framework is especially significant; as Michael Warner notes, the unknown ends of circulation enable hope for transformation.

Texts and Paratexts

The media circulation that scholars of public culture describe is not linear; nor is it confined to a single text.[87] Rather, publicness is dynamic and elusive. Clive Barnett describes circulation as a "process of scattering and dispersal," a process whose medium is discourse.[88] The idea of publics as formed through a concatenation of texts speaks to more recent methodological approaches to media studies, which focus not only on screen media texts but also on the paratextual satellites orbiting them: industrial discourse, promotional materials, audience forums, and criticism.[89] Circulation sites for film—mall multiplexes, art-house cinemas, informal DVD markets, university screening spaces, state-run cinematheques—act as vehicles for the dissemination of one form of discourse (filmic texts), and they are also sites for the exchange of paratextual discourse (e.g., promotional materials, Q&A sessions with directors, or conversations among audience members).[90] While the term "paratexts" suggests a subsidiary relationship that privileges the main attraction of the feature-length film, I would like to propose a model in which the term draws from its roots in "parallel," meaning side by side rather than auxiliary. For alternative cinema cultures whose feature-length films find few venues for exhibition, such paratexts are often the *only* access viewers might have to particular works. This awareness of the existence of films, coupled with their absence from widespread exhibition, creates a relationship between films and their publics that is based on a prospective, rather than actualized, connection.[91]

Spaces of circulation become critical venues for cultivating this sense of prospective connection, though many scholars have argued that the internet might be the more relevant space of public discourse in the present. While this may accurately describe the current moment of film consumption, physical spaces still hold the subjunctive promise of public culture. Geographer Doreen Massey describes the concept of open spaces as parallel to the notion of democracy yet to come, due to its characteristics of openness and uncertainty.[92] Within this model, place becomes "an ever-shifting constellation of trajectories [that] poses the question of our throwntogetherness," holding the *potential* of public unity.[93] This, in part, explains the film scene's attention to physical spaces for alternative media circulation in early-aughts public discussion, even at a time when domestic viewing dominated and online streaming was beginning to become more available (2005–2012).[94] Through public discussion of their plans, possibilities, operations, and, often, their closures, these physical distribution and exhibition spaces accrue sociocultural meaning, becoming texts in and of themselves. They index the relations among alternative film texts, their makers, and their present and projected audiences.

These issues around projected audiences came to the fore in a 2010 anthology titled *Philippine New Wave*. Filmmaker Khavn de la Cruz published the volume through an imprint associated with an arts festival he runs, the MOV International Film, Music, and Literature Festival. The anthology's interviews with filmmakers discuss a range of topics. Interestingly, the question of audiences emerges repeatedly, and the filmmakers' reflections oscillate between urgency and cynicism. Lav Diaz, for instance, attributes the mass audience's absence to the "feudal setup" of the mainstream industry, perhaps drawing from his own experience working as a director for Regal Films in the 1990s: "Digital leveled the field. The very feudal setup of making movies vanished. But we are suffering from a great cultural debacle. The masses remain ignorant. . . . The people don't know how powerful the cultural effect of cinema is. It can be a cultural tool to educate our masses."[95] This language references the hacienda system of land ownership, a social structure founded on colonial racial hierarchies. In his view, if the mainstream film industry become the *hacienderos*, filmmakers wielding digital tools become the agents of social change. The discussion here metaphorically links the absent national audience to broader national histories. While the length of many of Diaz's films precludes their access to industrial circulation channels, he remains concerned about the problems of domestic reception. His discussion here implies a speculative desire for circulation and the publics it would construct. It highlights a tension between the realities of the present (an industrial exhibition infrastructure that precludes long films, a public that may not be interested in such works) and an implied, speculative future, in which such films are used as tools of education.

The power of this paradox is also apparent in director Ato Bautista's comments; Bautista makes films that are closer in nature to accessible genre pictures, though with more darkness and violence than is typical in Philippine mainstream cinema. (Bautista counts the American director Martin Scorsese's *Taxi Driver* as a major influence.) In theory, it could be easier for his work to move in wider channels than the films of his counterpart, Diaz; but Bautista is also concerned with an absent domestic audience. He notes, "Out of 94 million people, not even 0.5 percent have seen our works. It may even be at .00 percent or something. So the things we do for the country—are they even able to watch it? It's an absurd idea that maybe it's just us who understand each other."[96] Despite the vast differences in their filmmaking styles, Bautista shares Diaz's critical view of mainstream films. However, Bautista's perspective is asymptotic. He envisions the present as a future history, its failures to reach potential audiences reflected in the class status of the makers. He argues that if someone were to research the current generation of filmmakers in the future, "they'll find out we came from the middle class. Let's say, I'm a kid, and 20 years from now, I research on a certain filmmaker. I'll find out that the reason he was able to get a full house [in the cinema] was because he didn't have to worry about buying a toothbrush, buying Colgate, soap, or what he'll eat every day because he's from the upper middle class. What about me? How is that going to be possible?"[97]

Matters of form and content are certainly critical in these discussions of audience. The films of the early aughts ranged across a spectrum of formal and narrative innovation, and this affected their circulatory trajectories. Critical reception of form and content became one aspect of circulation, mapping the parameters of films' movements through national and transnational space. On one end, films like *The Blossoming of Maximo Oliveros* (dir. Auraeus Solito, 2005), received praise from international and domestic critics for its universalism. The low-budget Cinemalaya feature employs the realist aesthetics associated with accessible indie filmmaking, while telling a story that transgresses the norms of the more mainstream studios.⁹⁸ Its main character is Maxi, a young cinephile who would fall into the social category of *bakla* within Philippine culture. As Martin Manalansan describes, *pusong babae*, or female heart, "encapsulates what is perhaps the core of the social construction of the bakla," that of being a man (or in this case, a young boy) with a female heart.⁹⁹ Maxi's mother has passed away from cancer, and their father Paco makes a living selling stolen cell phones. Their home life is a happy one. They skip school, spending time in a neighborhood screening room, watching old Filipino movies with other children. Maxi befriends an idealistic rookie cop, Victor, developing a schoolchild crush. Victor wants to insist on clear binaries—between right and wrong and between male and female. The film's ultimate message demonstrates his misguidedness, endorsing the blurred boundaries of Maxi's identity and their family's occupation. The sometimes-questionable but never transgressive child-adult friendship is tested due to Victor's investigation of a murder involving one of Maxi's older brothers.

Relative to other works associated with the burgeoning alternative film scene, *Maximo* fared well among domestic audiences. This had much to do with its form; Manila film critic Oggs Cruz explains the film's appeal as grounded in its universalism.¹⁰⁰ Disdaining what he sees as the more exploitative tendencies of other, similarly themed works, Cruz points to the film's tempered experimentation with portraying prepubescent romantic desire. Moreover, as Cruz describes, the film balances its depiction of a "gritty" urban setting with its simultaneous portrayal of that setting as a tolerant "Utopian paradise." *Maximo* offers difference, while undercutting that difference with familiarity. The film became the first Philippine film to play at the Sundance Film Festival, going on to win fifteen international awards. Like many of the works of its production companies, UFO Pictures and Unitel (one of its two local distributors), the film mixes universality and specificity. This balance owes much to its critical success both locally and abroad, an unusual combination for the recent wave of independent films.

If *Maximo* represents a negotiation between familiarity and difference, another film released in 2005 occupies a point further toward the margins. The same year, director Raya Martin released his first feature film, *A Short Film about the Indio Nacional (or the Prolonged Sorrow of the Filipinos)*. Conceived while Martin was a twenty-one-year-old student at the University of the Philippines, the film mimics the style of early cinema, depicting village life during the 1890s era of Spanish colonization. The majority of its ninety-minute run is shot on 35 mm, black-and-white celluloid, save for a framing device, which occupies the first twenty-two minutes. Shot in color on digital video, this sparse, three-shot opening sequence involves a man who tells his restless wife an allegorical story of the Philippines as she tries to sleep, with only the sound of crickets in the background. The man's story tells of an encounter between an old man and a young boy. In his story, the old man represents the Philippines, and he carries a heavy load that represents fraud, poison, and corruption. The film then becomes a simulacral relic of silent cinema, taking place during the 1896 Philippine Revolution. It is divided into three parts according to the age of its protagonist, who is portrayed as a boy, an adolescent, and a young man. Loosely linked scenes depict a nationalist iconography: a friar is tossed into a river, Katipuneros (an anticolonial resistance movement) foment rebellion, and a performance troupe depicts the mythological Bernardo Carpio, a giant who appears in nationalist author Jose Rizal's novel *El Filibusterismo* and will lead Filipinos to revolution. Brief, animated sequences depict a winking sun and moon, who watch over the film's hero. The film had a successful festival run, playing at Locarno, Rotterdam, Hong Kong, San Francisco, and Venice. Critics found the film compelling, if opaque. It drew comparisons to early filmmakers, such as Edison and D. W. Griffith, as well as the contemporary Canadian filmmaker Guy Maddin, whose work similarly evokes silent cinema.[101] These films represent two ends of an aesthetic and narrative spectrum of film practice that emerged as the millennium turned. Predictably, their circulation patterns reflected their form. *Maximo* was well known for an alternative film, while *Indio Nacional* played primarily in international festivals, largely due to a lack of alternative venues at home.

In the *Philippine New Wave* volume, these questions of content and form are less significant than the absence of exhibition and distribution channels. In his contribution, Khavn de la Cruz is explicit about this lack of alternative circulation infrastructures, pointing to the compensatory roles of informal mechanisms for distribution:

> Is the Filipino audience ready for that level of cinema? I don't think so. Not at this point. They've been spoon fed by GMA7 and ABS-CBN for so long. They're used to being boxed in. They like that box. They're not aware that there's something outside that box. They're not stu-

pid, just clueless. That's actually one good thing about piracy—the accessibility of all forms of cinema. Of course, the bulk of pirated movies still leans towards Hollywood.... Force-feeding them is probably not the right way to go, but the viewers should be given more options. How exactly? I don't know. There was one proposition that Film Appreciation classes should be taught in all schools nationwide. Efren Penaflorida, the CNN Hero of the Year, had a good idea. But instead of pushing around a cart with books, fill it up with DVDs of films, great films.[102]

Obviously, the problems of inequality underpinning this divided public go well beyond matters of access. Cruz's own films, for example, are highly experimental, with little attention to matters of textual accessibility. Nonetheless, for him, the problem of audience lies with the lack of infrastructural access to education, exhibition, and distribution.

What interests me about these passages is their emphasis on the circulatory matrix, rather than the text, as the crux of this film culture's meanings. *Maximo* and *Indio Nacional* generated a range of discussions about their relative merits as films; at the same time, they were defined by the circulation networks that moved them—festival programs, successful or unsuccessful local runs. If world cinema *is* circulation, aspirational national cinemas, it seems, *would become* circulation, even if their mobility is stalled due to alienated mass audiences and poor distribution and exhibition infrastructures. Alternative film culture is a product of this friction, defined and constituted by the rhetorical tensions between past, present, and future visions of cinema's social role. These frictions hold particular power in places where the divide between the middle classes and the majority has become a formative part of national discourse and where alternative films can offer new forms of global visibility to national cultural industries and governments.[103]

This dynamic is not limited to the Philippines. It occurs in many settings where under- or misrepresentation within global media culture heightens the stakes of foreign visibility, and where histories of colonial exploitation coexist with present conditions of global economic marginalization, intensifying the cultural politics of local-global interaction. For example, in her influential work on translation, Rey Chow notes the cross-cultural politics of Fifth Generation Chinese filmmakers, whom nativist critics fault for pandering to "foreign devils."[104] Similar undercurrents are discernible in the reception of other recent

Southeast Asian independent films as well. Gaik Cheng Khoo notes that the local audience for Malaysian independent films is usually "the urban middle class, arts and film students"; Khoo also quotes Malaysian director Amir Muhammad, who defines a Malaysian indie film as "one that is accepted to foreign film festivals but not at the Malaysian Film Festival."[105] In a study that encompasses rifts among transnational, urban, and rural scales, Benedict Anderson describes the divided reception of the Thai festival favorite, Apichatpong Weerasethakul's *Tropical Malady*, which middle-class Thai audiences in Bangkok reproached as being made for foreigners.[106] Meanwhile, rural upland viewers were far more interested in the work, accepting the art film's jungle settings as mundane reality, rather than stylized fantasy. Such trans- and intranational rifts among diverse audiences structured Manila's early-2000s alternative film scene, and circulation strategies became a means of coping with them. As in many contexts, the spaces of exhibition and distribution that emerged to push against these circulatory limits faced tremendous challenges, including state censorship; vast, difficult-to-navigate megacities; and the understandable indifference of the majority of city dwellers. But the desire for wider audiences at the national level persisted, as the passages above demonstrate. These tensions depict how the problems around alternative film circulation resonate with the incompleteness of modernities and publics.

Publics in the Global South

I am interested in how the public sphere concept captures an isomorphic relation between the incomplete modernities of the global south and the paradoxes of its alternative cinemas. Historically, the concept itself has long mediated the impasse of public-formation within class-riven and ethnically divided societies, where it takes on a subjunctive, aspirational dimension. In the Philippines, Jose Blanco argues that the contradictory idea of a united public represents the impasse of colonial modernity: modernity requires the consent of the governed, but it is also based on racial exclusion of the "native" population.[107] This paradox is its perpetual crisis, creating a pedagogical relation between elites and the mass population. To use Arvind Rajagopal's term, such publics are "split," and this fissure becomes "a heuristic in thinking about an incomplete modern polity, standing for the relationship between the configuration of political society desired by modernizing elites and its actual historical forms."[108] Rajagopal's heuristic shares much with postcolonial scholars such as Partha Chatterjee, who discusses the hiatus between civil society and political society as a mark of non-Western modernities. Echoing Lav Diaz's comments above, within Chatterjee's model, the elite are engaged in a pedagogical relation to the rest of society; the question then becomes how to conceive of a domain outside modern civil society, without falling into an essentializing binary between modernity and tradition.[109] These notions of pedagogy find parallels in Reynaldo Ileto's work on Philippine historiography, which call for a "non-linear emplotment" that would move away from more developmentalist models. As Ileto writes, "With *ilustrado* [turn-of-the-century, Europe-educated nationalist revolutionaries] writing . . . Philippine history became progressive, linear, and to some extent, 'purposive.' The people, or its vanguard intelligentsia, could help push history to its goal by education/reform or revolution."[110] As Ileto argues, subsequent histories have followed this template.[111]

As these discussions suggest, public cultures are inherently contradictory, fractured, and *projected*. These fissures exceed the idea of publics as divided and multiple. They suggest a *temporal* order, in which class dictates the parameters of a fantasized, future public. Middle-class filmmakers critique the problems around film distribution and exhibition, lamenting the reception-vacuum it creates. At the same time, they project the desire for a future, unknown public. The concept of speculative publics seeks to acknowledge this rupture and empower its contradictions. It does not smooth over alternative cinema's impasse—its paradoxical radicalism and elitism, drawn across the divide between texts/production and reception/circulation. But this homologous relation between alternative cinemas and incomplete modernities might provide a more complex context, one that neither dismisses alternative cinemas as an elite enterprise, compromised through foreign funding and circulation, nor isolates alternative cinemas as the only films of value in a rich domestic mediascape. Rather, it constructs alternative cinemas' paradox as the inevitable outcome of an always-unfinished modernity.

Passionate Observation and Writing against Film Culture

This book provides a concentrated picture of recent cultural history, taking shape over a period of time that saw profound changes in Philippine film culture. The years 2005–2012 were a period during which an emergent cinema was being debated and discussed, sometimes critically, often hopefully, and almost always with a sense of its innate possibility as a national cultural form, working in the contexts of intranational divisions and transnational flows. The struggles to create sites of exhibition and systems of distribution were crucial parts of these ongoing efforts.

The book covers a very specific time in internet history, which has played a crucial part in its archive. As Patrick Campos has observed, "virtual networks have fostered spaces for immediate, spontaneous, and sometimes sustained exchanges by highly film-literate Filipino Internet users."[112] Because I am interested in the public dimensions of film culture, I focus on observation at events and sites, as well as analysis of circulating, public discourse. In popular journalism, as well as on blogs, message boards, and comment threads, these discourses mark the internet as another "site of circulation," not for filmic texts but for the public imaginaries that surround them.[113] Like their brick-and-mortar counterparts, many of these spaces have disappeared. While notions of nationhood evoke the *longue durée* of history, these online sites are a part of what Paul Grainge calls "ephemeral media," which are transitory and evanescent.[114] In this way, their temporality parallels that of the film cultures they helped make.

Another aspect of this project's scope is audience and authorial positioning, which I raise here because of the importance of these issues within Philippine studies.[115] Given my background as a scholar based in the U.S. academy, this book is written with an audience outside the Philippines in mind, in the hopes of introducing elements of this film culture to cinema and media studies readers who may be unfamiliar with this setting. As such, I explicate background information that will be common knowledge to Filipino readers. Although I have familial ties to the city and lived there as a child, I was very much an outsider, even with the generosity and openness of many in the local film and activist communities, who became friends and acquaintances. As a researcher, my outsider status was sometimes useful for garnering explanations of cultural phenomena that seemed a given to my Filipino friends but which were sometimes enigmatic to me.

Thus, the critical-analytical stance I take in this book is that of passionate observation, a slightly tongue-in-cheek, paradoxical term I offer here less as a theoretical meditation on method than as a means of acknowledging both the analytical distance of observation and the affective binds that inevitably develop through this kind of work. This type of reflexivity is standard practice in feminist anthropology, though less common in cinema and media studies. The phrase I suggest is a slight play on the anthropologist Ruth Behar's idea of the "vulnerable observer," a term she develops to move beyond the distanced, objective observer of her discipline's classical period, toward ethnographic empathy.[116] My work is not ethnography per se, and I hesitate to use the word "vulnerable" to describe my intensely privileged position as an academic based first in Singapore and then in the United States, at well-funded research universities. I find claims of either detachment or immersion specious when describing my own experience as a researcher. My investment in Manila and its cinema is not purely intellectual, but I hope to avoid the allure of diasporic romanticism, a view that can slide into Orientalism.[117] If the book's tone is more descriptively analytical than normative, it is because I am also somewhat dubious of certain forms of long-distance nationalism, which make prescriptive claims about a homeland from the comforts of a distant academic post. Moreover, my work is in cinema studies, and while culturally valuable, cinema's broader social impact is circumscribed. I do not want to oversell the medium.

The idea of passionate observation is meant to capture a critical stance grounded in the interstices.[118] As Lila Abu-Lughod writes in her essay "Writing against Culture," the problem with "writing culture" is that such a method distinguishes between self and other, a problematic binary for feminists and "halfies," those whose "national or cultural identity is mixed by virtue of migration, overseas education, or parentage."[119] Thus, as she proposes, I endeavor to write against (film) culture, in order to investigate the multiple, often conflicting sectors of a film scene loosely cohered around shifting affiliations of nation, class, region, generation, or mode of production. In May 2010, I interviewed the film archivist and Cinema Committee Chair of the National Commission for Culture and the Arts (NCCA), Teddy Co, over drinks at the Coffee Bean and Tea Leaf in Quezon City's Trinoma mall. Co used the charged word "tribal" to describe what he viewed as Manila's sectarian film culture.[120] The term was used for rhetorical flourish rather than to describe specific practices; Co related the difficulty of getting projects off the ground, saying it is "because we are all working separately."

Such separation could apply to art scenes in many parts of the world, but the description does address the fragmentation that is an important part of alternative film in Manila. Hardly a coherent whole, the film scene is a multifaceted assemblage, which unravels the binary between the removed researcher and the holistic "object" of study. This makes the task of research less about finding commonalities among differences in the name of explanation than about tracking how these varied components inform one another. The classifications that offer useful critical traction for academics and rhetorical impact for pundits—national cinema, independent film, mainstream cinema, Hollywood—are often conditional and strategic, deployed by filmmakers, policy makers, exhibitors, and programmers within particular circumstances. These contingent, multifaceted situations variously embrace and expel the researcher's position, and insider or outsider status is never a settled matter. In this context, what ties the researcher to the work is the ability to negotiate affective binds, while also recognizing the inevitability of distance. The key relation is not that between self and other but between passion and observation—critical modes rather than essential identities.

Chapters

The chapters that follow examine how film circulation sites, initiatives, and discourses construct speculative publics within the contexts of transnational cultural trajectories, global economic flows, and intranational social divisions. The first three chapters investigate grassroots or informal spaces that attempted to integrate alternative film circulation and the city. Acting as transnational hubs for foreign and domestic cinemas, these sites constructed their speculative publics through the interface between urban crowds and circulation space.

The neoliberal cityscape's effects on alternative film culture become evident in the book's first two chapters. Chapter 1 tracks the significance of the mall as a space of film exhibition in the city. I examine Metro Manila's transition into what urbanists dub a "revanchist city," premised on massive privatization and the punitive excision of the poor from public space. The chapter argues that the principles associated with the revanchist city have entered the mall multiplex cinema and the speculative publics associated with it. The revanchist cinema became a microcosm of the city outside the mall's doors, mirroring its values of top-down surveillance and bourgeois decorum. This made it a key site for regulating and contesting visions of audience. Across various sectors (exhibitors, audiences, the film community, the state), the multiplex became an arena for envisioning the transformation of Manila's crowds into consumers, taxpayers, antipiracy vigilantes, and, in their most idealized projection, the egalitarian publics of a new national cinema. The tensions among these competing visions demonstrate how the multiplex exhibition space mediated debates about what a domestic cinema's public could and should be, within the contexts of a neoliberal cityscape. For the Independent Filmmakers' Multipurpose Cooperative (IFC), this public should include the vast crowds to be found in the mall's arcades, and the multiplex became a strategy for attracting them. Scholars in both geography and cinema studies have argued that publics are made possible through chance and contingency. Framing the mall as a space of chance, where passersby might happen upon the screening space, the IFC established Indie Sine, a mall multiplex screen dedicated to alternative cinema. This project was ultimately short-lived, but it left behind a trail of images and discourse—speculation about what alternative cinema's mall publics might become.

The second chapter also traces reactions to the neoliberal, revanchist city, though they take a different form. The chapter examines Quiapo, a working-class district in the "old city" that became synonymous with Manila's pirated DVD trade in the early 2000s. Against the backdrop of a neoliberal cityscape, Quiapo is a nationalist emblem of the city's past. Its former life is visible in its repurposed midcentury architecture, surrounded by the informal stalls that marked its socioeconomic decline. Dominated by the Muslim ethnic minorities who had fled the southern regions to escape war and poverty, the DVD trade brought middle-class cinema shoppers to the area for the first time since its midcentury heyday. Narratives of the Quiapo DVD journey created a new imaginary for the neighborhood, grounded in a rhetoric of authenticity that portrayed a democratizing space for a highbrow culture of consumption. Authenticity is a common trope of alternative art and its consumers, distancing them from mainstream, industrial production; outsiders also ascribe authenticity to urban spaces, where it connotes an imagined, prelapsarian past. Many cinephiles came to Quiapo seeking not only cheap DVDs but also the experience of shopping in a space of authenticity and difference—an underdeveloped part of an overdeveloped city that offered a safe, celebratory vision of the country's multiculturalism. I trace two forms of urban-cinematic authenticity at work in millennial Quiapo: fantasies of media access, which envisioned Quiapo as a site of globalized media abundance available to all; and pluralist images of multiculturalism, which saw it as a site of cross-class, interethnic interaction through media commerce. Cultivating new networks of affinity and dissociation among cinephiles, ethnic minorities, and the modernizing, regulatory state, these dimensions of urban-cinematic authenticity allowed Quiapo to be held up as the site of a more utopian, inclusive, and speculative *counter*public for alternative cinema. At the same time, however, this vision of placid multiculturalism sometimes attenuated histories of interethnic violence and Muslim suppression.

Chapter 3 negotiates the tensions between alternative film culture's speculative and asymptotic dimensions, shifting to film initiatives located in small-scale exhibition sites. Like Indie Sine, the idea behind these initiatives was to bring nonmainstream films to the city's wider publics, a move that engaged with the inherent contradictions of alternative cinema—their political and aesthetic radicalism versus their narrow, sometimes privileged reach. However, the small, sequestered art enclaves that housed these initiatives were hardly accessible; nor were they spaces already populated by a mass crowd, as with Indie Sine and Quiapo. The fantasies of access that structured the previous two chapters were more difficult to maintain in these cloistered settings. Here, the initiatives I analyze harnessed the temporalities of film dissemination as a strategy toward reaching their audiences. As I discuss, many scholars of industrial film distribution argue for the significance of temporality as a means of staggering or synchronizing release dates, thereby creating patterns of affiliation or difference across space. In these spaces, more artisanal, semi-industrial modes of film dissemination used temporality to different ends: as a means of constructing prospective publics. I focus on two initiatives: Cinekatipunan, a daily screening series held at Mag:net Galleries and Café, a venue located in an area dense with universities and NGOs; and the Mogwai Cinematheque, a microcinema and café established in 2007. I trace three temporal modes that characterized these film circulation projects. I examine how Mogwai's sequestration in the city constructs a spatialized timeline, moving from an overdeveloped mallscape dotted with billboards of mainstream media stars to a hidden area of the city that evokes a previous era of cinemagoing. I examine the Cinekatipunan screening series and the Mogwai Film Festival in terms of regularity and ritual, engaging with performance studies work on how the repetition of the series format enables the cultivation of "micropublics." The final, shorter section of this chapter examines Sinemusikalye, a music and media event. Because of its open-air plaza setting, passersby in the district—club goers, workers, vendors, and street children—participated in the screening alongside Manila's bohemians. This participation occurred on their own terms, as viewers fleetingly engaged with the films in a state of distraction. While Indie Sine aimed to bring alternative cinema to the people via the multiplex, here the street allowed passing viewers to construct their own ludic, transitory experiences of alternative cinema. This mode of engagement projected another utopian possibility for cinemagoing's speculative publics, one that looked very different from more cinephilic visions. Each of these cases demonstrates how temporality constructed speculative publics based on shared urban rhythms and local histories rather than the global simultaneity of industrialized distribution networks.

As the first three chapters relate, the state often acted as an obstruction to film circulation initiatives. The Movie and Television Review and Classification Board (MTRCB) entered the multiplex through antipiracy measures and threatened the Cinekatipunan screening series. Chapter 4 investigates the competing speculative publics that emerged through conflicts between the MTRCB and the alternative film scene. Here, these speculative publics produce different versions of the body politic and the state. While the alternative film scene's activist sectors produced a vision of Philippine publics as liberating, educated, and informed, the Arroyo state produced a view of these publics as infantilized and hostile to the current order. Each side's case hinged on assertions of the other's irrationality and parochialism. I call the alternative film scene's constructions of a rational, potential public for independent cinema "strategic rationality," a tactical maneuver that responded to the Philippine state's historic instability. To assess these conflicts, the chapter unpacks a series of confrontations among filmmakers, social movements, and the MTRCB that took place between 2007 and 2008, a point when the Arroyo regime's vulnerability made it particularly draconian. As both an object of debate and a setting for events, circulation space again became an arena where speculative publics took shape. The confrontations I examine focused on the question of public exhibition, pointing to the significance of the live cinemagoing event for fostering public culture. The first two cases investigate the banning of *Rights*, a human rights anthology film set to screen at the activist Kontra-Agos Film Festival, and the domestic censorship of internationally lauded independent features. The discourses surrounding them rendered the MTRCB a provincial backwater within a cosmopolitan cartography of world cinema, depicting local audiences as more educated and rational than the state that governed them. While these first two cases deployed strategic rationality to make their cases against censorship, the final case presents a more complex picture. It focuses on the MTRCB's encroachment on the University of the Philippines Film Institute (UPFI), one of two censorship-free zones due to its educational mandate. The UPFI became a target because of its screenings of sexualized "gay films" to large, unruly audiences, raising questions about the kinds of speculative publics precluded in both state *and* alternative film discourse.

Despite its history of repression and instability, a more aspirational view of the state persists. The book's final chapter continues this discussion of the state and its relationship to film circulation and prospective publics. It covers a transitional period in the alternative film scene's early stage, when a desire for the state to take up its role in domestic film circulation emerged—despite its history of instability and repression. This desire was partly a response to the perceived paternalism of the transnational festival circuit, a critique made in two films the chapter analyzes: *Ang mga kidnaper ni Ronnie Lazaro* (*The Kidnappers of Ronnie Lazaro*, dir. Sigfried Barros Sanchez, 2012) and *Ang Babae sa Septic Tank* (*The Woman in the Septic Tank*, dir. Marlon Rivera, 2011). While transnational festivals and funding agencies had fueled the film scene's early years, these films parody the foreign festival circuit. They depict a transnational prestige economy that encourages art cinema homogeneity, thereby excluding domestic publics. This turn away from transnational festival circuit led to calls for greater domestic support; surprisingly, fantasies of the state as an "institution ideal" surfaced as a counterpoint to this transnationalism. They emerged in controversies that developed around the Cinemalaya Philippine Independent Film Festival and Foundation. Cinemalaya had been one of the key players in the new wave of production, funding new works and acting as a gateway to foreign festivals. But in 2012, many began to question Cinemalaya's partnership between the state and commercial media industry interests. For many filmmakers, Cinemalaya's connection to the state Cultural Center rendered it an institution "for the people," revealing the persistent view of the state as representative of

Philippine public culture. This idealized vision of the state continues in the final section, which examines the Film Development Council of the Philippines (FDCP) and its Sineng Pambasa (National Cinema) project. Building state-owned cinematheques in several provincial centers, the FDCP aimed to reach outside the capital city, creating a decentralized, state-run system of film circulation whose speculative publics spanned the archipelago. The notion that alternative cinema's speculative publics should be housed under the wing of the state suggests the persistence of the state as an imagined ideal for institutionalizing local film culture, especially within transnationalized contexts.

Each of these chapters unpacks the logic of speculation underpinning early-aughts Manila's film publics. The exhibition and distribution initiatives that follow were grounded in prospective, Filipino audiences yet to come. They were spatial manifestations of "wishful thinking," as Alexis's post had put it. Just a few years after he wrote his list, Quiapo and *Criticine* were gone. In 2011, Manila mayor Alfredo Lim cracked down on Quiapo's DVD vendors, in an effort to comply with the U.S. Office of the Trade Representative (USTR). The mayor worked with the state's Optical Media Board (OMB) to seize his own constituents' wares, raiding the district with armed OMB teams in a fierce display of state muscle. With the availability of torrents and streaming, the market's heyday had passed; the shutdown was perhaps more performative than strategic. Still, the vendors, many of them migrants from the war-torn south, were left uncertain about their options. Some gave tearful or angry testimony in TV news segments. Behind them, OMB teams threw sacks of confiscated discs onto trucks as U.S. Embassy representatives looked on.[121]

But by far the greatest losses were the deaths of Alexis and his partner, the Slovenian film critic Nika Bohinc, who were murdered during a robbery in their Quezon City home in September 2009.[122] Upon news of their deaths, tributes from around the world surfaced across the internet, from festival programmers, filmmakers, critics, journalists, and friends who remembered their generosity and commitment to film cultures in their respective homes.[123]

I unexpectedly encountered Alexis's wish list years after its initial publication, through the DVD commentary on Quark Henares's film *Rakenrol*. A coming-of-age story set within Manila's early-aughts music scene, the film was released in 2011, two years after Alexis's death. It played to a standing-room-only crowd at the Cinemalaya Film Festival.

Henares and Tioseco had been close, and as the credits rolled, the film's dedication read, "In loving memory of our good friends Alexis Tioseco and Nika Bohinc. And in fulfillment of Wishlist Item #98." *Rakenrol* was one of the few independent works distributed through a major studio, Regal Entertainment, Henares's former employer. Referencing his past status as a director in the studio system, Henares describes his move to the more personal *Rakenrol* as something Alexis would have valued, framing its release in the tragic temporality of "so close, but too late": "I really feel bad that we didn't get to show it. . . . And he was so close. We shot at his house. When I think about it, so close." *Rakenrol* itself had become a document of an obsolete, postmillennial arts scene. Seventeen minutes into its commentary, Henares and his cowriter Diego Castillo decide that they should take an inventory of the film's vanished spaces. They track eight shooting locations that had closed since filming, such as the Futures Café, Mogwai, and Mag:Net Bonifacio. Virtual spaces enter their catalog as well, as a character mentions Friendster. Just a few years after its production, the film had become an accidental record of art world precarity; but it had also become an artifact of collective filmmaking, as Henares and Castillo described the friends who lent them music, labor, and shooting spaces. *City of Screens* has become a similar document, a record of a specific, transitional era, when these short-lived spaces conjectured about what alternative cinema's publics might become. As the chapters that follow suggest, for those involved, this public culture of domestic film production, circulation, and reception was wishful thinking, but it was something worth working toward—impossible but necessary.

CHAPTER ONE

REVANCHIST CINEMAS AND BAD AUDIENCES, MULTIPLEX FIESTAS AND IDEAL PUBLICS

INTERVIEWER: In a lot of ways, *Service* is like an homage to a bygone time when people would go to an actual movie theater, not the ones inside the mall, to watch films.
MENDOZA: Yes, it is a tribute to that golden age. That's why the decaying building is symbolic to what's happening now. There are no more movie palaces, just the ones inside the malls. . . . The ritual of going to the theater is gone.

To go to the cinema in Manila is to visit one of the city's sprawling shopping malls, the outcome of neoliberal policies that reshaped the Metro over the course of the 1990s. Some have few windows, their open spaces oriented inward, toward the pedestrian walkways that have enclosed Manila's social life within sheltered consumer spaces. In the interview above, the director Brillante Mendoza refers to his 2008 film *Service* (*Serbis*) as a tribute to the stand-alone theater, recalling a time before this mallscape became the dominant venue for film exhibition. The idea of the film as an homage is surprising, given the darkness of its story and setting, but Mendoza's comments allow *Service* to be read as a critique of the Philippine exhibition sector's decay. The film is set in Angeles, a city whose role as a hub of the sex industry originated through its proximity to the former U.S. Air Force base Clark Air Field.

Now a special economic zone to encourage foreign investment, Angeles manifests a stalled transition from colonial to neoliberal space, its sex trade shifting from servicemen to tourists.[1] In *Service*, the people who populate the film's porn theater setting have themselves become a part of this shadow economy. Shot in the former Family Theater, a dilapidated, midcentury building that was once the hub of cinemagoing in Angeles City, *Service*'s stand-alone cinema has fallen into disrepair, operating as a site of prostitution. Now a shadow of its former self, the theater has become a space where Filipino bodies are atomized rather than galvanized, reducing the cinema's dream of collective experience to a ruin. The same neoliberalism that frames the Angeles sex trade has pushed the stand-alone theater's crowds to mall multiplexes, clinical sites that cannot replace the "ritual of going to the theater." Due to films that focus on spectacularized poverty, and later his participation in the authoritarian Duterte regime, Mendoza is one of the most controversial directors of Philippine cinema's revival.[2] Given the content of his work, his dismissal of the mall as a viable site for film culture may have been rooted in commercial spaces' vulnerability to state regulation. For him, cinemagoing's migration into the malls marked the end of a prelapsarian exhibition era, one that was "public" in the purest sense of the word—civic, communal, and unrestricted.

As this account suggests, the mall multiplex became a contested platform for cultivating Filipino film audiences. While Mendoza represents a more dystopian perspective, others felt that the film scene was obligated to contend with the space that had become the dominant form of cinemagoing for the audiences they hoped to foster. This chapter investigates how diverse sectors (exhibitors, the commercial film industry, audiences, and independent filmmakers) used the space of the multiplex cinema to imagine the transformation of Manila's crowds into audiences, variously framed as consumers, children, taxpayers, vigilantes, and, in their most idealized form, egalitarian publics formed through a new national cinema. Exhibition space became an integral part of this new audience imaginary, with the multiplex housing "bad audiences" marked in public discourse as absentee viewers in a declining exhibition sector, as pirates absconding with filmic texts, and as *masa* spectators refusing to conform to bourgeois protocols of public viewership.[3] These disciplinary discourses betrayed the fantasy of a counterposing "good audience," comprised of paying, behaving, middle-class consumer-citizens. Meanwhile, the alternative film scene evolved its own fantasy audience: an "ideal public" of national cinema. As I describe in what follows, in the early 2000s, global Hollywood dominated, due to the support of more affluent and middle-class audiences; meanwhile, the patrons of local commercial films were primarily middle- and lower-income audiences. As alternative cinemas grew, in 2007, the Philippine Independent Filmmakers' Multipurpose Cooperative (IFC) attempted to carve out a niche within the multiplex space through the founding of Indie Sine, a screen dedicated to alternative film.[4] For the IFC, this ideal public was to be found, perhaps counterintuitively, in the cooled arcades of the shopping mall.

While it may seem incongruous, that the mall is the site of these imagined transformations is unsurprising given its ubiquity. Urbanists have called Manila an extreme example of urban privatization; it falls into a category that the geographer Neil Smith terms a "revanchist" city, founded on the punitive excision of the impoverished majority.[5] Asymptotic film culture is a manifestation of these conditions; it represents the severe separation between rich and poor, exacerbated by the city's forward charge into enclosed, privatized, consumerist spaces. Such spaces project a specific sense of temporal order. As Neferti Tadiar describes, life within neoliberalism is shaped by the "temporality of finance, or the time of speculation. . . . The practice of speculation, as an investment of capital, involves an anticipatory time of realization of value in excess of the present value for which it is exchanged."[6] Thus, as Tadiar writes, neoliberalism contracts present and future, dissolves chronological or successive time, and colonizes the future.[7] Urban spatiality evokes this order, as cities become key sites of neoliberal restructuring, signaling progress and modernity through urban transformation.[8]

In its organization of the urban crowd, the multiplex reenacts the socioeconomic principles that have come to dominate the privatized, postcolonial city. In this setting, the multiplex cinema works within the contexts of an ongoing political-economic crisis and the deliberate segregation of the middle class into themed, consumer spaces. As I will argue, it has become a *revanchist cinema*, a mode of exhibition whose discursive imaginary siphons the crowd into "good" and "bad" audiences, paralleling the city.

For many in Metro Manila, to live in the city means organizing your life around two structuring features: expansive shopping malls and the dense crowds that exchange the heat of the street for the malls' air-conditioned arcades. The malls are an urban phenomenon, organizing the city through their punctuation of pedestrian and automotive thoroughfares, becoming markers of the city's layout. For instance, one of the country's long favored emblems of national ingenuity is the jeepney. Covered in colorful paintings and embellishments (beads, Virgin Marys, and the like), the former U.S. military vehicles have been transformed into highly decorative modes of public transport. Working within their own, decentralized spatial logics, they organize their routes around the malls. They operate independently, competing with other forms of transport (buses, shared vans) run by the hundreds of small companies that took over mass transportation in the privatized free-for-all that followed the decay of city planning.[9] There is no printed map for their routes, so their unwritten paths require a particular kind of local knowledge if one is to navigate the city successfully. Jeep windows and bodies carry the names of mall locations, such as SM Fairview or SM North, which serve as the primary indicators of these vehicles' paths. For example, within days of the opening of a new Ayala Land Inc. mall in my neighborhood of Pag-Asa, jeeps soon sported hand-painted, makeshift signs in their windows emblazoned with the name of the new, high-end shopping complex, Trinoma, as a point of destination along their routes. The sprawling, week-old structure had become a key signpost in the vernacular maps guiding the jeeps' unwritten paths.

During my stay in Manila, I shared an apartment in Bagong Lipunan (New Society) Improvement of Sites and Services (BLISS), one of Pag-Asa's few remnants of centralized urban planning, built in 1979 by the self-appointed minister of human settlements, Imelda Marcos. Inspired by vernacular architecture, the four-story buildings were intended to provide low- and middle-income residents with affordable housing.[10] These utopian schemes, of course, were coupled with the Marcos regime's systematic displacement of unsightly "urban blights"—the poor—that fell outside their City of Man vision. These efforts to "revitalize" the city under the state have since given way to privatized variations. BLISS now stands in the shadow of a massive mall, SM North Edsa, one of the mogul Henry Sy's ubiquitous mall complexes. In April 2007, the Ayala corporation opened Trinoma across the street, and SM set about constructing an additional wing, making its North EDSA branch the third-largest mall in the world.[11] Meanwhile, the land on which Trinoma sits was long a disputed territory, as it was formerly the site of a large, informal settlement, since demolished.[12]

Between the two malls, they house eighteen multiplex screens and an IMAX theater. Thus, the malls encapsulate the city that Metro Manila has become in late modernity: privatized, sprawling, and divided. It was in this site that alternative filmmakers attempted to intervene.

By 2007, independent cinema had become an established presence within Manila film culture, and filmmakers, critics, and cultural workers sought to establish what they would eventually term a "home" for independent films in the city. Thus, in January of that year, the IFC partnered with the local mall Robinsons Galleria. This somewhat unlikely affiliation had an objective that seemed promising for the future of independent films and local audiences: the IFC would occupy a single multiplex screen, dubbed Indie Sine. The screen opened with an inaugural film festival titled Bagong Agos (new stream). While the festival materials subtitled the word "agos" with "wave," it is more precisely translated as "stream" or "flow." "Agos" is an evocative term in Philippine literature because of *Mga Agos sa Disyerto* (*Streams in the Desert*), a milestone collection of Filipino short stories by mid-twentieth-century writers who worked against both the Westernized Filipino literary canon and the commercialism of local writing, adding new life, or "streams," to the "desert" of Filipino literature.[13] It was not the first time the term had been appropriated for film. The filmmaker-scholar Clodualdo del Mundo referenced the work in his 1984 article "The Film Industry Is Alive, Filipino Cinema Is Dead," writing, "Filipino cinema is in such a state that it needs more than a New Wave to revive it. It needs something stronger than a wave—and something more intense than an '*agos sa disyerto.*' . . . Filipino cinema needs a storm—'*sigwa*'—to drive some sense into the long dormant minds of filmmakers who have made films their business."[14] Del Mundo's essay sees these films as a break from the mainstream, a category of filmmaking he describes as the far end of a spectrum from center to periphery, with GMA and Star Cinema occupying its center. The Bagong Agos title thus links the festival to earlier interventions into Philippine art, and the event was also a cooperative alternative to the larger institutions that would follow.[15]

Evoking provincial celebrations, the IFC board member Paolo Villaluna described the Bagong Agos Film Festival as "a fiesta," showcasing the "films that make the current resurgence of creativity in Philippine Cinema exciting."[16] Marking the moment of film history as a point of transition, the festival's opening night included the usual proceedings associated with such events. A large crowd of filmmakers, audience members, and media wandered about a tableclothed buffet of hors d'oeuvres, which stood out among the popcorn and fast-food restaurants. Banners with the Bagong Agos logo flanked the space, and a screen projected the images of interviews taking place. Many photographers and videographers from local media were in attendance, getting sound bites from organizers and invited guests. Representing municipal government, Vice Mayor Herbert Bautista made an appearance. *Artistas* from both alternative and mainstream films, such as Meryll Soriano, Ricky Davao, and Bembol Roco, also chatted with reporters. With a mixture of both DIY informality and the conventions of a high-profile film event, the evening seemed to inaugurate a new, possible future for local alternative film circulation. That this site of local art was established in a site of global commerce was significant.

Many multiplex screens are integrated into the mall's arcades, with individual ticket takers posted at each entrance. As such, the Bagong Agos events were conspicuously sutured into the multiplex's environment of global consumer culture: shops, international fast-food chains, cardboard displays advertising Hollywood films, and posters for their local, mainstream cinema counterparts.[17] Densely crowded with strolling passersby, in some ways the Galleria space could be anywhere in urban Southeast Asia, where malls and multiplexes have blossomed to meet emerging middle-class markets.[18] The Bagong Agos festival encroached on this relatively standardized spatial genre, particularly with one piece of ancillary festival decor: *Imahe Nasyon*. Consisting of twenty shorts by alternative filmmakers, the omnibus film was organized by the filmmakers John and Carol Bunuan Red and shown on a loop on a television in the theater lobby, which is integrated into the general mall arcade. Produced to coincide with the twentieth anniversary of the EDSA Revolution, the film collection addresses the question "What Happened after 1986?" It examines the two decades following the end of martial law and the supposed reinstatement of democracy in the Philippines since. The works vary in genre, ranging from science fiction to social realism to melodrama, and include a diverse range of filmmakers (the animator Roxlee, the art-house director Lav Diaz, and the visual artist Poklong Anading). Placed in a conspicuous, heavily pedestrian area of the theater, the installation marketed the Bagong Agos festival's ties to national history and hailed its ideal public: the mall-going crowds.

This chapter proposes three critical terms for considering the relation between audiences and exhibition, particularly within the contexts of urban multiplexes and the development of the city under neoliberalism: the "revanchist cinema" and its unruly inhabitant, the "bad audience," and their counterpoint, the "ideal" cinema public. The geographer Neil Smith uses the term "revanchist city" in his analysis of gentrification in New York City. It describes a form of development that flies beneath the banner of "renewal" and "revitalization."[19] The revanchist city seeks to cleanse the urban environment of the poor, ethnic minorities, the working class (or in the case of cities in the global south, itinerant vendors and informal settlements)—any groups perceived as opponents of the bourgeois elite and their supporters.[20] The term has been highly influential in urban studies and has been adapted to settings in Europe, as well as Mumbai and Taipei.[21] For instance, Kate Swanson nuances Smith's ideas for an Ecuadorean context, where cities inspired by northern urbanism deployed stringent neoliberal urban policies with the mission of sanitizing the street of "urban undesirables, mainly the indigenous."[22] Swanson thus argues that in Ecuador, the localized version of neoliberal urbanism is the project of "whitening"; "dirty Indians" stand in the way of national modernity.[23] In Manila, these ideas are realized in vast mall complexes, which increasingly include condominiums, technoparks, schools, and armed guards to prevent the entrance of undesirable elements.[24] As a key node in this infrastructure, the multiplex becomes a revanchist cinema, founded on similar principles: denouncing audiences that are incompatible with its ideals of consumerism, top-down surveillance, and bourgeois standards of decorum. This becomes a counterpoint to the IFC's rhetorical construction of an ideal public.

Within this context, the idea of the cinema as a site of public culture becomes increasingly difficult. Historically, the movie house has long been linked to notions of the audience and public formation. Analyzing working-class immigrant consumers of silent cinema in the United States as an "alternative public sphere," Miriam Hansen argues that if public life is based on principles of openness, freedom of access, the multiplicity of relations, communicative interaction, and self-reflection, the cinema seems an ill-suited platform—it discourages interaction, self-representation, and participation.[25] But as Hansen notes, the spectator is doubly constituted. They are a member of a particular public sphere, the "ad hoc social audience" within an instance of exhibition; but they are also a part of an intersubjective public horizon. This horizon is the *potential* of collective reception. Within this model, the unpredictability of collective reception renders the cinematic viewing experience "public."[26] Hansen's argument implicitly references how the public is not fully formed within the space of the theater but remains a speculative possibility, formed through the notion of the ongoing circulation of texts and discourse.

For alternative cinema projects founded on ideas of speculation and possibility, this horizon for collective reception evokes a different kind of anticipatory temporality than the neoliberal, revanchist city. The tensions between the affirmative speculation of arts organizers and the financial speculation concretized in neoliberal city space dramatize the paradox of alternative cinema. The idea of the unpredictable, open-ended horizon of collective reception speaks to these frictions between different versions of what cinema might be. The IFC organizers established Indie Sine to envision an intersubjective horizon that reached beyond the rarefied audiences of alternative films; their strategy was to infiltrate the neoliberal, revanchist city that had intensified social divisions. For this, they relied on the notion of the mobile crowd, a formation that Vicente Rafael has called a "communication technology" in contexts of mass protest, here transfigured into the neoliberal city's consumerscape.[27]

These dynamics raise significant questions about the desire to form a national public through media circulation—in this instance, an artisanal cinema with explicitly nationalist designs. Scholars of public culture argue that publics are formed through the circulation of texts via mass media. Here, alternative film advocates seek to make boutique cinema a "mass medium" through its site of exhibition, trading the widespread, industrialized circulation of the text for the capricious, unpredictable circulation of the crowd. At the time of the period under study, the texts of alternative film production had proven highly mobile, but the networks in which they traveled were not ideal: local and international festivals, schools and universities, cloistered art-house enclaves. Their paths of mobility were constrained. The mall multiplex offered a different model, where the mobility that mattered was not that of the films themselves but of their *potential audiences*—the speculative publics that the multiplex form addressed. In the decades prior to the rise of alternative film in the Philippines, malls were reliably filled with crowds, and it was their routes that mattered for Indie Sine. The screen was an opportunity to capture the local audience.

This is not an easy objective, given the circumstances of urbanism in Manila, where public space has been "annihilated" through pervasive privatization and the subsequent deracination of the urban poor.²⁸ If one means of creating a "national" film culture is through rendering it a mass medium, this then begs the question of how to define and engage that "mass," particularly in a context where the majority is systematically excluded from the global city imaginaries that have transformed urban space and the mall-based media screens it houses. To recognize the context of the IFC's rhetoric regarding the ideal public, first we need to understand the rise of the mall and its relation to middle-class consumers and the urban crowd. These dynamics have played into constructions of the multiplex audience as a bad one from the perspective of cinemagoers, exhibitors, and even independent filmmakers.²⁹ This chapter ultimately suggests that the alternative film scene's ideal public is largely incompatible with the neoliberal urbanism underpinning the mall multiplex's rise. Revanchist urban development has drawn Manila's crowds into malls, circumscribing their transformation into the kinds of publics that nationalist film projects require.

City, Mall, Cinema

The revanchist cinema is part of larger patterns of urban development under neoliberalism that exacerbate severe fragmentation among social classes, and its mall setting is a symptom of these patterns. Class is a complex subject in the Philippine context. Koki Seki notes the Philippine middle class's ambivalence, caught as it is between the upper and laboring classes, wanting to migrate while also feeling hesitant to leave.³⁰ Marco Garrido, meanwhile, cites studies that assert that class identification is largely absent in the Philippines, with identity structured around either patronage or more horizontal ties such as kinship or province.³¹ Rather than "class," with its economic connotations, the more common means of identification is what Philippine sociologists define as "status." As Garrido observes, the alphabetical breakdown used by journalists and policy makers in the country ("AB" meaning upper, "C" meaning middle, etc.) is marked by status indicators, such as how well homes are constructed, occupation, running water, and commodities such as computers. The idea of status is more in keeping with studies in other contexts that take a more "constructivist" approach to social class, arguing that it is primarily about self-identification.³² Historians, meanwhile, have also problematized the term "middle class." Reynaldo Ileto argues for the importance of the middle class's roles in

Philippine politics, drawing from Temario Rivera's work and using the term "middle element," rather than middle class, to describe this locally rooted (rather than itinerant) social sector.[33] Studies also suggest that the middle class plays an important role in integrating the masses with civil society and the public sphere.[34] For the sake of consistency with the work that I employ in cultural and urban studies, I will use the term "middle class"; however, I admit that the term is an imperfect fit for the social conditions in the Philippines.

A complex class hierarchy is reflected in the divisions among malls themselves, which vary widely in terms of the class brackets to whom they cater. Take, for example, Cubao, the area of the city where the east-west Light Rail Transit (LRT) and north-south Metro Rail Transit (MRT) systems intersect.[35] Crossing from one line to the other requires walking through Gateway Mall, established by the Araneta Corporation in 2004 as a high-end addition to a rapidly changing area. Located on the mall's fourth floor, Gateway Platinum Cinema featured the Philippines' first La-Z-Boy cinema. This upper-level location is significant; malls in the Philippines often organize their establishments in tiers, with lower-level floors catering to lower-cost shops, and upper-level floors housing premier brands. For ₱350, moviegoers can recline as they watch a Hollywood film, while also gaining access to a lounge area with a bar. The forty-seat theater's ticket price reflects its exclusivity, given the usual ticket price of about ₱150 at most multiplexes. Gateway Platinum Cinema includes a garden area, available only to paying customers.[36] Called the Oasis, the climate-controlled area serves patrons of businesses such as Café Adriatico, an established Spanish-Filipino restaurant group; Cibo, a "modern Italian" eatery; and Sachi, which serves Japanese cuisine. An upper-middle-class space, Gateway offers the experience of what Dick Hebdige calls "mundane cosmopolitanism."[37] Just outside Gateway's doors, nearby shopping venues like Shopwise, the Ali Mall, Farmers Market, and Farmers Plaza cater to a less affluent clientele. The architectonics of Farmers Plaza differ from Gateway in telling ways. The box-shaped structure was built alongside the Araneta Coliseum, site of the 1975 "Thrilla in Manila" boxing match between Joe Frazier and Muhammad Ali, for whom Ali Mall is named. Farmers is a relic of an earlier model of shopping, lacking the fusion between indoors and outdoors that Gateway, and to a greater extent Greenbelt in Makati and the Fort in Pasig City, employ. Farmers was renovated in 1999, but it maintains distinctly class-affiliated differences from Gateway, its more recent neighbor. The color scheme in Gateway is monochromatic and white, and its arcades are relatively free from clutter. In contrast, Farmers Plaza is colorful and visually busy, its different levels painted to form a rainbow of colors as they rise. Stand-alone stalls crowd its arcades, creating a shopping experience that blends the enclosed mall with the sensibility of the neighborhood *palengke* (open-air market). One description on a 2005 blog post titled "Blessed Cubao" describes the place as a crossroads not simply for its position via the LRT and MRT but also for its delineation into "1st and 2nd class thingies (hard to find)" in Gateway, while Farmers Plaza houses "2nd-3rd class thingies (common items)." "Once you're in either posh Gateway or the humble Farmer's [sic]," the post promises, "the fun never ends!"[38]

As these examples suggest, the malls in Manila are not monolithic. They vary widely, catering to a range of clientele from various socioeconomic backgrounds. This diversity signals their ubiquity; across all social sectors, malls of various kinds have become a key site of urban life. Hence, urbanists argue that Metro Manila represents an extreme version of privatization.[39] Following local and federal governments' retreat from city planning, property developers have evolved large-scale "megaprojects" designed to cater to the city's growing consumer classes. As Gavin Shatkin argues, this form of development mirrors the private sector's imperative to seek profits by cutting through the decaying spaces of the "public city" to "allow for the freer flow of people and capital" and to "implant spaces for new forms of production and consumption into the urban fabric."[40] The idea of freely flowing crowds and capital speaks to the fiction of the progressive horizon not as distant but as proximate—already lived by some, within close reach of others, with still others excluded from its fixed, linear perspective.

A 1995 cartoon in the magazine *Asiaweek* demonstrates how the revanchist, sanitized city is grounded in hierarchical control, even as it espouses the free flow of the crowd (figure 1.1). Metro Manila mayor Alfredo Lim looks at the city from the aerial perspective of a helicopter. The caption reads, "Looking out, 'Dirty Harry' Lim realized the mature, modern mall had created what he could not: an urban area in which every inch was under the watchful eye of 24-hour surveillance cameras."[41] Given the moniker of the Clint Eastwood character for his reputation for being tough on crime, the cartoon presents the fantasy of the municipal panoptic gaze, realized not simply by elevation but by

1.1 "The Illustrated Prophecies." *Asiaweek*, January 27, 1995, 8.

the interiorizing of an entire city within the regulated enclosure of an endless mall. Informal settlements and street vendors are gone. Rather than being an unruly, disorderly mass, the crowd is so controlled as to be completely unseen, organized into air-conditioned consumer space. This space does not need to be continuous with the streets—it has completely overtaken them. That the image resembles a ghost town is particularly significant, given the forced, sometimes violent eviction of informal settlements that such megaprojects often require.[42]

Noting the mall trend in the Metro's development, Rolando Tolentino writes a decade later that the mall has become such a powerful signal of the country's development that the Philippines itself aims to become one "hypermall."[43] Within the often unpredictable, frequently inhospitable environment of the global southern city, it is perhaps unsurprising that citizens would flock to these enclosed spaces, as Tolentino further notes: "Inside the mall, the surroundings are brightly lit giving the impression that the sun is shining the whole day; it is clean, there is no garbage littering the streets; it is cool; there are trees; the toilet flushes; the service is good; and there are no crimes" (translation).[44] The mall itself is a vehicle—a defining component of Manila's spatial organization—transporting its citizens away from Third World space and time to a brightly lit universe of First World cosmopolitanism. While the street remains cut off from a mall's interior, that interior space is encroaching upon an ever-greater amount of urban space and time, particularly for the consumers who shop there but also for the workers, who are often employed under precarious conditions due to the creative manipulation of Philippine labor laws.[45]

In many ways, the mall embodies the class divides that existed before its emergence. Walden Bello has called the Philippine situation a "political economy of permanent crisis," in which local agents are unable to unite in support of a secure model of governance.[46] This divide is embodied in gated communities and condominium high-rises, flanked by the urban-poor communities who often provide domestic help for their wealthier counterparts.[47] In keeping with these patterns, further deregulation in the 1980s witnessed the growth of large-scale shopping malls, which have led to an increase in consumerism.[48] Howard Dick and Peter Rimmer note that Southeast Asian malls "were designed to encourage access by the mobile high-spending middle-class population and to discourage patronage by ordinary people who were for the most part window-shoppers."[49] The newest malls present a fusion of these residential and consumerist trends, attaching condominium high-rises to retail spaces.[50]

Such divides are premised on the mall as upholding a particular image of modernization, which requires a specific kind of citizen-inhabitant. The absence of urban planning and public space allows the mall to transform the "unruly crowds" of the street into a middle-class, cosmopolitan consumer market, in keeping with the *image* of the global city. Separated from the chaos of the street, the mall projects a fictionalized image of Manila as a controlled, global city, an image that requires a citizenry with buying power. If the IFC's aim was to construct an ideal public for a national cinema, the objective of many malls is to create the image of the global, middle-class consumer, even if this is more a "regulating fiction" than an economic reality.[51] The institutions comprised two opposing speculative publics operating at different scales: one nationalist and tied to visions of a citizenry united across class and education, another globalist and middle class.

Part of this regulatory fiction is the establishment of cinemas as a part of the country's mall development. Cinemas' trappings become a signal of malls' quality and branding. The largest cinema exhibitor in the Philippines is SM Prime Holdings, Inc., founded by Henry Sy, the wealthiest man in the Philippines until his 2019 death.[52] The 2011 annual report of SM Prime Holdings measured its expansion in "Gross Floor Area," describing its move to the provinces in terms of the placeless sites of global modernity and trade. In them, "call centers, special economic zones, logistic hubs, and industrial parks" created ideal environments for SM to set up shop, aided by the new, expendable income of families whose relatives send money home from overseas jobs. Within this globalized consumer setting, SM operated 228 movie screens as of 2011, counted 138,304 cinema seats, and had a 3.5 million average daily pedestrian count, measuring its planned expansion for 2012 as 466,930 square meters.[53] As the alternative film scene grew, the fantasy of a completely malled-over city seemed an impending reality. This fantasy engenders an imagined audience, a consuming citizenry existing in privatized space, adhering to the value systems and behavioral protocols that space requires.

The mall has thus become the privatized space of social life in the country. Alongside its role in urbanization, the mall multiplex has likewise become the primary way to watch films outside the home. As the vision of the malled-over city suggests, these trends in urbanization are a transition from a space of contingency to one of top-down control. In contrast, the romantic ideal of public space envisions it as a space of chance and openness. James Donald has argued, "We experience our social world as simply the way things are, as objective presence, because that contingency is systematically forgotten."[54] As theorists contend, disorder can be useful, as contingency is where the political is made possible.[55]

For geographer Doreen Massey, these ideas relate to spatiality in multiple ways. Her ideas connect to the open-endedness required for public formation, what Hansen describes as the unpredictability of collective reception. Massey argues that space makes this openness possible. The malls in Manila are privatized public spaces, a spatial category that aligns with very specific possibilities for interaction and use. In a discussion of public and private spaces, Michael Walzer argues for two kinds of space: "The first is *single-minded* space, designed by planners or entrepreneurs who have only one thing in mind, and used by similarly single-minded citizens.... The second is *open-minded* space, designed for a variety of uses, including unforeseen and unforeseeable uses, and used by citizens who do different things and are prepared to tolerate, even take an interest in, things they don't do."[56] As Walzer describes, "The government center, medical center, cultural center, shopping center are all single-minded; the forum, the square, the courtyard are all open-minded."[57] In many ways, Manila has become a city comprised of single-minded spaces, though consumers use them in various unsanctioned ways. I do not want to overstate the parallels between the mall cinema and the privatized city, but in the context of Manila, the scale of privatized urban development threatens to occupy an extreme proportion of the city. In the imminently malled-over city, the boundaries between exterior and interior are not blurred; on the contrary, they remain as severe as ever. At the same time, however, the protocols of the interior environment become increasingly viewed as normative: public and private are partnered; citizenship parallels consumer power; the crowd is an unruly mass that requires organization and control. Massey notes that it is important to avoid romanticizing public space as an emptiness that allows free and equal speech. I would further argue that while it is critical to value openness, we must also avoid the impulse to fetishize "chaos" itself, without adequate attention to the very real, unevenly distributed violence that it allows. Nonetheless, these theorists' ideas of contingency speak to the stakes of public space's erasure.

These are not novel ideas, but the degree to which they are adapted in the context of the mall cinema is compelling, and it suggests the persistence of the *idea* of the movie theater audience as a genre of collective gathering, despite its box-office decline. The disciplinary mechanisms of what Swanson called "whitening," the promotion of both top-down and bottom-up surveillance, and the maintenance of behavioral protocols present some suggestive parallels between the (privatized) city and (multiplex) cinema, which will provide an important counter to later imaginings of ideal publics. They are often conceived as the bourgeois public sphere, but as revisionist scholars such as Michael Warner and Nancy Fraser point out, the rise of a bourgeois public sphere is accompanied by a range of competing counterpublics—groups that organize themselves as publics due to their difference from dominant culture.[58] Thus, the bad (disruptive, unruly) audience of the revanchist cinema and the ideal public of Indie Sine exist in discursive opposition to one another. The former is not imagined as a public per se. Nevertheless, I would suggest that within these imaginings, the bad audience's stubborn failure to *become* a public, its refusal to engage in the ongoing circulation of discourse rather than the fleeting exchange of talk, becomes a part of how it is constituted as a counterpoint against which cinema advocates can imagine an ideal public via cinema exhibition. By paying for tickets and filling seats, the crowd becomes an index of film-industry health. At the same time, that crowd must align with protocols of theatrical exhibition that have been standardized according to the benchmarks of a global middle class.

The Revanchist Cinema

In the early 2000s, the mall multiplex had become the locus of global middle-class film culture in many parts of the world. As such, it fits within larger urban dynamics of revanchism, and these connections reveal the kinds of speculative publics that the mall multiplex constructs. As Gordon MacLeod and Kevin Ward describe, the revanchist city is structured around state policies combined with neoliberal, antiwelfare ideology, the insecurities of the risk society, middle-class "compassion fatigue," and the straits of the poor.[59] While it may seem too broad to apply this idea to the cinema, as we will see below, the multiplex becomes an arena for enacting ideas associated with revanchism on a microscale. We can see this in the exhibitors' and distributors' imaginings of the multiplex audience, which hinge on declining theatrical attendance, and how exhibitors envisage audiences as divided into "good" (citizens, taxpayers) and "bad" (pirates). The former shares theater managers' responsibility to excise the latter.

The Bad Audience: Absent Middle Classes and Pirates

During independent film's rise in the mid-2000s, the local box office returns for mainstream cinema were in steady decline.[60] For Philippine exhibitors, the promises of market growth and increased consumer spending had created an excess of screens, leading to falling box office performance. Audiences became the scapegoats for the slump. This decrease countered the increasing consumerism of the Philippine market as a whole.[61] The middle class in Manila had consistently grown since the 1980s, despite economic upheavals and a low overall income. A 2007 study by the Korea Trade-Investment Promotion Agency (KOTRA) aimed at penetrating ASEAN markets demonstrated that the Philippines' consumer markets had increased fourfold since 1990, with "luxury" as the primary framework for consumption due to the increase of overseas professionals, whose rising numbers had triggered a growing middle class seeking a "luxurious, Western lifestyle."[62] However, despite this increase in consumer spending, the number of Manilenyos frequenting movie theaters was steadily declining. A 2006

Nielsen Media Research Report stated that the ways in which Filipinos engaged media had changed due to consumers' living increasingly farther from their places of work, with many spending more and more time at home. While television viewing and DVD/VCR ownership had increased, cinema viewing had decreased to 34.9 percent in 2006, down from 36.9 percent in 2001 and 71.5 percent in 1996.[63] Similarly, the European Audiovisual Observatory reported that the Philippines had undergone the world's steepest drop in theater admissions, with a more than 50 percent decrease from 131 million in 1996 to 63 million in 2004.[64] As the alternative film scene struggled to find avenues for public exhibition, Philippine consumers were becoming increasingly discriminating about the movies viewed in cinemas, owing to the proliferation of pirated DVDs and VCDs, increasing tickets prices, and "frequent bomb scares in a number of malls where the movie houses are located."[65] In 2006, as alternative cinemas grew, movie theaters were at only 7 percent capacity, with an average of 121,644 viewers going to theaters daily.[66]

Many emphasized piracy as the reason for movie-house decline.[67] Exhibitor rhetoric regarding these numbers suggested a vision of the audience as an infantilized, disobedient consumer, imagined within class terms. For example, as the next chapter will discuss, disc piracy in Manila was a classed and ethnicized practice, which worked to other the informal industry and those within it. Piracy became a bane to be punitively purged; moreover, its eradication was the duty of rightful citizens, positioned in rational contrast to the irrational, pirate other. Ric Camaligan, who tellingly played a dual role as both Anti-Film-Piracy Council president and vice president for operations of SM Supermalls, warned: "Despite high capital investments in renovating and upgrading the cinemas, especially the audiovisual [equipment], we are trying to work with it and yet the attendance is going down.... I believe the government is not aware that they are losing over a billion pesos in amusement taxes... and the worst is more cinemas will be closing. Don't be surprised if Filipinos will one day watch movies again in Plaza Miranda if they will really be looking for big screens—that is if they will not do what they are supposed to do."[68]

Here Camaligan uses a framework of quasi-parental guilt: money is spent, but it goes unappreciated. He then cites an oblivious government unable to effectively regulate illicit movie circulation. Both audiences and the weak state, unable to collect its citizens' taxes, are figures of blame. Camaligan endorses an idea of the audience members as citizens, calling on "the people" to enact vigilante justice to compensate for state ineptitude. What Filipinos "are supposed to do" is adhere to the letter of the law: if they are distributors, they should refuse to provide prints to exhibitors in malls that sell pirated optical discs; if they are audience members, they should make a "citizen's arrest" if they notice viewers with cameras.[69] The quote thus demonstrates the regulatory environment of the mall making its way into the mode of viewership imagined within the multiplex space, wherein viewers act as proxy guards and security cameras. Moreover, Camaligan positions Plaza Miranda, the Quiapo site of Philippine political rallies that has become synonymous with the voice of the masa, as the unwelcome option awaiting Filipino audiences with the disappearance of the multiplex.[70] As the next chapter elaborates, the previously thriving downtown was the former heart of Manila and had been known for its bustling, local movie houses. Thus, he emphasizes the divide between this most public of Philippine spaces, located in Quiapo, the crossroads of the country, against the "big screens" of the privatized mall multiplex.

Camaligan's statement implies a shift from the public plaza to the shopping mall as the site of the Philippine mass public. As the idea of the malled-over city suggests, control becomes an organizing principle of the revanchist city. This wresting away of chance and contingency has had deep implications for the nature of space as a vehicle for public life. Camaligan's simultaneous dismissal of Plaza Miranda and his promotion of the mall multiplex delineates a transition from a space of chance to a space of control.

Robinsons Galleria, specifically, manifests this transition through its historical role as a setting for political revolution. While Indie Sine's opening in Robinsons Galleria ensconced the burgeoning national-cinema space within iconographies of global consumer culture, it also positioned it within an important site of national history, a site with overt links to ideas of the Filipino crowd. The connection between the mall and the crowd underpins the multiplex cinema, the exhibition initiatives it hosted, and the audience imaginaries that sprang up around those initiatives. If the multiplex is a revanchist cinema, structured by the same principles that came to define the city outside its walls, then it is crucial to understand that city's histories of urban development, particularly as they relate to class and to notions of the crowd. The historical relationship between the mall and the crowd informed Indie

Sine's exhibition strategy. Linked to the history of mass demonstration in the country, the crowd has become an archetype of Philippine democratic life. It has also become closely associated with the mall, due in part to the decline of public space. Urban development in Manila reflects a history of the state's selective retreat in the wake of dictatorship and the attendant rise of neoliberal policy, which has led to the rise of the shopping mall as a consumerist alternative to public space.

In 2001, over a million people gathered at one of the key sites of the EDSA Revolution that had ended martial law.[71] The crowds protested President Joseph "Erap" Estrada, who faced impeachment trials for corruption charges.[72] The erstwhile president had a penchant for alcohol, a reputation for womanizing, and a level of English-language proficiency that made him a target of class-based disdain. Organized largely via cell-phone text messages, the uprising took place in the shadow of the EDSA I shrine, a towering Virgin Mary statue that looms over a passing flyover, built in 1989; Robinsons Galleria was erected a year later. This historical trajectory demonstrates the connection between the mall and the notion of the Philippine public, inscribed here as the crowd. During the EDSA II protest in January 2001, the crowd itself broke down any discrete barriers between the mall and the street, lending the mall and its crowds a symbolic power that would inform the later discourse about Indie Sine's ideal publics.

In a much-cited essay, the scholar Vicente Rafael argues that within the context of the coup, the cell phone and the crowd became twin parts of the middle class's "telecommunicative fantasies."[73] These fantasies reveal two pervasive beliefs among the middle classes: first, that such technologies as the cell phone could bypass the lack of urban infrastructure and the subsequent urban crowds; second, that they could control their relation to the masses and harness the power of the crowd to communicate middle-class demands. The mall became a key setting for this interaction between masses and the middle class. Though his mention of the mall is brief, Rafael shares an account in which the protester "Flor C." portrays her experience moving in the anonymous urban crowd that gathered along the EDSA freeway.[74] She describes moving from the street to the inside of the adjacent Galleria shopping mall, where she is "shocked and thrilled" to hear the rally cry "Erap resign!" emanating from the food court. As she puts it, "The mall became black from the 'advance' of middle-class rallyists wearing the uniform symbolic of the death of justice."[75] Everyone was happy to hear the protest call, from shoppers to the smiling security guards. Rafael analyzes this account, contending that the streets and the mall—a space designed to keep the streets at bay—are united. Rafael argues, "As shoppers, they consumed the products of others' labor and constituted their identity in relation to the spectacle of commodities. But as demonstrators, they now shed what made them distinct: their identity as consuming individuals. They are instead consumed and transformed by the crowd."[76] This is the mall as an open-minded space of chance, the contingency that, in this instance, would lead to political change.

Within this space, the crowd becomes a kind of technology in and of itself, beckoning potential participants to join. Rafael states that for all but the city's poorest, the anonymity of the crowd means that it is impossible to differentiate according to social categories.[77] Through this anonymity, the streets obscure social hierarchy. This account of the crowd as a technology of communication is fitting for a discussion of Indie Sine, as the ability to win an audience would thus transform nonstudio films from obscure, boutique cinema to a boutique cinema that happened to circulate widely. As in Rafael's account, the crowd would thus form a kind of medium through their bodies and, in this case, their box-office impact, communicating between independent filmmakers and the broader nation they hoped to reach—state officials, local industries, distributors, exhibitors, and potential viewers. Such works would be the perfect candidate for both prescriptive notions of national cinema as reflective of national culture, as well as descriptive ideas of national cinema as something that viewers watch.[78]

The ideal of a nonhierarchical crowd is in some ways the ideal of that cinema public—in Flor C.'s utopian vision, rallyists, onlookers, and even smiling security guards—could ostensibly move from the scene of the Galleria mall, viewed here as a seamless continuation of the public streets, right into the multiplex. The problem is that this utopian vision is only fleeting, contingent upon the circumstances of the ephemeral, cross-class protest event. Moreover, as Rafael points out, the crowd's communicative utility depends on their perceived voicelessness. This perception proved misguided in the subsequent "Poor People Power" rally of armed crowds paid by Estrada; the elite, English-language news depicted them as disorderly and uncivilized, making no effort to acknowledge or hear their voices, which were loud and clear.[79] Thus, class interests thwart the utopian possibility of the crowd, a possibility only realized within the ephemeral event of cross-class political protest. Any kind of mass, pedestrian gathering is made increasingly difficult by the lack of walkable public space in the Metro, which is dominated by private automobiles and the privatized mass transit of jeeps, buses, tricycles, and taxis. The privatized, surveilled mall is not a continuation of the streets; as Rafael relates, managers play music at a deafening volume to remind mall goers that they are not in the streets and are being watched.[80] Thus, the utopian variation of the egalitarian urban crowd is largely a middle-class fantasy; this fantasy underpins the speculative notion of an ideal cinema public.

This utopian fantasy of the crowd found its opposing counterpart in state and corporate discourses of the bad audience. Five years after Camiligan's Plaza Miranda comparison, the OMB and the Intellectual Property Office (IPO) intensified their strategies to cut down on piracy. Rather than calling on audiences to surveil their fellow moviegoers, the IPO director general Ricardo Blancaflor announced to the media that intellectual property (IP) enforcers would patrol cinemas wearing night-vision goggles, advising: "This is a warning; perpetrators will not even notice they are being monitored."[81] Industry fears of piracy quite literally transformed the cinema into a space of surveillance, in which both citizens and officials were tasked as sentries against dubious moviegoers who did not belong. The discourses established a set of protocols that divided moviegoers into "good" audiences (those who are there to consume, their only labor in the service of multiplex security) and "bad" elements (those who are there to work, in a form of labor some would call parasitic, others symbiotic).[82] Importantly, the notion of the divided audience allows some to participate in its constitution as a public, while precluding others. If a public is constituted through communication, that communication circulates between exhibitors and their audience-taxpayer-citizen-consumer-vigilantes. This, of course, means that pirates, occupied with a task that requires concealment and anonymity, can only be the object of that discourse rather than its subject.

Absent within this rhetoric was the film industry's own critique of the state's heavy amusement taxes, as well as the contention that theaters themselves were responsible for decreased attendance because of high admission fees. The high cost of tickets and taxation became the primary campaigns in the Roadmap for Philippine Film Development, a movement spearheaded by the IFC and the Fair Trade Alliance, a network of NGOs. Representative Florencio Noel observed that the high cost of admissions was "one of the factors that is driving away our movie patrons from theaters and [forcing them] to patronize pirated DVDs."[83] He thus located the reasons for declining cinema attendance in state taxation and with exhibitors rather than with the audiences, who are scapegoats in narratives like Camaligan's. Noel urged, "This is hurting even our local film industry. There should be a middle ground between box-office profit and providing affordable public entertainment."[84]

The Bad Audience: Pang-Masa *and Female*

The disregard for arguments about admission costs and overtaxation, coupled with the emphasis on controlling the public through enforcing compliance to normative, institutional modes of comportment and consumption, reflects the class issues at the center of multiplex cinema consumption in Manila. As scholars have long recognized, audience comportment marks social status. Vicente Rafael relates accounts of the Filipino audience during the Spanish colonial period as distracted but not indifferent, alternating between disruption and attentiveness.[85] During nineteenth-century theatrical *comedias*, "there was no 'audience' in the sociological sense of a group that consciously sees itself to be separate from the actors on stage, constituting itself by judging what it sees."[86] This description complements Richard Sennett's arguments regarding the nineteenth-century transformation of audiences in the United States and Europe, who had previously acted as an "active force" participating in the event; in the new era, "restraint of emotion in the theater became a way for middle-class audiences to mark the line between themselves and the working class."[87] Within the contexts of the mall multiplex, such divisions mirror the mall's function as a contested First World shelter from the Third World city, shedding light on how global cinemagoing as a practice (in addition to global cinema's status as a body of texts) becomes folded into existing social structures. Moreover, as I will discuss below, local industry hopes about middle-class audiences who patronize Filipino films demonstrate another version of the bad audience: one whose operations within the market have caused them to stray from their national responsibilities as moviegoers. This is a somewhat different picture from usual accounts of "cultural imperialism," which are often framed in global-local terms and centered on production, the box office, or textual representations.[88] The social protocols of exhibition, as well as industry expectations about "responsible" cinemagoing add to these arguments, allowing matters of class, gender, and ethnicity to enter the global cultural fray.

In discourse about the behavior of middle-class audience members, the good audience is one that adheres to standardized restraint during a middlebrow Hollywood picture. For example, one columnist describes her preference for the more affluent multiplex of the Shangri-La mall, positioning herself as a consumer and thus adhering to a system of rights and obligations (I paid; therefore, I expect the audience to follow the rules):

> Movie tickets at the Shangri-La Plaza cinemas are more expensive than tickets in other cinemas. A lot of people think it's part of the high-class image and the AB market of the mall. It isn't, actually. Why do I sound so sure of that? Well, it takes money to pay a sufficient number of people to see to it that everything is maintained in an orderly fashion.... Although seats are numbered, from experience, people find ways to disregard the seat numbers if they happen to be assigned to seats that do not have a very good view of the screen. Hence, a sufficient number of ushers and usherettes mean a lot. Compare that to the hundred or a P120 you pay at moviehouses in, say, SM Megamall, the difference seems justified.[89]

The column reveals the author's expectation that her "more expensive" tickets can bankroll her away from the undesirable elements. The author cites the cinema's cleanliness, maintenance, and the prohibition of viewers' staying for more than one showing, a common practice: "Filipinos like repeating movies they enjoy without paying extra (and some think that a single movie ticket entitles them to a comfortable seat and air-conditioning for the entire day)."[90] She condemns this type of audience behavior because it encourages distracted viewership. Spectators use their cell phones more during repeat viewings. They constantly come and go, which also decreases the staff's ability to clean the theater after each screening.[91] Interestingly, the author insists that higher costs are unrelated to class and contribute to the "orderly" maintenance of the space, reflecting obliviousness to the classed associations connected to certain forms of comportment. That the desire for a comfortable seat and air-conditioning might indicate a lack of these accoutrements of middle-class modernity outside the theater seems a moot point to the author. Indeed, moviegoing fans of "superstar" of the masses Nora Aunor nostalgically describe staying in the cinema all day in the 1960s and 1970s.[92]

A more direct wish to render the multiplex a space safe from the masses also appears in an article by a columnist for the *Manila Times*, who sarcastically describes the "helpful" nature of "talking movie house ladies" who interpret plot points or describe the scene on-screen: "At first I thought that the talking-movie-house-ladies phenomenon was only confined to the *pang-masa* or less-expensive theaters. So the wifey and I started paying double for 'premiere' theaters—those with comfy, numbered seats and free popcorn—thinking that these places can buy us some peace and quiet. It was a foolish assumption of course, and we only ended up trapped in our numbered seats as LSBYTTHS [Lady Sitting behind You Talking to Her Seatmate] kept up a merry commentary behind us."[93] Candidly citing a desire to escape the undesirable, and in this case, gendered *pang-masa* (of the masses) crowd, the author's annoyance parallels that of the previous columnist. The crowd is unruly, feminine, and, what's more, ignorant of the language of global cinema and the behaviors that accompany it:

> The good thing about watching a movie in the Philippines is that you don't need subtitles for those times when you didn't quite get what Nicole Kidman said.
>
> Nicole Kidman: "He said 'the teacher will . . . (garbled) . . .'"
>
> Lady Sitting Behind You Talking To Her Seatmate (LSBYTTHS): "He said 'the teacher will never leave this room alive' *daw*!"
>
> Seatmate: Hah?
>
> LSBYTTHS: *Hindi na daw s'ya makakalabas ng buhay*! (She said he'll never get out alive!)
>
> Seatmate: Ahh . . .
>
> . . . This will go on all throughout the movie, with LSBYTTHS repeating the dialogue in a voice loud enough to be heard by everyone within a three-seat radius. It's like having your own interpreter, free of charge. This can be very helpful, especially if you're hearing impaired or don't understand English. (Incidentally, the title of this particular movie is *The Interpreter*.) Sometimes, if you're lucky, LSBYTTHS will even point out key visual details that you might have missed. Again, this audible exchange can be very helpful, especially if you're blind and your seeing-eye dog somehow made the mistake of leading you inside a Philippine movie house. What is it with these

talking movie house ladies—and they're always ladies, from my experience—that makes them want to, I don't know, show off their English comprehension? Practice their diction and voice projection? Annoy everyone to the point of wanting to plot murder?

This sarcastic assessment of the pang-masa desire to "show off" their understanding of English is one of the most common indictments of one's class standing.[94] These movie patrons' blunders are twofold: first, in the need to translate the language of the Hollywood production and, second, in interacting during the film. As Miriam Hansen has discussed in her work on audiences of silent cinema, and as Rafael has elaborated in his analysis of historical Philippine modes of viewing, the interactions among audience members and between them and the screen are signs of discord with bourgeois and colonial normative behavior.[95] That these discordant moments of movie viewership garner criticism from middle-class viewers speaks to the class hierarchies playing out in the multiplex arena. They demarcate a line between "us" (the good audience and, ostensibly, the reader of the columns) and "them" (the bad, disruptive audience, once again an object of public discussion rather than a subject).

It is important to point out that these divides between classes, while rife, were hardly as stable as they might have appeared. A 2006 report on reaching affluent markets in the Philippines, plainly titled, "The Rich Share Similar Tastes with the Masa," states that while a majority of elite markets attend the cinema once a month, with foreign films preferred, there is also a demonstrated "taste for Filipino culture," a taste not commonly associated with the "AB markets" frequenting the cinemas of Shangri-La.[96] The study notes that the wealthy "don't watch [Filipino] movies in [the malls of] Rockwell, Gateway or Podium. Once the DVDs are out, they sneak that in and watch it," suggesting the "guilty pleasure" status of local, presumably commercial cinema, enjoyed in the privacy of one's home rather than in the cinemas of affluent malls.[97] Interestingly, while the rich become more local and thus more *masa* in their consumer practices, possibly because "some of them may be influenced by the people who work with them in the house," the masses imitate the upper classes as they increase their purchasing power.[98] Whether a growing masa fondness for foreign cinema paralleled this *elitista* affection for local cinema is unclear. The configuration suggests a more symbiotic relation between classes than might be thought from reading the accounts above at face value.[99] What these contradictions suggest is that the cinema becomes a site for regulating norms of gender, class, and, in the case of piracy, ethnicity, thus demarcating and policing the bad audience. At the same time, however, this regulation is largely performative, restricted to the public, rather than domestic, sphere.

The Savior Audience: A Middle-Class Patron of Local Cinema

The dynamics of class, foreignness, and moviegoing presented a difficult situation for the local movie industry. On the one hand, the ideal audience was the composed, relatively affluent middle class, defined through their consumer practices; ostensibly, however, while some stars cross class boundaries, in the early 2000s this bracket generally preferred foreign cinema, at least in terms of public cinemagoing.[100] Thus, the actual "good audience" that circulated in public discourse was a bit of a unicorn—a moneyed, middle-class moviegoer who consumes Filipino films in theaters. For many years, the Metro Manila Film Festival (MMFF), a holiday showcase of studio films that involved a two-week, citywide blackout on foreign cinema, filled theaters. I will discuss the MMFF in more detail in chapter 3; interestingly, the audience consists primarily of lower-income viewers, many of whom can only afford a theatrical outing once a year. Many mainstream films address spectators as consumers, rendering some degree of purchasing power integral. These films thus function largely as an extension of the mall space, often breaking the tenets of classical form to conspicuously display sponsors. As writer Nonoy Lauzon describes in his assessment of the MMFF: "No account of MMFF 2014 can be complete without mention of shameless product placements in certain entries. At the rate this annoying practice was resorted to by some festival films, it might as well cease to be regarded as a filmmaking flaw, and instead be marked as a defining, certainly embarrassing, attribute and characteristic of a mainstream Filipino film."[101]

Thus, in the local, middle-class imagination, mainstream cinema was largely defined by its reputation for "crass commercialism," thus precluding Filipino middle-class theater audiences from its viewership. However, this did not necessarily suggest a desire for highbrow alternatives; rather, the middle-class audiences often chose the high production values of Hollywood films. While the local film industry generated ₱1.423 billion in total receipts in 2006, the total receipts of foreign films were almost double at ₱2.6 billion.[102] In 2003, 109 local films competed with 266 foreign productions.[103] As plans for Indie Sine were underway three years later, the highest-grossing movie was *Superman Returns*. The film earned ₱300 million in domestic ticket sales and competed with only 30 local productions.

However simplistic, this division of cinematic fare into local versus foreign (mainstream films) provided the framework for much discussion of cinema screens' disappearance in the Philippines. While this has largely changed, in these mid-aughts accounts of the cinema's decline, the presumption was that "local cinema" meant "local commercial cinema," as these were the films that competed with the onslaught of global works. Dominic Du of the National Cinema Association of the Philippines, an exhibitors' organization, lamented this saturation of foreign (i.e., Hollywood) cinema, stating, "What is written here [in the movie schedules] is a testament to the collapse of the Philippine movie industry."[104] Speaking in 2007, Du reported that while seventeen Filipino movies were scheduled through June, he had scheduled twenty-one foreign films for the first half of the year from just one Hollywood studio, Columbia Pictures.[105] A former movie producer, Du recalled the Philippine industry's production of over two hundred films per year prior to the 1997 IMF financial crisis.[106] While Hollywood had had a foothold in the Philippine film industry for decades, he reported, many believed that this was the worst the situation had ever been, with Hollywood "bulldozing" the local market.[107]

The Film Development Council of the Philippines (FDCP) presented a more positive outlook, stating that box-office revenues for the entire film industry had risen 5.6 percent in 2006: "Of this amount, revenues of local films grew by 40.2 percent to ₱1.437 billion from ₱1.025 billion previously, accounting for 32.5 percent of total industry revenues from 2005's 24.5 percent. In contrast, domestic sales of foreign major studios decreased by 4.9 percent to ₱2.37 billion last year from ₱2.492 billion in 2005, while those of so-called 'independent' foreign producers—largely smaller Asian and European film outfits—fell by 8.03 percent to ₱607 million from ₱660 million."[108] This is one of the few studies that differentiated between the "foreign major studios" and "independent foreign producers," perhaps because as a government agency, a part of the FDCP's mandate concerns the production of local, "quality" films. In contrast, the Film Academy of the Philippines countered that although some growth may have occurred, movie-industry workers did not feel these positive developments and instead suffered from low wages and job instability. In 2007, the FDCP stated that the box-office revenue of the local film industry grew 40 percent in the previous year, the first time in the last seven years that local box-office revenues had increased, "outgrowing even foreign major studios whose sales in the Philippines dipped to P2.370 billion last year from P2.492 billion in 2005."[109]

Given the multiple interests of these parties, with the state-based FDCP accountable to the president for improving the condition of the local film industry and the Film Academy representing film-industry workers, the data presented perhaps reflect these conflicting concerns. However, these somewhat inconsistent media discourses reflected the vexed, unstable nature of these trends: increasing middle-class consumerism, falling numbers of cinema screens overall, SM Supermalls' opening thirty-three new screens in 2008, the decline of the local Filipino industry owing to Hollywood's "bulldozing," and, according to the FDCP, this same local film industry's growth in the past year, particularly in relation to its foreign competitors.

These circulating ideas about the state of the multiplex in Manila, while conflicted, depicted the complexity of public discourse on cinemagoing in the Philippines in the early 2000s—narratives of a once great, now dying industry whose demise was reflected in the closure of multiplex cinema screens. That these multiplex closures signaled the end of the industry—or at the very least, a turning point—suggested the dependence of the local industry on these multiplexes, which had long been the only way to see movies outside the home. Independent theaters that catered to broad, thriving audiences during the 1980s, such as the Paramount, Circle, and Delta theaters in Quezon City, had either closed or been converted into makeshift church venues for Christian organizations; major mall operators inherited this market.[110] Camaligan asserts, "When SM opened eight theaters in SM North [in the mid-1980s], the movie patrons opted to watch there. It's more convenient, there is a better quality of entertainment, it's clearer and colder."[111] Hence, the multiplex market had long been virtually the *only* cinemagoing market under discussion within these debates. It was the logical extension of the revanchist city, recreating its stratifications and absences on a microscale.

Speculative Publics, Both Cosmopolitan and Isolated
The revanchist cinema is not confined to the Philippines. For example, because the academic work on Philippine cinema exhibition is primarily historical, providing a crucial context for later practices, the body of

scholarship with the highest number of parallels to the contemporary Philippine setting is on India.[112] While the parallels are perhaps unexpected, the burgeoning of the Indian multiplex over the past decade has aimed toward an up-market, middle-class family viewership, and the urban environment has been reoriented toward international capital. Likewise, there is a fundamental connection between the multiplexes and emerging models of speculative property development.[113] In India, urban leisure has evolved into a "two-tier leisure infrastructure," in which multiplexes "solve the 'problem' of the cinema from a middle-class perspective," leaving the older cinemas to the lower classes, thus exacerbating class separation.[114] As Adrian Athique and Douglas Hill describe, "The multiplex, therefore, is just the latest part of the history of the cinema hall which, in totality, provides a useful weathervane pointing to the prevailing currents in India's urban ecology over the last century—in turn accommodating (and thus spatialising) colonial and caste elites, a proto-nationalist public, urban mass migrants, subaltern agitators and, in the form of the multiplex, a willfully segregated 'consuming class.'"[115]

Their work suggests several parallels between the established "major emerging economy" of India and the "minor emerging economy" of the Philippines. Both are caught in deceptively celebratory, transnational discourses of sudden affluence, making reference to wealth concentrated within a fraction of their middle- and upper-class populations.[116] Indeed, Tejaswini Ganti has described the evolution of the Bollywood film industry from the mid-1990s to the present as a process of gentrification, borrowing the spatial, urbanist term to describe the ways that "Hindi cinema is part of a broader socio-historical conjuncture where urban middle classes are celebrated in state and media discourses as the main agents, as well as markers of modernity and development in India."[117] Similar patterns of liberalization and development are evident in the Philippines, where they are instantiated in cultures of multiplex moviegoing. While the parallels may be crude, I raise them here because discussions of urbanization within globalization often hinge on either the uniqueness of the postcolonial city, or on matters of convergence with *Western* models (Disneyfication, suburbanization, edge cities).[118] These ideas of global convergence underpin discussion of the multiplex, their cosmopolitan aspirations informing the kinds of publics that they constitute.

One form these aspirations take is themed space, which further separates the mall multiplex space from the city. Charles Acland's discussions of theming provide one example of how localized contexts lend nuance to the meanings of global multiplexes' architectural conventions. Due to the ways they are woven into mall arcades, I would argue that multiplexes in Manila present what Acland calls "semiotic clutter," based on ideas of themed space, a notion with links to the medium's early days as a cinema of attractions.[119] Rather than offering coherent meaning, themed environments suggest interpretations of the space, applying genre to everyday life in a way that presumes a knowing viewership.[120] Acland contends that the primary function of theming is not to give meaning but to "give difference to public life," in "a process of division for civic and commercial coordinating and structuring."[121] Just as the multiplex reflects and creates a divided cinema, the themed environments of the mall reflect and create a divided city, in a process of scaling that works across local and global, poverty and affluence, material reality and aspirational fantasy.

As this section has proposed, in sites like the Philippines, the contexts of ongoing political economic crisis and the deliberate segregation of the consuming class via the movie theater lend further resonance to the notion of theming public life. In Manila's revanchist cinema, the theme, as it were, is not simply spectacle or entertainment but global modernity, which necessarily precludes the mass publics—the crowd—that exist outside the walls of the mall. To participate in the protocols ascribed by the mall and its multiplex cinemas is to participate in the tenets of globalism.[122] Thus, the theming of public life suggests the middle classes' eventual retreat into the depths of controlled commercial environments, as the discourses on the pirating, pang-masa audience indicate; ultimately, such discourses signal a greater remove from civic culture in the future that this trajectory would follow. Certainly, I do not want to suggest that audiences are passive, that activists must avoid malls and live lives of rigid ideological consistency, or that commercial culture cannot coexist happily with more civic impulses. It is very obvious to suggest that the more normalized a privatized environment becomes, the more intolerable the deviations from it. But I would submit that the more abstracted the idea of the "masses" and *"their city"* becomes, the easier it is to imagine them as pitiable and voiceless rather than recognizing their demands, as Rafael describes above. The multiplex spectacle divides one not only from mundane everyday life but also from the pressing crises that constitute the country's ongoing civic struggles. If, as in India, the multiplex provides a "weathervane" to the country's urban ecology, the speculative publics it portends do not exactly bode well for civic life in the city.[123] In this case, the primary hierarchies are those between the cosmopolitan middle classes and the respective majorities of their countries rather than (or in addition to) the hierarchies between local and global cultures. I raise these points of connection here to suggest that the revanchist cinema may be viewed as a product of neoliberal urbanism, particularly when such urbanism is manifested in the global south. While every context requires its own nuances and distinctions, many share the key dynamics of a middle-class elite minority and impoverished majority, state corruption and/or weakness, and the globalization of modes of cinemagoing (sometimes, though not always, accompanied by the globalization of film texts). Through condemning the bad audience, the revanchist cinema infers a speculative public that is globalist in its orientation, while also being local in its (mainstream) film consumption. This vision provided a consumerist counterpart to the revolutionary crowd. The mall was the natural habitat for these dueling speculations, and it was here that the alternative film scene staked a claim.

Indie Sine and the Ideal Cinema Public

If the mall multiplex is a revanchist cinema, achieving its archetypical state through enforcing protocols of surveillance, silent decorum, and the banishment of the masses, this would ostensibly seem an odd place to erect a "home" for a burgeoning national cinema that privileges art over commerce. But by the time Indie Sine opened with the Bagong Agos Film Festival in 2007, it had become clear that local distribution mechanisms dominated by Star Cinema were not going to provide feasible options. Thus, Indie Sine seemed like an apt solution: a permanent screen that could bypass standard distribution models. The screen provided an opportunity to harness the untapped crowds of the mall, and in so doing, position a burgeoning indie cinema as both an art cinema and a mass medium. If Indie Sine had succeeded, it would have achieved the seemingly impossible task of becoming a national cinema across economics, reception, text, and criticism.[124] Its unusual juxtaposition with its surroundings could be an asset. National cinema is defined largely in terms of what it is not (for example, Hollywood).[125] Indie Sine could continually proclaim its identity as Filipino and non-mainstream, purely by being so blatantly ensconced amid the foreign, commercial cinemas of its neighboring screens.[126] Thus, as an inaugural

1.2 The Bagong Agos Film Festival program likens waves to eyes, paralleling new waves and new forms of vision.

festival, Bagong Agos set about establishing Indie Sine's version of an ideal public for this new national cinema. The contours of this ideal public are visible in the space's evocation of the idea of the mall as home, references to the jeepney route and the urban crowd, and pedagogical allusions to audiences and history. Much of this discourse is found in the promotional materials surrounding the event, particularly the accompanying program (figure 1.2). As promotional materials, the essays and programming descriptions display a utopian vision of the festival, perhaps due to the multiple roles many of the organizers played as both festival programmers and filmmakers, an overlap necessitated by the small number of participants in the alternative film scene.

A Home along the Jeepney Route

Ideas of home permeate the Indie Sine discourse. While, in this context, the public space of the city is the site of neoliberal policy, consumer rationality, and other markers of late modernity, the *home* is often imagined as outside those formations (even if such calls to domestic authenticity are merely constructs). Through metaphors found in the festival's paratextual surroundings, the notion of home is inserted into the idea of the city street; the cinema-home becomes a stop along a jeepney route. If the idea of the revanchist cinema brings the neoliberal urbanism of Manila into the multiplex, these allusions are an attempt to expel it. As Warner argues, the creation of publics involves "poetic world-making," specifying texts' circulation not just through the claims those texts make but also through the *forms* in which these claims are made.[127] Metaphor thus acts as a discursive means of bringing the city street into the mall multiplex rather than promoting either its eradication or the encroachment of the mall space onto it. This move constructs a specific variation of speculative film publics; they become passersby, inhabiting the street, opening the multiplex space to chance and contingency.

The program accompanying the venue's launching festival includes a statement on the concept behind Indie Sine, written by the IFC chairperson at the time, Emmanuel Dela Cruz. Dela Cruz describes theater manager Michael Go's inquiries: "If we put up a cinema exclusively for independent films, will there be enough content to sustain it? Can the independents organize themselves?" His own reply: "Despite myself, [I] gave a resounding 'Yes!'"[128] Entitled "Indie Sine: Home to Brave New Works," the essay describes the multiplex screening space as a prime opportunity to create links between mainstream audiences and Philippine independent cinema:

> Here's the chance we have been waiting for. Here's a prominent cinema chain, inspired enough or mad enough to give a permanent home to the homeless. Grab it! Kidlat Tahimik, in a film conference challenging the head of another well-known cinema franchise, said, to create a route, one has to put a jeepney regularly at a stationed place so that passengers can come every time, with a certainty that a jeepney will always be there. In time, that jeepney becomes a promise. What Kidlat was saying was, build it and they will come.
>
> The prospect of having a regular venue for non-mainstream and alternative films, side by side with Hollywood blockbusters and local mainstream films solves one major problem of these filmmakers/producers who are forced to self-distribute and release their work. . . . The Indie Sine, like that jeepney, will be a beacon for our audiences.[129]

Dela Cruz's statement elaborates the reasoning behind Indie Sine within canonical filmmaker Kidlat Tahimik's spatial metaphor. The jeepney provides the primary mode of public transport for lower-income Manilenyos; unlike the highly regulated fantasy of a completely enclosed, malled-over Manila absent of jeeps and their passengers, this envisions a jeep as a promise to the moviegoing public, offering an alternative future for the city. This utopian promise of a home for nonmainstream films, playing alongside local commercial and Hollywood works, opens the possibility of a promise to "the crowds, who spend time in the malls," as producer Moira Lang put it.[130] Dela Cruz further articulates this idea in a statement to the press at the venue's launch: "Aside from [providing more choices], Indie Sine would showcase the talents of Filipino independent filmmakers to more audiences, since we all know that many people go to the malls. . . . So when Robinsons Galleria offered us a cinema last year . . . that was the fastest 'yes' that I said in my entire life."[131]

These statements locate the mall within the geography of the "crowds," of the "many people." Moreover, the passage from the program positions Indie Sine within Philippine culture more broadly. Referencing the canonical Filipino experimental filmmaker Kidlat Tahimik and his allusion to the iconic, ubiquitous jeepney, the statement imagines a Philippine cinema that is both independent of commercialism, as it is set apart from its mainstream neighbors, yet available to a broader Filipino audience that is figured as inhabiting the space of the mall. Unlike the middle-class columnists denouncing the pang-masa theater, the organizers position Indie Sine as a space for the mass audience that uses the jeepney to navigate the city, who in this case would use the Indie Sine screen to navigate the enclosed First World landscape of the mall. The mall becomes the public streetscape of the city, and the cinema a mode of transportation. Moreover, Tahimik's reference to the jeepney, if read in relation to his own filmic work, highlights the jeepney as a symbol of Filipino resourcefulness.

In *Perfumed Nightmare*, a landmark work of experimental cinema in the Philippines, Tahimik's protagonist, a role he himself plays, describes the jeepney to an American who asks about the "multicolored taxis," saying, "These are vehicles of war, which we've made into vehicles of life." Read into the history of Philippine cinema, the multiplex movie screen, once a vehicle of cultural warfare, becomes a vehicle of life—a home for localized, independent cinema. This notion of a "home for independent cinema" emerges repeatedly in the discourse of the Indie Sine. Actor Rustom Padilla stated during the opening ceremonies, "The real home of the film industry is independent films." Meanwhile, during an acceptance speech for the festival's Daluyan Award, Ed Cabagnot announced, "This is your new home." The statement is telling, particularly considering Cabagnot's affiliation with the Cultural Center of the Philippines (CCP); he thanked the CCP, a state institution, directly after his declaration of Indie Sine as the new, privatized residence for Philippine cinema.

The idea of an independent cinema-home is also evident in the programming, which includes a section called "Family-Oriented Films." Entitled "Blood Is Thicker than Water," the programming notes speak of the works in terms of their distinctly Filipino subject matter, implicitly situating this "Filipinoness" within a broader cultural context in order to ultimately celebrate its national-cultural peculiarity: "No man is an island, and that truth is all the more delightful for Filipinos: the umbilical cords connecting us to our families are never truly cut. Our familial ties are so strong they define our culture: parochial, maternal and all those Freudianisms. And we are the better for it—because we can go on living our own individual lives, and at the end of the day, whether we are poor, rich, gay, straight, depressed, demented or happy, we know that there is a family willing to go through it with us."[132] The passage unifies the national populace across class, sexuality, and psychological state, within the most fundamental unit of Philippine society, the family.[133] It also alludes to the normative notions of family put forth by Western psychology's "Freudianisms," an important point in the context of international criticism of the Philippines for corruption, sometimes attributed to an overemphasis on the clan in lieu of the state.[134] The passage celebrates Filipino difference from these foreign norms.

Through these promotional paratexts, Bagong Agos launched a new home for Philippine independent cinema within the cityscape that Manila has become: privatized, globalized, and largely—though, as Indie Sine's birth intimates, not exclusively—commercial. Acland argues, "Film is a set of conditions, unfolding in time, as much as it is a sequence of images and sounds. The film varies across time and across consumption contexts and carries a great deal of unpredictability with it."[135] If this is the case, contexts of exhibition play a large part in informing the meaning of cinema texts. If these texts are held up as the emblems of a burgeoning national cinema, and their new home is within the space of the multiplex, one way to harness the inevitable "unpredictability" that comes with such a contextual configuration is through the production of dialogue about these possible discrepancies and blurred boundaries. Therefore, the ancillary products and mundane elements of such events as the festival—statements in accompanying programs, the eruption of festival accoutrements within the existing, everyday space of the mall—play a large part in the integral roles of framing and contextualizing. The mall becomes the site of the Philippine populace, mall goers become potential audience members, and blurred boundaries between "mainstream" and "independent" become opportunities to cultivate new viewers, imagined here as publics, engaged in the circulation of discourse.

Cinema Pedagogy

Ultimately, the Bagong Agos festival also presented Indie Sine as a site of unofficial cinema pedagogy, inserting its filmmakers into an established historical frame and amid a canon of recognized filmmakers. This is a significant move, considering that, as we will see in the next chapter, filmmakers, cinephiles, and cultural institution workers have referred to the piracy markets as the unofficial school of Filipino independent filmmakers. While these markets introduce them to established world-cinema canons, independent filmmakers themselves have little opportunity to distribute their own films within these networks (though some have tried).[136] Thus, the idea of pedagogical access that did not quite work under piracy finds new possibilities with the mall multiplex screen. As Villaluna writes:

> In the late 70s and 80s, a cultural revolution began—Lino Brocka, Ishmael Bernal, Peque Gallaga and Mike De Leon together with indie giants like Kidlat Tahimik, Raymond Red, Nick Deocampo, Roxlee, and a host of other filmmakers unsettled the mainstream industry by making films that truly underlined how Cinema is an artform and not just a Business. Interestingly, in 1986, The Wave Festival was held at Farmer's Theater and was led by a group of young independent filmmakers. 20 years later, as destiny would have it, we now come full circle: the *Bagong Agos* Film Festival is a child of that revolution—and its filmmakers have picked up a new tool: the digital technology.[137]

Alternative cinema is given a teleology, beginning with the second-golden-age Wave Festival in 1986, the same year that martial law ended. Two decades later, filmmakers have traded their 16 mm cameras for low-cost digital video, "the new technology," which "undoubtedly took away the monopoly of filmmaking from only those that can afford [it]."[138]

The process of canon formation is always tenuous, as it stands to cement hegemonic, enclosed ideals of cinema history. I would argue that the IFC seeks to elude this possibility by positioning *themselves* as students. Thus, the IFC granted Daluyan Awards as "part of the Independent Filmmaker's Cooperative's endeavor to underline how previous efforts of living personalities have helped shape the current generation of filmmakers."[139] The award consisted of a statuette in the shape of a wave, mirroring the Bagong Agos festival's logo. The word *daluyan* translates to "flow," which the IFC explains: "Using the analogy of current filmmakers as vessels, hoping to carry their individual visions on land, Daluyan would then refer to the flow, or wave that makes the vessels reach their destination. The Daluyan Awards is given to those whose lifelong efforts in promoting, inspiring and educating filmmakers and the audience are crucial to the development of the Independent Movement. They are the Daluyan of our humble vessels."[140] Awardees included Raymond Red, Mike De Leon, Mario O'Hara, Nick Deocampo, Ben Pinga, and Roxlee and also festival and film-education organizers (Tikoy Aguiluz, Ed Cabagnot, and the sole woman on the list, Virgie Moreno, a founder of the University of the Philippines Film Center). Many of the recipients played dual roles in organizing film culture and in the production of films. The awards aim to position these predecessors as the driving force behind the present crop of independent filmmakers, who presumably are either influenced by these previous works or supported by the awardees' affiliated institutions. Thus, Indie Sine's ideal public is configured within ideas of historical literacy and a national cinematic canon.

In the Bagong Agos festival's talk of jeepneys, its evocation of EDSA I via *Imahe Nasyon*, and its framing of the mall multiplex as independent cinema's new home, the IFC implicitly positions Indie Sine's ideal public as the urban crowd. These are complicated aspirations. In his work on the public and the cinema hall in India, S. V. Srinivas cites Partha Chatterjee, who argues that the signal of non-Western modernity is "an always incomplete project of 'modernization' and of the role of an enlightened elite engaged in a pedagogical mission in relation to the rest of society."[141] There is always a tension between the interventions of *civil* society's version of democracy, which is framed via the project of modernization, and *political* society's notions of democracy, where it is seen as a mode of mobilization that tries to channel and order popular demands.[142] With the Bagong Agos festival, the freshly opened

Indie Sine had not yet negotiated that tension, evoking both the notion of the agential crowd, which holds transformative possibilities, and more reformist ideas of cinema-educational enlightenment. As we will see in chapter 4, later projects made moves toward the political-society end of the democratic spectrum.

Indie Gambles and Ethnicized Industries

During its tenure, Indie Sine programmed a range of films by Manila's independent filmmakers. The most popular were the "gay films" that catered to specialist audiences, an ironic turn given that the majority of these films adhered to "sexploitation" genre aesthetics rather than more conventional ideas of national cinema.[143] After three years of operation, Indie Sine closed its doors in March 2010, citing difficulties in finding audiences and working within the business models of the Robinsons chain. Speaking to the *Philippine Inquirer* newspaper, IFC members described the vision of access to a broader audience that had underscored their move into the mall. The IFC chair Paul Morales explained, "We have to face the realities of business and hence redouble our own marketing efforts to break through and reach a wider audience."[144] Similarly, the filmmaker Adolf Alix lamented, "It's sad because for a while it was the most accessible venue where people can watch independent films. It's really a struggle as indie films are still finding their audience, along with a concrete distribution system."[145] While the vision that inaugurated Indie Sine was that of breaking ground on a new cinematic home, this home proved fleeting and unstable in the mall context that regulates Filipino public life. Indeed, independent filmmaker Pablo Biglang-awa stated his problems working with the multiplex operators, positioning the attempted collaboration as an ineffective gamble for winning the imagined mall viewership: "The only upside [about Indie Sine] is the rare opportunity to show to a mall audience. Sadly, with the present setup, it's like buying a lotto ticket . . . even worse."[146] The IFC had taken a gamble on marrying art and commerce, which had eventually proven unsustainable.

Even more potent was the frustration displayed two years later among other independent filmmakers when they were asked about the Movie and Television Review and Classification Board's (MTRCB) ratings system.[147] In 2012, the MTRCB reviewed its classification system to include an R-16 rating; this addition meant that SM Malls could screen films with more mature content, as R-18 works were banned there. Filmmakers were skeptical that this change would have any real effect on local production, exhibition, or audiences. Here, mass audiences go from being the objects of national (independent) cinema desire to being scapegoats for the failure to develop systems of distribution and exhibition. As one filmmaker protested:

> How can we possibly grow as an audience or gain greater sophistication and education with the flow and progression of world cinema if we are stuck with GP, PG up to R-13 movies? . . . We will be eternally stuck with these diabetically sweet, sickening wholesome romantic comedies until we barf our digestive systems out of our oral cavities. So with the absence of mature movies done by Filipino filmmakers in the mainstream cinema . . . and the non-showing of foreign films that have substantial thematic challenges to the viewer (and not only a display of tits and asses), what we have is a form of community retardation. Do you think this would benefit the audience? How can it not benefit the audience when we start weaning them away from a 100 percent diet of recycled junk food?[148]

Another filmmaker asserted an ethnicized view of industry hierarchies: "There is NO film industry. Just Chinese importing Hollywood films, for the consumption of starving Filipinos. And it's a good business considering that 2 days of *Avengers* yielded 101 million pesos. Do you think this would benefit the audience? I don't know what the audience wants. The audience does not know what it wants. It can consume all the corny comedies and mushy love stories churned out by big studios for all I care."[149] The severe rhetoric of these quotes is ultimately aimed at industries and institutions: mall multiplex operators, distributors, local commercial studios, and the state censorship board. Nonetheless, mass audiences become collateral damage, viewed as textually determined and powerless. Once again positioned as a medium, the crowd is maligned for their failure to communicate the "right" message. This consumer viewership is dumbed down, infantilized by a lack of mature movies, and unconscious of what it wants (though Hollywood and a derivative, "recycled" local cinema seem to be candidates). This has become the alternative film scene's notion of a bad audience.

The statements reveal how prescriptive the ideals of a "national public for national cinema" can be. The vision of the film industry pictured is hardly an inclusive one, and here, ethnicity refracts the usual divides between a dominant cinema and a passive, infantilized audience. Movies are American, exhibitors are Chinese, and audiences are the starving Filipino masses. This rhetorical move has a long history. As Caroline S. Hau argues, the shifting meanings of "Chinese" in the Philippines underpins a logic of "selective inclusion and exclusion" that developed in relation to shifts in global and regional historical contexts.[150] The statement does not figure "Chinese importers" as hyphenate or mestizo, accessing outside power without being consumed by it.[151] Rather, their Chineseness becomes a means of dismissing the existing mainstream film industry as prone to foreign influence, and thus incompatible with ideals of nation premised on specific frameworks around ethnicity and power.

Here, bad national audiences are figured as part of independent film's failure to become the economically sustainable national cinema that these filmmakers envision. While the passages above are in no way representative of the film scene as a whole, they posit alternative film's speculative publics as failed markets. In that sense, this framing of the audience mirrors that of the commercial exhibitors discussed earlier in this chapter. Even as the speakers vilify the commercial industry, they scapegoat bad audiences, rendering their discourses more similar than they might imagine.

The IFC's chosen home proved untenable, but it established the multiplex as an integral front line in the ongoing race for screen publics that underpins national-cinema formation. As the next chapter's discussion of the Muslim-led informal DVD district will demonstrate, an uneasy politics of ethnicity also underpins other formations of nation, class, and alternative film culture. If the mall's globalism became a means of establishing "indie" difference as a contrast, the nationalist authenticity ascribed to the ethnicized informal DVD marketplace became an unexpected point of affiliation.

CHAPTER TWO

THE QUIAPO CINEMATHEQUE AND URBAN-CINEMATIC AUTHENTICITY

Concert, *teleserye*, music videos, anime
Sex scandals, foreign films, subtitled, boxed sets
Lahat ng hinahanap mo [Everything you're looking for]
Lahat ay nandito [Everything is right here]
dibidi ma'am dibidi sir, dibidi dibidi dibidi X
Action, dramedy, science-fiction, documentary
Suspense, rated r thriller, horror, Oscar nominee
Lahat ng hinahanap mo [Everything you're looking for]
Lahat ng ay nandito [Everything is right here]
Dibidi m'am, dibidi sir, dibidi, dibidi, dibidi X!
—SANDWICH, "DVD X," 2006

While the IFC's Indie Sine project envisioned the ideal public of national cinema as a nonhierarchical crowd united across class, this was not the only speculative public circulating in early-2000s Manila film culture. In the informal street markets that acted as counterpoints to the mall, pirated DVD vending became linked to ethnicity in ways that cultivated another version of alternative film's speculative public, one imagined as transcending both class and ethnicity.[1] Beginning in the early 2000s, the neighborhood of Quiapo, a predominantly Muslim, working-class district in the Old City, became a hub for pirated media. Run primarily by the Muslim Moro minority that had migrated to Manila from the south, the informal media distribution industry thrived, luring cosmopolitan cinephiles to Quiapo for the first time since the district's midcentury heyday, when it was Manila's shopping and entertainment center. Quiapo had since fallen several rungs on the socioeconomic ladder, but as the new millennium turned, the district became a space where cinematic cosmopolitanism and urban multiculturalism mutually informed one another, laying the foundations for a nascent alternative film scene. Captured in popular media, blogs, message boards, and independent filmmaking, the district's burgeoning, cinema-fueled imaginary drew from the interaction between the informal media industry and the space it occupied. Within these discourses, the district became a site to experience cultural heritage and ethnic difference, alongside hard-to-find, pirated art films. As such, this media-circulation space was grounded in ideals of authenticity that came to play an important role in discussions of Philippine alternative film. In many ways, this is not unique to the Philippines; authenticity often plays a part in discussions of art, including cinema. At the same time, it is also common in discussions of urbanism, playing an integral role in designating areas of the city as reflections of cultural identity. What is less common is seeing how these overlapping spatial and cinematic concepts of authenticity inform one another, through the film-circulation site, and how this interaction engenders particular ideals of public culture formed in opposition to an "inauthentic" other (the mainstream film industry, state regulators, the overdeveloped city). Discussing the spaces where alternative films meet their audiences reveals the significance of these sites in lending meaning to bodies of films *and* to the identities of those who consume them. In settings where independent cinema's meaning hinges on debates about nationalism, culture, and collective identity, the question of authenticity is crucial. Like the constructs of the mall multiplex's "good" and "bad" audience, notions of authenticity demarcated parameters of belonging and difference, establishing the contours of the speculative publics that emerged alongside the Quiapo DVD market.

Developing alongside the concept of modernity, "authenticity" is a contradictory concept. It alludes to mythic origins, tying it to the past; it also suggests creative innovations, orienting it toward the future. Quiapo functioned as an arena for chance encounters across class and ethnicity, constructing a perspective on public culture that hinged on a particular kind of speculative public. In this case, an imagined, multicultural "we" took shape within a marginalized cinema space, across class and cultural difference. This poses compelling questions about what it means to imagine a cinema public within a stratified, diverse society. Much analysis positions the public sphere as an unrealized ideal rather than an actual, historical formation. Michael Warner and Nancy Fraser point out that the rise of a bourgeois public sphere is not monolithic; it is accompanied by a range of competing counterpublics.[2] For Fraser, the interactions between bourgeois publics and counterpublics are always antagonistic.[3]

In a Philippine context, scholars have written about ethnic minorities as antagonistic counterpublics, which troubles any easy visions of multicultural unity. Dale F. Eickelman and Jon W. Anderson argue for a Moro public formed via the intersection of new media and Islam, while Smita Lahiri analyzes the formation of an Indio, subaltern public sphere during the late nineteenth-century Spanish period.[4] Class is a critical dimension of the counterpublic as well. Raquel A. G. Reyes has argued that *ilustrado* nationalism at the turn of the twentieth century was constituted through tensions between anxieties about Westernization and *urbanidad*, the new, middle-class way of life in Manila, which involved a range of social protocols and capital accumulation as a means of performing bourgeois status.[5] Signs of distinction such as "property, propriety, and social polish" maintained the borders of class, sex, gender, and nation, borders that life in the city made threateningly porous.[6] Building on this work, Denise Cruz writes that because this status was a key rationale for national independence, ilustrados were alarmed at Western prognoses such as that of the sexologist Richard von Krafft-Ebing's *Psychopathia sexualis* (1886), which depicted Malays as "savage races."[7] Many elite nationalists claimed Malay ancestry as a means of drawing distinctions between themselves and the country's more "savage" groups, such as Muslim Moros of the South, as well as highland indigenous peoples like the Igorots and Negritos.[8] In its formative years, national identity took shape within these frictions of class and ethnicity. Elite nationalists sought to separate themselves from ethnic minorities in a bid for modernity, while ethnic minorities created subaltern, antagonistic public spheres to cultivate independent identities.

Thus, the rhetorical cultivation of Quiapo as a space of interethnic encounter and counterpublic connection became a fertile ground for rejecting this historical narrative and its ethnicized ties to elite nationalism. Narratives of the informal DVD market rewrote these hierarchical histories of class and ethnicity, trading them for a speculative variation of public culture grounded in new patterns of affiliation. What is interesting about the Quiapo DVD market discourse is its simultaneous rejection of bourgeois models of public culture alongside an implied, speculative *counter*public. In this case, it is that multicultural counterpublic that functions as an unrealized ideal, tied to a discourse of Quiapo's authenticity. This discourse constructed a new constellation of affinities, rhetorically linking art film aficionados and Muslim minorities, who together opposed the regulatory state's Optical Media Board (OMB), the mainstream commercial industries of the Philippines and Hollywood, and the less-discerning consumers who could not recognize Quiapo's charms. Knitting these two sectors together provides the grounds for a speculative counterpublic imagined in antagonistic relation to "bourgeois" norms of law-abiding, mall-frequenting, commercial-cinema-consuming citizens. Of course, these disparate groups of citizens were the vast majority of consumers who purchased informal DVDs in the early 2000s, seeking access to entertainment media, primarily of the domestic, Hollywood, and South Korean varieties. Informal circulation enabled their participation in popular cosmopolitan film culture, just as high ticket prices and other protocols excluded them from the more gentrified multiplex experience. Intellectual, middle-class, and middle-class-aspirant consumers were particularly drawn to Quiapo for pirated, hard-to-find art films, and this new availability became tied to a discourse linking that availability to authentic, intercultural experience. The Quiapo DVD marketplace's prescribed authenticity allowed it to function as a speculative counterpublic, predicated on distance from a range of mainstreams: the state, commercial cinemas, overdeveloped parts of the city.

When attributed to film, authenticity signals the autonomy of both practitioners and consumers, whose patterns of production and consumption ostensibly operate outside (or in spite of) industrialized systems. When ascribed to city space, it often harkens back to an imagined, folkish past; here, distance and unfamiliarity render this folk authenticity visible. In Manila, the millennial transitions of both alternative cinema and urban development engendered new imaginaries, each with its own value systems, which pivoted on notions of authenticity. For alternative film cultures in the Philippines and elsewhere, authenticity entails a cultivated, sometimes performative distance from mainstream film production, both domestic and global. While it could be nationalist in its orientation, celebrating particular aspects of local or national history, it also combines with a preference for obscure, difficult-to-find works of world cinema. Such preferences distance intellectual, middle-class cultural consumers from their more working-class counterparts. However, spaces of circulation create the possibility of spatial, if not cultural, proximity. In the "trip to Quiapo" narratives that emerged alongside the DVD marketplace, the neighborhood's old world, ethnic multiculturalism negotiated its links to cosmopolitan taste cultures, tying arty, middle-class visitors to national history and to working-class ethnic minorities, even as they perused the newly available, pirated world cinema canon that would link them to cosmopolitan taste cultures abroad. Through discourses of authenticity, Quiapo offered a democratizing space for a highbrow culture of consumption, allowing that culture to negotiate its contradictions.

In Quiapo, discourses of authenticity emerged in relation to both the media being distributed (alternative works) *and* the space in which these new networks were forged (an underdeveloped section of an unevenly developed city, with a rich national history). Millennial Quiapo was a space of lavish, globalized media abundance. Here, urban and cinematic variations of authenticity took two forms: fantasies of media access and pluralist images of multiculturalism. Both constructed a vision of an inclusive counterpublic for the Philippines' burgeoning alternative film culture. Through the production of urban-cinematic authenticity, Quiapo's new imaginary made claims to a more "authentic" speculative counterpublic, a fantasy that played a crucial role in fashioning the alternative film culture that was beginning to take shape in the early 2000s.

In many ways, this was a cause for celebration: a "decaying" neighborhood, revived as a nationalist paradise lost, providing newfound access to alternative media in the global cultural periphery. This more celebratory perspective makes sense. There are important, even liberating dimensions to what was happening in Quiapo at the turn of the millennium. As this chapter will show, much of the popular discourse about the district's new role in global film distribution focused on the more affirming aspects of this transition. But I am also interested in the more complex, contradictory underpinnings of these dynamics. The alternative, urban-cinematic imaginary created around the district reveals how ideals of authenticity can leverage cultural power, legitimizing claims to identity and creating hierarchies of artistic production and reception. This has important implications for understanding the role of circulation in alternative film culture, conveying how it functions not just as grassroots or industrial practice but also as a reified cultural construct, attached to certain ideals of public culture.

Thus, this chapter argues that the intertwined discourses of cinematic and urban authenticity produced Quiapo as a hub for cosmopolitan, alternative film culture, while simultaneously decentering the histories of interethnic violence and marginalization that created its conditions of being. This contradiction reflects the ambivalence at the heart of alternative film culture: its simultaneous radical potential and elite underpinnings, its tendencies to embrace cultural and aesthetic difference while flattening that difference into a consumable text. These discourses of authenticity became a two-pronged form of speculation, working as both a mode of imagination and a wager on Manila's film culture futures. Such utopian visions of Quiapo's DVD marketplace implied a multicultural, nonhierarchical film counterpublic, formed in opposition to the bourgeois publics associated with the overdeveloped city, mainstream cinemas, and ethnocentric state policy.

My argument stems in part from a desire to critique my own encounters with the space. Quiapo was at its height as a DVD distribution center when I lived in Manila in the early 2000s. It was often one of the first places I would take visitors from abroad, in efforts to convince them of the sprawling megalopolis's hidden charms. In a cityscape whose most obvious markers consist largely of malls connected by a web of congested, billboard-lined roads, Quiapo was one of the few areas where I could hold up an image of the city for my foreign guests, offering them an experience of Manila that spoke to travelers' desires for a preconceived notion of authenticity. Elsewhere, air-conditioned mall arcades produced their own sense of local space. But Quiapo offered deeper difference. It afforded a view of old Manila, presented in the ramshackle form that visitors often seek, proving their traveler mettle by breaching class and ethnic borders. The tour might include a stop at Ma Mon Luk, a 1950s-era Chinese Filipino eatery, to eat *siopao* under fluorescent lights. Afterward, we could head toward particular DVD vendors, venturing into a dense crowd of shoppers making their way through the street stalls (figure 2.1). Upon reaching our desired DVD vendor, I would point out specific titles, those that might be sufficiently jarring to foreigners: pirated Criterion films or collections of Hollywood

2.1 Quiapo DVD vendors, 2007. With permission of the photographer, Sidney Snoeck.

war movies compressed onto a single disc, its title awkwardly translated from Chinese into "Cruel, Irritable."

In these moments, my desire to prove Manila's overlooked charisma—the cultural syncretism that could render its appeal legible for a wider audience—overtook my wiser, more ethnographically informed instincts. As Caroline S. Hau might say, I had succumbed to a diasporic tendency to present the Philippines as text—depthless and distanced.[9] While Quiapo's importance to Philippine history is clear, the view that promoted the district's "charms" was grounded largely in class and ethnic difference. For the great majority of people in Quiapo, there to work or to shop for low-cost groceries and the like, the features that made the neighborhood "colorful" were simply an ordinary part of city life. For the district's newer southern migrants, the neighborhood's difference might register in other ways, setting it apart from their own, distant homes. Given the long history of Moro minorities' oppression, such difference is by no means trivial. It speaks to an ongoing political context of deracination, impoverishment, and, under the influence of the United States, an association between Moro insurgency and terrorism. These were the geopolitical currents flowing beneath the innocuous surface of commerce and exchange, the violent infrastructures enabling Quiapo's synesthetic pleasures. On my visits to buy pirated DVDs, I occasionally spotted other intraurban travelers, capturing the market's bustle with their upscale, digital SLR cameras. I avoided bringing mine, as my friends had warned me of street theft. To be celebrated, the district's transgressive consumer flows could only move in one direction.

The following sections track a line of inquiry that began with this ambivalent encounter. I first examine Quiapo's history as a site of alterity, which informs its later position as a hub for alternative film culture. Through its connection to Manila's Muslim community, the site has been distanced from state institutions. This alterity translated to its later transformation into the cinephile imaginary of the "Quiapo Cinematheque," constructing pirated DVD consumers as both distant from the state and its mainstream media allies, while also connected to multiculturalist versions of national identity. This dynamic of distance and proximity constituted the circulation site's "urban-cinematic authenticity," which drew together the authenticity associated with its nationalist past while also implying more utopian, possible futures that existed outside the overdeveloped city and mainstream media institutions. The fantasies of media access and abundance that Quiapo provided created a fantasy of new counterpublics that would connect laterally across ethnicity and class, simultaneously opposing more hierarchical, bourgeois variations. However, such utopian possibilities had their limits, as consumers' ethnicizing of the district suggests.

Quiapo Alterity

Quiapo's role in Manila's alternative film culture grew out of its long history as a destination in the city. This history informs the district's later incarnation as an authenticating touchstone for film producers, consumers, and their visions of more pluralist national publics. It constructs the neighborhood's distance from the state, as well as its ties to minority cultures that both the state and the mainstream film industry have deemed deviant, opening space to imagine alternative affiliations across class and ethnicity.

The Muslim population that would come to dominate Quiapo's informal DVD market settled in the area following World War II, as traders moved into the adjacent district now known as Palanca. At the time, Quiapo was a lively commercial hub for middle-class Manilenyos, housing a number of first-run cinemas playing both Hollywood and Tagalog films, department store shopping, and Quiapo Church, the city's largest Catholic cathedral.[10] The Muslim community consists of a Maranao majority, with a much smaller population of Maguindanaons, Tausūgs, Badjaos, and Samals.[11] Immediately following the declaration of martial law in the early 1970s, the Muslim National Liberation Front rebelled in the southern region of Mindanao, with the aim of separating the predominantly Muslim island provinces of Mindanao, Sulu, and Palawan from Philippine territory. The war prompted the exodus of Mindanao Muslims to Quiapo, a common entry point for intranational migrants from around the country.[12] The already sizable Muslim population in the district grew, leading the Office of Cultural Minorities to construct the Golden Mosque in Quiapo in 1977.

Public discourse figuratively maps Quiapo as the peripheral space of the Other, a reputation that plays into its later role as a site of alternative film culture. Part of this otherness stems from Filipino Muslims' relation to the state and, through this connection, to the mainstream media industry. Muslim communities have long existed in a tenuous relation to the Philippine state, from times of Spanish colonization to the present.[13] The community's highly visible presence in the informal media industry sustained this distance from centralized state institutions. Meanwhile, the state's desire to quell informal media distribution emerged from its own transnational networks. The Philippines was on the USTR's "Priority Watch List" from 2001 until 2006, when it was moved to the "Watch List" due to the Arroyo administration's 2003 transformation of the Videogram Regulatory Board (VRB) into the OMB, a body designed to "regulate the manufacture of optical media in all its forms and impose stiffer fines and penalties for its illegal reproduction."[14]

For years, these bodies had little success, despite highly publicized, theatrical OMB raids and celebrity leaders from the mainstream media industry, such as Senators Ramon "Bong" Revilla, Eduardo "Edu" Manzano, and Ronnie Ricketts, all former action stars. Trafficking in hypermasculine, performative tropes of action cinema, OMB leaders would arrive in warehouses and street markets with sunglass-wearing, machine-gun-toting SWAT teams, confiscating wares in a televised show of state bravado. Such highly mediated public acts created a visual dichotomy between Muslim DVD vendors (and implicitly, the off-screen consumers who support them) and the state/mainstream-media dyad, represented synecdochally in the figure of the action-star-cum-OMB-chair. Moreover, this dyad was also complicit with the U.S. media behemoth, through its compliance with the USTR. A David and Goliath model emerged.[15]

This model positioned alternative filmmakers on the side of the underdog, performing a counterpublic in formation posed against bourgeois, law-abiding citizens. For example, a portrayal of media abundance occurs in Marie Jamora's 2006 music video, "DVD X," whose lyrics begin this chapter. One of the few women directors working in the independent cinema scene, Jamora would go on to direct the coming-of-age feature *Ang Nawawala (What Isn't There)* in 2012, when she was fresh from her MFA in filmmaking at Columbia University. *Ang Nawawala* is a coming-of-age love story set against the backdrop of Manila's alternative music subcultures. Its vintage-wearing protagonists reference local bands (its soundtrack was released on vinyl), comics (Gerry Alanguilan's *Elmer*), and martial-law-era films (Mike de Leon's *Kisapmata* [1981]), while also alluding to their love of foreign, cult favorites like the American television show *Twin Peaks* and the 1982 Hollywood film *Blade Runner*. The "DVD X" video presages this intertwining of local and global alternative media, while also drawing connections between two forms of alternative cultural production (music and movies). A staple of the Manila music scene, the pop-punk band Sandwich's lyrics commemorated the wide swath of films newly available on the gray market. As the song's lyrics reveal, these bootlegged optical discs present a wide-ranging taxonomy of media genres: foreign films, documentaries, local teleseryes (prime-time television soap operas), Oscar nominees, and subtitled box sets. The lyrics imagine a burgeoning culture of cinematic consumption, suggesting a speculative counterpublic characterized by newfound cosmopolitanism and democratization among genres.

While the video does not allude to Quiapo per se, its satirical depiction of an OMB raid says much about how the spectacle of pirated, cinematic plenty constructed an antagonistic relationship between cinephiles and the state, which furthered the cinephiles' "oppositional" character (figure 2.2). The music video includes a cameo appearance that is both a reference to local, commercial cinema and to the state's attempts at regulation. As the band plays their song in an industrial interior, the video cuts to a man in a suit. He approaches in slow motion, his face just outside the shot. At the song's climax, the camera dollies into a medium close-up, revealing the identity of the intruder: Eduardo "Edu"

2.2 Band members as pirates in the "DVD X" music video.

2.3 The OMB chair Edu Manzano guns the band down.

Manzano—former action star, game-show host, and, at the time, chair of the state's OMB (figure 2.3). Manzano pulls two guns from beneath his blazer. The band goes down in a slow-motion hail of bullets, and Manzano shoots a haughty, cautionary look directly into the camera. With its two-fisted guns and slow motion, the sequence is an homage to Hong Kong action director John Woo's films, a subtle reference to the international cult cinema that the gray markets provide. The reference emphasizes the notion of piracy as a means of film access and education, furthering the divide between, on one side, the band and the cinema consumers they represent and, on the other, the regulatory state and the local mainstream industry, personified in Manzano.

Though the video does not depict actual vendors in its celebration of media access, the band members themselves become stand-ins for the informal industry. Their costumes allude to pirates; each wears a white suit with a black eye mask, evoking cartoonish depictions of burglars or bandits. The lead singer Raymund Marasigan points a small consumer video camera of the kind that might be used to make a "cam copy" during theatrical screenings. Theirs are the bodies that bleed in the fictionalized raid. For the purposes of the video, they *become* the pirates. This iconography signals the web of alliances that the pirated DVD market engendered: alternative cultural producer-consumers, embodying the "pirates" that had granted access to the assortment of world media. They align with those pirates against a figure who represents both the state and the mainstream film industry. In this representation, piracy offers distance from mainstream culture and media institutions, while also allowing new networks of affiliation to emerge: between alternative media consumers in the Philippines and abroad, and between cosmopolitan, middle-class consumers and the pirated DVD markets that create their conditions of being. These two networks could seemingly oppose one another; one transgresses national boundaries, while the other is firmly located within local culture. But here, localized piracy culture negotiates cosmopolitan media culture's foreignness, tempering its potential elitism through their shared alterity and allowing claims to authenticity.

Quiapo's space also plays a significant role in constructing its otherness, in this instance from the rest of the city. As the previous chapter demonstrates, Manila has become a malled-over city, divided into air-conditioned, sanitized, globalized interiors and hot, polluted, infrastructurally deficient exteriors. As such, palengke-style shopping in a place that evokes the premall city becomes a powerful experience of spatial, sensory, and, importantly, ethnic difference. While Quiapo is deeply embedded in national histories, it is also a transnational outpost in the city, acting as a hub for intranational migrants with connections to their own international trade networks, which offer a gray market counterpoint to the OMB-USTR association above. These networks become a material part of the city space itself, through businesses that cater to particular ethnic communities, the products available in the street markets, and the overall sensorial experience that marks the neighborhood's difference from the rest of the city. The DVD market was a critical part of this difference. While the wares themselves were a mix of the commonplace (multiplex blockbusters, Korean dramas, local teleseryes) and the unusual (pornography, the world cinema canon), their distribution infrastructure positioned Quiapo as a space that is central in terms of geography while being peripheral in terms of culture.[16]

Tilman Baumgärtel's research on Quiapo reveals the extensive, transnational trajectories its cinematic wares followed before reaching the hands of Manilenyo movie viewers. As one of Baumgärtel's informants shared, the pirated DVDs entered the country through two main routes, the "Chinese connection" (Hong Kong) and the "Muslim connection" (Indonesia or Malaysia). The latter would come in a single master disc and then enter the country hidden in the belly of tuna fish or in barrels of shrimp on fishermen's boats in small island areas controlled by the Moro Liberation Front, a Muslim guerilla organization. The discs then made their way to Davao, the major city of Mindanao, the southern region of the Philippines. The master would go to Manila, to one of the piracy centers in Quiapo, Pasig, or Caloocan City, where it would be duplicated upon arrival. "Especially in the neighbourhood of Quiapo, where the biggest pirate market in all of Manila is located," Baumgärtel describes, "the duplication machines can only run between 8 A.M. and 6 P.M., because otherwise the noise they make might attract unwelcome visitors."[17] As Baumgärtel's research suggests, the pirated cinema trade followed a long journey on its way to the capital city, across multiple versions of modernity. Moreover, his account highlights the industry as an embodied, material practice. However apocryphal it might be, his image of fish bellies hiding illicit copies of global media is not the usual picture of abstract cultural flows at work. Nor is the cacophony of the duplication machine a common factor to consider when imagining deterritorialized spaces of globalization. The material space of the media-circulation site created a sensorium of sounds, smells, and images, making it ripe for aestheticization in the imaginaries of capital-city cinephiles. Such aestheticization lends itself to discourses that position Quiapo as a more authentic alternative to the malled-over city.

The Quiapo DVD market laid the foundation for alternative cinema's reawakening in millennial Manila. Public discourse constructed its alterity by counterposing the district against the state, the mainstream media industry, and the rest of the city. As I will demonstrate, notions of authenticity underpin this construction and implicitly inform the production of alternative film culture, thereby revealing the role of place in that production. Work on art-house cinemas, for example, has discussed how food, decor, and ambiance can play a major role in attracting and constituting particular kinds of bourgeois publics.[18] In the case of Quiapo, a rhetoric of authenticity did similar cultural work for the entire neighborhood rather than a specific screening site. Unlike a mall multiplex or art-house movie theater, Quiapo's authenticity requires not the purposeful refashioning of material space to draw specific consumers but a particular point of view on the existing material space, a perspective predicated on class and cultural distance.

Through its representation in public discourse, Quiapo became part of a symbolic system that cultivated an intertwined, urban-cinematic authenticity. Discourses of authenticity tied to the city allowed a cosmopolitan, alternative film culture to be folded into local settings, despite its potential alienness. With cosmopolitan cinema consumption attached to a discourse of local urban revival and national multiculturalism, Manila's emergent alt-film culture mitigated its potential exclusivity and foreignness, charged issues for the Philippines' evolving film scene (as we have already seen). As this chapter suggests, trading exoticism and danger for multiculturalism and authenticity is not a simple process. E. San Juan Jr. argues that the problem with multiculturalism is the concept's presumption of an equality of opportunity in the public domain.[19] Such models certainly fail to account for cultural and socioeconomic asymmetries—particularly, in the context of the Philippines, between Muslim minorities and the Catholic majority.[20]

Urban-Cinematic Authenticity

Scholars of independent cinema—and, indeed, of alternative culture more broadly—have demonstrated the significance of ideologies of authenticity in legitimating both bodies of work *and* the reception cultures they produce. Often, the perceived authenticity of these alternative spheres of production and consumption is not only a product of authorial bona fides or aesthetic originality but also draws from the spaces of exhibition and distribution in which such spheres take shape as a culture. The spaces of exchange inform the production of authenticity alongside the cultural products themselves.

In a postcolonial setting in the global south, these dynamics take on the weight of national history and cultural identity. Urban authenticity has long been ascribed to Quiapo, which houses the ruins of the Philippines' midcentury affluence, while also portraying the ingenuity of the ethnic working classes who make their living there.[21] Visions of the neighborhood offer up the city as a consumable text, existing outside the hegemonic, global urbanism that stands in for modernity outside its borders. Quiapo presents the remnants of the country's former affluence, manifested in its retrofitted art deco architecture. It also presents the country as a pluralist, multicultural place, combining the Philippines' Catholic, Chinese, Muslim, and indigenous influences.

Due to its long history, the district lends itself to the kinds of mythologizing associated with claims to authenticity. In theories of memory, history, and urban studies, authenticity acts as a measure of mythic origins, harnessing history to form collective identities. As Walter Benjamin argues, the idea of authenticity is rooted in place and time, in a primeval way. As such, it is not an organic characteristic, innate to objects or events.[22] Rather, it is a socially accepted construct, one that constructs the past as malleable, produced through the vagaries of memory.[23] Importantly for the discussion here, this collective misremembering has a strong basis in place, wherein history is written as a series of events materially tied to specific locations.[24] Paradoxically, authenticity is in some sense invented and can be mobilized toward ideological and consumerist ends.

Cultural representations have long played a part in "inventing" Quiapo's role in Philippine culture. Take, for example, writer Nick Joaquin's description of the district. Joaquin is perhaps the principal chronicler of the city; his book *Almanac for Manilenyos* provides an urban counterpart to the almanacs of farmers in the provinces. Joaquin describes a trip to Quiapo as a devotional, civic journey: "Cubao and Makati may also have shops and first-run movies and restaurants, but not the 'thereness' of tradition; whereas a trip to Quiapo is still always partly a pilgrimage, even in the civic sense."[25] He dubs the district, particularly its central square, Plaza Miranda, the "crossroads" of the country. Sociologist Fernando Nakpil Zialcita builds from this vision of Quiapo as a site of nationalist pilgrimage. In his 2006 anthology, *Quiapo: Heart of Manila*, Zialcita sought to establish the site as a point of pride among Filipinos through the development of both heritage and tourism in the area. Zialcita argues for the importance of Quiapo by discussing its multiple cultural influences: "Quiapo is compelling as an ensemble. . . . The district serves art, history, religion, entertainment, and commerce in one colorful mix."[26] These accounts describe Quiapo in terms of Manilenyos' collective reminiscence, positioning the district as a link between the present and a primordial, national past. Joaquin constructs a narrative of transition from the "dreamy and quiet" streets of the area's past to the "jungle" that it was at the time of his writing, and Zialcita follows suit in his attempts to establish the district not as an area known for street crime and poverty but as the locus for Filipino national identity.[27] Quiapo becomes a remnant of a more desirable, more authentic national narrative.

In the early 2000s, cinema became a part of this connection to the past. For example, an article designating the district the "Quiapo Cinemathque" came from a June 2007 feature in the Sunday magazine of the *Philippine Inquirer* newspaper. Like the cinematheque designation, the story's headline referred to the French New Wave: "Quiapo Mon Amour." Referencing the 1959 Alain Resnais film, the headline sat beneath the Sunday Magazine's title, *Romance in the Old City*. Melding a piece of canonical French art-house cinema with a neighborhood in the "Old City," the allusion asserts Quiapo's cosmopolitan pedigree through a reference to international "prestige" cinema, fitting this cinema within accompanying maps of the Old City. It explicitly fuses the district's dual ties to alternative cinema and mythic nationalism. Positioning that nationalism within the terrain of myth enables a form of nationalist affect and remembrance that is distant from present conditions. This distance thus further constructs Quiapo as a counterpublic space. Moreover, the reference to the Cinematheque Française of the French New Wave, coupled with the allusion to a herald of modernist art cinema, *Hiroshima Mon Amour*, situates the article's mode of address within specific horizons based on education and international cultural literacy. The ability to appreciate the "romance" of the Old City requires a public with critical distance from, rather than proximity to, the images depicted.

These depictions also aestheticize the district by linking it to a multicultural, national history. While pluralist images highlight the district's lateral interconnections among the Philippines' diverse ethnicities and religions, there is also a more hierarchical process at work here. Such depictions become a means of aesthetic judgment, setting Quiapo apart from not only the rest of the city but from the forms of urban development that characterize it: malls, foreign chains, and other markers of global capitalism and its local outposts, including the multiplex. If discourses critiquing malls' globalism indict such spaces for their inauthentic, simulacral spectacle of global middle classness, Quiapo's DVD market provided a window into a different, possible future, which drew from the country's history. Thus, authenticity here implies not simply continuity with the past but also a break with the present, predicated on a "nonmainstream" status deemed preferable to it. Quiapo became a site that was authentic in both senses of the term—it was a tie to national origins, while also being an innovation on the status quo. The selective remembrance of its past becomes a signal of its value in the present.

This dynamic reveals much about the role that material spaces of film circulation play in forging alternative film culture and the speculative (counter)publics that emerge alongside it. As a space of film circulation, Quiapo played an important part in negotiating alternative culture's contradictions. As discussed, notions of "indie" and "alternative" rest on a fundamental contradiction. On the one hand, such terms embrace a radical sensibility that breaks new ground and subverts dominant systems of industry, politics, and aesthetics—this constitutes its claims to authenticity. On the other, the term often involves a culture of boundary drawing, grounded in levels of education and affluence, particularly at the point of consumption. The term carries a fundamental tension between its democratic and elitist tendencies. This divide is difficult to overcome; as Michael Z. Newman observes, popularity threatens independent artists' credibility, their works' status as outsider art, and, most crucially, their consumers' sense of being separate from the dominant culture. In the case of Quiapo, these contradictions inspire the discursive production of a speculative counterpublic for alternative cinema, one whose prospective status enables it to evade these inconsistencies. This is not merely a matter of distinction; as Fraser points out, historically, the "ethos and practices" of the bourgeois public sphere functioned as status markers, in Pierre Bourdieu's sense, by separating a "universal class" of men from the older elite aristocracy.[28] The discourses surrounding Quiapo are not merely trying to achieve status, but for the most part, neither are they purposeful interventions into public life.

Discussions of independent film in Asia tend to focus on its more radical potential, due to the contexts of state censorship and political repression that many of the films depict on screen and contend with off screen.[29] This is an important aspect of film production. At the same time, film scenes are not monolithic, and some sectors within them can also entail a recuperative, rather than transformative, stance toward national history, rejecting globalist modernity while stopping short of more revolutionary calls to social transformation. Accounts describing film consumption and reception reveal this tendency. As I go on to demonstrate, consumers can establish their alternative authenticity through the process of consumption, and the space of Quiapo played a key part in this.

But while this process might allude to the more exclusive tendencies of alternative film culture, the space of Quiapo allowed for its more democratizing inclinations: it linked consumers with the working-class ethnic minorities who ran the informal industry, and it also tied them to a version of the city that sat outside the present, connecting them to a national past. Hence, for consumers, the *process of attaining* alternative cultural productions became an important way of demonstrating cultural autonomy from mainstream industries and institutions. In this way, authenticity is not just attached to cinematic texts and practitioners but to the *consumers* who constitute alternative film culture through paratextual narratives that envision their own authenticity (e.g., describing journeys to attain obscure films, discussing and ranking their finds, demonstrating their knowledge of the obscure parts of the city where they seek their wares). The journey to Quiapo to seek obscure cinema becomes a celebration of a national past, as well as a way of separating from the homogenizing global urbanism that constitutes moviegoing in the present. It also entails supporting an industry run by an oppressed ethnic minority, creating moments of both solidarity and friction.

Fantasies of Access and Autonomy

As I have argued, in settings like Manila, where the socioeconomic divides between mass viewership and alternative cultural practitioners are often vast, and where nationhood is an ongoing project, alternative film's tensions between democratizing and hierarchizing tendencies become critical. Because the middle class is a small minority, criticizing popular culture means dismissing the mass majority, for whom mainstream film and television are a significant part of their everyday lives.[30] As May Adadol Ingawanij argues, establishing a national film culture means creating a space to imagine potential futures within a shared territory.[31] I would suggest that, as points of public dissemination, sites of film circulation become one of those spaces, providing an arena for envisioning national film culture's speculative publics. But the spaces for imagining potential futures are sometimes more inaccessible than their organizers may intend; indeed, accessibility was part of the rationale for the Indie Sine multiplex screen. It is therefore crucial to unpack not only such spaces' resistant tendencies but also their more contradictory dimensions.

While the discourses of authenticity surrounding both alternative cinema culture and urban space posit Quiapo as a site of alterity in the

2.4 Rita in Raya Martin's *Now Showing*.

city, thereby establishing it as separate from the dominant mainstream that the rest of the city represents, they also reveal a need to institute its role as a point of media access for a broader swath of people. The Quiapo Cinematheque became a celebrated site of media abundance; this abundance appeared in alternative films being produced during this period. For example, Raya Martin's 2008 film, *Now Showing*, depicts the Quiapo marketplace as an aestheticized urban backdrop (figure 2.4). Screened in the Un Certain Regard program of the 2008 Cannes Film Festival, the film is self-reflexive about the medium. Shot on digital video, it includes a sequence in the middle of its meandering four hours that involves a fragment of archival footage from the first "Golden Age" of Philippine cinema, played backward, lending an elegiac tone to the film's take on cinema history. If the film presents this decaying archival fragment as the partial artifact of a lost history, it contrasts this filmic fragment with the sheer media abundance of the present. The film follows a girl named Rita from childhood to adulthood. One sequence depicts Rita at her job, working the nightshift as a DVD vendor in Quiapo. She disembarks from a jeep, and the camera follows her in a long take as she traverses the nighttime marketplace, passing stall after stall. Upon her entrance to an interior shopping center, she passes arcades wallpapered with discs. Visibly bored, she sits and waits out her shift, occasionally helping customers find fictional titles; DVDs occupy virtually all the space around her. Depicted as mundane ordinariness, the portrait of extreme media plenty presents a stark contrast to the precious seconds that the archival footage offered.

This discourse of newfound access and availability worked at multiple levels. Consumers of alternative cinema framed Quiapo as an access point to cosmopolitan, alternative film culture unavailable in the rest of the city. At the same time, as we will see below, these consumers also framed working-class vendors' newfound access to these same films as a source of the district's socioeconomic, cultural transformation. Beyond simply pointing to the economic prosperity that the market created, they imagined the circulation of shared taste in films as a means of bridging cultural divides between middle-class lowland Christian buyer and working-class Moro Muslim seller. This utopian view undercuts notions of distinction that accompany alternative cinema. The issue becomes not one of aesthetics and taste but of availability. The problem of authenticity becomes not just a matter of autonomy from an imagined, industrial mainstream; it becomes a matter of making *that autonomy itself* available to other people, who may not have access to nonmainstream film consumption otherwise.

Thus, fantasies of access became a significant part of Quiapo's new imaginary, rendering it the foundational site for the speculative publics of Manila's burgeoning alternative film culture. By the mid-2000s, both local and foreign cinephiles imagined the district within ideas of newfound access to obscure films, in discourses that parallel information-rights perspectives on the global knowledge economy. For example, in a festival blog entry, Rotterdam International Film Festival programmer Gertjan Zuilhof speaks of his 2008 trip to Quiapo with reverent enthusiasm: "In Bangkok, Kuala Lumpur, Jakarta and above all in Manila, I had seen pirate DVD shops that were larger and with a wider range than legal stores in Amsterdam or New York. And that's what I wanted. An audience seeking calmly and choosing from immense stocks. The new model of cinephilia. The school of the young Asian film makers."[32] Here, consumer access is seen as an educational prerequisite of film production, linking the site of cosmopolitan film consumption to the burgeoning, local production scene.

This fantasy of access also translated locally, leading Filipino journalist Eric S. Caruncho to give the district its nickname, an allusion to the Cinémathèque Française, the educational institution of the French

New Wave filmmakers: "One thing that anti-piracy advocates neglect to mention is the appalling lack of choice of titles in legit DVDs. Go to any legit video store and chances are, all you'll get is mainstream Hollywood product. Not so at the Quiapo Cinematheque.... French new wave? Italian neo-realism? Film noir? Hong Kong action? '70s Japanese bondage films? Zombie cannibal splatterfests? Korean romcoms? Silent films? Got 'em."[33] As the market grew, blogs and message boards shared this discourse of longed-for access to global cinema, positioning the pirated marketplace as the city's sole source for a particular kind of cinema. These were not typical media consumers; rather, they were consumers who valued Quiapo (and piracy more generally) because it allowed access to titles unavailable elsewhere. Quiapo became an access point to a specific kind of foreign culture, one grounded in a wide-ranging view of film history—and the distinction that this view implies.

Moreover, urban space became part of this dynamic, melding cosmopolitan film culture with a mythically national space. If Quiapo has been viewed as the consummate site of urban nationalism, a rare destination in an overdeveloped city, the following accounts provide a parallel discourse about the cinema it offered. Quiapo may have been the consummate local destination, and the films it offered might have been a diverse assemblage of world cinema, but they shared the distinction of obscurity. In accounts on online message boards and blogs, urban space and the film culture it housed became rare gems unavailable elsewhere:

> Pirated DVDs and CDs provide access to hard-to-find classic, foreign and art films. Since these classic and hard-to-find films are already out of print or at least not available in major video stores, they can be had through piracy. This way, it becomes easier to get access to such movies.[34]

> As long as the legal local releases consist mainly of bad B-movies (yes Virginia, there is such a thing as a "*good*" B-movie) and forgettable Hollywood fluff, there'll always be a paying audience for the Quiapo goods.[35]

> As it was only my second time in Quiapo, I still found the huge number of DVDs strewn about overwhelming. Cartoons, Asian films, indie films, classics, live concerts, animes, old TV series, reality shows, latest blockbusters—you can find just about everything in that place.[36]

Where else can you buy an Akira Kurosawa collection in Metro Manila? Or critically acclaimed film *Marty*? Or even the film *300 Spartans*?[37]

DVD pirates, Quiapo and Art films gone loco! I am really not that fond of artfilms at first because of the lack of exposure and the availability of materials in local video rental shops. It's true! Go to any decent video shop and ask if they have, let's say, *Amelie*, most of the time, they would only shake their heads faster than a tree shedding it's [sic] leaves in autumn. It was the Hollywood schlok that ruled the nest. Even during the vcd era, there were not a lot of artflicks other than the asian horror genre. Back then, it was what? *Ringu*, the *Phone*, Pang Brother's *The Eye*. But that was it. It was only after I got hooked on dvds that I learned to appreciate artfilms as a whole. The first film i bought was Cuaron's *Y Tu Mama Tambien*, followed by *Crime of Padre Amaro*, and the rest was, well, history.[38]

As these passages assert, gray markets did not replace existing distribution channels but instead created new ones. This model follows discussions in postcolonial and critical legal studies, where considerations of piracy's ethics turn away from ideas of property, instead focusing on its transformative potential.[39] As Ramon Lobato demonstrates, these discussions frame piracy as a nonoppositional, ordinary means of survival.[40] This is an important perspective for considering piracy in the global south, especially during its early-aughts height. What is interesting about the new imaginary surrounding Quiapo is that it frames piracy as enabling a nonmainstream taste culture. As these discourses illustrate, the Quiapo Cinematheque's value lay in its status as a gateway to transnational, *alternative* film culture. Designations such as "art films," "hard to find," "classic," "indie films," and "critically acclaimed" serve as a contrast to "Hollywood schlock," "bad B-movies," and "forgettable Hollywood fluff." Referencing media from Japan, Mexico, the United States, Hong Kong, and France, from a range of historical periods, these consumers' rationales for piracy were based on the presumption of cosmopolitan (media) knowledge as a public good.

While Marxist readings of piracy view it as oppositional to mainstream media industries and, more indirectly, resistant to mainstream cultural norms, the Quiapo marketplace works differently. It is nonoppositional, but not because it is ordinary and everyday; indeed, the district is often framed in terms of its special place in Philippine history and its difference from the rest of the city. Rather, its alternative status rested on its proximity to cosmopolitan alternative cinema, combined with its distance from those cultural products regarded as mainstream. Like alternative cinema more broadly, Quiapo's new imaginary entailed a paradox between two impulses: the more democratizing (access for all, even those with little means) and the more elite (access to an established canon).

However, the space also acted as a means of negotiating this core tension of alternative film culture. While cinephile consumers venerated the district's alternative film offerings, they also imagined this access as available to a wide range of social classes and backgrounds. Specifically, they credited this access by transforming the district, through providing alternative films to working-class, Muslim vendors. One blogger, a visitor to Manila, relates how a host shared this narrative with her:

> Romeo . . . told me that the Muslim section of Quiapo used to be so scary he wouldn't go there. Shootings every week, nearly, between Muslims and Christians, tension tension. Then, the pirated DVDs came in. People started braving the crazy-ethnics section of town to get cheap flicks, but that wasn't the deal. The deal was that everyone in that part of Quiapo suddenly had access to films: Hollywood, art films, kiddie flicks, documentaries. The shop owners watched movies incessantly, as did their neighbors. The cultural savvy of the entire neighborhood leapt upward. Suddenly, upper/middle class artistes like Romeo could talk about the great European masters with Quiapo shop owners because the latter had gotten in a series of BBC artist biopics. Christians and Muslims could argue about camera angles, rather than shoot each other. (Well, not really, but imagine!)[41]

A posting on another blog, entitled, "How DVDs Create World Peace," discusses analogous ideas, constructing DVD shopping in Quiapo in comparable ways.[42] Similarly, a 2009 headline reads, "Pax DVD in Quiapo," illustrated with an image of a DVD superimposed with a peace sign, flanked by a Christian cross and Muslim crescent.[43] "What centuries of diplomacy and military subjugation failed to do, the pirated DVD has achieved in Quiapo," journalist Stephanie Dychiu writes, observing the ongoing commercial activity during Ramadan.

While the neighborhood's increased security likely had more to do with its economic prosperity, these accounts also attribute this peacefulness to attaining the knowledge that DVDs provide. Here, the fantasy of access involves elevating the "cultural savvy of the entire neighborhood." Quiapo's new imaginary and its role within alternative film culture entailed not simply circulating a rarefied form of cinema, thereby allowing consumers to establish their autonomy from a mainstream. Rather, it entailed circulating that autonomy itself, through access to alternative films.

It is important to note that in these discourses, access to specific films stands in for access to broader resources: education, synchronicity with global culture, and a shared taste culture that would ostensibly provide common ground among citizens. This fantasy is one of pirated (alternative) cinema creating a new public sphere: Quiapo's pirated DVDs would educate filmmakers and working-class film vendors alike, creating a shared public culture, grounded in alternative film consumption. Access does not necessarily lead to participation, however. The notion of media access as a structural precondition for publicity has found criticism in scholarship that questions its underlying premises: that the social structure is flexible, able to accept new members, and amenable to change.[44] Quiapo's fantasies of access seemed to provide a way out of alternative film culture's impasse between democracy and exclusivity. But as with most encounters across the borders of class and ethnicity, the more inclusive aspects of this negotiation had their limits, as we will see.

Difference, Authenticity, and the Limits of Cosmopolitan Film Culture

Purity and Distance

Quiapo's class and ethnic alterity played a significant role in its aestheticization. Quiapo not only offered access to newly obtainable films; as urban space, it offered access to a particular experience of the city, aestheticizing it in a manner that suited its new, film-fueled, cosmopolitan identity. Ethnic difference played a significant part in this dynamic, as the ability to aestheticize this experience was predicated on distance.

Quiapo's evolution, like many spatial transformations in Manila, cannot be seen in terms of simple gentrification. As D. Asher Ghertner observes in his analysis of gentrification's applicability in the global south, the concept's conventional emphasis on rising rents and correlated types of market-induced displacement obfuscates the political economy of land that underpins such processes.[45] Informality of the kind seen in Quiapo upends this broader view of gentrification. Moreover, the district's transformation was not based on new residents, as its "destination" status shows. Nonetheless, the models of authenticity that apply to certain perspectives on urban space do apply here. As the urban sociologist Sharon Zukin observes, "We can only see spaces as authentic from outside them. Mobility gives us the distance to see a neighborhood in terms of the way it looks, enables us to hold it to an absolute standard of urbanity or cosmopolitanism, and encourages us to judge its character apart from any personal history or intimate social relationships we have there. The more connected we are to its social life, especially if we grew up there, the less likely we are to call a neighborhood authentic."[46] Zukin argues that outsiders secure in their own social status ascribe authenticity to the "downwardly mobile."[47] This divide aligns with discussions of alternative media cultures. Borrowing from anthropologist Mary Douglas, Stephen Duncombe asserts that a dynamic of "purity and danger" develops around indie culture.[48] Purity involves autonomy from industrial control over authorship; this becomes a guarantee of authenticity. Danger entails the corruption of that autonomy through mainstream, industrial "co-optation." Like indie cinema notions of "purity" as synonymous with low budgets and low-fi aesthetics, here a neighborhood's remove from capital-intensive development becomes a signal of its cultural value. The value of purity moves from production and text to circulation context, creating a symbiotic relation between film culture and circulation space. This value becomes most apparent in discourses that frame the circulation space as an intraurban travel destination, thereby highlighting the distancing dynamic that Zukin observes. The designation of authenticity requires not only visitor status but an uneven distribution of power across the border between insider and outsider.

In Quiapo, these class-based dynamics intersect with factors such as race and ethnicity. For example, middle-class cinephiles' journeys to Quiapo entailed not only purposeful homages to national history, as in Nick Joaquin's narrative above, but also more inadvertent, physical experiences of difference:

> i like palengke-style shopping, i don't mind it at all. but at the end of the day i desperately needed a shower![49]

> I don't pretend to be an expert on Quiapo (I don't go very often) and I don't discount that it's an exhausting place to visit (jeepney is not my favorite form of public transport). . . . [But] those of us who

are drawn by its magic believe that it is a place worth visiting again and again.[50]

So, be sure to send a postcard on your next trip to Quiapo.[51]

Here, Quiapo becomes a destination point within the city, separated by the physical discomforts of travel, by geography, and by its "magic." In these imaginings, it is temporally and spatially partitioned from the rest of Manila; by implication, the city outside becomes the space of contemporaneity and ordinariness, rendering Quiapo the site of outmodedness and the event. Mirroring Zukin's model above, the version of authenticity at work here exists within the frameworks of travel. This is not uncommon. Indeed, many users posted maps to favored vendors, demonstrating both selectivity about desired films and the unfamiliarity of the space for those who might seek those works (figures 2.5 and 2.6).

As Zukin suggests, this insider-outsider dynamic operates across uneven power relations. Much scholarship discusses how travel and travel writing function as technologies of colonialism and modernity.[52] Within much of that discussion, Western privilege makes possible the narratives describing travel within "other" places and encounters with their inhabitants. Furthermore, such technologies contribute to the development and consolidation of that privilege, which is internally split by categories of gender, race, and class. Clearly, intraurban travel by Filipinos to Quiapo occurs very differently. Nonetheless, as the quotes suggest, this movement can sometimes involve similar dynamics on a smaller, intranational scale, as urban, educated, middle-class Manilenyos seek authenticity through encounters with religious and cultural minorities, encounters that, in this case, took place via the cinema-shopping interaction.

Importantly, while Quiapo's spectacle of cinema circulation captured a vision of transnational art cinema and multiculturalism, this spectacle also obfuscated a long, difficult history. As San Juan Jr. observes in his analysis of these struggles, "The situation of the Moros (now 10 million of 88 million Filipinos) may be taken as exemplary of the problematic nature of a formally plural (not yet genuinely pluralist) society constituted by violent dispossession and subalternization."[53] San Juan Jr. argues that Filipino Moros may be "one of the most brutalized victims of colonial domination and religious chauvinism in world history."[54] Politically and economically dispossessed, as well as culturally

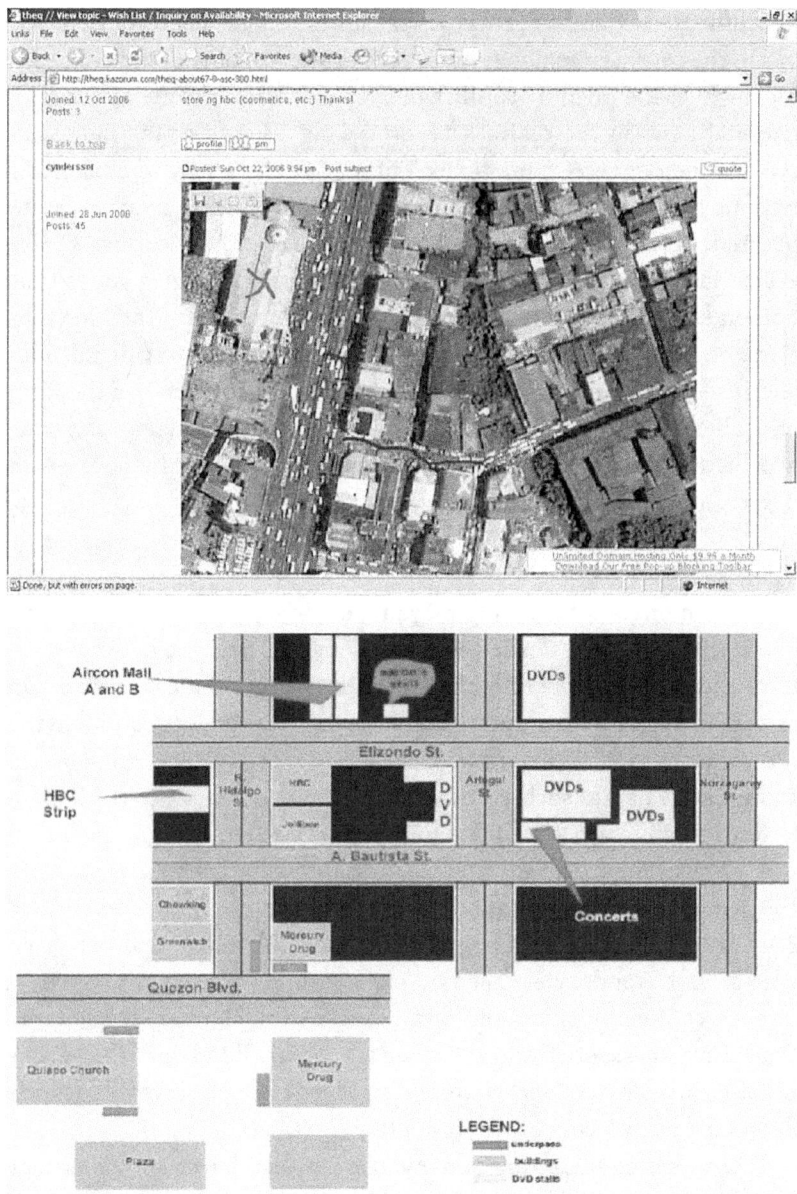

2.5 and 2.6 User-produced maps of the district, circulated on early-aughts message boards.

discriminated against during colonization and its neocolonial aftermath, the southern region is one of the country's most impoverished.⁵⁵ Meanwhile, the ongoing conflict in the South has become a fixture of national news in the capital city, producing a figure of the Bangsamoro as a homogenized, premodern other, an obstacle to the placating notions of national pluralism in which Quiapo cinema piracy was implicated. There is an irony, of course, that while the Moro pirate is a premodern figure in the popular imagination, the bootleg goods they offered served as an entry point into global modernity. This, too, has class connotations. Rolando Tolentino argues, "The pirate again intrudes and inserts himself or herself, in Philippine modernism—as the filter to enable the imagination by the nation-state and its citizens of having achieved the simulacrum of middle classness," which he goes on to describe as an affective feeling of class belonging.⁵⁶

"Abu-Suki"

This sense of class belonging played a significant part in discussions about DVD vendors themselves. Assertions of difference between vendors and customers pointed to ambivalent interethnic relations. On the one hand, talk surrounding the Muslim DVD vendors connoted the idea of camaraderie between vendor and buyer in shared antagonism toward state bodies such as the OMB. Consumers described the *suki* relationship, in which regular customers and vendors designate one another by the Filipino term "suki" to indicate a habitual relationship. On the other hand, many accounts of DVD shopping in Quiapo exoticized Muslim culture, emphasizing the district's otherness and perceived danger. Both tendencies relied on markers of difference, which reflect a more complex relationship with the district's Muslim inhabitants than simple aestheticization. Authenticity of the kind described above requires insider-outsider relations, but these relations reveal the limits of Quiapo as a placid outpost of multiculturalism.

Discourses emphasizing camaraderie between buyer and seller may be rooted in the Philippine state's token moves to combat the piracy trade. Raids on DVD markets placed the state in an oppositional relation to both Muslim vendors *and* their customers, complicating the ties between those selling pirated wares and the shoppers who dub them "Abu-suki." While "suki" references the habitual business relationship; "Abu" demarcates ethnic difference between vendor and buyer as an ethnicizing term. For instance, one DVD shopper posted, "pagpasensyahan nyo na mga abu suki kung mainit ang ulo nowadays . . . Ramadan kasi at malamang di pa kumakain yun" (You all be patient with the abu-sukis if they're hotheaded nowadays . . . because it's Ramadan and perhaps they still haven't eaten).[57] The term thus indicates the complexity of this customer-vendor relation, which teeters between respectful amity and divisions into "them" and "us."

Beyond the presence of vendors themselves, markers of difference in the way of atypical cuisines and languages also indexed the district's foreignness. Visitors mapped the DVD areas through their proximity to curries and halal meats, which became a key part of the cinemashopping experience. "Dinner and a movie" became curry and a pirated DVD, a variation on the familiar, long-standing links between food, taste, and cinema.[58] The accounts of Quiapo posit the foreignness of the DVD-shopping interaction as a key part in the experience, indexed via foods, languages, and cinematic genres:

> When you go to the area selling dvds there are also *carinderias* selling Muslim food (curries and such).[59]

> Our artist hosts for the day . . . took us to the Muslim area of Quiapo, near the mosque, to eat Halal chicken (mmmmmm) . . . near the pirate DVD shops.[60]

> Taking pictures here [around the pirated DVD stalls] is definitely not recommended! It is quite tricky if not plain dangerous. I tried it and it was met with anger. One shop owner started shouting at me and soon a little mob assembled. I didn't understand what they were saying but I moved on as quickly as I could . . . I guess they thought I was working for the FBI. ;-)[61]

> And, as was customary whenever I go buy movies, I asked one lady if they had *Felicity*. The lady, while busy gobbling La-la [fish crackers], hollered to some guy in another dialect, turned back to me and said yes, they did.[62]

> And, of course, Quiapo is the pirated CD (audio CD, VCD, and DVD) capital of the universe. I once brought two Ilonggo *barangay* chairpersons there to buy karaoke CDs. They were so afraid of the Muslims they hardly spoke and looked at the merchandise. Funny. Since

my sister in law converted to Islamism, Quiapo is also where I would buy her and her family *halal* meat. Chicken, beef and veal are sold in a Pakistani-owned shop there.[63]

In addition to the "Golden Mosque," Quiapo now boasts a Hindu temple. Needless to say, because of this, Quiapo has become THE place to find the best *halal* meat and latest Bollywood movies.[64]

As with the narratives of travel, the Muslim (and Hindu) markers of difference separated the district from the rest of the city, which lent the space its value. In keeping with the locale's connection to both exoticism and crime, many bloggers wrote of the site's danger, warning foreigners to avoid the place unless accompanied by a local: "Note to the Foreigners Reading this Blog: Please do not even attempt to go to Quiapo alone. It is not a place friendly to outsiders."[65] Others provided warnings for potential visitors:

> Nerds like me scoured Quiapo for bargains, carrying only enough money for a few good finds and jeepney fare (as a precaution against muggers).[66]

> My friends would say I court an element of danger every time I go here but danger is exciting and I get to love manila all the more because of it.[67]

> Dress simply meaning "no-frills" clothing will be best. Best to go also in sneakers or slip-ons. . . . Stick to the main roads. Stay where there are most people to avoid getting mugged.[68]

Perceived danger was thus a large part of the Quiapo experience. Some of this discussion may have been related to a desire for "street cred," with participants in this aspect of alternative film culture demonstrating their knowledge of an obscure part of the city. On a more practical level, the blogs encouraged readers to blend in with the site's masa surroundings to avoid robbery but also, as one posting put it, "because Muslim merchants are wary of giving discounts to *coños*."[69] The derogatory term for wealthy Manilenyos distances the writer from that class bracket. In a trope common to travel narratives, he becomes a guide for middle-class visitors to the district, able to fluidly navigate both inside and outside. If the class dynamics of the district are predicated on encounters between the upwardly and downwardly mobile, this writer's mobility is multidirectional, indicating their expertise. As with much travel writing, claiming the ability to navigate both worlds implicitly reinscribes difference, elevating the "neighborhood guide" above both visitors and locals.

Specifically, this idea of risk was related to street crime rather than the district's pirated merchandise vendors. While OMB discourse posited the site as a home to criminality based on illegal trade, consumers and vendors existed in a kind of familiarity and shared investment in the illicit exchanges taking place. One writer observed that vendors warned shoppers to "take care." Moreover, mutual disdain for the OMB created a kind of camaraderie between vendors and shoppers. Though many blog posts mocked OMB efforts, dismissing them as mere show, others expressed trepidation about buying pirated goods in case of raids. Quiapo Pirated DVD (QPDVD) provided an online guide to shopping the district's DVD stalls (figure 2.7). Members posted news of raids; others responded with comments, such as "Ni-raid daw ang Qdessy kanina? Grabee naman. Kawawa sila manong." (They said there was a raid at Qdessy earlier? My goodness. Poor vendors.) Such expressions of empathy and degrees of loyalty toward the vendors also appeared in remarks reporting a fire at a regular DVD site: "Kaninang umaga para raw yung sunog. Kawawa naman ang mga Muslim vendors doon." (It was said that there was a fire earlier this morning. Poor, poor Muslim vendors over there.)[70] Some days later, a comment updated fellow members as to where the vendors at that particular spot had moved. This empathy toward vendors was not entirely consistent, however, as one post referred to the raids as a positive thing "which favors us," that is, the consumers, because of the smaller number of shoppers in the district, which would make haggling easier.

In a way, Quiapo allowed its cinemagoing visitors to have their cake and eat it too. It enabled film consumers to access international films (mainstream and boutique), while also making these purchases in excursions to their city's most historically rich, culturally diverse setting, without engaging in the interethnic conflicts that inform its conditions of being. It allowed the differences of class and ethnicity to be framed as markers of urban-cinematic authenticity rather than reminders of a difficult history. At the same time, it is important to consider the impulse behind the multiculturalist dimensions of the Quiapo Cinematheque. As Zukin asserts, the search for the authentic city is often a search for the urban village, "the low-key and often low-income

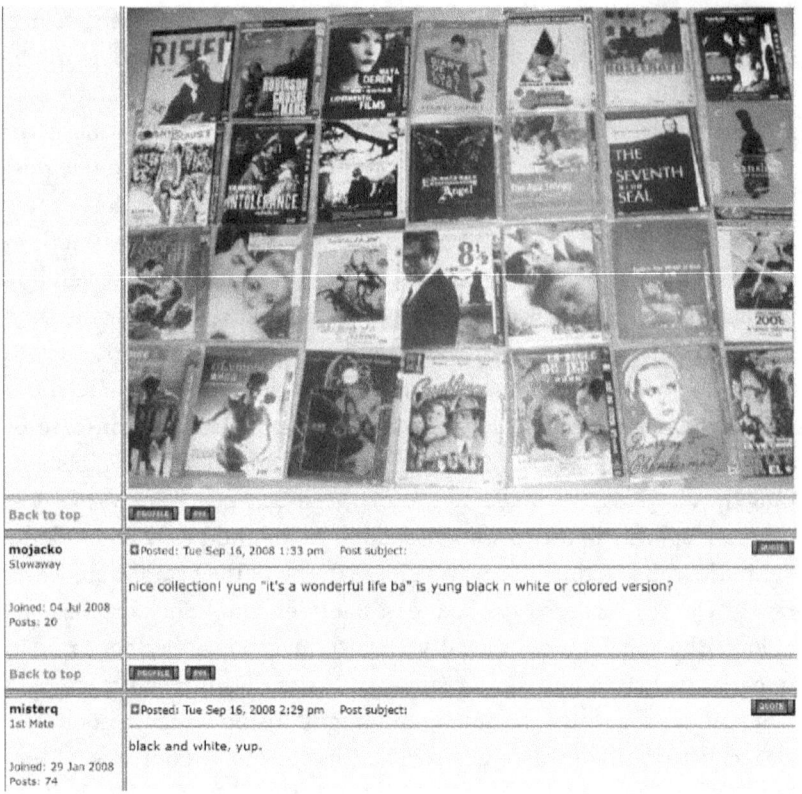

2.7 A spectacle of world cinematic abundance, displayed on the QPDVD website.

neighborhood, the culture of ethnic and social class solidarity, and the dream of restoring a ruptured community. It is in many ways the local response to globalization."[71]

The symbolic system that Quiapo's new imaginary engendered may have been doing some reparative work, negotiating the circulation of global cinema with a turn to the perceived purity that alternative film culture values. In this instance, interactions with a minority community became one vehicle for this purity. This turn to authenticity reflects the concept's most contradictory dimensions—its simultaneous radicalism and elitism, its democratizing and exclusionary tendencies. Quiapo became a space where a nascent alternative film culture could negotiate those contradictions, envisioning a speculative public that crossed class and ethnic lines.

The End of the Quiapo Cinematheque

As with many of the sites in this book, Quiapo's reign eventually faded. Manila mayor Alfredo Lim first saw to the abolishment of the Animist vendors surrounding Quiapo Church. That Lim was also the omnipotent eye in the previous chapter's 1995 political cartoon is fitting; his campaign against Quiapo's informal street markets worked toward his dream of a completely surveilled, malled-over city. Eventually, in 2010, he and the newly appointed OMB chair Ronnie Ricketts offered Quiapo DVD vendors a one-month grace period before the OMB would carry out large-scale raids on the district. On the morning of July 1, 2011, Lim, Ricketts, members of the media, and representatives from the U.S. Embassy confiscated 10 million pesos' worth of pirated discs.[72] News cameras captured the scene as representatives from the state's Optical Media Board filled trucks with countless bags of DVDs. Television news interviews showed a community of vendors expressing anger, doubts, and apprehension about their abilities to earn a living. Most of them spoke regionally accented Tagalog, their voices marking them as migrants to the capital city.

Lim himself embraced a very different kind of foreignness, sporting a "Los Angeles" T-shirt for the cameras. This was an ironic sartorial choice. Transforming his body into a reference to the center of global media production, the mayor spouted tough talk against the informal industry that had raised his district into relative prosperity. Meanwhile, his own constituents saw their livelihoods disappear onto government trucks. In this scene of obstructed circulation, Lim, the U.S. Embassy, and the commercial film industry (through Ricketts, a former action star) align with one another against an ethnicized Filipino other. This spectacle of state obstruction was staged to present a dominant, dramatic narrative of illicit pirated-media circulation, portraying it as a battle waged across multiple scales: piracy was a problem that had emerged from the national hinterland, which could be eradicated through alliance with a global power.

While the Quiapo Cinematheque imaginary constructed media circulation within fantasies of access and multicultural authenticity, this display of state force staged an altogether different kind of intercultural encounter. Again, urban space and media circulation inform one another. If Quiapo had once provided a concentrated, geographic symbol celebrating the Philippines' archipelagic multiculturalism, the raid portrayed this same interculturalism as deviance. Through tropes of action heroism and state machismo, the carefully executed scene attempted to transform a national public, urging it to identify with a different, more powerful transnational alliance than that imagined over the past decade. It encouraged viewers to trade the more utopian notion of counterpublic solidarity between Christian consumers and Muslim vendors for affiliations between Filipino filmgoers and transnational IP enforcement.

This scene suggests the possibilities of what spaces like Quiapo can provide, momentarily. It highlights the complexity of a film culture that is both speculative and asymptotic, depicting its possibilities and its failures. Cultivated through the lens of urban-cinematic authenticity, Quiapo's new imaginary offered one means of negotiating the tenuous relation between middle-class Manilenyo cinephiles and the Muslim vendors they patronized. When scholars discuss media circulation, the classical model is that of circulation as a centripetal force, cohering viewers through the mass consumption of shared texts, creating a collective, imagined community—in this instance, crossing the divides of class and culture. This is certainly one of the imaginaries that circulation engenders. As this discussion suggests, in Quiapo, this imaginary is predicated on ideals of authenticity, a contradictory concept used to negotiate the tensions inherent to both revitalizing urban space and alternative cinema. The Quiapo Cinematheque would provide access to alternative films for Manilenyo cinephiles. Moreover, it would create alternative film culture as a new, multicultural, counterpublic sphere, based on shared peripheral status. This model provides an important counterpoint to more dystopian images of state power. But it also privileges the smoothness of flows, obscuring the frictions created through differing literacies, industrial infrastructures, and long histories of intercultural conflict.

Unlike the imaginary that drove Indie Sine, which involved entering the existing space of the malled-over city, the Quiapo Cinematheque was predicated on intraurban travels. This imaginary embraced the spaces and people that the mall, with its disciplinary constructs of the good and bad audience, had left behind. Quiapo offered a different kind of media-circulation space, cultivating not a unified mass public, drawn from the mall's arcades, but a speculative counterpublic predicated on distance from the mallscape and the reinsertion of the middle class into an older version of Manila urbanism. This spatial logic also translated to alternative film exhibition sites that emerged during the early years of Philippine cinema's revival.

CHAPTER THREE

ALTERNATIVE EXHIBITION AND THE RHYTHMS OF THE CITY

To Cinekatipunan's detractors we say, you can raid us anytime but for as long as independent films are created by artists and activists we are committed to provide the needed venue.
—MAG:NET GALLERIES, 2007

Cubao X. The artist community. A state of mind, a sense of place. A term coined by a filmmaker during a gathering (no staid, formal meetings here, just people sitting back, relaxing, drinking the drink of their choice and chatting unhurriedly with likeminded people). Cubao X refers to the group of artists running their own shops inside the historic Marikina Shoe Expo at the Araneta Center, but it has since come to mean the epitome of creativity and cooperativism.
—*CUBAO-X*, 2007

The quotes above describe exhibition sites that emerged in the early years of Philippine alternative cinema's growth: Cinekatipunan (2006–2009), a by-donation, daily screening series held at Mag:net, a restaurant and gallery located in the university area of Quezon City; and the Cubao Expo, a small enclave of independently owned businesses located in a shopping district that had seen better days. In the mid-aughts, the Expo became a hub for niche commerce, drawing crowds attracted to its vegetarian-friendly café, bars, vintage shops, and comics store. The

3.1 These stills from a deleted sequence of the Quark Haneres 2011 film *Rakenrol* depict the Cubao Expo as a regular haunt among Manila's early-aughts bohemia. The film introduces the space through contrasting the shoes with the later art scene.

Mogwai Cinematheque (2007–2011), an alternative exhibition space owned by filmmaker Erik Matti, was situated among these alt-leisure offerings.[1] Both sites were spaces for cultural production, for the circulation of artworks and artisanal commodities, and for community building around shared political or artistic ambitions.

Each site represents specific versions of urbanization. Here, community requires retreat from the institutions and economies of urban life. In the first quote, urban life entails state surveillance. In the second, it requires the hustle of capitalist work and consumerism. The screening initiatives provided a respite from both of versions dystopian urbanism. While their spatial separation from the rest of the city is clear, the sites also establish their peripheral status through a deliberate temporal divide. Here, participants can "sit back," "relax," "chat unhurriedly with likeminded people" in a censorship-free space, liberated from the Movie and Television Review and Classification Board (MTRCB) and premised on using film to forge alternative futures (figure 3.1).

This spatiotemporal partitioning underscores the sites' identities in Manila's alternative film cultures. Cloistered away from the urban fray, these spaces of cinema exhibition are selectively attuned to alternative circulatory rhythms, both local and foreign. Scholars of exhibition have long established that screening environments affect audience encounters with films. More recently, scholars of distribution have analyzed the staggered temporality of films' dissemination to audiences, examining how delivery dates align with audiences' social hierarchies.[2] Films make their way from the wealthiest to the poorest areas of the city, their timing mapping audiences according to long-established inequalities.[3] Much of this research deals with the macro view of distribution temporality, examining both informal and official industrial practices. In this chapter, I am interested in more artisanal, ad hoc temporalities that attempt to synchronize the circulation of films with the wider rhythms of the urban spaces they inhabit and the communities they target. Thus, I am not interested in distribution as an industrial process so much as dissemination as a semiformal practice tied to particular exhibition sites.[4] Here, the temporalities of the city play a much more significant role in establishing the relationships among time, public culture, and films' dissemination to Manila's intellectual and art audiences.

While the so-called Quiapo Cinematheque's media piracy engendered fantasies of access that envisioned a counterpublic for alternative cinema, niche exhibition sites suggested a different approach to drawing out Philippine alternative cinema's speculative publics. Like Quiapo, the sites generated a slew of discourse in popular media, blogs, and message boards, cementing their status as key venues in the city's burgeoning early-2000s alternative film culture. Also, like Quiapo, they are founded on palimpsestic readings of the built environment that tie the spaces to the past. They establish their separation from the unevenly developed city both spatially and temporally. Unlike Quiapo, however, the initiatives described in this chapter are not as interested in melding local historicity with global simultaneity (e.g., pirated access to new theatrical releases and art cinema reissues). Rather, they foster a vision of the alternative exhibition space as embedded in a kind of temporality constituted in binary opposition to mass consumer cultures. This opposition to mass consumer cultures speaks to the kind of speculative publics created within these spaces. Indie Sine was built on a strategy of contingency and stealth encounter—the crowds are in the malls, so for those in the alternative film scene, infiltrating that space meant drawing mass consumers to the alternative cinema screen. Through chance encounters, Indie Sine hoped to create a broad public that reached across social class. The Quiapo DVD market's discourse took a different tactic, fostering an imagined counterpublic comprised of middle-class cinephiles and ethnic minorities bonded through shared antagonism toward international IP enforcement. This chapter's accounts of film exhibition and consumption dramatize an escape route from the paradox of alternative cinema, narrating the possibility of unified national publics for a burgeoning, alternative cinema.

The accounts achieve this in several ways. Unlike the multiplex cinema, they do not synchronize with what Charles Acland describes as the "felt internationalism" of global information-communications technologies.[5] Instead, they embrace an alternative temporality that combines an orientation toward a shared, localized past with a cosmopolitan connection to other parallel enclaves abroad, which cultivate their own alternative temporalities. Such temporalities have utopian aspirations, though they do not always play out in the ways that organizers imagine. In their built environments, educational strategies, screening technologies, and programming schedules, the film initiatives in this chapter produce a kind of temporality tied to a collective memory. Selectively synched to the rhythms of the city, this temporality—of nostalgia, urban walks, schedules and programming, and the city's subjunctive mood—presents itself as a counterpoint to the globalized, homogeneous time of mass consumer culture. The sites are not aligned with that global consumer clock, but with a counter-consumer-culture temporality that is no less transnational in its orientation. This is not the kind of synchronicity predicated on speed, acceleration, and simultaneity, as with globally concurrent release dates for Hollywood blockbusters. Rather, tied to a revaluation of lost urban and cinematic histories, this is about the slow, long-term duration that certain kinds of historicity afford, a duration that has become its own kind of transnational, subcultural currency. Outmoded projectors, references to national history, and vintage wares become a part of the exhibition experience. In this way, while the screening initiatives attempt to synchronize to a more local setting in order to attract broader viewerships, these efforts are circumscribed by the sites' subcultural status.

I track three different initiatives here. In the first section, I investigate the role of urban nostalgia in mapping the Cubao Expo onto a broader map of Manila. If malls and billboards filled with stars constitute the city's major thoroughfares, these cloistered spaces call back to the city's past. This juxtaposition creates a spatial chronology of film and urban history that moves from the mall-studded center to the art-house periphery. Second, I examine how two film initiatives appropriated existing urban rhythms in their programming, in an attempt to cultivate publics for alternative cinema. Screening six days a week at 5:00 P.M., Cinekatipunan folded itself into the repetitive temporal structure of the workplace and the university. Meanwhile, the Mogwai Film Festival appropriated the temporality of the Metro Manila Film Festival, an annual mainstream moviegoing ritual that coincides with the Christmas holiday. Lastly, the shorter, final section examines how a one-off event in Remedios Circle, the downtown and former bohemian section of the city, created a liminal, expansive exhibition event that displayed what Victor Turner describes as the city's subjunctive mood. In each of these cases, competing temporalities become a crucial part of alternative film circulation, allowing a cosmopolitan, middle-class film culture to claim local territory. This film culture harmonized with local rhythms that worked outside the standard tempo of revanchism. Given the long-standing critiques of Philippine independent cinema as insufficiently local and made primarily for foreign viewerships, this attempt to sync with the city's rhythms becomes a way to stage a more local version of alternative film culture through practices of circulation.

In this way, discussions of urban temporality are useful for considering how circulation can enable alternative film cultures to negotiate their relationship with imagined national publics. While such film cultures are cosmopolitan, they are often deeply invested in particular ideas of locality, which become a part of their symbolic systems. As one observer put it, Cubao was a "cosmopolitan," "uniquely Filipino," "local Greenwich Village."[6] This moniker is not just easy shorthand for bohemian life; it trades one form of urban temporality for another. In her study of Greenwich Village, Sally Banes writes of the idea of a "bohemian community" as an urban alternative to the pastoral idea of community. Rather than being bound by religion, work, and family, the Greenwich Village community of the 1960s looked to "folk, popular, and transgressive subcultural styles, as well as to religious ritual, for means to reject the values of both the previous generation of artists and the socio-political establishment."[7] She argues that the sensibilities created in the Village might only be viable in the city, in the middle of the gesellschaft; they are not local but instead are eclectic, hybrid, and "plugged into what Marshall McLuhan termed the 'global village' being created by the electronic mass media."[8] This evocation of "the folk" evokes a counterintuitive combination of time (lost, pastoral, ritualized) and space (cosmopolitan, mediated). This synthesis of time and space operates within these alternative exhibition spaces as well. As we will see, locality and the speculative publics that it represents become not just a matter of space and scale but of time and history.

Film-Circulation Temporalities

A cosmopolitan, middle-class turn to ritualized time is in part a response to the transformations of the ever-expanding revanchist city and its regulation of urban publics. The spaces under discussion here point to the multiplicity of urban temporalities in cities like Metro Manila, temporalities that often exist in antagonistic yet interdependent relation to one another. A key claim of this book is that alternative film culture is a temporal process that constructs a futurist vision, one that is both speculative and asymptotic. Such film cultures are grounded in possibility, but that possibility's achievement is perpetually stalled in the political-economic conditions of the present. Through their engagements with time and history, the alternative exhibition spaces elaborated in this chapter mediate these conditions. They engage with temporal modes that work in opposition to those of the wider city.

Speculation becomes one of these temporal modes. By recalibrating urban time via ritual, programming, and evocations of collective memory, these spaces refract the revanchist, neoliberal city's forms of speculation, offering countervariations. Neoliberalism is an economic order grounded in anticipation, dismantling the tidy linearity of past, present, and future. Neferti X. M. Tadiar writes that as a system of political and economic rationalization, neoliberalism constructs a "circuit of money advanced as credit."[9] This circuit creates "a temporality of finance, or the time of speculation, that shapes the form and experience of the neoliberal *homo economicus*."[10] Drawing from the work of political scientist Melinda Cooper, Tadiar argues that the practice of speculation as capital investment constructs value through *anticipatory time*, inverting the power of past and future, production and profit. Within finance capital, future profit births the past of production: "The contraction of past and future, the evaporation of chronology or successive and cumulative time in the infinite extension of present action, the colonization of the future as a means of present realization, such temporal features of life under neoliberalism are, in my understanding, an accounting of the subjective experience of a subject inhabiting money as capital."[11]

If this describes the time of the neoliberal city, the spaces here offer a contrapuntal variation of evaporated chronology and anticipatory time. Modernity has always been multisided, describing both market-driven industrial economies and the cultural-aesthetic forms that emerged to oppose them.[12] This relation is at work in the spaces here, setting them apart from other exhibition spaces that acted as alternatives to the multiplex norm. For more lux, aspirational viewing experiences, there were the lounge cinemas discussed in the chapter 1. On the other end of the spectrum, third-run theaters in areas like Quiapo became popular cruising sites for gay men.[13] State-funded spaces such as Film Development Council theaters and the Cultural Center of the Philippines, which I will discuss in chapter 5, provided other alternative, cinematheque experiences for middle-class moviegoers. What sets the spaces in this chapter apart are the specific kinds of temporalities they sought to cultivate, which worked outside the deterritorializing velocity of the revanchist city and its globally synchronous cinemas. These alternative spaces evoked older forms of communal life and, thus, a return to ritualized time, suggesting a fantasy of permanence. Writing in a very different context, Charles Baudelaire asserts that urban modernity is "the ephemeral, the fugitive, the contingent, the half of art whose other half is the eternal and immutable."[14] The sites discussed here reflect this perspective, evoking older, "immutable" forms of ritual time whose permanence might enable new futures for alternative, protomodern film cultures. Their proprietors kept them small scale and artist run in order to stay outside the bounds of state regulation and capital-intensive investment. This left them in a state of precarity while also, paradoxically, enabling their existence. Such alternative art sites enter the world with a limited life expectancy, even as their turn to ritual time alludes to more durable forms of public existence.

This paradoxical, contrapuntal temporality works in two main ways in the discussion here. First, through programming and scheduling, these alternative film initiatives engage in processes of synchronization that attune to local, rather than global, rhythms. The film initiatives described here are not striving for global synchronicity but deliberately turn to other rhythms that constitute the city: to the everyday of work and school, to leisure time, or to seasonal rituals. As with Quiapo's images of media abundance, these are projects that involve fantasies of access and the broader publics that access might engender. These rhythms also play a part in constituting film publics, their centripetal energies working as a counterpoint to industrial distribution's stratifying tendencies. Much recent work on film distribution has sought to examine how industrial distribution processes divide audiences according to market value, through differential rates of delivery. In his study of La Paz, Bolivia, Jeff Himpele observes that imported film prints make their way from more affluent to poorer neighborhoods.[15] Deb Verhoeven similarly argues that films "'descend' through social hierarchies" due to the zone-run-clearance system of theatrical distribution, reaching the least privileged last.[16]

These practices affect the formation of media communities on a transnational scale. Charles Acland's work on the internationalization of distribution analyzes how industrial networks establish zones of consumption defined by the speed at which new commodities arrive.[17] Capitalism is "not a totalizing flow" but circulates unevenly.[18] These flows create what Acland terms "popular cosmopolitanism," a "structure of feeling" that allows audiences to feel synchronized with imagined, distant populations, enabling them to negotiate nationhood with the dominant experiences of globalization.[19] Of course, such synchronicity differs across class, income, and other forms of intranational, collective identity. The temporal dimensions of industrial film distribution profoundly affect cinema's ability to form wider, more meaningful collectives. For these scholars, the acceleration or delay of circulation constitutes audiences—and hence, potential publics—differentially.

But disseminating films to audiences does not just happen at an industrial level, where novelty is the prime value. The initiatives and events in this chapter work within more localized rhythms. Geographers have long discussed cities as nodes within ongoing networks of trade, migration, and exchange rather than static objects.[20] This idea of the city's own rhythms is key. In the film initiatives I describe, it manifests as the urgency of political oppression, the quotidian schedule of the workday, and the ritualism of the holiday season. These are temporalities that work alongside the global capitalist flows that drive industrial distribution patterns, and it is these temporalities that the alternative film-circulation initiatives follow.

The second temporal strategy involves these sites' allusions to the past. Through evoking urban and cinema history, these sites of alternative film culture allude to collective, public memory. Such evocations of a broad, collective memory construct a speculative, future public. While the cultural products the sites circulate are rarefied objects to be shared among the few, the antiquated experience of the city they evoke is more wide reaching. Through allusions to a shared urban history, these wider publics become a part of the sites' "future perfect vision," the "will have been" or conditional "would have been" that they register.[21] Revisiting older parts of the city and viewing them through the lens of nostalgia, embracing vintage technologies for their cultural value rather than their use value, acknowledging long histories of film and popular culture—these practices construct ideas of what might have been and what still might be, creating a different sense of anticipatory time. As Henri Lefebvre observes, "Space is nothing but the inscription of time in the world."[22] For the projects in this chapter, this inscription means hailing the possible audiences that alternative cinema had yet to find. The sites become aspiring, subjunctive spaces, the events they house embracing a utopian form of speculation that works in the future perfect tense. Their rituals of moviegoing took on the impossible task of overcoming alternative cinema's paradox, trading the uneasy combination of limited circulation and textual radicalism for a more enticing admixture: communal village life hidden in the revanchist city, localized ritual time amid the globalized time of neoliberalism. They constructed anticipatory spaces of public film circulation.

Spatial Timelines and Residual Exhibition

The neighborhood of Cubao provided a fitting space for those seeking a premall version of Manila moviegoing. Indeed, Cubao's layered, semiotic density informed the Mogwai Cinematheque's identity as an exhibition site. Nostalgia became a key facet of Mogwai's art-house temporality, operating across scales, from the exhibition site to the small shopping center that housed it, to that shopping center's surrounding neighborhood and beyond. As scholars of exhibition have long demonstrated, the contexts of the screening event inflect viewers' encounters with the cinematic text. Here, such arguments expand to the multiple scales of space that surround the exhibition site, in part because Mogwai was a cloistered, hidden destination in the city. Online users shared maps to the Cubao Expo shopping center, like Quiapo, telling tales of searching for the location—taking public transportation, describing it as "this nice hidden place," getting lost in a rarely visited neighborhood

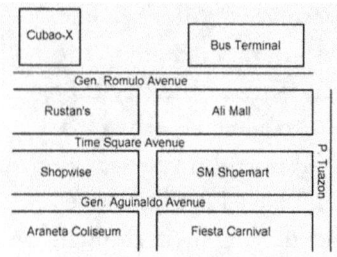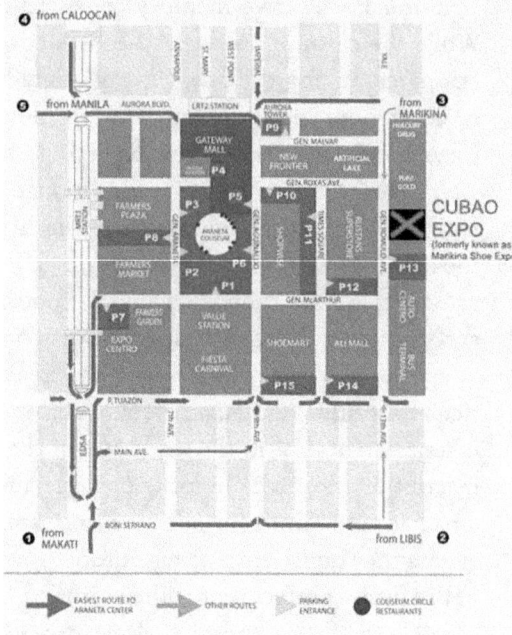

3.2–3.4 User-generated maps to help find the Cubao Expo.

that was well past its prime (figures 3.2–3.4). These accounts thread the Cubao Expo into a longer travel narrative that moves across both space and time: from contemporary mallscape to midcentury ruins to bohemian outpost and, sometimes, to a microcinema bedecked in midcentury art-house trappings. Embedded in nostalgia, the Cubao Expo's allusions to the past become a means of negotiating past and present. They offer alternative timelines that operate in the subjunctive, alluding to a speculative present that might have been.

Manila film culture parallels this spatial movement from present to past. Urban travelers would move through visual manifestations of mainstream media (the present) to reach their alternative arts enclave (the past—and a utopian, speculative future). To travel around Manila is to travel the city's tangled, arterial highways, clogged with slow-moving vehicular traffic. It is also to be surrounded by massive, looming billboards displaying the country's stars. When I lived in Manila, scantily clad Sam Milby, a mestizo Filipino American who found fame on *Pinoy Big Brother*, adorned enormous advertisements for Bench, a local clothing company. K. C. Concepcion, the daughter of the superstar Sharon Cuneta, had just returned to her home country after college in Paris. Her entree into local show business included advertising campaigns for the clothing company Bayo, which towered over EDSA, the city's main thoroughfare. On one billboard, Bayo congratulated her on her new film, the 2008 Star Cinema romance *For the First Time*, highlighting the star's role as mediator between film and consumer culture. The Philippines' mainstream media industry was visually omnipresent in the city, as aspirational images of health, wealth, and beauty towered above a congested network of human and automobile traffic. This mammoth height is fitting. In line with Tadiar's observations, the infrastructure projects designed to push Manila into the flows of global capital have involved literal elevation through elevated motorways, which create a vertical caste system of travelers divided across forms of transport.[23] Looming above the fray, these mammoth billboard stars would sit at the top of this hierarchy.

In this way, the mainstream media industry is woven into the fabric of Manila's urban visuality, with stars punctuating the failing transnational-national infrastructures that date back to Marcos-era development projects.[24] If, as Paul Virilio has argued, "the view from the windshield is cinema," in Metro Manila, that cinema is of the mainstream variety.[25] In this context, one strategic move for the alternative film scene was to create Indie Sine, melding with these spaces of global consumerism and mainstream cinema; another strategy involved cloistering itself away, in a spatial separation from the rest of the city. This separation allowed not only a means of escaping the malls but also a visual, sensory separation from the mainstream media industry emblazoned across the cityscape. This division had temporal dimensions as well. For middle-class intellectuals, the overdeveloped city and its mainstream cinema represented lost opportunities; a return to an urban past represented a chance to rewrite old timelines, locating them within a localized setting more amenable to aspirations of a national film culture.

That Cubao became the center of this revision is not surprising, given its history in the city's cinemagoing and consumer culture; moreover, its socioeconomic status had fallen in previous decades, lending the neighborhood a poignancy particularly suited to middle-class nostalgia. The wealthy Araneta family developed the area in the 1960s, and at the time it was intended as an alternative to the increasingly crowded streets of downtown Manila. As a former center of urban leisure, Cubao played a role in the city's midcentury film culture. New Frontier Theater became Quezon City's first first-run theater in 1968, and it was soon followed by the Nation Cinerama and others. By the 1980s, many of these theaters had become screening venues for local soft-core pornography. By the time Mogwai opened its doors, several of these decaying structures were still there, retrofitted into other businesses, such as thrift stores that sold imported clothing donations and a budget hotel. The former Cinema 21 became a dilapidated Protestant church, its banner outside promising miracles to its working-class patrons. The area also had a reputation as a haven for the gay sex trade. As Bobby Benedicto describes, "Cubao was seen as a place 'respectable' people did not go at night, if at all."[26] It was known for "run down go-go bars with broken neon signs, for the brothels masquerading as massage parlors, and for giving rise to the term *'bakal* (metal) boys,' a reference to the hustlers who used to stand by the steel railings around Araneta Coliseum."[27] By the early 2000s, Manila's bohemia had made its way to the area, settling into an environment that recalled the city's former prosperity, while also registering the district's descent into seediness. Early-2000s Cubao was a spatial palimpsest, layering mid-twentieth-century affluence, late twentieth-century working-class repurposing, and postmillennial urban art subcultures.

The neighborhood's spatial timeline of urban evolution provided a fitting center for the Mogwai Cinematheque. Mogwai opened its doors in 2007 in the former Marikina Shoe Expo, a small, U-shaped shopping complex that had changed its name to the Cubao Expo, or "Cubao X." This transition reflected the structure's move from being the home of inexpensive, Filipino-made shoes from the neighboring city of Marikina to its state as a mix of a few remaining shoe stores alongside a frequently changing roster of bookshops, antique and vintage stores, a comic book and toy store, art galleries and collectives, and cafés. The shoe industry collapsed due to the liberalization of the Filipino economy in the 1990s, which increased the flow of low-cost, Chinese-made shoes into the domestic market.[28] The Marikina Shoe Expo was already well past its prime when it opened its doors to other vendors in 1997 due to the Asian financial crisis, which caused many shoe stores to close.[29] Thus, the Expo itself is an artifact of a preliberalization economy, in which domestic production and consumption led to a thriving local industry. It is a museum of localized commerce from a previous era, rendering it a fitting site for a local alternative film scene envisioning local audiences.

Much of the Cubao Expo's identity as a haven for Manila's bohemian or counterculture crowd stemmed from its slightly worn veneer, created not simply through its relatively recent additions of vintage and antique shops but also through its positioning within a dated version of Manila's shopping history: the surrounding, large-scale department stores, the shoe stores that acted as reminders of the Expo's previous existence, and the *ukay-ukay* (thrift) stores that catered to shoppers driven by price as well as those looking for unusual, vintage finds. The cult of nostalgia surrounding the Cubao area prompted recollections from those reminiscing about its former incarnations. Bloggers wrote lengthy tributes to the area, one noting, "The place hasn't changed much in the past 20 years. It didn't help that the tinny trebly speakers that served as the PA system was [sic] blaring old 80s pop songs like Van Halen's 'Jump' and Yes's 'Owner of a Lonely Heart.' Nostalgia galore."[30] Another compares the Expo's current incarnation to its past life, using the space to mark a transition between generations: "Cubao. I lived my childhood on one of the streets named after a city abroad. . . . The now popular Cubao Expo, the venue or more like the 'house' of vintage shops, artistry, antiques and much more, was but Markina Shoe Expo to me and my friends. . . . [I] have witnessed how it blossomed for another generation."³¹ Similarly, another writer discusses how the space registers the passage of time:

> I drove to the Marikina Shoe Expo in Cubao on a lovely, sunny Saturday afternoon and attended a short meeting, an orientation of sorts. . . . My mother and I used to regularly go to Cubao, every two weeks, on the dot. . . . In the late 1980s, Cubao started changing. . . . Now, there's the well-air-conditioned Gatewall Mall and the loud, imposing supermarkets. . . . But the best surprise is the Marikina Shoe Expo. I do remember going there once or twice long ago. . . . Nowadays, it is the Marikina Hip Expo (Cubao X, they call it), with art galleries, a bookstore, cool gift stores, and an exalted Italian restaurant.³²

As these selections demonstrate, the nostalgia surrounding Cubao plays a significant part in constituting its identity within Manila, as a place that was once a hub for shopping and commerce, whose reputation in the "fast lane" was replaced by newer areas of the city, and that has since become a focal point for Manila's "underground" culture. It is a space that is separate from the "loud, imposing supermarkets" and the "well-air-conditioned" malls. As Christine Boyer argues, knowledge of the built environment is based on collective memory, which enables users of urban space to create meaning from it.³³ In the case of Cubao and Mogwai, this collective memory was grounded in nostalgia for an era of consumer culture predating the rise of neoliberal globalization. Using nostalgia to reject a teleological, globally ordered spatiotemporality is not necessarily radical; indeed, nostalgia is often deemed a conservative, reactionary impulse. But as Hamid Naficy writes, it can also be a response to the displacement wrought by neocolonialism, imperialism, and transnational capitalism across the world.³⁴ While Naficy refers to exile, I assert that nostalgia can also function on a more figurative, local level. For residents in changing cities and neighborhoods, it can become a means of asserting agency, allowing them to reclaim "symbolic ownership."³⁵ In an unevenly developed city like Manila, organized around malls and their globalized forms of commerce, symbolic ownership through nostalgia becomes a means of reconnecting with a localized past. It thus offers a subtle critique of the present. For the middle classes that populate vintage, bohemian enclaves, nostalgia becomes a structure of feeling that projects lost futures. It becomes a counterpoint to popular cosmopolitanism's outward-facing, affective ties, turning them to a shared past and the national publics that this shared past implies.

3.5 Made to promote the Cinemalaya Philippine Independent Film Festival, the promotional short *Cinemalaya Pulutan* was shot in Mogwai, suggesting the connections between the café and alternative film production and exhibition. The iconic screen star Joel Torre makes a cameo appearance.

This was a fitting setting for the Mogwai Cinematheque, which positioned itself as an inheritor of an older kind of cinemagoing, as well as a new hub for the city's growing alternative film scene (figure 3.5). Its visual allusions to an older form of exhibition suggested a novel timeline, a history of local film culture that moved not from "Golden Era" to mainstream multiplex but from this era to an alternative microcinema asserting its art-house DNA through programming and interior design. This is not to suggest that Mogwai had an antagonistic relationship to local mainstream media. This connection was not so much antagonistic as ambivalent, reflecting the film work of its owner, Erik Matti. Much of Matti's career took place in the commercial industry; he became known for cowriting a 1996 fantasy film, Star Cinema's *Magic Temple*, which he authored with another director who works at the interstices of commercial and independent filmmaking, Peque Gallaga.[36] Matti cofounded Reality Entertainment in 2005 as an independent studio, but it also maintained ties to the commercial industry through his partner, Dondon Monteverde, the son of "Mother" Lily Monteverde of major studio Regal Films.[37] Matti's relationship to the mainstream industry is not quite oppositional, but it is not entirely unified either.

Nonetheless, Mogwai's programming and decor lent the space a distinctly art-house veneer. Like Cinekatipunan, Mogwai functioned at a distance from Manila's established cinematic institutions, in particular, the MTRCB. Unlike Cinekatipunan, this distance was a product of the screening space's commercial, rather than political, practices. Mogwai's Cinematheque operated through memberships, which were available in multiple forms, via various monthly or annual rates. This membership system was a way of maneuvering around the restrictions of the MTRCB, which required fees for screenings. As with the Quiapo Cinematheque imaginary, alternative cinephile consumers distanced themselves from the state in ways that were not necessarily oppositional but which asserted a separation nonetheless. Mogwai's mission statement explained that in addition to being run by practicing filmmakers with "film scholars as consultants," the Cinematheque was "the only other cinema aside from the U.P. Film Center and Cultural Center of the Philippines to have no censorship restrictions in the country."[38] Thus, Mogwai existed at a remove, however ambivalent, from both the mainstream industry and the state, cementing its alternative status in a way that was not simply cultural, aesthetic, or geographic but institutional.

The site's programming furthered this distance from mainstream media industries and state institutions. In addition to hosting local independent films fresh from their festival travels, the Mogwai Cinematheque had a markedly international program, promoting itself as a hub for "films from Hollywood classics to underground cinema, art-house fare to *Pinoy* grindhouse flicks," thus mixing local independent fare with alternative cinemas from Hollywood and elsewhere. In addition, the venue's launch included outdoor projections of the Cannes collection of shorts by thirty-six directors, *Chacun son cinéma*, thus establishing the exhibition of works from an international canon as a part of its mandate. One review of the venue explains: "The second floor is home to the screening room, a cozy little private cinema that regularly shows movies that would never make it to our cinemas. . . . There's no better place to catch movies considered 'off-the-beaten-path.' It's hard to find any place that's showing *Glengarry Glen Ross* or *Chacun Son Cinema*."[39] Like Quiapo, fantasies of access become a part of the site's identity; sites like Quiapo and Mogwai allowed potential viewers to see films that would otherwise be inaccessible in early-aughts Manila.

Unlike Quiapo however, this access's curation was tied to local auteurs rather than the whims of transnational piracy networks. While the programming was often international, Filipino filmmakers also played a significant role in the lineup, drawing from a long history of alternative cinema. Screenings with Filipino artists as guest programmers featured such films as Troma studios' *Tetsuo Body Hammer* (1992), shorts by the Quay brothers, and a four-hour documentary on Andy Warhol. In this way, these artists became "hosts" for nonmainstream international movies, which were integrated into the repertoire of local, alternative taste cultures.

Nods to film history were also evident in its decor. Mogwai mixed a more unconventional screening layout with aesthetic connotations of the midcentury art house. While the downstairs was primarily a bar and restaurant, Mogwai's upstairs was designated specifically as screening space, with a video projector, surround-sound system, and piles of large, amoeba-like floor pillows where viewers would sit and, usually, lie down to watch the show. The space was small, with a maximum occupancy of thirty people, and upheld a no-shoes policy, with shoe racks outside the doors. The screening experience was thus cloistered, collective, and bodily, with patrons bringing in food and drink from downstairs, surrendering their street shoes, and lounging on the ground in a vaguely slumber-partyish atmosphere.

At the same time, the Cinematheque also gestured to the midcentury movie palace, a nostalgic design that evoked the history of its Cubao surroundings. Its walls were covered with deep red, brocade-patterned wallpaper, and its doors were covered in tufted black vinyl. A row of movie-theater-style seats sat against the back wall. Most prominently, its facade featured an old-fashioned movie marquee, which glowed like a beacon in the Expo's small, U-shaped arcade. Its membership options referenced the traditional movie palaces of midcentury downtown Manila, dividing into a rolling scale with choices ranging from "Loge," to "Balcony," to "Orchestra." The construction of a movie palace, even if only through the rhetoric of its marketing materials, suggests a regard for cinemagoing as it "once was," outside of the mall multiplexes that comprise the vast majority of cinemagoing opportunities in Manila. It evokes a return to older forms of urban leisure.

Mogwai thus housed a form of nostalgia specific to Manila, and perhaps to other urban settings in the global south, where an educated middle class bridges a complex divide between an outward-facing, cosmopolitan modernity and an inward-facing pull to more localized variations. This nostalgia complicates cinema studies ideas about alternative, art-house exhibition, which focus primarily on class. In the Western settings where most of this research has taken place, the art house has historically been seen as a site of social reproduction, drawing an audience of older, more affluent white cinemagoers before its 1960s decline.[40]

Its contemporary versions recall this past, sometimes occupying repurposed, midcentury cinemas, whose value lies in their status as urban heritage. Certainly, there was a class dimension to the bohemian enclave surrounding Mogwai. But the space also conjured a history of urban leisure whose loss takes on a different meaning in cities like Manila, where, as we have seen, malls have created a revanchist city, their globalized, "popular cosmopolitanism" exacerbating conditions of severe inequality.

From a certain middle-class perspective, there was something elegiac in Cubao's repurposed, consumerist ruins, standing in the shadow of a more recent, affluent mall. When the district began to revive, media coverage celebrated its return, frequently dubbing the Cubao Expo "Bohemian Manila." As one proprietor of a vintage shop observed: "I think by the statement that we attract the Bohemian-type actually means we attract people who are not afraid to look for something as different as Cubao Expo. People will go out of their way to get here; you have to admit it takes time to get here. But like I said, the people who take the time, who allow themselves to be pulled in by the magnetism of the Expo, are the ones who have the Bohemian spirit in them to go here."[41] This statement reflects the consensus in early-aughts media and blog postings about the space: those who frequented the place sought "something different," were drawn to it because of an innate affinity for its particular kind of "magnetism." The fact that artists and the like found this particular area appealing speaks to their middle-class status—as in Quiapo, by looking for "something different," they also crossed class borders. But class was not the only dynamic at play.

I would argue that the art-house exhibition space's nostalgia held multiple meanings, existing in tension with one another, embedded in both its elite and progressive tendencies. As Stuart Tannock contends, there is a need to recognize nostalgia's heterogeneity, the myriad ways it has been put to use in the service of political projects: "The nostalgic subject turns to the past to find/construct sources of identity, agency, or community, that are felt to be lacking, blocked, subverted, or threatened in the present."[42] In a setting like Manila, the distinction associated with the art house works in tandem with a longing for the preliberalization economy that the Expo represents. Written into the built environment and the events it housed, this past became the site of collective memory. As such, it alluded to a broader Manilenyo public, while also cloistering itself away from a film culture that had come to be defined primarily by the multiplex cinema. As a space, its dynamism was simultaneously centripetal and centrifugal. The built environment's "veneer of pastness" cultivated an identity that, like alternative film culture itself, hinged on a tension between the elite and the radical, the cloistered and the inclusive, a nostalgic turn to the past and a utopian staging of the future.[43] Mogwai's identity as an exhibition site was both spatial and temporal, existing in a balance between the innovation of the new and the collective memory that vintage aesthetics recall.

This nostalgia created a speculative counterpublic that was both localized and cosmopolitan. Cloistered away from the mainstream city, the Cubao Expo and Mogwai created a chronology that was most recognizable to those within the culture, who had grown up with the memory of the space as it once was. The layout of the built environment created a route of passage for its visitors, from globalized-mall modernity to a historical modernity of a different sort, a consumer culture that might have been. Embedded in this imagined timeline, the Cubao Expo offered a subjunctive space, and Manila's film culture grafted onto this route of passage. The transition from billboard-lined, star-studded highways to Mogwai's re-creation of the midcentury movie house produced a speculative public that was cosmopolitan in its consumption and localized in its collective memory.

Regularity and Ritual

While the semiotics of space evoked nostalgia, the rhythms of programming also produced their own temporality. As Jeff Himpele argues, the idea of creating a public through cinema is difficult, because cinemagoing events are ephemeral; gathered from disparate places, audiences enter and exit the theater before cultivating the more enduring identities that would lead to public formation.[44] For Himpele, the cinemagoing public is as ephemeral as the screening event itself. Thus, for programmers and screening organizers seeking to foster an alternative film community, regularity became a temporal strategy. Though they worked in very different ways, the screening initiatives of Cinekatipunan and the Mogwai Film Festival drew from existing urban rhythms to cultivate audiences, viewerships who were already worked into the city's tempos through their roles as students, office workers, and cinemagoers. Projecting an ideal public forged from the mobile, urban crowd, the initiatives counteracted the ephemerality of the cinema event through their series format and the annual ritual.

Repetition and Publics

The Cinekatipunan film series used its daily screenings to build from the publics that already existed in its surrounding area, which were organized around activism or education. The series was connected to social movements due to organizers' affiliations with the activist media organization Southern Tagalog Exposure, and it was also integrated into the academic community, due to its location amid several universities as well as a screening night dedicated to student works. In this way, it differs from the other spaces under discussion here, in that it acted as a hub within independent, transnational, and activist social and media networks. Cinekatipunan's venue, Mag:net Galleries and Café, was owned by the artist Rock Drilon. The Katipunan Avenue location was not the first; two previous locations, Mag:net ABS and Mag:net Paseo, had closed. It was named for its initial function as a "magazine network," which would allow subscribers to foreign periodicals to purchase their subscriptions through the network for a lower price. Due to this function, Mag:net was a cosmopolitan space.[45]

This cosmopolitanism also owed much to its location. Situated on Katipunan Avenue, a main road that houses three of the city's major educational institutions (the University of the Philippines, Miriam College, and Ateneo de Manila University), Mag:net catered to a large student market as well as others of Quezon City's café and gallery clientele. The area is middle to upper-middle class; both Ateneo and Miriam are known for their wealthy student bodies.[46] Like most middle-class areas of Metro Manila, it is intended for vehicular, rather than pedestrian, traffic, so the crowd's orbit around the venue was relatively confined. Though many of Mag:net's events might have had customers spilling onto the pavement outside, the relative lack of public street life in the vicinity rendered them some of the few inhabitants of this small spot of Katipunan Avenue, beyond shoppers at Rustan's, the café's neighboring high-end grocery store, customers going in and out of the Starbucks that shared Rustan's building, or the area's few street vendors—street children selling small towels made of scrap fabrics or women with carts selling fish balls. Thus, while the gallery was one of the few spaces like it along Katipunan Avenue, the logistics of its layout rendered it a somewhat enclosed space, calling little attention to itself, its lights often dwarfed by the glow of its grocery-chain neighbor. Despite its location on a major road, it was a site for cloistered, subcultural gatherings.

The interior of Mag:net was quite small, built in a narrow shotgun style with few windows, save for those facing the street in the front. It divided into two narrow floors. The downstairs portion served as a gallery space for local artists and a small magazine and bookstore selling local and international publications—from art magazines to books on U.S. politics. Postings and signs covered the narrow stairwell leading to the second-floor bar and restaurant, announcing film screenings, art exhibitions, and the like. The stage in this upstairs portion provided a site for a wide range of performances, including stand-up comedy troupes, dance pieces by the young dance collective AirDance or the established dancer Myra Beltran, and local bands that ran the gamut of Manila's early-2000s music genre offerings, from the Filipina folk-rock artist Cynthia Alexander's collaborative show with Manila-based Indian musicians to a tribute show honoring the classic New York punk band the Ramones, to Manila's own, mid-2000s indie staples, such as Up Dharma Down and Sandwich.

Cinekatipunan shared this stage space with its daily screenings of predominantly local cinema produced outside the mainstream studio system. The screening series took regularity as one of its primary values, enabling it to work its way into the ongoing schedules of the surrounding universities. Screening six days a week at five o'clock in the evening, before the venue's later events, the series was the project of a young, local independent filmmaker and human rights activist, Kiri Dalena (figure 3.6). As one blogger wrote: "Cinekatipunan at Mag:net is a daily affair, and is just about the only place where you'll find a constant stream of independent video screenings whose make and treatment vary from the avant-garde to college theses to hard-hitting social documentaries. Initiated by independent filmmaker Kiri Dalena of the group Southern Tagalog Exposure, Cinekatipunan seems to be slowly gaining ground and a steady audience, not just from the universities around the area, but from among groups of independent filmmakers, creative folk from all walks, and film enthusiasts."[47]

This "constant stream" is a key aspect in public formation, which relies on the everyday temporality of ongoing circulation. In her work on performance and utopia, Jill Dolan argues that the "festival or series format extends the temporary public the audience constitutes across a longer period of time, a condition that facilitates utopian performatives," creating "more opportunities for critical and affective discourse around performances that a familiar group of people shared."[48] In this

3.6 Cinekatipunan's calendar, November 2007.

view, the festival or series model offers a counterpoint to Himpele's doubts about the cinema's ability to form publics. Repetition creates a level of ease among audience members, who may become "micro civil societies," sustained by group identities more confined than citizen, working class, or "the mass consumers of the nation," connected through mutual responsibility.[49] As we saw in chapter 1, a desire for permanence and regularity drove the Indie Sine film initiative to the mall; this desire also drove Cinekatipunan's organizers, given Mag:net's location in an area already filled with university students, faculty, and activists. The mix of work screened was varied, ranging across a wide spectrum of alternative filmmaking practice, but its daily screening time was its constant, encouraging regular attendance.

While the screening series was quite successful, drawing a significant number of viewers every time I attended, it was not without its troubles. These problems stemmed mainly from being targeted by government institutions and anonymous threats. Dolan's account of how the series format itself leads to "micro civil societies" may be a shade idealistic. In the case of Cinekatipunan, the organizers already had group identities that existed beyond the film screenings. The screenings played a role in *extending* rather than producing these affiliations. The series created a new means of establishing collective identity rather than new identities themselves. This proved threatening to state authorities.

In November 2006, agents of the MTRCB appeared in Mag:net and informed organizers that they would have to stop the screenings unless they could produce a permit.⁵⁰ This was no empty threat; as Dalena shared in an interview, members of Southern Tagalog Exposure had been interrogated by paramilitary forces before. The organizers met with the MTRCB chair and members of the board, who stated that the body had no problem with the project's mission to give "a venue and support to Philippine indie filmmaking and filmmakers" rather with the entry fee.⁵¹ The MTRCB conceded that the screenings could continue as long as there was no admission fee, though the 50-peso contribution from the series to the filmmakers was small compared to the local multiplex fees of the time, which could be 150 pesos or more.

The series continued its daily screenings unabated, celebrating its one-year anniversary at the end of that year. It also amplified its commitment to social movements in the coming months, due to the heightened suppression of activists. In April, Jonas Burgos, a thirty-six-year-old activist affiliated with leftist underground movements, was abducted from a Quezon City mall by the Philippine military. Cinekatipunan responded by preceding its regular screenings with a short film about this forced disappearance. In August 2007 Mag:net began to receive angry phone calls and threats of closure if Cinekatipunan did not cease its screenings.⁵² In the café's newsletter, screening organizers theorized that the regular programming of activist films had much to do with this unwanted attention: "Could it be because Cinekatipunan has programmed one of its screening days to show advocacy films, some of which are quite political and incriminating? Or could it be because it allows screening of some films censored or banned somewhere else? Or could the reason be because Cinekatipunan has recently preceded its daily programming with Jonas Burgos 30-second ad clips and has committed to run them till Jonas is found and till the government can address and do something to put a stop to the increasing cases of disappearances and summary killings of journalists and activists?"⁵³ Consistency became one of the key strategies of the series. The article ends with the statement quoted at the beginning of this chapter, the pledge to continue its screenings: "To Cinekatipunan's detractors we say, you can raid us anytime but for as long as independent films are created by artists and activists we are committed to provide the needed venue." The declaration maps the position of Cinekatipunan's exhibition space against the commercial or mainstream cinema supported by the MTRCB, as well as the violence of the Arroyo administration. In this instance, government cinema bodies demanded compliance with a political status quo. In the context of Arroyo's Philippines, this status quo encompassed a political regime responsible for the disappearance and extrajudicial execution of dissenters, many of whom were closely connected to the organizers of the film series. Urgency became a driving force for the series, connected to the films it played and to its daily temporal structure.

These daily short films depicted a state of ongoing, immediate risk. As Susan Stewart observes, the temporality of everyday life involves a contradiction. It is linear, moving forward indefinitely; it is also repetitive and predictable.[54] Within these films, the contradictory temporality of the everyday—its indefinite linearity, combined with its cyclicality—takes on a grave urgency. In this instance, repetition reflects conditions of ongoing violence, and its endlessness is an unthinkable possibility. For example, Sigrid Andrea Bernardo's one-minute film *Lost and Found* presents an immediate call to action.[55] It begins with black-and-white, handheld documentary footage. Protesters clash with police wearing riot gear. Quickly edited documentary shots of protest performances flash by. Shirtless, hooded protesters kneel with ropes around their necks. Crouched around coffins, others hold portraits of the disappeared that speak to unremitting daily violence. Signs by members of the League of Filipino Students, a long-standing anti-imperialist organization, indict the president, demanding, "Gloria, who are your next targets?" and "Hey! Hey! PGMA, how many civilians did you kill today?" The film's form then switches, moving from an aesthetic of liveness to a more elegiac mode. A contemplative song by Jess Santiago plays over color footage of street vendors. Close-ups lend poignance to everyday objects: a camera, a hat, a bandana. The vendors place them carefully on a blanket, beside a sign reading, "Lost and Found, 10 piso." The objects are synecdoches for missing activists, their banal physicality emphasizing their "lost" owners' bodily absences. The screen dissolves into a collection of portraits of the disappeared, labeled with their names. One by one, the images disappear from the black screen, over sounds of physical struggle. A larger photo of Jonas Burgos appears, and a title card reads, "Lost and Not Found." Shorts like this became a defining aspect of the Cinekatipunan film series, depicting the social world in which the series took shape. This world is one of conflicting temporalities: ongoing violence, immediate calls to action, and irrevocable, permanent loss. At only seventy-five seconds long, the repeated microduration of *Lost and Found* reflects a time frame in which rapid, widespread dissemination was critical. The daily series provided an embodied, physical space of exhibition that complemented the shorts' release online.

Within this context, I would suggest that an important part of the threat that the screening series posed to the state was its synching with the metronomic cadence of official, everyday time: the school day and workday. With its six-days-a-week, 5:00 P.M. screening time, it worked within the temporal structure of its surroundings, an area dense with universities and NGOs. The film series harnessed the cyclical, indefinite duration of everyday life, but it punctured that predictability with its films, which operated within a logic of disclosure and information dissemination. Cinekatipunan's role in persistently disseminating information allowed it to function not just as an exhibition site but in a mode similar to print journalism. Certainly, a film takes more time to produce than a journalistic article and thus lacks the immediacy of a newspaper. The parallel here is admittedly rough. But the idea of topical films, exhibited on a regular basis, emphasizes the *rhythms* of exhibition. Michael Warner argues that the regularity of discourse allows it to punctuate daily rhythms. "The temporality of circulation," he writes, "is not continuous or indefinite; it is punctual. There are distinct moments and rhythms, from which distance in time can be measured."[56] This is crucial for creating the sense that this circulation is occurring in an active, rather than a passive, sphere.[57] It invites a public to act, intervening in an ongoing stream of discourse. While the public sphere is often discussed in spatial terms, its temporal dimensions are crucial, allowing consumers to recognize its dissemination to strangers through the reflexive, cross-citational field created via reviews, criticism, and—importantly here—controversy.[58] While the parallel between film and print is imperfect, Warner's print-based analysis offers a fitting model for thinking about nonindustrial patterns of film dissemination and their meaning.[59] Removed from the framework of staggered windowing or day-and-date releasing, regularity and repetition are meant not only to attract viewers but also to confer agency onto them. This strategy allowed the Cinekatipunan screening series to harness the temporality of circulation in an effort to create a utopian, "micro civil society"—the speculative, future publics that could, ostensibly, upend an oppressive state.

Festival Ritual

Creating a community of viewers was a key goal for both Cinekatipunan and the Mogwai Cinematheque. Both succeeded in drawing their art-practitioner/aficionado clientele, though their reach beyond this circle was perhaps limited. Mogwai's programming was more varied, but I would like to focus here on how the site appropriated one of Manila's mainstream cinema rituals. If Cinekatipunan was oriented to the urgency of the political present and the possibility of an activist future, the Mogwai Film Festival operated within a different temporal logic, reworking a troubled past to pose alternative futures. As we saw in the previous section, part of this was based on an aesthetics of the past. But for the Mogwai Film Festival, it also involved inverting the branding of an older film festival with a long history in the city, one with a very specific model of exhibition.

The late Canadian Filipino film critic Alexis Tioseco organized the 2007 Mogwai Film Festival (MFF) in reference to the commercially oriented Metro Manila Film Festival (MMFF), announcing his initiative with the declaration "One M is better than two" on his widely read cinephile blog. The MFF was, in part, a temporal reinvention, aimed at a speculative public for alternative cinema. This worked in two ways: appropriating ritual and alluding to the past. The Mogwai Film Festival harnessed the power of ritual in order to reference an annual moviegoing rite, one that would have been familiar for the vast number of Manilenyos. Moreover, while the MMFF had become an object of scorn for many by 2007, its history suggests a more utopian origin. Thus, alluding to MMFF's unmet potential becomes an oblique reference to the past, framing it as a lost opportunity. Importantly, this lost history is one of local mainstream cinema and mass audiences. That this becomes a historical model for a new alternative cinema demonstrates one of the key tensions underpinning any clean divides between mainstream and alternative film: a latent desire for mass audiences, even within the confines of a cloistered art-house venue.

The Metro Manila Film Festival is a studio-sponsored, commercial cinema fiesta that involves a two-week blackout on foreign films in multiplexes across the city, as well as in other parts of the country. Throughout the blackout, all theaters in Metro Manila play only the seven movies associated with the festival, creating a brief period that exclusively showcases local commercial movies.[60] This blackout earned P305 million in 2007, demonstrating Manilenyos' love of local commercial cinema. Ostensibly, the festival would be a prime example of national film culture in the making. But the festival's history demonstrates the difficulties of cultivating any such culture, due to institutional corruption and class divides.

Started as the Manila Film Festival in 1966 by Manila mayor Antonio Villegas, the all-Tagalog event was the city's biggest attraction until 1974, when it became mired in local politics.[61] President Marcos removed Villegas and enlarged the festival to include the other municipalities in the newly founded Metropolitan Manila.[62] It was renamed the Metro Manila Film Festival and declined, before Mayor Mel Lopez revived it in 1991, with only moderate success. Controversies around rigged awards three years later returned the event to the media spotlight, albeit in a controversial way. Since then, the festival has been successful commercially, though local critics find that the films it features leave much to be desired.[63] Tying these failures to mainstream studios' visions of their audiences, writer Jessica Zafra said of the MMFF's 2012 iteration, "There are good commercial movies, and there are bad commercial movies. The bad outnumber the good because the studios think the viewers are idiots."[64] For many critics, the MMFF has become a symbol of the film industry's unrealized aspirations.[65]

Despite these perceived problems, the Metro Manila Film Festival holds a unique place in the city's social life, due largely to its timing. Beginning each year on December 23, the MMFF has become a fixture of the Philippine Christmas season, known as the world's longest (beginning in September) and most lavish (as one CNN story put it).[66] The festival provides a kind of cinematic follow-up to the centuries-old Catholic Simbáng Gabi ("night mass"), which runs from December 16 to 24.[67] It is deeply integrated into the traditions of the season, a time of year that blends commercialism with religious and folkloric practices, a fitting combination for a mainstream film festival with holiday associations.

Despite issues with institutional corruption and purportedly poor-quality filmmaking, the MMFF retains the shadow of its initial utopian promise. This is particularly evident in the mass audiences associated with it. In keeping with the festivities of the season, the MMFF begins with a street parade of floats for each film, an event that weaves together national history, mainstream movies, and notions of the cinema as a spectacle for "the people." The Parada ng mga Artista (Parade of Stars) begins at Manila City Hall, a building located in the heart of the capital city's government district, and ends at Plaza Miranda, the working-class Quiapo square known as the heart of Manila, the crossroads of the country, and the home of the people's voice, due to its history as a site of martial-law-era political rallies.[68] After its two-week run, in keeping with its populist image, the festival ends with an audience vote that plays a large role in the selection of best picture.

Essentially, each year, the Metro Manila Film Festival stages a utopic, nationalist vision of local film culture. It acts as a halt on Hollywood distribution, rendering the Philippines a temporary obstruction in global distribution networks. It trades this form of circulation temporality for another, replacing global synchronicity with local ritual. As Charles Acland argues, "Corralling screens across continents into coordinated openings and closings of films paints an image in which the variegated traces of cultural expression connect people to geographically distant and temporally synchronized communities."[69] If this is the dominant temporal logic of global cinemagoing, the MMFF offered an alternative. Embedded in geographically proximate communities, the MMFF replaces the desire for global synchronicity with a more localized temporal experience—in this instance, the annual rituals of a holiday season.

Viewing the MMFF as a missed opportunity, the Mogwai Film Festival sought to use the MMFF's symbolic density, evoking its blend of annual ritual, Filipino films, eager local audiences, and, as Tioseco saw it, lost opportunities for national film culture. As he pointedly described: "From December 25–January 7, cinemas in the Philippines are polluted by an event known as the Metro Manila Film Festival. . . . More than just a venue for less than stellar films, the 'festival' is a den of corruption, with the rules, regulations, selection criteria, and awarding criteria changing unannounced every year to suit whoever is in the organizer's favor."[70] While the festival content was, to Tioseco's mind, lacking, its structure and broad, guiding principles were compelling. Tioseco commended the policy of blacking out foreign films in favor of local cinema, stating, "Handled properly, an event with a policy such as this could be a source of national pride—no country that I know does something as daring, let alone at this time of the year . . . but given its current state, [the festival] is an extreme form of oppression."[71] This rather ascetic divide into mainstream versus alternative cinema sheds light on the strategic use of the MMFF as a means of marking this divide. From this perspective, the commercial industry and the MMFF had been given a chance and squandered it, opening the door for an alternative counterpart. In this way, the Mogwai Film Festival was an inverted riff on this project, once again offering local films to local audiences but doing so in a manner that would sidestep the commercialism of its would-be predecessor. This history frames the Mogwai Film Festival as an event founded on lost possibility.

While Tioseco's writing suggests an austere divide between "high art" and "low art," within the context of Philippine cinema, this austerity was rhetorically useful, given that many in the early-2000s alternative film scene felt the mainstream industry needed to be recuperated. Part of this recuperation involved the creation of, as Tioseco put it, "a community of informed and active viewers," and the Mogwai Film Festival's screenings were free of charge.[72] The festival exhibited a range of independent works, from those "that have been praised and shown around the world," to "ones that deserve more attention locally," to works that have "been praised, but rarely considered (i.e., written about)."[73] Running from December 28 to January 13 to mirror the MMFF, the 2007–2008 MFF lineup presented a kind of "boot camp," strictly for alternative film, concluding in a day of discussion.

Programming choices often evoke ideas of canon, and certainly, film festivals' tendencies toward canon creation have been critiqued.[74] Part of the MFF project was to find foreign audiences' local counterparts—when I attended the festival, the attendees were the usual crowd of discerning cinephiles or "captive" students required to attend for class. Nonetheless, appropriating the temporal structure of its mainstream predecessor, the Mogwai Film Festival revealed its aspirations: to salvage what Tioseco saw as a lost film public, the holiday moviegoers immersed in a national ritual. His dedication to creating an active, cinemagoing public was clear in his writing, as he rallied, "Let this be an occasion not just for viewing cinema, but also for writing, blogging, debating and arguing about it! That is, if we believe it matters." He maintained a solemn belief in the transformative possibilities not only of cinematic production, but also of communities of moviegoers, in specific circumstances of exhibition and reception.

The Mogwai Film Festival created a clear divide between commercial-industrial and alternative-artisanal modes of filmmaking, a gulf based on the perceived shortcomings of the contemporary, mainstream film industry. But the festival's strategic use of the MMFF as a reference point suggests that the borders between the one- and two-M events are not as finite as they might seem. Both share the goal of a national audience. While it might be easy to dismiss the MMFF as having purely commercial aims, its earlier incarnations suggest an event equally invested in cultivating a local film culture. When Alexis titled his article "One M is better than two," he referred only to Mogwai. But the Manila Film Festival of the 1960s *was* another "MFF," one that preceded the institutional corruption of its Metro Manila successor. Commercial or not, both MFFs shared aspirations for a local audience of local cinema. In this way, "one M" also references a lost past and a possible future, rather than simply a divide between mainstream and independent.

As I have suggested, the formation of community among audiences and filmmakers became an integral element in the development of alternative cinema culture in Manila. Temporality was a crucial part of this process: Cinekatipunan deployed repetition and regularity, and the Mogwai Film Festival grafted onto an existing ritual of moviegoing. These nonindustrial models of distribution and exhibition demonstrate how temporality becomes a mode of intervention into existing film infrastructures, allowing circulation practices to map themselves onto different forms of synchronicity. If the transnational simultaneity of multiplexes evokes global collectivity, these alternative exhibition sites used regularity and ritual to evoke collectivity of a more local kind. Nonetheless, these two circulatory modes are similarly aspirational. They both work within a subjunctive space, even as their visions of modernity's futures privilege collectives formed at different scales. For screening organizers in Manila, the collective they seek is one predicated on memory of the city, involvement in ritualized events, shared investment in political futures, and participation in educational or professional institutions.

This collectivity has its limits, and it is important to note that film exhibition is primarily conceived as leisure time, existing outside of work. As such, support staff working at screening spaces may not experience these sites' temporal interventions in the same way. Discussing the frequency of Cinekatipunan's screenings, Mag:net's newsletter referred to an inadvertent melding of film education and service labor: "There is a joke, the waiters and personnel of Mag:net have already become film critics."[75] This offhand remark is a reminder of exhibition sites' "backstage." In a cultural context where service-industry workers and patrons described as "filmmakers, film students, and film lovers" often have very different educational and socioeconomic backgrounds, this passing comment is a reminder of the divergent ways that viewers sharing these spaces might experience a film scene's collectivity.

In her recent study of global temporalities, Sarah Sharma builds from Doreen Massey's touchstone framework of "power geometries" to unearth the uneven politics of temporality, which she terms "power-chronographies."[76] As Sharma argues, the contemplative, intersubjective time of the deliberative public sphere is valorized as the appropriate mode for political space, which fails to recognize the uneven temporalities that make that space possible.[77] Theories of the public sphere, she contends, are not just about space but about free *time* enabled by others' absented labor.[78] The contemplative time-space of the alternative exhibition site is made possible through the commitment and dedicated labor of proprietors and screening organizers. In addition, all such art spaces are also enabled through the less visible labor of those who cleaned the seats, cooked the food, and carried the trays, who may or may not have caught a glimpse of the screen in their peripheral vision. This is another audience inhabiting these sites, one whose experience works within a different variation of time and space. Exhibition spaces act as a place of escape for some and a place of work for others. For alternative exhibition sites with broader cultural aspirations, the collectivities they seek to cultivate are in formation—taking shape for the future, but often limited in the present. These divisions between labor and leisure time become blurred in the discussion below, where a plaza exhibition site assembles its cinemagoers from the informal economies of the street.

Sinemusikalye and Street Temporalities

While nostalgia was a constitutive part of Cubao and the Mogwai Cinematheque, it operated not just as a call to the past, but reshaped the present to gesture toward possible futures. Such speculative gestures are particularly heightened in exhibition events that disrupt the everyday life of city spaces. In 2008, an event titled Sinemusikalye moved the alternative exhibition site from the cloister to the street, suggesting other possibilities for imagining audiences. This strategy was common in the alternative film scene. In some ways, the move to "take the cinema to the public" recalls Indie Sine's insertion into the mall's arcades. A few years later, the Film Development Council would develop similar approaches with their mobile cinema initiative, which I will discuss in chapter 5. For Sinemusikalye, the spatial disruption of the street exhibition event became a way of bringing together diverse audiences, thereby evoking what Victor Turner calls the city's subjunctive mood. Sinemusikalye (loosely translated: "movie, music, street") was a cinema, music, and digital media event that took place in Remedios Circle in Malate, the pedestrian-friendly, "old Manila" section of the city formerly known as the bohemian district. The Cinema Committee of the National Commission for Culture and the Arts sponsored the screening, in keeping with state-driven efforts in Malate's urban renewal.

Rows of plastic chairs filled Remedios Circle before a long, wide screen. Three projectors combined to create a panorama of digital film, scored with sound artists and electronic musicians. A flier for the event pointed to its melding of media and mobility, featuring an old-fashioned suitcase filled with optical discs and celluloid reels, alongside an image of a street surface. The image conveyed porousness and fluidity among media platforms and between media and space. The suitcase suggested the portability of even ostensibly immobile forms of "old media," like celluloid film, while the image of the street indicated a move outside the confines of the conventional theater. Works exhibited included *videoS* by Lyle Sacris (a cinematographer who co-owned Mogwai alongside Erik Matti) and Mark Mijares, manipulated live by artists Tad Ermitaño and Blums Borres. Musicians Malek Lopez and Caliph 8 scored animated films from Mowelfund, the Movie Workers Welfare Fund that action star and former president Joseph Estrada started in 1974. Elements and the Children of the Cathode Ray scored animated films from the lauded filmmaker Roxlee, while electronic musicians Moon Fear Moon and Trojan Whores provided audio for a video deconstruction by Blums Borres. Experimental filmmaker John Torres began the event with a "triptych" version of his essayistic, autobiographical video work, *Years When I Was a Child Outside*, which had premiered at the Berlin International Film Festival.

Unlike the slow cinema or social realist experimentations that characterized much independent film at the time, these were predominantly works predicated on some form of audiovisual spectacle, achieved through both the on-screen image and the contexts of exhibition, which included music, lights, and the unofficial, ancillary attractions of wandering food vendors and conversations among patrons, who engaged with the films in a state of semidistraction.

As an event, Sinemusikalye staged a utopian variation of media exhibition, conveying the city's subjunctive mood. The anthropologist Victor Turner describes two "moods" of the city that stir beneath the surface of urban life.[79] One is rational, referring to the representation of actual things and events as evidential. The other is subjunctive, presenting the possibility of social change. For Turner, the "liminal" spaces of ritual, carnival, fiesta, theater, and cinema present a subjunctive mood, one that expresses desires and reassembles everyday life's facticity. The distance of these liminal spaces from everyday life enables their occupants to reflect on the existing social order. I would argue that Sinemusikalye's subjunctive mood stemmed less from the works themselves than from the site's openness to its setting. This openness allowed the screening to *disrupt* the cyclical rhythms of the neighborhood and the street rather than folding itself into them, as with Cinekatipunan's regularity. In addition to attracting a more diverse viewership, this openness allowed chance, contingency, and play to enter the exhibition event.

As Turner argues, if everyday, ordinary life is in the indicative mood, the performance event creates a chaotic, liminal space, a "storehouse of possibilities . . . a gestation process."[80] Created not just through the text but through the interactions among text and audience, the performance event holds the potential for social change. When the performance event is a film screening, this model contrasts with the vision of the art house or art gallery as privileging the filmic text. Janet Harbord contends that such exhibition sites are dialectical, forming their institutional identities through their relationship to the multiplex.[81] As she argues, this, in turn, creates another binary—between film as a discrete, "pure" object and film as an experience, dissolved into ancillary products for consumption.[82] Exhibition events like Sinemusikalye offer a third model, one in which ancillary experiences create a ludic cinema event, whose openness to contingency rests in part on its street location. This is significant for a setting like Malate, where the street is a site of labor, as well as leisure.

Moreover, for Sinemusikalye, nostalgia and collective memory became a critical part of this reaggregation of everyday life. The city itself became a part of the exhibition site as text. This was due in part to its Malate setting, which referred to Manila's bohemian past while also offering a cross section of the city. While Cubao became the center of Manila's mid-aughts counterculture, Malate had served this role in previous decades. Since its 1980s bohemian heyday, Malate had since become better known for its proliferation of older, white male tourists with young Filipina companions, often employed at the neighborhood's numerous "girlie bars." The area has also become one of the city's primary gay districts, featuring many gay bars and clubs, which also cater to foreigners.[83] Remedios Circle itself is a popular cruising spot.[84] The state has countered these trends with urban renewal projects targeting upper-middle-class domestic and foreign tourists. Malate has also become home to a number of Korean-owned businesses.[85] The area thus caters to a hierarchy of clienteles, configured along lines of gender, sexuality, class, and nationality.[86] Perhaps by accident, the Sinemusikalye event offered a compelling example of alternative exhibition's public possibilities, because of this street culture. It created a speculative counterpublic that was, by virtue of its setting, strikingly inclusive. Perhaps accidentally, the event overcame alternative cinema's inherent paradox, if only for a brief moment.

For Malate's informal sex workers and vendors, the street existed within the temporality of labor. Possible customers, meanwhile, used the street as a route of passage, moving among bars, restaurants, and hotels. As a highly visible, public event in a heavily trafficked plaza, Sinemusikalye momentarily disrupted these dynamics. Due to its positioning in an area of the city thick with pedestrian traffic, the event drew not only the familiar faces of Manila's alternative film scene but also passersby on their way to the Malate's many bars, restaurants, and clubs.

Groups of street children gathered to watch the show. More interested in the laser lights that were a part of the audio set-up, the children passed their hands back and forth amid the beams of light, which became toys, privileging the ancillary technology over the cinematic "main event" (figures 3.7 and 3.8). Hardly an environment focused on the sanctity of the moving image, the occasion used cinema exhibition to create a kind of social crossroads. There are very few places in Manila that would welcome this broad a spectrum of cinemagoing behaviors or that would entice this wide a variety of spectators, from gay club goers, to tipsy tourists, to working-class vendors, to established Filipino artists of a variety of ages, mingling, circulating, passing through, or relaxing amid the plastic chairs spread across Remedios Circle's cobblestones.

The street children who participated are perhaps the clearest example of audiences normally positioned just outside the paths of middle-class

3.7 and **3.8** Ludic cinemagoing.

Manilenyos and foreign visitors. Children who work on the street are often viewed as a nuisance, as they attempt to sell Sampaguita flowers or ask for money.[87] Adult vendors see them as competitors, while police and government officials view them as a violation of public order: they vend without licenses, bother passersby, illegally beg, violate antivagrancy laws, or use drugs in public.[88] They are seen as blights that the modernizing city must expel or conceal. Because Sinemusikalye unfolded on the street, it allowed them to fleetingly participate in the leisure temporality that middle-class ideas of childhood take for granted. This is not how these children are most often seen in public space or imagined in disciplinary state discourse. The conditions that necessitate these children's labor also preclude their being viewed as children, rather than as abject violations of public protocols.

While I do not want to make too much of it, genres of leisure are unevenly distributed across the city, and Sinemusikalye did allow these particular children momentary participation in a collective event. Critics often see the homogenization of the audience before the screen as regressive, upholding cinema's antidemocratic tendencies. In this instance, such unifying tendencies work to create a screening event that was a counterpoint to the revanchist cinema of the first chapter, welcoming and folding in the viewers that other modes of cinemagoing seek to excise. Removed from the theatrical structure itself, the fleeting possibilities (if not quite realities) of cinematic exhibition that Dudley Andrew would describe as "democratizing" emerge.[89]

Ephemeral Exhibition

Emerging in the early years of Philippine alternative cinema's rise, Cinekatipunan, the Mogwai Cinematheque, and events like Sinemusikalye staged the exhibition site as a kind of utopian encounter between audiences and alternative cinemas. Through repetition, ritual, and nostalgia, they used temporal strategies in attempts to mitigate their spatial separation from the mainstream spaces of the city. Selectively tied to specific rhythms of the city (a seasonal film festival, the workday or school day) and to urban history, the sites existed as a response to immediacy, acceleration, novelty, and global synchronicity. Their alternative temporalities became attempts to reach wider audiences and to signal a kind of longevity—through the spaces' imagined connections to the urban past, if not through their actual life spans.

One crucial aspect of these alternative exhibition sites was their ephemerality, which destabilized their more long-term, utopian inclinations. Perhaps because public discourse imagined these sites as prelapsarian, talk of their eventual demise circulated widely, even at the height of their popularity. Cinekatipunan eventually ended its run, and Mag:net relocated to Bonifacio Global City, an antiseptic, new-urbanist enclave in the southern part of the city. Built on the site of the United States' Fort McKinley, the space was renamed after a major figure of the Philippine Revolution, Andrés Bonifacio, in 1957. In 2003, the Spanish Filipino Ayala family partnered with the Bases Conversion and Development Authority, a government corporation created to transfer former U.S. military bases into civilian use. Together, they built a Global City named for the nationalist revolutionary leader, on the vestiges of the American imperial project. Condominium high-rises, embassies, wealthy shops, and even a Venetian Grand Canal mark The Fort's transformation into one of the Metro's wealthiest areas, a space with global aspirations that invites Manilenyos and foreign transplants to "live, work, and play in a city made for great minds and passionate hearts."[90] The cinema includes both recliner and 4DX options, offering a luxury variation of moviegoing that matches its surroundings. Mag:net eventually closed its doors, but it lived its final days in a very different version of utopian visioning, a cloistered space isolated from the rest of the city and founded on the promise of the foreign. In 2008, The Fort's Fully Booked, a local bookstore chain, began hosting a screening series of foreign and local independent films called U-View Cinema.[91] The Fort is difficult to reach by public transportation; it is good that such events found another home, but this kind of space changed the dynamic, placing the screenings within a different chronology of urban space.

The Mogwai Cinematheque also shut its doors, preceded by anxieties about the Cubao Expo's closure. In early 2007, several friends sadly told me that the Cubao Expo would close and face demolition to make way for the Araneta Center's high-end condominium high-rises, Manhattan Garden City, planned by the appropriately named developer Megaworld Central Properties, Inc., the same company involved in Bonifacio Global City. These allusions to gardens in Manhattan and world domination through property are suitable for a development in Cubao, where roads are named after the posher of U.S. locales. For months, I expected to walk up New York or Harvard Street to the Expo only to find an empty lot in the early stages of construction. Even postings on various websites alluded to this idea that the Expo was about to become paradise lost: "CubaoX (Marikina Shoe Expo) . . . about to be gone because of Manhattan Gardens City"; "They just had their yard sale everything must go last week, i think idedemolish na sila [they will demolish it] soon to give way for Manhattan Garden towers . . . closed na yung kalahati ng mga stalls after nung sale [all the stalls will be closed after this sale]. Closed for good!"[92]

Manhattan Garden City now towers above the Expo, which still stands at the time of writing. This forecasted demolition did not occur, though many of the original art spaces closed after a 2007 change in the Marikina Shoe Expo's management, which resulted in a 40 percent increase in rent, from ₱18,000 to ₱25,000 per month.[93] The art galleries Kukuada and Future Prospects shut their doors, as did the comics store Chunky Far Flung. The popular discourses pitting Cubao X against its developer foe were common. It is a narrative of impending loss, a familiar one for many cities.[94] Unlike the cosmopolitanism of Manhattan Garden City, whose marketing pronounced, "a new city is born," which will be "New New York in Asia!" the cosmopolitanism of Cubao Expo worked not through the building of a "New New York" on the rubble of an old city but through the recuperation of a localized urban history, as an antidote to globalized modernization's destruction of local histories.[95]

The Mogwai Cinematheque eventually closed its doors in 2011, not to make way for a condominium development but for reasons that remain ambiguous, at least publicly. One filmmaker told me the building's owner wanted to use the property for other purposes, while a film professor attributed the closure to a raid by the MTRCB for illegal screenings. Mogwai's loss cultivated its own version of urban nostalgia. In an article titled "Memories of Mogwai," a writer for the *Philippine Daily Inquirer* observed, "Mogwai was a lot of things to a lot of people. So it came as no surprise that when news that the Cubao X favorite had closed started to spread slowly last Tuesday, there was an outpouring of grief on Facebook, Tumblr and Twitter."[96] A young writer set up a Storify site called "Mogwai: Our Collective Memories," which gathered these online reminiscences. Some stories recall the site's status as a community space:

> It was a bar, it was a cinema, it was a café, it was a restaurant, it was a hangout. It was a place for cheap beer and serious talks, good food and great movies, chilling with old friends and meeting new ones.[97]

Mogwai was where you can immerse yourself in great Filipino culture. A place where one can't help but participate in the rapture of living the experience of life, and it's a little unsettling to see purveyors of taste and the performing arts lose another home.[98]

Other recollections deal with cinema.[99] As one post recalls, "I spent one Halloween in Mogwai, watching Roman Polanski's *The Tenant*. I had my own films screened in Mogwai. . . . I have to admit I've taken Mogwai for granted. I thought it would always be around."[100] Mogwai had become an everyday fixture of Manila's cinema circulation; screenings of foreign and local alternative works were incorporated into community gatherings and their "immersion into great Filipino culture."

The utopianism of these sites was based on the idea that they acted as foundations—initial stages in a Philippine cinema timeline, predicated on its possible futures. In this way, their loss becomes a part of the naturalized cycle of ongoing struggles to create sustainable infrastructures for local circulation. In these collective memories, they become visions of what people once believed was possible. Such foggy recollections lend themselves to romanticism. But as Richard Dyer argues in his analysis of queer subcultural spaces, "I don't say that romanticism, with its passion and intensity, is a political ideal we could strive for—I doubt it is humanly possible to live permanently at that pitch. What I do believe is that the movement between banality and something 'other' than banality is an essential dialectic of society, a constant: keeping open of a gap between what is and what could or should be."[101] Like Jose Muñoz's notion of utopia as "something that should mobilize us, push us forward," Dyer sees value in the affective registers of passion, desire, and longing, the engines that drive social life from the ordinary to the extraordinary.[102]

This dialectic is what is missing in many elaborations of alternative film: the complex interplay between what is now, what could be, and what should be. While the cultural economy resigns alternative cinemas to an elite network of cultural value and prestige institutions, this is not the only sphere in which these texts operate. Many idealists on the ground are also involved in building paths for circulation, often using a limited supply of monetary, human, and affective resources to enable them. To be sure, these paths are asymptotic: undoubtedly circumscribed, inadvertently hierarchical, and often short-lived. The neoliberal cityscape in which they take shape dissolves linear chronology, colonizing the future with its predictions of risk and investment. Within this setting, the most idealistic forms of counterspeculation are born with a limited life span, bound to the vagaries of capital. Independent art spaces sought to reshape the city's spatial timelines, offering a return to a lost, collective past in order to construct alternative ideas of possible futures. They synchronized with local temporalities, distancing themselves from the globalist currents that had overtaken the malled-over city.

As the paratexts I have discussed suggest, these momentary spaces for cultivating present and possible viewerships fostered a community of sentiment that will outlast the sites themselves. Alternative film culture involves a complex spectrum from antipublic exclusivity to market-driven populism, and exhibition initiatives like those discussed in this chapter work within the interstices between these poles. Alternative films are isolated and exclusive; this is certainly an accurate critique. But often, they are also surrounded by initiatives that try to propel them, taking on the impossible task of pushing against their circulatory horizons.

This necessitated a great deal of optimism, of course, due to the numerous obstacles such circulation ventures faced. These obstacles included, as we have seen, dealing with the vagaries of the state censorship board. The communities of sentiment these alternative screening initiatives sought to create were grounded in ties to urban pasts and filmic histories, forms of affect more often associated with an aesthetics of nostalgia than with political volatility. But other sectors of the alternative film scene had more activist intentions, as Cinekatipunan indicated. As the following chapter discusses, public exhibition—the live gathering of the crowd—stoked Movie and Television Review and Classification Board fears.

CHAPTER FOUR

"NOT FOR PUBLIC EXHIBITION"

CINEMA REGULATION, ALTERNATIVE CINEMA, AND A RATIONAL BODY POLITIC

It's not [for the MTRCB] to judge the [film's] content on whether or not it undermines the public's faith and confidence in the government. It will be up to the audience to decide that.
—**CRISPIN BELTRAN**, party-list representative and labor leader

The previous chapters describe struggles to forge encounters between screens and their prospective audiences, whether through envisioning a home for independent film in the revanchist space of the mall, through imagining a multiculturalist, national past in spaces of film circulation, or through synching alternative spaces for Manila's film culture with the ongoing rhythms of the city. Such ambitions faced a number of obstacles—an absence of exhibition and distribution infrastructure outside the mainstream studios, a lack of film education among audiences, the aesthetic or narrative difficulty of some film texts, and obstructionist state regulation. These initiatives' aspirations included the ideal publics that would constitute a national cinema from production to reception; this proved difficult to maintain. However, if the alternative film scene were to overcome the contradictions inherent in its combination of radicalism and isolation, it would need those audiences. One critical barrier to reaching them was the state's Movie and Television Review and Classification Board (MTRCB).

National culture became the domain of a striving alternative film scene and its speculative publics. Its territories were circulation spaces that tied alternative film culture to an imagined national past or that linked it to the city's mass crowds. In these spaces, the state's role was one of obstruction. The MTRCB brought state surveillance into the revanchist cinema, projecting the idea of a bad audience as a part of their antipiracy campaigns. It partnered with the U.S. Office of the Trade Representative to eradicate piracy in Quiapo, creating a fantasy of affiliation between the alternative film scene and Muslim DVD vendors, united against the state. In dealing with alternative screening venues, the MTRCB used screening fees, review policies, and sometimes threats to halt potentially incendiary screening events, constructing its vision of audiences as volatile and dangerous. While the alternative film scene's circulation projects were predicated on bringing national audiences into being, the MTRCB's obstructions aimed to eradicate that latent potential.

This chapter focuses on the MTRCB to examine the conflicts between two speculative publics: one seen as liberating, emanating from the alternative film scene's social movement ties; the other seen as threatening, infantile, and subject to base instincts, originating in the Arroyo state's censorship board. Each side's cases pivoted on assertions of the other side's inability to interpret textual meaning and audience potential. For the film scene, it is the state, *not* the potential film public, that is brash, corrupt, and parochial, indictments that discredit the institution's right to govern while furthering the film scene's claims to represent "the nation." Such charges invalidate MTRCB regulation and the danger of mass uprising that is its premise. Meanwhile, the alternative film scene's speculative public is not the MTRCB's unruly mob but an informed, knowledgeable, educated public, one whose sedition could only lead to liberation. This paradox was predicated on particular spatial configurations: the immediacy of the live screening event; the transnational festival circuit as a rationale for loosening regulation at home, thus creating unevenly scaled cartographies of cinema censorship; the possibilities of educational settings for screenings, where captive student audiences might transform into ideal publics.

Several cinema and media studies scholars have called for the need to view censorship as "productive," as well as "prohibitive," breaking down the neat lines between creation and cutting to consider how censorship practices inform production choices, create genres and classifications systems, establish viewing norms, demarcate cinema's cultural "function," and, most important for the discussion here, conceptualize the moviegoing public.[1] But censorship does not just affect texts—like the film initiatives chronicled in the previous chapters, censorship produces space, through allowing or prohibiting public exhibition. Because of its link to exhibition and audiences, censorship is a spatial practice premised on regulating the latent affective power of mass gatherings, whose live encounters with films in space become a means of imagining alternative futures. If Manila's masses hold dormant political potential, then in the contexts of an unstable state, controlling these unstable crowds is vital. As with the alternative screening spaces in the prior chapter, regulating texts and audiences means regulating exhibition space and the temporalities of dissemination, which ultimately means controlling cinemagoing as a collective experience. While the previous chapter discussed initiatives that emerged from below, this chapter examines top-down strategies and the challenges that rose to meet them. The state and alternative filmmakers become territorial in a literal sense, laying claim to sites of circulation where audiences' and texts' paths might intersect.

To examine these tensions, I assess a discursively dense, historically bounded series of confrontations that took place among filmmakers, social movements, and the Movie and Television Review and Classification Board (MTRCB) between 2007 and 2008, a moment that provides a compelling case study of a state responding to the threat of overthrow. During this time, the film scene's countercensorship tactics were specific to the Arroyo administration. While I refer to the MTRCB's practices as "censorship" in this chapter, it is important to note that its duties are officially limited to classification; its practices during this historical window acted as a form of tacit, covert censorship. Moreover, subsequent relations between the MTRCB, the state, and the alternative film scene worked differently. Upon his 2010 election, President Benigno Aquino appointed Grace Poe-Llamanzares as chair of the MTRCB. Poe-Llamanzares is the politician daughter of Fernando Poe Jr., an action-film icon. Her appointment was significant, given her late father's loss to Arroyo in the 2004 presidential election. Two months after the loss, Fernando Poe Jr. requested that the Supreme Court annul Arroyo's election due to fraud; he passed away in December of that year. As head of the MTRCB under Aquino, Poe's daughter provided a distinct counterpoint to the Arroyo administration that had preceded her, describing an "open minded board" that would consider the film and television industry's well-being. As she put it, "I will try to strike a balance between the rights of the filmmakers and the viewing public. I hope my dad (Fernando Poe Jr.) will be proud of me."[2] Poe-Llamanzares left her post to run for the Senate in 2012; her campaign was often framed in light of her father's allegedly fraudulent loss to Arroyo. Her successor, Ateneo de Manila University law professor Eugenio H. Villareal, took a similarly liberal approach. He described the MTRCB's role in familial terms: "There will be no censorship. We will just classify content. Grace's advice was to wear a parent's hat."[3] Even MTRCB chairs appointed under the administration of Rodrigo Duterte have embraced a rhetoric of openness, even if that openness is mixed with paternalism.[4] These more recent tendencies suggest a stronger affinity between the MTRCB and the film industry, combined with a greater level of separation between the MTRCB and the state.

While conflicts with the MTRCB have continued, the tenor of those taking place at the end of the Arroyo administration were particularly intense, in part because of that administration's increasing instability as its term drew to a close. The debates below demonstrate the fraught narratives that emerge when states and the local intelligentsia come to blows over an internationally circulating domestic cinema. Within these narratives, the state became an enemy of the people, the alternative film scene became their savior, and transnational arts circuits became an ally of the just and good. While justified within certain historical circumstances, this can be an unsettling narrative, placing the onus of alternative cinema's limited audience on an oppressive nation-state, while directing hopes for its future in unencumbered flows of global networks. This is a common dynamic in globally circulating art cinemas; it manifests such cinemas' tenuous relation to location. Here, however, it works a bit differently; transnational flows became instead a means of justifying domestic circulation.

In this way, the debates that took place in 2007 and 2008 demonstrated how speculative publics are formed relationally, through the contentiousness of and affiliations among various institutional players, both domestically and, to a lesser extent, abroad. At the core of this discourse was the question of how to define the role of local cinema in Philippine culture—its relationship to state and nation, its connection to a viewership comprised of international elites, and its shaping of a local, masa public. These conflicts engendered specific kinds of discursive strategies for dealing with film regulation. I will track three of them here. First, I discuss the construction of cinema as rational knowledge, a move that relied on comparisons to the newspaper and on the immediacy of the cinemagoing event. I look at the 2007 banning of *Rights*, an anthology film on human rights. The work was scheduled to open the Kontra-Agos Film Festival, an activist event that took place in the Indie Sine multiplex screen. For activist media, online circulation was not enough—the organizers needed a live event to cultivate the publics they aimed to reach. In this way, censorship created the film exhibition space as part of a transmedia assemblage of activist media, predicated on discourses of liveness.

Next, I examine how film censorship rescaled the circulation of media. Here, international festival accolades for locally censored films (*Imburnal* [dir. Sherad Anthony Sanchez, 2008] and *Death in the Land of Encantos* [dir. Lav Diaz, 2007]) became a rationale to combat the MTRCB. Transnational channels were not the aim; rather, they functioned as obligatory paths that films had to take to accrue the status that would find them domestic exhibition venues. Local censorship rescaled the circulation of alternative cinema, pushing it from domestic exhibition channels to foreign prestige circuits.

For the alternative film scene, each of these conflicts cultivated a vision of the potential film public as rational and disciplined, a move that positioned the state as irrational and unruly. This discourse was strategic in its embrace of rationality, framing the Philippines as an imminent, if not already-existing, modern polity. As we have seen, the notion of a bifurcated public has been a key characteristic in discussions of the global south's "incomplete" modernities, with modernizing elites adopting a pedagogical view of the masses.[5] As previous chapters suggest, in this initial phase of postmillennial alternative film culture in the Philippines, this bifurcation was evident. But it was often positioned as a problem of film infrastructure rather than audience readiness. In 2008, Rolando Tolentino wrote a piece in the Tagalog-language media outlet *Bulatlat*, discussing the middle-class "culturati" youth audience for independent films and lamenting the lack of diverse venues for exhibition.[6] Similarly, writing in 2010, scholar Bienvenido Lumbera observed, "So far, the limited accessibility of [independent filmmakers'] output in the established exhibition venues has generated an audience of mainly young people, students and fresh graduates of urban colleges and universities. Nevertheless, it is a growing audience and one looks forward to a future when accessibility will cease to be a liability."[7] As Lumbera's hoped-for future suggests, the "actually existing" film culture of educated, young urbanites was not necessarily the anticipated ideal, in which alternative films would reach beyond an educated culturati. As was often the case, the aesthetics and content of many of these films were not the focus of these discussions; rather, the discussion hinged on a lack of adequate infrastructures for distribution and exhibition, highlighting the critical role of circulation in film culture imaginaries.

Within this model of circulation, censorship became a critical factor, framed as an unnecessary preventative measure that exacerbated the gaps in a faulty infrastructure. The early-aughts discourse on film framed cinema publics as rational, shifting their image from an *indefinitely* stratified, heterogeneous, and domestic audience to a model focused on *imminent* alternative cinema audiences—the speculative publics that had framed so much of early millennial film culture in Manila. Here, the film scene's discourse about speculative publics took a slightly different tack. Within this rhetoric, the problem was not that wider audiences were not ready for these films, as the censorship board argued. Rather, the issue was framed as a matter of access: this broader audience simply could not see the films, due to gaps in the country's circulation infrastructure. These charges parallel those made against the MTRCB in the midst of the Arroyo presidency. While the MTRCB stance depicted an infantile public, those promoting unfettered film circulation produced an image of a rational, ready audience, one that was not in any need of uplift. This was not a pedagogical relationship between elites and mass audiences but a discursively constructed, contingent relation of equivalence. This discourse of rationality presented a variation of speculative publics that reconfigured conventional images of the Philippine body politic. As I will discuss below, the model of the Philippine body politic was often predicated on elements of emotionality and embodiment, from which the film scene had strategically distanced itself.

While strategic rationality was a response to censorship discourse in the moment of Arroyo's presidency, the final case I will examine demonstrates its limits as a rhetorical strategy. This last section assesses a messier conflict, which took place around the University of the Philippines Film Institute (UPFI). Alongside the Cultural Center of the Philippines (CCP), the UPFI is one of the country's two censorship-free zones, due to its educational mandate. Its screenings of "gay films" to raucous audiences made it an MTRCB target, leading to much debate about the kinds of publics an educational site should allow. Here, both censorship *and* the alternative film scene designated particular spaces as the domains of education and culture, thereby precluding the mass publics outside those domains. This preclusion persisted despite these publics' economic possibilities. Once the domain of dedicated third-run theaters that doubled as cruising spots, low-budget "gay films" had provided a reliable source of income for independent exhibition spaces in the early aughts. For example, at an Independent Film Summit held at the end of 2008, members of the media, academics, state arts and culture agencies, and film practitioners discussed the future of cinema in the Philippines; once again, the problem of a projected domestic audience was a key point of discussion, here tied to the economic sustainability of the industry. Interestingly, filmmaker Nick Deocampo described gay audiences as a potential economic market, noting that the adult "gay films" screening at Indie Sine had constituted the top five box-office draws. Deocampo elaborated: "That's the power of niche marketing. . . . Gay films cater to a specific and loyal audience."[8] In the alternative film scene's early years, the gay audience raised complicated questions about the kinds of niche audiences the alternative film sector wanted to cultivate. Despite gay audiences' financial potential, as the controversy around the UPFI suggests, mass gay viewerships held a complex place in early-2000s alternative cinema imaginaries.

During the period that comprised these events, the alternative film community, the local intelligentsia, and the MTRCB waged a public struggle for both discursive and spatial territory. Within the contexts of the Arroyo administration's decline, local cinema's rise within international circuits, and efforts to cultivate a national cinemagoing culture at the local level, the MTRCB and the alternative film community competed for the hearts and minds of an imagined mass public. Both sides claimed the role of mediator between the masses and the state. Alternative cinema's oppositional relationship to the state accrued meaning through a dynamic of regulation and resistance. Importantly, this relationship played out through struggles over circulation that designated sites of exhibition and, thus, the audiences that films can reach. The friction between them became a discursive battle over constituting or suppressing speculative publics. Within this rhetoric, speculative visions of film publics refigured the body politic, shifting its conventional alignments of reason, affect, state, and populace. This refiguring points to the difficulties of negotiating the state's role in "national-cinema" imaginaries.

The Unstable State and the Stakes of Film Censorship

This discussion is less about the structure and policy of the MTRCB than the rhetoric that emerged at a historical moment, rhetoric that configured the relation between state, society, and cinema in telling ways. The discourse around film censorship at the end of the Arroyo presidency created a contrast between reason and passion, staging alternative film advocates, mass audiences, and state censors in an unusual way.[9] In previous chapters, circulation initiatives envisioned speculative publics that were premised on notions of national becoming, with film organizers projecting images of prospective, alternative cinema audiences yet to come. Here, these visions took a different form, as images of an already existing, reasoned audience became central to anticensorship rhetoric. The conflicts between the MTRCB and the alternative film scene provide a compelling case study for examining film censorship within contexts of state instability. As state censors became more draconian, the alternative film scene produced an image of the body politic that reversed its typical design.

The metaphor of the body politic—the state as the rational head of an unruly corpus—is a touchstone of political theory. In the Philippines, this metaphor has taken on specific characteristics through public imaginaries of the laboring classes, which have become synonymous with the mass citizenry. Several scholars have touched on this dynamic, in both informal and theoretical ways. In an essay titled "Phantom Limbs in the Body Politic," Joel David tracks foreign film representations of Filipinos, contextualizing these representations within the history of overseas Filipino workers (OFWs), whose remittances keep the national economy afloat.[10] The local elite remains silent about foreign interference, while sending "pliant, versatile, long-suffering, essentially feminized" workers abroad.[11] Benjamin McKay deploys the metaphor more directly, analyzing the "mirrored metaphors" of the Philippine and Singaporean body politics through the films *The Flor Contemplacion Story* (dir. Joel Lamangan, 1995) and *The Maid* (dir. Kelvin Tong, 2005). McKay cites the Malaysian journalist Karim Raslan, who writes, "The ... imbalance between the different parts [of the body politic] makes the Filipino irrational and emotional: the opposite of his Singaporean counterpart who is a monster of 'reason.'"[12] McKay argues that Singapore views the Philippines as "a weak irrational entity, with a propensity to emotionalism." Meanwhile, the Philippines produces an image of the nation as the "Madonna-Martyr" via the OFW, "a wounded woman ravaged by a cold hard man who disguises his brutality as rationality."[13] Though one view is critical and the other celebratory, both are grounded in notions of national affect, framing each as excessive or transcendent. These imaginaries are thus speculatively constructing a portrait of Philippine mass publics defined by emotionality and embodiment.[14]

As these analyses suggest, the dichotomy between irrationality and rationality has specific meaning in the Philippine national imaginary: emotional and physical labor have become emblems of the national self, constructed in opposition to hyperrationalized others. This dynamic foregrounds the mass population's embodiment as a form of both cultural identity and monetary value. The state is implicated in this system. Rolando Tolentino has theorized the role of "body capital" in the Philippines' state-society relations. The concept describes a system of value in which beauty pageants, swimsuit competitions, talent and game shows, and reality television have presented the laboring classes with "the possibility of moving socially upwards using bodily traits that meet the standards of the service sector industries."[15] This system finds its counterpoint in the presidential body: a strongman, during the era of Marcos, who was obsessed with the physique of his youth.[16] Later, Corazon Aquino's body was constructed as maternal, "giving birth to a clean moral national slate after a dark period of the nation's history."[17] Ramos surrounded himself with phallic symbols, to remasculinize the presidential body. Arroyo became associated with rash aggression. Writing in 2009, Tolentino observed: "Gloria Macapagal Arroyo's (2001–present) periodic apologies for her short-tempered outbursts ... her unapologetic declaration of a state of emergency early in February 2006, and her strong commitment to maintaining the military status quo all contributed to an aggressive image of presidential readiness. But her rule has been questioned repeatedly and dubbed illegitimate—both in terms of her winning office despite massive electoral fraud, and her highly questionable defense of political appointments, government contracts, and national development."[18]

As the figurehead of the state, Arroyo's presidential embodiment was not associated with strength, stoic machismo, or maternity, constructs that could be seen as the products of careful public performance. Instead, she was noted for her quick temper, her corruption, and her reactionary turns to violence. Though she was seen as efficient and calculating, these traits were coupled with charges of emotional volatility, indictments that reflect the state's institutional weakness.

Given the history of these discourses about embodiment and their relationship to mass publics, when the MTRCB heightened its regulatory measures toward the end of Arroyo's term, the alternative film scene discursively reconstructed the body politic, realigning ideas of emotion, rationality, state, and populace. Within this context, making strategic claims about audience rationality reworked established conventions of national self and other. Claims of the state's illegitimacy personified it as an irrational institution whose decisions were arbitrary, its approach fascist, its reactions impulsive and extreme. It became an institutional other to a national self, figured here as its opposite. This self was constructed as a conjoined "alternative film scene and mass audience," their union framed as a site of rationalism and ethical fortitude. In this way, the body politic was reversed. The state was not the cognitive, controlling "head," ruling over an embodied, emotionally driven populace. The alternative film scene had taken on that cognitive mantle, and because their anticensorship claims relied on the rationality of audiences, the wider national public joined them.

This binarism was largely performative rather than reflecting the institution's actual operations. Although the state and the MTRCB were intimately linked, the state was not coterminous with the MTRCB as a whole. Neither is a monolithic institution; their varied components and players often conflict with each another. Just two months after calls for President Arroyo's impeachment sounded from the thirteen thousand people who flooded the streets during a February 2008 interfaith rally, Laguardia's colleagues at the MTRCB began their own demonstrations. Their protests contested Laguardia's firing of Mina Nacilla, the head of the MTRCB Employees Association Inc., and her assistant, Roberto Jacobe, who had filed formal complaints with the Office of the President for Laguardia's violations of MTRCB laws. Wearing black armbands and holding weekly gatherings outside the President's Tower of the MTRCB's Quezon City office, the state censorship board's employees called for their own regime change.[19] As an institution, the board itself was fractured. The interests of its leadership and those of its employees were frequently at odds. The public discourse surrounding censorship viewed the MTRCB as a cohesive entity, setting aside these internal clashes.

In the Philippine context, political instability gave further weight to local discussions of censorship. The creation of a resistant mass public was a particular threat in a country that had seen two "People Power" uprisings since the end of martial law and over a dozen attempted coups. While the MTRCB often attributed its X ratings to sexual content, it could also apply to political critique. As I will discuss below, the rating had significant impacts on a film's exhibition possibilities, prohibiting it from theaters. Alternative works often included both sexual and political content; part of their claim to the "independent" label was their distance from mainstream norms—aesthetic, industrial, cultural, and, for some, political. Given the troubled nature of Arroyo's tenure, any moves to destabilize the state were quickly suppressed.[20] Within this political setting, the Arroyo regime's protection of its interests was urgent, and the cultural arms of the state became players in this process. Prescribing reason to audiences is certainly tenuous, and the visions of speculative publics below emerge through a process of accelerated uplift (the mature mass audience) and rhetorical excision (the raucous gay audience).[21] But, employed as a rhetorical maneuver, prescribing reason to audiences operated as a strategic response to state corruption, constructing a specific version of the Philippine body politic that reversed the idea of the state as its rational head. Spaces of exhibition played a role in this construction.

I have previously suggested that film censorship is in part a spatial practice; likewise, the body politic is a spatial metaphor, constructing boundaries of inside and out, while creating hierarchies between affect and reason.[22] During the period under discussion, exhibition sites lent a spatial dimension to anticensorship discourse. The mall multiplex, conventionally conceived as a site of unthinking consumerism, became a space for social movement building and debate. Conversely, the university, an arena of knowledge production, became a space for sexual excitement. During Arroyo's tenure, these spaces of film circulation became spaces of film regulation, signaling the presence of the state in the city.[23] They evoked the idea of the city as analogous to the body politic. As previous chapters demonstrate, urban forms shape political imaginaries, which in turn construct the prospective publics anticipated in film circulation sites, events, and initiatives. Unfettered mobility was an unspoken assumption within these imaginaries. In their own way, previous chapters' sites were premised upon the free movement of films and audiences: from transnational festivals to domestic exhibition networks, from mall arcades to multiplex outposts, from overdeveloped to historical parts of the city. Films and audiences would move from established channels to the burgeoning detours being offered via alternative cinema culture.

The discussions below foreground the ongoing circulation of information and audiences. Such ideas are in keeping with long-standing theories of the city as a space of circulation, models that connect with ideas of the city as a correlate to the body politic.[24] Edward LiPuma and Thomas Koelble, for example, conceptualize the urban cultural imaginary as a "space that is created in and through the relationship between these forms of circulation [of goods, people, services, and capital] and the practices of stabilization that seek to objectify the city as a totality."[25] Deleuze and Guattari likewise argue for mobility as the defining aspect of urban spaces.[26] Within these models, the interplay between stabilization and circulation shapes urban space, and this dynamic is central to the image of the body politic as a mirror of the city. Conventionally, the mass publics that would compose potential film viewerships constitute the city's lifeblood, connecting to circulation as a normative value. Manila's major north-south highway, EDSA, is known as the artery of the city, while the Quiapo plaza and marketplace, as we have seen, has been called its heart. Both thoroughfares are spaces of mobility. Historically, they are also spaces of mass uprising, which have since become affective sites of national history.[27]

In the accounts below, censorship becomes a part of these urban, circulatory imaginaries; it functions as a symptom of state control over the movements of films and audiences. State regulation becomes an obstruction to the city's ongoing flows, acting as a counterpoint to spaces associated with affective practices of national remembrance and mass consumption. Within this context, the discourses of state irrationality and rational publics strategically reconfigure such models. In other settings, the state might typically be conceived as a resource for the urban infrastructures that would enable the flows of people, goods, and information. Here, anticensorship discourse portrays the state as a barrier to the city's organic rhythms, a trespasser in spaces of free exchange among citizens.

Cinemagoing as Knowledge Dissemination: Rights and the Kontra-Agos Film Festival

At the end of Arroyo's troubled presidency, reason became a critical aspect of alternative cinema's speculative publics. The exhibition space shifted from a space of affect to one of critical engagement. One form that this strategic rationality took was linking cinema to other forms of information dissemination. This positioned the circulation space as an arena for deliberation and debate, a model of cinemagoing that differed from that suggested in the Arroyo/Laguardia MTRCB's heavy hand. For the MTRCB, regulation was necessary to quell the dangers of the live event's unruly crowds. In the alternative film scene's discourse, cinema paralleled other forms of media based on topicality and knowledge dissemination, a resemblance furthered in the immediacy of the live cinemagoing event. Such parallels imply a strategic vision of these activist films' ideal publics as both revolutionary and reasoned, an image furthered through contrasts with MTRCB capriciousness.

Cinema Disclosure

In September 2007, filmmakers involved with the Cinekatipunan screening series and the Free Jonas Burgos Movement prepared for the release of their anthology of sixteen public-service announcements, titled *Rights*. Inspired by similar works created by Amnesty International in commemoration of International Human Rights Day, the groups produced the series in collaboration with local independent filmmakers. Organizers planned the collection of shorts to coincide with the thirty-fifth anniversary of Ferdinand Marcos's declaration of martial law. The *Rights* anthology's release was to take place across two venues: the two-year-old streaming service YouTube and the Indie Sine multiplex screen, which had opened in January of that year. The screening event would include a forum reflecting on the years of the Marcos dictatorship.[28] On September 19, the *Rights* organizers received word from the MTRCB that their human rights video project had been barred from public circulation. A letter to the filmmakers signed by the MTRCB's then chair Consoliza Laguardia stated, "Scenes in the film are presented unfairly, one-sided and undermines the faith and confidence of the government and duly constituted authorities, thus, not for public exhibition [sic]." Laguardia herself was under scrutiny for her own prolonged term at the MTRCB helm; while her post had officially ended

4.1 The Kontra-Agos program. The camera breaking through the water suggests a more transformative shift from the discourse of new waves.

in November 2006, she had stayed on as "acting chair," a move that one journalist attributed to the influence of her aunt, Sophie Macapagal, who was married to Judge Demetrio Macapagal, a cousin of President Gloria Macapagal Arroyo.[29]

In the week that followed the ban, popular and alternative media, blogs, and cinephile websites wrote of their support for the *Rights* filmmakers. In the midst of this heavy press coverage and comparisons to martial law, the MTRCB lifted the ban on *Rights* a week and a half later, following a second review that allowed its public exhibition, provided the viewers were over thirteen years of age. At issue was not only the banning of these specific films but the irony that despite the passing of two decades of Philippine democracy, the state maintained its dominance in designating the kind of cinematic work that was fit (or unfit) for exhibition to the Filipino public. Two months later, the organizers involved with the *Rights* anthology arranged Kontra-Agos: Resistance Film Festival (figure 4.1). Translating to "Counter Stream," it was meant as a continuation of the Bagong Agos (New Stream) Film Festival that had taken place earlier that year. Chitz Jimenez of the Independent

Filmmaker's Cooperative (IFC) opened the event, stating that while the previous year's festival "was a reaction to mainstream culture," Kontra-Agos was intended to demonstrate that "it's not enough just to react, we must resist.... We welcome everyone to the resistance, because dissent without action is consent."[30] Jimenez's comments differentiate between reaction (an impulsive, spontaneous response) and resistance: a tactical, measured means of counteraction.

The festival's encounters with the MTRCB underscored this call for resistance. Just as they had only two months earlier with the banning of *Rights*, the festival organizers received word that three more of the programmed films had received X ratings: Southern Tagalog Exposure's *A Day in the Life of Gloria Arroyo*, a humorous, animated short depicting the president repeating the phrase, "I am sorry," after which her nose grows, surrounded by twinkling sparkles and the sound of harps, until it becomes a tree branch in which a bird nests; *Mendiola*, a journalistic, documentary short by the activist filmmaking organization Sine Patriyotiko that draws parallels between the 1987 Mendiola Massacre, when state police violently dispersed a farmers' march on the presidential Malacañang Palace, and Arroyo's calibrated preemptive response policy requiring rallies to have permits; and *Holy Bingo*, a roughly composed, primarily handheld, first-person short documenting gambling in a provincial church, during which church officials attempt to prohibit the filmmaker from recording in the building, verbally threatening violence on church steps as a crowd looks on.[31]

While MTRCB regulation was premised on institutional logic and sound governance, the institution was more capricious than this founding assumption implied. This inconsistency furthered the alternative film scene's posture of rational knowledge dissemination. *Holy Bingo*'s rating was later changed to PG-13 following a second review. Such changes are not uncommon, leading filmmakers to submit films for second reviews in hopes of receiving a more sympathetic screening committee. Filmmakers must pay for each review, making multiple submissions to the MTRCB a costly procedure for those working on shoestring budgets. Following a later X rating of the independent horror feature *Three Days of Darkness* (2007), the producers of the film referred to *Holy Bingo*'s ratings switch as an indicator of the ratings process's arbitrariness: "How could [the MTRCB] justify one version of one film getting two vastly different ratings in so short a time? It becomes a game of numbers that unjustly puts the filmmakers at the mercy of chance. All we can do is hope that the reviewers assigned to our works be 'open enough' to appreciate our artistic intentions, and not those who have the tendency to throw x-es on just about anything non-traditional, non-conformist and non-Catholic, like what happened to Noriel Jarito's short film 'Holy Bingo.'"[32] Hardly an impartial, consistent calculus, the ratings system is instead a "game" for the MTRCB and a gamble for filmmakers, leaving them to the "mercy of chance" as board members haphazardly "throw x-es."

The Kontra-Agos filmmakers and festival organizers protested the x ratings in statements to the media, labeling the Arroyo state "fascist." The post-martial-law government has been called a return to "cacique democracy" with Aquino and Ramos, as well as "lumpen populism" in reference to Estrada.[33] Referencing the instability of Philippine democracy, Nathan Gilbert Quimpo calls the post-martial-law era "contested democracy," alluding to the struggles over governance that have marked it.[34] In the case of Arroyo, particularly in relation to the MTRCB, several activists and public intellectuals spoke of her administration as "state fascism."[35] The label connotes extremism and demagoguery, alluding to a political system that combines authoritarianism with appeals to popular sentiment. Again, it is an indictment of the state's irrationality. Perhaps even more than the screening of the films, their being banned from public exhibition demonstrated the proximity between the Arroyo and Marcos administrations, an irony that was not lost on those in attendance at the Kontra-Agos festival's opening night, many of whom pointed to a return to martial-law politics. The parallel is pointed—for many, the Marcos regime's authoritarianism and violence is cemented in national memory. The films thus circulated within a context of heightened political urgency, and debates around their censorship worked to establish the MTRCB as a biased, unpredictable regulator.

Liveness and Public Exhibition
Throughout this conflict, questions of space became critical. The recently reworked mall multiplex became a space of information disseminnation and debate rather than a space of mass consumption, and this was predicated, in part, on the liveness of the exhibition event. This foregrounding of public exhibition presents a counterpoint to discussions of media transition as a linear, historical move away from live exhibition, toward the greater immediacy and "liveness" of television and new media. Most often theorized in relation to news coverage, the

notion of liveness describes the sense of mediated access to "the now" as produced through audiovisual tropes, such as sensational on-screen text and handheld camera footage, which create a sense of urgency.[36] It is not an inherent function of the medium but works through intricate ideological and discursive operations, which create a sense of immediacy and "authentic" access to the real. I would argue that liveness is not limited to textual representation, however; it extends outside the text itself, to the event of its exhibition in space and time, which lends a topicality or urgency to textual content. In the case of these activist films, the liveness of the screening event underscores the urgency of their textual representation. Like the newspaper, the cinema becomes a source of immediacy and knowledge dissemination, through the act of public exhibition that the MTRCB would try to prohibit. Comparisons to the newspaper build the film scene's anticensorship argument on the legalities of free expression while also constructing the filmic public as strategic, rational, and ready to engage with state corruption.

Many of the censored films were available online, but the live screening event was seen as a necessity, nonetheless. When I attended the Kontra-Agos festival's forum on censorship, the makeup of the forum demonstrated the significance of the live event for framing a body of films. The forum had assembled a more unusual crowd within the Indie Sine multiplex. Many attendants sat in groups according to their organizations, wearing T-shirts with political slogans. When the emcee introduced particular people, many stood to face the crowd and raised a fist, communicating solidarity and resistance. A panel of filmmakers (Clodualdo del Mundo, Nick Deocampo, Carlitos Siguion-Reyna, and Rojo Malaya) provoked a lively discussion with the audience, much of which hinged on finding venues for independent films that could work "under the radar" of the state. Participants had different views of the Indie Sine screen that provided the forum's setting; as a commercial venue, the location was beholden to MTRCB approval. While this regulation led some to express doubts about its possibilities, others were hopeful that the venue could reach a wider audience. Others asserted that independent films should not be relegated only to the University of the Philippines and the Cultural Center; despite its vulnerability to censorship, many felt Indie Sine would be a key venue for disseminating films. As one audience member stated, with Indie Sine, "we were very hopeful that somehow the films can be made available to a broader audience. This doesn't mean that we are compromising the vision of our film, but we were truly sincere in just in wanting to have a broader audience *na* walk-in." The Indie Sine space was premised on fantasies of access to prospective audiences, even if this meant risking the prohibitions of state regulation. In both its format and its content, the event foregrounded the urgency of public exhibition and the city as a space of circulation. It conveyed the kinds of publics it hoped this exhibition could grow—walk-ins, who may not have had a preexisting predilection toward those kinds of works.

Censorship, of course, disrupted these fantasies of access, mapping state encroachment into urban circulation. Because of the lack of access to commercial venues, the organizations involved declared their commitment to exhibiting the films on their own. Many discussed educational settings as an alternative to MTRCB-vulnerable sites, pointing to the idea of these films as knowledge. In collaboration with the Free Jonas Burgos Movement, a partner organization in the *Rights* project, the filmmakers and activists released a statement affirming the groups' efforts to "continue to reproduce and distribute copies of *Rights*, holding a series of public screenings for the 'benefit of the people's right to know.'"[37] Kiri Dalena of Southern Tagalog Exposure stated that she and the other filmmakers would show the films in schools and small group gatherings.[38] Commenting on the X ratings of *Mendiola* and *A Day in the Life of Gloria Arroyo*, Southern Tagalog Exposure's Mabilin said that the groups would continue to resist all forms of censorship, utilizing alternative venues, such as schools, to propagate their films.[39] Tellingly, these film-circulation cartographies place alternative cinemas in the school, a site of knowledge dissemination.

These school screenings accompanied comparisons to other forms of media, furthering the idea of cinema's informational, educational function. Following the X rating of *Rights*, the National Union of Journalists of the Philippines (NUJP) condemned the MTRCB censorship at a press conference, suggesting ties between these activist films and other media forms. The NUJP secretary general Rowena Paraan urged "our friends in media to protest this violation of the constitutionally guaranteed right to free expression."[40] Carlitos Siguion-Reyna, chair of the IFC, also drew connections between alternative cinema and ideas of information dissemination: "X is simply censorship. They are hiding behind the semantics of classification. There are no visible acts of violence. They are all criticism of government policy. This is a form of legitimate airing of grievances. They should be given the same space as any editorial in the newspaper."[41] Within the framework Siguion-Reyna proposes, exhibition spaces for alternative films parallel the workings of a free press, mirroring the kind of deliberative argumentation that an editorial would ostensibly provide. The censorship of *Rights*, *Mendiola*, and *A Day in the Life of Gloria* acted as unifying events for many in the media, independent film, and activist communities. Upon a second review, *Rights* received a PG-13 rating, a change that came about because of public pressure and critical media coverage.

These accounts construct an urban cartography of film censorship, one that deviates from typical descriptions of film, the city, and the state. The institutions mentioned above—journalism and the school—are meant to be antithetical to emotional display. While the former is intended to provide a system of accountability between state and society, the latter is conceived as a public good, supported by the state while free from its direct intervention. In their ideal form, their objective is education, and education is conventionally positioned as a rational, epistemological enterprise, premised on reasoned, logical debate.[42] Formalized spaces of education are meant to be uncorrupted by the vagaries of emotion. Evoking these ideal models of democratic debate positions the alternative film scene's exhibition events as correctives to an obstructive, irrational state. They become spaces where information can circulate freely, producing knowledge and constructing rational, speculative publics through the exchanges taking place among citizen-audiences.

State Parochialism and Obligatory Transnationalism

While the activist films above circulated in channels affiliated with social movements, the MTRCB also extended its reach to the feature-length films that had marked the return of Philippine cinema on the international stage since the early aughts. The films I discuss below, Sherad Anthony Sanchez's *Imburnal* (2008) and Lav Diaz's *Death in the Land of Encantos* (2007), played primarily in international film festivals, while facing MTRCB censure upon their return to domestic circuits. This prohibition from domestic channels frames transnational circulation as an obligatory path for filmmakers forbidden from local exhibition. Like the emphasis on public exhibition above, censorship takes on a spatial dimension, one with critical implications for the filmic publics the MTRCB administers. Censorship rescales circulation, pushing it from national to transnational paths. Their foreign travels only highlight the films' absence from domestic screens.

As we have seen, controversies around cultural identity surrounded the independent features that composed Philippine cinema's millennial revival. As such, siphoning these films into foreign channels was no small matter. But viewing these paths as at least partly obligatory rather than chosen renders this cinema exilic instead of expatriate. For some works, inordinate transnationalism becomes a byproduct of state intervention into domestic circulation channels. Amid allegations that such films pandered to festival juries and foreign viewerships, discussions of the MTRCB portray a film scene whose cosmopolitanism is, in part, compulsory. Its relationship to domestic publics is aspirational rather than indifferent, obstructed by a brash, corrupt state. While the comparison between the newspaper and the cinema above constructed an ideal, deliberative domestic public ready to receive these films, the discourses below turn to the state. They emphasize its parochialism, thereby furthering the divide between this ideal, national film public and the regulatory state that disciplines it. This is a practice that has a long history. As Joel David has written, martial-law-era filmmakers used festival accolades to make a case for domestic screenings of politically controversial films.[43] While less common in the early, postmillennial moment of Philippine cinema, a similar practice is being used in the accounts below.

Imburnal

Sherad Anthony Sanchez's digital work *Imburnal* (Sewer hole) was shot in Aplaya Matima, in the southern region of Davao, Sanchez's home province. Told in an experimental style with a nonlinear narrative, the four-hour digital film is a coming-of-age story that portrays two impoverished eight-year-old friends who find refuge in the sewers. The film also depicts *desaparecidos* ("the disappeared"), activists who are kidnapped by paramilitary forces. Just forty-five minutes before it was scheduled to premiere at the Cinemanila International Film Festival, festival organizers received word that the MTRCB had given the film an X rating for scenes depicting sex and nudity. Thus, the work was not shown in its entirety during the festival, despite appeals from the festival director Tikoy Aguiluz, asking the board to reconsider.[44] Festival audiences saw only the first ten minutes of the film.

Despite the ban, *Imburnal* won Cinemanila's Lino Brocka Grand Prize in the festival's Digital Lokal section. The following month, the film also received the top award at Manila's 2008 Cinema One Originals Digital Film Festival. *Imburnal* had received an R-13 rating upon a second review, following edits and deletions of scenes. Unlike the other entries, which received multiple commercial screenings, the film had only a limited release as the Cinema One closing feature in Robinsons Galleria's Indie Sine. The director Sanchez explained, "We don't want to show the cut version as much as possible. . . . That's why, to be safe, we will run the movie only once . . . but in time we will try to push [a screening of the uncut version]."⁴⁵

At a press conference in Quezon City's Gusi restaurant, Cinema One head Ronald Arguelles discussed the MTRCB's decision. His comments suggest that the board lacks an understanding of cinema as a medium: "*Pero* for me, *mas* shocking *ang* film language niya kasi pinu-push niya ang [his film language is more shocking because he pushes the] viewers to another kind of filmmaking style."⁴⁶ While the MTRCB fails to comprehend cinematic form, Arguelles envisions potential film publics very differently, stating, "We are showing the film in its entirety at U. P. and I hope the public will love it."⁴⁷ The filmmaker and the festival organizer maneuvered around the MTRCB's rating with both an obligatory version of the work and a director's cut. While they had little power over the required edits, they did have some control over the films' paths of circulation, limiting the screenings of the edited version, warning possible viewers of the censored version, and promoting the screening of the director's cut at the University of the Philippines. Pointing to a formal experimentation that only the public (not the MTRCB) would understand, Arguelles constructs a view of local cinemagoers as cinema literate, discerning, and willing to seek out alternative fare, a view he contrasts with the state's. Again, the alternative film scene makes claims upon the educational institution, and the state becomes the ignorant counterpoint to a rational public.

The MTRCB's censorship of *Imburnal* contrasted with the film's international acclaim. Some of the commentary the ban received in public discourse directly addressed this divide between foreign and domestic reception. Following the film's ban at the Cinemanila film festival, the *Inquirer* newspaper ran an "exclusive interview" with Rebecca Zlotowski, who attended Cinemanila as a member of the selection committee for the Director's Fortnight section of the Cannes Film Festival. Zlotowski criticized the MTRCB's X rating, stating, "I can understand now how difficult it is for Filipino independent filmmakers to make movies."⁴⁸

Zlotowski attested that she found it inexcusable that "these films are received well in Cannes and other international festivals, but they can't seem to find an audience in their own country." Echoing many in the local industry, she continued, "The 'x' rating seems too harsh. It's nuts that these films can't be shown in commercial theaters. . . . I feel it's our [international programmers'] responsibility to bring them to the world's attention."[49] Zlotowski's claim that circulation must fall into international hands due to the failures of "nutty" state institutions frames films' transnational circulation as a necessity.[50] These patterns of exhibition are more than simply a means of moving the works to more audiences or of accruing cultural capital. To an extent, these transnational paths are the *only* option for filmmakers whose works may be banned from local exhibition.

Death in the Land of Encantos

Lav Diaz's nine-hour black-and-white digital video work, *Death in the Land of Encantos* (*Kagadanan sa banwaan ning mga Engkanto*), also received an X rating from the MTRCB, though members reportedly failed to sit through the entire film. This X rating contrasted with the film's reception abroad, and its numerous foreign accolades became a rationale for commentators' critiques of the MTRCB. In particular, *Encantos* became a touchstone for constructing the MTRCB as a remnant of Philippine feudalism, a parochial body predicated on notions of the Philippine public as an infantile, "peasant" audience. In anticensorship discourse, foreign awards invalidated MTRCB bans, provincializing the board and the corrupted state it represented.

Death in the Land of Encantos tells the story of poet returning to the Bicol region of the country, which suffered without adequate government response in the aftermath of December 2006's typhoon Reming. Mixing a fictional narrative with documentary footage and interviews with those who had survived the storm, the work blurs the lines between fiction and documentary. It also includes content that could prove questionable to the Philippine censors' board: a powerful critique of a corrupt state, a scene in which one of the government's men beats the protagonist while singing the Philippine national anthem, and naked bodies.

The latter became the board's rationale for its ban, a move that infantilized the audience and, for Diaz, foregrounded the MTRCB's role in reproducing social stratification. The MTRCB report on the film stated: "The scene where the woman was shown in bed naked with her breasts and vagina (genitalia) are exposed is against the rules and regulations of the board—No exhibition of the genitals [sic]." In response, Diaz commented in a statement to a local entertainment journal: "I don't believe in censorship. The existence of the board of censors is very fascistic. . . . Censorship is a very feudal act. . . . I will not change anything [in *Encantos*]. The real struggle is to make good films for our people."[51] Posing the duty of the filmmaker to make meaningful work for the Filipino people, Diaz likens the operations of the MTRCB to feudalism and fascism, shorthand ways to suggest an antimodern, authoritative system that imagines its people—in this case, potential audiences—as the bottom of a social and political hierarchy.

These references to feudalism occurred once more in a very public setting, again suggesting the power of the live exhibition event for providing opportunities to frame the alternative film scene. Despite the ban, *Encantos* competed at the Cinemanila Film Festival in October 2008. Diaz took the opportunity to take his critiques to a very public level at the festival's opening night. When asked to lead the invocation, he preceded the prayer with words that elicited laughter from his audience of film industry members and cinephiles, saying, "I'm not used to doing invocation, *baka* [maybe] provocation."[52] He continued, closing with a jab at the institution that had censored *Encantos* days before: "This is the tenth year of Cinemanila. We are celebrating a landmark year for Cinemanila and Philippine Cinema, our culture, our country. Let's ask Bulol God . . . this is very important . . . Let's ask Bulol God to abolish the Board of Censors!"[53] The MTRCB chair, Laguardia, was present in the audience. Diaz's invocation of the indigenous Bulol God acts as an oblique indictment of MTRCB feudalism. The reference positions "Philippine Cinema, our culture, our country" within an ancient, precolonial past, one often imagined within a collective social structure of *bayanihan* rather than the stratified, colonial feudalism that followed. This historical vision positions alternative cinema as the true inheritor of the nation, while tying the state—represented here through the MTRCB—to the illegitimacy of the country's colonial residue.

Diaz is one of the more established alternative filmmakers working in the Philippines. Hence, the ban on *Encantos* was met with commentary in various forms of media, much of which drew comparisons between the film's domestic and foreign reception. Armida Siguion-Reyna, a former chair of the MTRCB who was deposed for her liberal practices, published an article commenting on the X rating. She laments that despite the crises occurring across the world, "in the Philippines, we're still focused on breasts and vagina in a film that's clearly nothing close to pornography."[54] Here, the MTRCB becomes an island of provincial priggishness, focusing on the minutiae of physiology as crisis grips the world.

The board's crude take on sexuality also enters Siguion-Reyna's discussion of the MTRCB as unable to fully comprehend the meaning of artistic "creativity." She used *Encantos*'s X rating to point to the censors' lack of context for their practices, warning of the dangers of "anti-obscenity" bills in the House and Senate, bills that MTRCB members had supported. While purporting to protect women and children, the terms of the bills are so broad, Siguion-Reyna argues, that their basic purpose "more dangerously seeks to strangle all forms of creativity." She quotes problematic passages from the bills' texts, which condemn all forms of media (including those "future technologies to be developed") "which are calculated to excite, stimulate or arouse impure thoughts and prurient interest, regardless of the motive of the author thereof."[55] Unlike the ideal variations of Philippine film publics above, the bills envision the audience as a mass of "excitable" bodies.

Siguion-Reyna creates an opposition between the MTRCB-supported bills and the Philippine artistic community, linking this artistic community to more rational observers from abroad. Like Arguelles's discussion of *Imburnal* as beyond the MTRCB's comprehension, Siguion-Reyna suggests that the board lacks artistic understanding, pointing to the bill's proposition that authorial intention and context are irrelevant. Turning to international press coverage, she quotes Ronnie Schieb's *Variety* review of *Encantos*, warning her readers: "This bill becomes law and we completely slay the creative energies of the few remaining Lav Diazes. This bill gets passed, and gems where 'stark black-and-white digital compositions frame a landscape so bleak and boulder-strewn, so empty of habitation that it is hard to believe the land was not barren from time primordial. Painful flashbacks to the region's past resurrect a lost Eden. The only thing more shocking than the extent of the damage is the ages-deep acceptance in the eyes of the survivors' is forever judged in terms of breast and genital exposure, and filmmaking be damned."[56] Siguion-Reyna's assessment of Diaz's banishment from Philippine screens is clear; her quotation from the *Variety* review stresses the irony that, even as an international viewership lauds the film, it is banned within its own country. Reflecting on her own tenure with the MTRCB, she condemns those who failed to help her broach the issue of censorship previously, holding them responsible for what she views as the industry's demise: "I wonder what [the MTRCB member and former actress] Amalia Fuentes feels, helping kill the industry that made her? . . . I wonder what they feel, now that major films cannot be screened? Death in the land of the encantos, indeed. HB 3305 and SB 2464 is murder, regardless of the motives of its sponsors. It cannot be allowed to pass."[57]

Siguion-Reyna drew on *Death in the Land of Encantos*'s international reviews as evidence of the film's value. In her estimation, the local audience was left out of its own cinema's international renaissance because an unsophisticated state institution was fixated on nudity. Like Diaz's assertions of state feudalism, the turn to transnational circuits positions the state as premodern and parochial. This discourse severs the ties between nation and state, while underscoring those between national and transnational audiences. More than positing opposition between the state and the imagined national audience, this framework enlarges the scale of the discussion, using foreign reception to shame state institutions for how they have conceived of Filipino audiences. State censorship becomes a refusal to participate in the modern transnationalism of world cinema culture, where Philippine film is already playing an important role.

Siguion-Reyna was not the only critic to respond to *Encantos*'s ban. Perhaps because Diaz was one of the most internationally respected Filipino filmmakers, local viewers and critics met the banning of *Encantos* with particular ire. Upon its prohibition, many commentators in blogs and popular media framed the X rating as the MTRCB's means of provincializing its own compatriots, excluding them from the publics that their own cinema had generated across the globe:

> The film *Death in the Land of Encantos* has brought honor to the country when it won numerous awards abroad. However, it was hindered from being screened in the Philippines when it got an "X" rating from the Movie and Television Review and Classification Board.[58]

> Apparently not caring about the rights of the Filipino movie-viewing public—the little that's left—to see what won the Special Mention prize in the 2007 Venice International Film Festival's Orizzonti (Horizons) section, the MTRCB banned it from screening.[59]

> As with government, we seem to get the leaders we deserve, but when it comes to honoring and paying respect to our Real artists

(and not the "artistas") I'm thinking that perhaps our country doesn't deserve to have an artist with the courage and talent of Lav Diaz. *Death in the Land of Encantos* won the Orizzonti second prize at the 64th Venice International film festival (2007), the oldest and one of the most prestigious festivals in the world next to Cannes and Berlin film festivals.[60]

The quotes suggest the belief in a local prospective movie audience laying claim to a cinema regarded as simultaneously local and international, a cosmopolitanism that is not merely the product of multiple influences and hybrid cultural products but also of necessity.

This obligatory cosmopolitanism was a key factor in shaping the early stages of Filipino cinema's rebirth. This form of cosmopolitanism stems from compulsory patterns of circulation, imposed by the prohibitions of state censorship. As the institution behind the MTRCB, the state was an implicit factor in Philippine cinema's ties to international audiences and programmers, who feel it is their "duty" to circulate the works, given local conditions.

In terms of such films' aesthetics, the idea of cosmopolitanism is not always a welcome designation, whether obligatory or not. As Jigna Desai writes, "The phenomenon of the art house is based on positioning 'foreign' films as ethnographic documents of 'other' (national) cultures and therefore as representatives of national cinemas."[61] There were some moves to address the issue of national circulation, in both local and international terms. In 2008, the Paris Cinema Festival held a retrospective of Philippine cinema. At the festival, several alternative filmmakers spoke to Nestor O. Jardin, president of the Cultural Center of the Philippines (CCP), sharing their problems with local distribution. Alongside the UPFI, the CCP is one of two screening spaces in the country outside MTRCB jurisdiction.[62] Jardin helped arrange the two-part Independent Film Summit held later that year; the first session focused on the problems of local distribution and exhibition of indie works, while the second session strategized how to market independent cinema within international circuits. The former chair of the IFC Clodualdo del Mundo noted the importance of combining the business of moviemaking without sacrificing the "indie spirit," stating, "Our movies have to be seen. We have to reach our audiences, here and abroad."[63]

The regulation of local screening space thus underscores and heightens the requirement of the global audience, represented here by the film festival network that provides the major outlet for these works. The global audience is, to an extent, always a necessity for works that fall outside the mainstream, with festival stamps becoming requisite markers of "quality cinema" for films traveling the film festival circuit before finding runs in the art-house cinema screens (sometimes within local multiplexes) and specialty DVD distributors. As we have seen, these paths have only been intermittently available to Philippine alternative works. Thus, these international festivals played a pivotal role in the Philippine alternative film scene, not just as markers of a work's international "success" and access to foreign audiences but also as funders of local works. For instance, the International Film Festival Rotterdam's (IFFR) Hubert Bals Fund has supported Khavn de la Cruz's *The Family That Eats Soil* (2005), Lav Diaz's *Heremias* (2006), Ramon Mes de Guzman's *Balikbayan Box* (Returned compatriot box) (2007), Raya Martin's *Now Showing* (2008), John Torres's *Tempestad* (*Tempestuous*) (2012), Joanna Vasquez Arong's *The Sigbin Chronicles* (2012), and Jet Leyco's *Leave It for Tomorrow, for Night Has Fallen* (2013). As scholars and critics have pointed out, the producer role that international festivals often take within the cinemas of the global south can sometimes involve complex relations of power, with selection committees favoring works that convey a narrowly "authentic" view of national culture.[64] But in a context where an unstable state fears local circulation, foreign channels become a secondary stopgap, leaving local audiences' latent political energies untapped.

Gay Film Publics and the Limits of Anticensorship Discourse

While the discourses above positioned the state as parochial and potential film publics as rational, these constructs became more complex when one of the country's two censorship-free venues came under fire in a way that complicated strategic turns to rationality. In discussions of gay film audiences at the University of the Philippines Film Institute (UPFI), a marginalized community's failure to meet behavioral protocols rendered the space a target of censorship. Alongside the Cultural Center of the Philippines, the UPFI is classified as a censorship-free zone due to its educational and cultural mandate. Because of this positioning outside MTRCB jurisdiction, the UPFI remains one of the few places that allow the exhibition of censored films in their original, uncut versions. Thus, the university cinema provides not only an important venue for the screening of alternative works, but also a key setting in narratives of the battle against the MTRCB. Its reputation also draws from the university's history as a hub of anti-martial-law activism, which positions it as a bastion of collective action under authoritarian rule. Due to these conditions, the UPFI is an important site in Manila's cinema imagination, held up as a last stand against oppressive state censorship. While censorship sought to crush the circulation of knowledge, art, and culture, the UPFI stood outside its jurisdiction as a free space. When censors threatened its sovereignty, filmmakers and cinephiles recalled the UPFI's role in their own cinephilic memories. Such recollections positioned the site as a hub for the controversial, sometimes international, cinema that the MTRCB was too provincial to appreciate. The director Aureus Solito recalled his memory of seeing Derek Jarman's *Caravaggio* (1986), his "first viewing of a totally beautiful queer film," as well as the Lino Brocka film *Orapronobis* (1989), censored by the post-martial-law Corazon Aquino government. A blogger remembered seeing Martin Scorsese's *The Last Temptation of Christ* at the University of the Philippines in 1998. The MTRCB's then chair Manoling Morato had rated the film X for nudity. Due to a planted piece of false information, he had rushed to the UPFI Film Center upon hearing of its screening, only to realize that the film had screened the night before. As the story goes, a sign on the door read, "Welcome to the Manoling Morato Memorial Film Center," and the joke appeared in the college newspaper the *Collegian* the following week.[65] Thus far, this seems in line with the discussions above. In this alternative film culture imaginary, films reach their ideal publics in an educational setting with a nationalist history, the last bastion of a resilient nation, girded against a corrupted state. Meanwhile, the MTRCB plays the fool.

While these recollections of the UPFI offered a familiar schematic of Manila's alternative film scene and its relationship with an oppressive state, the complexity of this view was revealed in early 2009, when the UPFI's regular screenings of local films catering to gay audiences came under scrutiny. Media coverage from the local entertainment press deemed the UPFI a clandestine "gay porn haven." Mario E. Bautista, an entertainment contributor for various newspapers and magazines in the city, wrote in the *Philippine Journal*, "We're alarmed because the U.P. Film Institute is fast getting the reputation of being a haven for pornographic films. . . . It's not within the jurisdiction of the MTRCB so they can show whatever they want."[66] Rather than limiting his critique to the "full frontal nudity" and "simulated sex acts," part of Bautista's criticism stems from the films' perceived lack of quality: "We're also against censorship but only if a film is artistically well done.... We're not homophobic, but even in the name of artistic freedom, most of these sleazy films don't deserve to be shown in the country's premiere state university.... Can't a committee be formed to screen the gay films that they show and make sure that only those with artistic merits be allowed for exhibition?"[67] It seems that the speculative publics such films evoked were not of the preferred sort.

Following these criticisms, the MTRCB informed the UPFI that the board had received word that the Film Institute was charging admission fees to screen films without permits, informing the Film Institute that the MTRCB would now "monitor" films exhibited at the university. If any works deemed pornographic were shown, the MTRCB would file complaints in court.[68] The MTRCB called for the directors of three narrative features to appear before the board: Adolf Alix for *Aurora*; Monti Parungao for *Sagwan* (Paddle); and Jowee Morel for *Latak* (Dregs). The latter two were films with "gay themes" that combined nudity and sex with indie sensibility (economical production values, on-location shooting) and film festival play. The board accused the filmmakers of "commercially" screening the works at UPFI before receiving permits.

In this instance, the alternative film scene's focus on education, knowledge, and rationalism was at odds with the MTRCB's target—the gay audiences that visited the university theater for "libido stimulation." Whether the UPFI charged for the films was not the primary point of discussion in the discourse surrounding MTRCB monitoring. Rather, conversation focused primarily on issues of quality, questioning the criteria for labeling sexual content "porn." For example, the University of the Philippines College of Mass Communications professor Marichu C. Lambino wrote a widely circulated blog entry critiquing the MTRCB for attempting to regulate which materials the Film Institute should be allowed to teach. Lambino listed "advice" to the board, asking them to consider what constitutes pornography, pointing out that many of the films screened include celebrated, mainstream stars. ("It might be big movie news to find out whether these actors have suddenly made a career shift to porn.")[69] She also asked the MTRCB to tell her which works they would classify as "porn," using the films' international accolades to justify their legitimacy, listing such awards as *Serbis*'s (dir. Brillante Mendoza, 2008) Palme d'Or prize at Cannes,

Masahista's (dir. Brillante Mendoza, 2005) win at Locarno, and *Sikil*'s (dir. Ronaldo Bertubin, 2007) screening at the San Diego Asian Film Festival.[70] She then posed a question: "Which one or which ones of these have utterly no redeeming social value or utterly no artistic, literary merit? More important, does the MTRCB have jurisdiction to tell U.P. what it can teach and how to go about it?"[71]

The judgment of a work's value is a specific part of the MTRCB's language, which states that the board's assessment of whether a work is "fit" for public exhibition is whether it holds artistic, cultural, or scientific merit. Because of these international accolades, the films listed certainly met the "quality cinema" designation, demonstrating the obligatory cosmopolitanism of Filipino works screened outside national borders and prohibited on local ground. Lambino's arguments picture a cinema that is inclusive, democratizing, and catering to the interests of art over commerce, common rationale in arguments against cinema regulation. Such anticensorship discourse was a crucial tool in the fight against the MTRCB. Emphasizing films' quality and potential film publics' rationality served a strategic purpose for the alternative film scene. At the same time, it also important to consider how this rhetorical approach, while unavoidable, may have precluded other, less rational, more bodily kinds of engagement with the medium.

These issues became a point of contention in discourse within parts of Manila's gay community. Again, questions of artistic merit were central. Commenters implied a desire for the composed, rational public that quality cinema would constitute. This created an aspirational contrast with the raucous, oversexed gay audience that had become the bogeyman in the MTRCB's UPFI censorship. For example, the author of a blog titled *The Bakla* (gay) *Review* described the fervor of this niche cinemagoing audience:[72]

> For the past year, many X-rated films have enjoyed packed premiere screenings at UP—sometimes a new movie every week. Today, filmmakers reserve slots at U. P. even before getting a rating, in anticipation of a hard time with the MTRCB. It's somewhat become standard practice, especially since it's also an effective promotional scheme in capturing a core audience.[73]

The author noted that despite the scandal surrounding "gay porn," many of the films, while banned for sexual content, are not necessarily about sex or about gay characters. He surmised that the gay films "raised eyebrows" in part because "they attract such an excitable crowd during these premieres."[74] The excitable crowd became the perceived threat.

Like their discourses involving the mall multiplex's bad audience, the MTRCB deemed UPFI's gay film crowds a problematic public. The author also points to holes in the "artistic merit" reasoning through references to mainstream, commercial cinema. Comparing the alleged trashiness of the gay-themed works playing at the UPFI to mainstream, commercial cinema sharing the same venue, he relates his viewing of a "terrible Dingdong Dantes and Marian Rivera romance" the previous year, arguing that he would not deny the film to those who may have enjoyed it, because "you have to weather the bad, because only in such a free environment can good films also thrive." Rather than appealing to an internationally lauded quality cinema to make his point against censorship, the author points to inconsistencies in criteria for cinema regulation—inconsistencies that would apply to "quality cinema" arguments coming from both the MTRCB and the alternative cinema community.

Beyond the *Bakla Review*'s arguments concerning value judgments based on artistic quality, the author also makes a case for the need for an exhibition space for gay cinema due to the practical logistics of exhibition in the Philippines, which leave little room for works outside the mainstream. Like the discussions above, he foregrounds the importance of public exhibition space. Stating that "Filipino gay sex films are already on the fringes," he notes that the genre is almost exclusively "the territory of the independents," with lower budgets to compensate for the smaller niche market and for their limited commercial runs. The films screen primarily in larger cities, outside the country's biggest cinema chain, SM Cinemas, which will not exhibit R-rated films. As the author points out, films rated X exist within "the fringe of the fringe." Moreover, the author notes the difficulty of reaching UPFI's out of the way location: "Most people, even those interested to watch them, don't even brave the traffic and distance to U. P. in Quezon City. As it is, the setup for X-rated films is already unfriendly."[75]

Ultimately, for the *Bakla Review*, the question hinges on the lack of exhibition spaces and these works' rights to screen: "The issue is not art or trash. It is not X or R. The issue is not exploitation of actors or unfit professional practices, though it deserves its own inquiry, of course. The issue is that in the event a film does get an X-rating, where will it go if U. P. chooses not to accept it? . . . It's not even simple censorship, it's banishment. It's throwing an entire work into limbo, never to be seen or heard from again."[76] Again, censorship is a spatial practice, creating an exhibition vacuum for works that have no way to reach their audiences.

The description of "Filipino gay sex films" adds another dimension to the future of Philippine cinema brought about by the advent of the digital and the subsequent proliferation of alternative works. However, unlike their more "highbrow" counterparts, this film subculture cannot turn to the logics of quality to justify their right to circulate. They are on the periphery, with few options in terms of public exhibition. As such, they index the heterogeneity of works dubbed "independent" or "alternative" film. In the case of these gay sex films, the primary idea of a Filipino public is not as a mass, prospective audience with rights to information and education via cinema; rather, the public is a space from which some of these viewers feel separate, as the posts below further indicate.

The *Bakla Review* article was met with many comments, some on the site, others on its partner blog, *Hot Men in the Philippines*, most of which discussed similar matters of where gay films would screen if they were banned from UPFI. Some of them also pointed to the lack of quality in the "gay sex films" at issue, discussing the idea of whether the films' artistic merit would make it easier to justify their screening home within an institution of higher education. One commenter lamented in Filipino, "The novelty of gay films is truly lost. You can't count them now, nor are they exciting! Before, gay movies were considered an 'event movie,' each featured exposure caused a ruckus. . . . Now they don't, because now a lot of movies are like that, but they're all worthless! . . . The U.P. theater is becoming a dumping ground for so-called art films."[77] Describing a cinema valued precisely for its "prurience" and for its positioning outside the legitimizing "art film" status, the comments suggest the idea that these works should be screened, but within a setting more appropriate to their nature. They are deemed outside the aspirations of Manila's alternative film culture, occupying, as the writer above stated, "the fringe of the fringe."

Other commentators mirrored these ideas. Echoing the arguments that emerged in discussions of the bans of other cinematic works, one poster argued that "censorship has no place in a democratic society where free speech is guaranteed." However, he continued that quality *should* be a principal factor in deciding what cinema should screen where: "We need both bad and good films, art and pornographic films and whatever adjective you may attach to it, but they need not have their over hyped premiers at UP. The way the buzz some of these films generate with words like full frontal, uncut . . . you are obviously going to attract a crowd more interested in libido stimulus than an intellectual discourse or an artistic uplift."[78] The writer describes an unruly public constituted in the exhibition of these films, a discrepancy within the educational, cultural mandate of the university, which is supposed to generate "intellectual discourse" and "artistic uplift." Other posters worried that these films' unruly audiences would only harm the reputation of the wider gay community as well as the status of the alternative cinema community with which it had become affiliated:

> Yes there must be a place to show topics or works of arts—no matter how controversial it may seem, so that we would know, that even in a country such as ours, there is still freedom of expression . . . but what these films show is the negative image that society at large claims that the gay community stands for. It removes what respect the community has gained with the general public. . . . Even in as free a community as the gay community, self-control is needed.[79]

> As for the quality of such gay indie films, we have to admit, most are really crap. Some stereotype the whole gay culture, some sensationalize our whole existence, others settle for mere uncalled-for frontal nudity. I am not playing my Pilate card. I just want better films. I do hope that UPFI screens its movies though, we don't want to see the demise of the whole industry, and drag UPFI with it.[80]

The comments here demonstrated concerns similar to those addressed in the previous sections, discussing the role of censorship in a democracy. However, in addition to these overtures concerning censorship and democracy on a more general level, the comments also exhibited contentions around the issue of gay mainstreaming within the context of "gaining respect" from the "general public." Salacious marketing, the possibility of exploitative production practices, and a raucous audience interested in "libido stimulation" rather than "artistic uplift"—these are factors largely absent from the wider discussions of Philippine alternative cinema practices and publics. While the cases cited above condemned MTRCB regulation, some of the viewers here, whom the regulation at UPFI would ostensibly affect, demonstrated more mixed feelings. Due to these works' affiliation with a marginalized community, many within that community wanted to keep them out of circulation to the broader public in order to "save face." These discourses reveal a speculative public housed within the gay community itself. They demonstrate a concern with the imminent threat posed to a censorship-free space for art films. While they are against censorship, they also distance "low-quality" films and the modes of cinemagoing they encourage.

It may be useful to consider this discussion of cinemagoing within broader dynamics of gender, sexuality, and class in the Philippines. Describing *kabaklaan* culture, Robert Diaz writes, "Despite being traditionally associated with a range of marginalized sexualities such as the lower-class *bakla*, the parlorista (or hairdresser), and the trans* woman, *kabaklaan* can also be defined as a type of performance that exceeds these identitarian constructs. It instead indexes ways of overacting, of being over the top, of being aware of one's being over the top, and of asserting a distinctly queer sensibility about the travails of everyday life."[81] Modes of expression like "*biyuti*" (beauty) are "the queerness that the state cannot automatically co-opt to make trans* life respectable to the masses."[82] The crowds in the UPFI cinema may or may not have overlapped with the communities portrayed in Diaz's analysis, and undoubtedly, the practices described are of a very different sort. But his article's discussion opens provocative questions for considering the modes of filmmaking and collective cinema consumption pushed to the peripheries of alternative film scenes. It tracks the frictions between notions of respectability and forms of expression and entertainment deemed excessive, a tension reflected, however broadly, in the discussion above. Rather than positing a framework in which the MTRCB works for the state and against both cinema practitioners and the publics they represent, calls to excise these kinds of films (and their audiences) inadvertently position MTRCB censorship as a means of keeping out the bad films, thereby consolidating a version of gay representation that is more acceptable within a broader public.

Censorship, the Unstable State, and the Strategically Rational Nation

Ironically, given the uphill battle his film faced, *Imburnal* director Sherad Anthony Sanchez was one of the few filmmakers able to attend an awards ceremony for 2008 Cinemanila winners at the presidential headquarters, the Malacañang Palace. Arroyo herself presented the winners with cash prizes and Bulol trophies depicting the Ifugao rice god holding up a film reel; this is the same god that Lav Diaz invoked at the Cinemanila opening ceremonies in his call to end the MTRCB.[83] Prohibited from the festival itself, the director's cut of *Imburnal* was screened a month after the Cinemanila ceremonies, at the UPFI Film Center. Sanchez's presence at the Malacañang ceremony captures the contradictions of state censorship within the unstable Arroyo regime. Cinema censorship became a nonsensical farce; as a counterpoint, the alternative film scene adopted a strategically rational role as the true mediator between national publics and their cinema. Through an emphasis on cinema as knowledge dissemination, exhibition events like the Kontra-Agos Film Festival and public discourse around films' obligatory, transnational paths construct a speculative, national public grounded in reason and rationality.

This is a different vision than that offered in images of nationalism as affective attachment.[84] Nationalism is often seen as the domain of sentiment; meanwhile, the state is the domain of institutional bureaucracy and rationalism. The alternative film scene's anticensorship discourses challenged this dichotomy, inverting common configurations of the nation-state. This reversal became a means of legitimizing their speculative vision of a national public for alternative cinema. Strategically deploying the notion of the Filipino film public as tempered, deliberative, and mature enough to handle incendiary content, the alternative film scene created a vision of national cinema based on clearheaded audiences and artistically ambitious texts. This strategic representation was, in part, a product of the state it opposed—an administration whose corruption and violence rendered it an irrational, parochial counterpoint. Censorship also mapped a geography of cinemagoing. Discourses on public exhibition emphasized the circulation site as a crucial aspect of film culture, while discussions of international circulation framed transnational routes as obligatory. Through censorship, the MTRCB produced an imaginary of film-circulation space.

Within this discourse, the censorship board became a symbol of state power, a claim that tied targeted film scenes to a more authentic, purer vision of nation. In one sense, this dichotomy would seem to work against the notion of the irrational state and the rational populous. Ideas of national identity are known for the contrast between their emotional power and their conceptual paucity; the rational administration of the public sphere (the state) becomes a counterpoint to the affective culture of the private sphere (the nation). But as Paul

Willemen and Valentina Vitali point out, one strain of national cinema discourse invokes the metaphor of the national body and narrates the nation in a progressivist way: the nation is born and develops, and its cultural practices mature.[85] Alongside this model, the film industry functions as a metonym for the industrialization of culture and for modernity.[86] The discourses in this chapter offer a model of national cinema predicated on a late stage of national becoming, characterized by audience maturity. The state becomes here an obstruction to the nation's organic progression, and the boundaries of the body politic are strategically redrawn. As the cases above suggest, within certain circumstances, this kind of rhetoric has merits. It can function as a strategic means of framing state corruption. But this rhetoric also has limits; it can inadvertently delineate boundaries around the kinds of audience engagement welcomed within this model.

The following chapter also examines a spatial imaginary produced by the state, one that entails more utopian aspirations. This geography turns inward, toward the country's provinces, constructing an expanded, archipelagic variation of the national body politic. I examine a vision of state-controlled circulation through analysis of the Film Development Council of the Philippines' Sineng Pambansa (National Cinema) project, which constructed government-owned cinematheques and mobile cinemas throughout the archipelago. If ephemerality defined the sites in previous chapters, the fantasies that follow are based on aspirations of permanence, enabled through the state—an unexpected turn, given the instability of state institutions.

CHAPTER FIVE

"HOLLYWOOD IS NOT US"

NATIONAL CIRCULATION AND

THE SPECULATIVE STATE

By 2010, the Philippines was in a state of transition, both in terms of the cinemas that had made their mark internationally and in terms of the state that had provided so few avenues of government support for these films. In May, Gloria Macapagal Arroyo's eleven-year tenure as president of the Philippines ended. She would soon face charges of election fraud and plunder, fighting her national "house arrest" with claims of a rare bone disorder requiring treatment abroad. The local media would fill with photographs of Arroyo in a hospital bed, sporting headgear and a neck brace, images whose questionable legitimacy embodied the corruption of her decade of rule. The photographs signaled the end of a troubled era in Philippine politics.

    The Arroyo regime's inheritors were more familiar than might be expected, especially for a transition described as the dawn of a new political epoch. Winning 40 percent of the vote, Benigno "Noynoy" Aquino III became the Philippines' fifteenth president.[1] The son of Corazon and Benigno "Ninoy" Aquino, icons of post-martial-law democracy, former senator Aquino was persuaded to run in the wake of national mourning upon his mother's death from cancer in 2009. He met the announcement of his victory amid cheers in the Senate chamber, wearing a barong Tagalog embroidered with a yellow ribbon that evoked his mother's campaign color. His siblings accompanied him, including the television host and actress Kris Aquino, whose national fame has given her the unofficial titles "Queen of All Media," "Queen of Talk," and "Box Office Queen." The election was both a presidential victory and a coronation, uniting state and media in a blend of idealized history and speculative future.

Kris Aquino was not the only familiar media figure flanking the president's triumph. Aquino's closest competitor in the election was also a recognizable face, deposed former president Joseph "Erap" Estrada, who followed with 25 percent of the vote. Despite being ousted on corruption charges in 2001, a move that promoted then vice president Arroyo to head of state, the former action star had recently returned to the country to reinvigorate his political career. In addition, Imee Marcos, daughter of Ferdinand and Imelda, was elected governor of the clan's Ilocos Norte Province. Meanwhile, her brother, Ferdinand "Bongbong" Marcos Jr., won a Senate seat. Not to be outdone, the pair's eighty-year-old mother, Imelda, became a member of the House of Representatives, stating her aim to be "a grandmother for our country."[2] A generation earlier, Marcos's allies had gunned down the newly elected president's father upon the exiled activist's return to the Philippines from the United States; his martyrdom would stir the nation to elect his widow, Corazon, in the first People Power revolution. Now the Marcos and Aquino families would be two key players in what they promised would be a new era of statehood, based in part on old political and show-business dynasties. A new phase in alternative filmmaking paralleled what was to be a brief moment of middle-class optimism in Philippine governance.

If the disillusionment of the Arroyo presidency affected the initial tenor of the Philippine independent cinema's birth, the election of Benigno Aquino III aligned with a new stage in Philippine cinema's postmillennial transition phase. I would locate this stage at the beginning of Aquino's tenure, from approximately 2010 to 2012, its end point marked with the entrance of the term "maindie" into public film discussion. A portmanteau of "mainstream" and "independent," "maindie" would come into widespread public circulation in 2012, to describe a new direction in filmmaking: films produced outside the mainstream studio system but embracing more mainstream sensibilities and aiming for a wider audience. The period in this chapter presages this later shift, marking it with a turn to self-reflexive representations of alternative film production, growing criticism of key film institutions, and, for some, a surprising turn to the historically erratic, oppressive state as an agent of change. Alternative cinema's publics became a part of this transition. While the film movement's early-aughts beginnings tended toward neorealist depictions of the masses, this intermediate phase contested these imaginaries, refiguring the film scene's strategies toward reaching new audiences. These new strategies involved visions of a nationally dispersed cinema that would be decentralized, both geographically, beyond the Metro, and aesthetically, beyond the tropes that had become associated with the "independent" label. It was a vision that encompassed a range of speculative publics—those that would be found outside the capital city and those that more difficult aesthetics excluded.

This chapter focuses on two main shifts that capture this phase of Philippine alternative filmmaking and its relationship to a national film culture, built through circulation. First, there was a move from smaller-scale sites to the desire for large-scale institutions for domestic cinema circulation. The previous chapters focused largely on fragmented, grassroots efforts to build local circuits for Philippine alternative cinema. In the period under discussion here, the film scene's demands took a slightly different tack, as state institutions presented another alternative to the foreign-festival network that had begun to dominate circulation.

This desire for state institutions is partly a product of the second shift: a change in how the alternative film scene viewed the transnational funding agencies and distribution circuits that had supported local production. Several years into alternative cinema's rise, this transnationalism shifted from being seen as a driver of newfound cinematic diversity in a context dominated by local studios and global Hollywood to being seen as an agent of paternalism, perpetuating a different kind of aesthetic homogeneity and excluding domestic publics. If transnational festivals, funding agencies, and awards bodies had entered and reconfigured the Philippine alternative cinema scene in its earliest years, by this time, this variation of transnationalism had settled into Philippine film culture, raising complex questions about national cinema formation at the local level. While the international festival circuit remained a robust component of the Filipino film scene, the difficulties of local distribution and exhibition persisted, as the previous chapter on censorship indicated. Moreover, by this time, the majority of the film distribution and exhibition sites discussed in the first four chapters of the book no longer existed, and new sites had risen in their place. As I have suggested, this cycle was driven by the speculative ambitions that aimed to expand alternative cinema's publics with each new screening initiative. This cycle's persistence raised the question of institutionalizing cinema circulation and what that might mean for the project of Philippine film culture. Meanwhile, the established place of the transnational festival circuit within local film culture also led to questions of its institutional and cultural legitimacy.

What emerged is a demand for an *idealized* version of the state to establish its role within national cinema formation, at the levels of production, distribution, and exhibition. The relation between the state and Philippine cinema was not new. Critics have pointed to the irony that one reason for the rise of "Second Golden Age" filmmaking during martial law was the support of the Experimental Cinema of the Philippines (ECP), a state body headed by Imee Marcos.[3] But by this point during the postmillennial transition period, the state had been largely proscriptive, entering film culture via censorship policies or antipiracy legislation. If the Optical Media Board and the MTRCB offered dystopian images of authoritarianism, the Film Development Council of the Philippines' (FDCP) plans offered the promise of a more utopian counterpart, tempering the proscriptions of the former with ideals of a functioning, benign state institution, representative of its constituents. This is not necessarily how this institution functioned in actuality but, rather, how many in the local film scene and players in the government itself projected it. These visions proposed *fantasies* of a government, as one filmmaker puts it below, "for the people." Thus, this is not a chapter about the actual workings of government arts initiatives but about the speculation underpinning these projects' possibilities. This speculation was structured around visions of an ideal public for national cinema. This positioning of the state as the decisive through line for domestic cinema circulation, despite its often problematic, sometimes violent place within Philippine history, reveals the persistence of the state as an *imagined ideal* for institutionalizing local film culture, particularly within a transnationalized context. The progression in this chapter is not meant to be teleological, culminating in the state; rather, it addresses the persistence of the state as a fantasy, a model institutional form.

This final chapter examines the envisioning and reformulating of three institutions concerned with domestic cinema production and dissemination: the foreign film festival circuit; Cinemalaya, a national public/private foundation; and Sineng Pambansa (National Cinema), a state-sponsored film-circulation initiative. With each of these institutions, the question of publics became a controversial point of contention. As previous chapters have suggested, the transnational festival circuit's role in alternative cinema production and circulation had evolved into a contentious point of debate, leading to questions around cultural authenticity and the impact of domestic censorship. The problem of the elusive local public became key, and Cinemalaya and Sineng Pambansa emerged as potential resources for dealing with it. Each of these institutions had ties to the state, allowing a speculative vision of a benign state to emerge.

First, I look at the local transformation of the transnational film festival circuit. In these filmic critiques, foreign festivals' prestige economy encourages young, middle-class filmmakers in the global south to make the "poverty porn" films that will garner awards. This tendency underscores the notion that the films are made for foreign, rather than domestic, audiences. Specifically, I analyze two films that have critiqued this festival circuit: *Ang mga kidnaper ni Ronnie Lazaro* (*The Kidnappers of Ronnie Lazaro*, dir. Sigfreid Barros Sanchez, 2012) and *Ang Babae sa Septic Tank* (*The Woman in the Septic Tank*, dir. Marlon Rivera, 2011). Second, I examine the controversies surrounding the Cinemalaya Foundation and Philippine Independent Film Festival, a mixture of state, private-sector, and academic participants. Debates about the festival's mixture of art and commerce reveal the persistence of filmmakers' and audiences' visions of state institutions as for the people. This vision reflects a speculative vision of the state as both producing and representing the national publics that the alternative cinema scene hopes to reach. Finally, I look at the government-based Film Development Council of the Philippines, focusing on its Sineng Pambansa (National Cinema) initiative. Envisioning a national, decentralized, state-owned cinematheque circuit, the Sineng Pambansa project revealed another ideal of cinema and nation: a translocal variation that reaches into the provinces and across national borders.

I am interested in the conflicting, prospective versions of alternative cinema publics these three institutions suggest, viewing them as *speculative institution-ideals*—reified systems within particular public imaginaries, carrying overt symbolic identities. Because they are ideals, they are less grounded in the extant reality of the present than they are in the potentiality of the future. They are always in process, and the *ongoing process* of institutionalization itself becomes a site of meaning. In some ways, this aligns smoothly with the kinds of aspirational projects that occupied the previous chapters. The Indie Sine multiplex screen, Quiapo Cinematheque imaginaries, art-house screening venues, and activist film festivals all created specific encounters between screens and audiences. These encounters were fertile grounds for a host of possibilities about what these projects could engender: building communities of moviegoers-cum-citizens, preserving culturally "authentic" urban histories, creating an economically sustainable film industry outside the major studios, or expanding political projects. Within these aspirational blueprints for a national film culture, the state was primarily an obstacle to overcome.

The idea of an institution-ideal in this chapter differs from these previous endeavors, because of its scale (an emphasis on longevity and reach), as well as its ties to idealized versions of state infrastructure, which are largely chimeric in Philippine contexts. Like many settings in the global south, the Philippines has had what Patricio N. Abinales and Donna J. Amoroso describe as "a long history of institutional weakness."[4] As they argue, the modern Philippine state that came into being during the American period is "a colonial state creation as well as a nationalist imagining."[5] This somewhat contradictory relationship between an imposed colonial order, on the one hand, and an ideal of nationalism, on the other, is reflected in approval ratings suggesting a conflict between public anticipation and realities. Studies conducted during this time indicated that a majority of Filipinos continued to trust in state institutions generally, despite a high rate of income inequality and a low rate of change over time; voter turnout was reported at 75 percent for the election that brought Aquino to power.[6] The film scene's turn to the state during this period signaled this persistent sense of the state's potential, its untapped ability to give rise to the publics that had been speculated about for several years. Within the context of cinema, the state's ideal form rested on its ability to manifest those publics, clearing the frictions between "nation" and "state" that the previous chapter captured.

In this way, the institution-ideal borrows from sociological and anthropological discussions of the state as a culturally specific social construct rather than an empirical universal.[7] I expand these concepts to apply to media institutions, which function here as proxies for an idealized version of benevolent state power. Theorists have long viewed state formation in postcolonial contexts as a process that mixed precolonial and European structures of power and belief, blending the deep, affective structures of ritual with the imposed frameworks of rational bureaucracy. In his work on what he calls the "magic of the state," for example, Michael Taussig analyzes the tendency to view the institutional structure as a kind of fetish, highlighting the religious impulses of a supposedly secular system.[8] Like the commodity fetish, for its subjects, the state holds a "peculiar sacred and erotic attraction, even thralldom, combined with disgust."[9] In the context of the Philippines, this mixture has a long history. In his work on state formation in sixteenth-century Philippines, Vicente Rafael argues that religious conversion helped to create the Spanish colonial state.[10] The desire for security and life after death motivated compliance to Spanish priests and the Tagalog ruling class, or *principales*, suggesting the culturally specific, affective foundations of Philippine state formation.[11]

While the mixture of affect and rationality may take specific form in postcolonial settings, it is by no means confined to them. Rather, this combination is a fundamental aspect of how states function as both ideology and institutional networks. Timothy Mitchell argues that the state is an object of study that exists as both a material structure and an ideological concept.[12] Rather than separating these two dimensions into the "state-system" (its material operations) and the "state-idea" (its symbolic identity), as previous research proposed, Mitchell argues for the need to see these two dimensions as inseparable parts of the same process. "The phenomenon we name 'the state,'" he contends, "arises from techniques that enable mundane material practices to take on the appearance of an abstract, nonmaterial form."[13] Mitchell is interested in how state power becomes internal and subjective, while also having the appearance of external, objective structure.[14] This is what he terms the "state effect"—how practices and processes (e.g., dividing space, allocating bodies, directing movement) make a state apparatus (e.g., the military or, in this instance, government-supported art institutions) appear to be greater than the sum of its parts, independent of those individuals who constitute it.[15]

Appropriating these concepts for a discussion of media institutions may seem tenuous, as the state is a very specific kind of entity, with a particular set of disciplinary and governmental powers. Nonetheless, I would suggest that because utopian aspiration played such a crucial role in driving the early-2000s alternative film scene—particularly its visions of national film publics—the notion of ideal state institutions fits into a larger framework of speculation.[16] Moreover, in this context, the state and entertainment media are particularly intimate in their connection. As the account of Aquino's 2010 inauguration suggests, the drama of state transition stemmed from both the familial connection to a post-martial-law national narrative, as well as the melding of governance and the entertainment industry, personified by Kris Aquino's presence. In his analysis of Kris Aquino's stardom, Rolando Tolentino argues that the combination of showbiz and politics has created what he calls a culture of mobility ("kultura ng mobilidad"). Images of success promise progress, an achievement most accessible in either show business or politics.[17] If Kris Aquino embodies the promises of mobility under the state and the entertainment industry, I would argue that likewise the state, in this case, embodies the promises of film culture, which entails a different variation of progress. This is not the developmentalist progress of economics but a movement toward an elusive ideal of national culture. Envisioned as a steady, ongoing relay among filmmakers, texts, and audiences, this particular version of film culture hinges on circulation to domestic publics under the (stable, benevolent, speculative) state.

Within these discussions, the foreign festival circuit becomes the bête noir; meanwhile, Cinemalaya and the Film Development Council become proxies for the hopes of governance. Their abilities to both produce films and, theoretically, to circulate them become part of the "effect" of an ideal Philippine state. This does not work in quite the same way as the theorists above describe. In this instance, this effect is not about the actualized operation of state power, as it was in the previous chapter's discussion of censorship. Rather, the effect is about counteracting that *idea* of authoritarian state power, through envisioning an *ideal, aspirational version* of the state as representative of its subjects, the nation-state in its latent democratic form. What better evidence of an ideal state than its ability to fulfill the ideal mandate of national cinema: to enable the domestic production, circulation, and reception of "quality" films. This is the state effect in the context of film—the notion that the state might overcome the paradox of alternative cinema, widening film circulation without a recourse to monetary commerce. As multiplex screens folded, microcinemas lived their short lives, and the university faced censorship, the state became a prospective, asymptotic object of desire.

This prospective, speculative status explains much of the ambivalence surrounding the role of the state in alternative film culture. While many commentators framed Cinemalaya and the FDCP as ideals of the state's potential, the film scene did not wholly embrace either institution.[18] Some felt that the state offered a promise of longevity that more decentralized, short-term projects could not, providing an institution that would, in theory, be removed from the market interests of more commercial entities. Others, however, felt that faith in the state was a fool's bargain, given its history of authoritarianism and instability. Any optimism about its prospects for sustaining national film culture was unfounded. Moreover, the FDCP's vision of a national film archive involved absorbing collections that activists had taken years to develop; this strategy evoked top-down, Marcos-era approaches to arts and culture. Thus, this desire for the state was complex and contradictory, operating in multiple ways within a heterogeneous film scene. This desire works across a spectrum between rational and affective registers, reflecting the state's inherent dualism as system and idea. It translates to the kinds of cultural institutions that filmmakers would place within the state's purview.

The desire for this ideal form is particularly acute given the contexts of obligatory transnationalism that characterized much of the alternative film scene at this point, largely through the foreign festival circuit. I am interested in how an aspirational state functions in the ideal models of screen culture proposed by some sectors of the film scene. Thus, this chapter begins with a consideration of how filmmakers, government institutions, and audiences respond when the transnational (foreign film festivals, awards, and funding sources) becomes an established and, for some, tiresome part of a local screen culture rather than a novel means of financial support and cultural capital. Here, the state is envisioned as a remedy to cinemas viewed as too heavily entangled in the value systems of local commercial industries, global Hollywood, and transnational cinema circulation.

Film Festival Markets and Foreignness Fatigue

As the previous chapters suggest, the most recent iteration of Philippine alternative cinema was fueled in part by the funding and distribution resources provided by foreign film festivals. While the local film institution Cinemalaya, a mixture of state and private-sector funds that I will discuss in the next section, played a significant role in spurring production, the foreign festival circuit was an important counterpart, acting as a funding source and a means of accruing prestige through transnational circulation to specific kinds of foreign publics.

There has been a great deal of recent work on international film festivals as institutions of production, distribution, and exhibition, much of it based on their role in creating "world cinema" through production funding and dissemination. More recently, many works allude to the potentially problematic role of the festival circuit within national industries, particularly around matters of the domestic audience. As this work argues, festivals might become a crutch, preventing economically sustainable, domestic film industries.[19] European festivals favoring filmmakers from the global south can sometimes adopt a patronage role, as filmmakers create work catering to festival criteria.[20] While studies of the festival circuit's role within world cinema often focus on the workings of international festivals themselves, I am more interested in the reverberations of transnational festival institutions within the domestic film industries they support. During this time in the Philippines, they were understood less as individual events and organizations, and more as a generalized signifier of foreignness. Thus, the approach I take differs from many discussions of media institutions, in that it examines not the specific workings of particular organizations, but their amalgamation into a general category in a particular local culture. Broadening the idea of institutions to include the nonmaterial aspects they entail (cultural values, social norms) reflects the function of the transnational festival circuit as not only a circulator of Filipino cultural goods but also as an engine driving their production. As the Philippine alternative film scene took shape in the early 2000s, this process created a proposed value system for ideas of local and transnational filmmaking. Critics felt that the festival system required films made for foreign juries; what emerged in these critiques was the indictment that these films had ignored local publics. Thus, winning local audiences became a part of this alternative cinema value system, framed in opposition to the foreign festival circuit.

One way that filmmakers began to comment on their positioning within the transnational system of festival patronage was through films themselves; they offered self-reflexive commentary on the local film scene's more cosmopolitan ambitions. Here I focus on two films: Sigfreid Barros Sanchez's *The Kidnappers of Ronnie Lazaro* (2012) and Marlon N. Rivera's *The Woman in the Septic Tank* (2011). Beyond simply commenting on the aesthetic tropes of independent film that evolved over the course of its emergence, they also linked these formal clichés to the power of the transnational festival circuit and the elite, foreign publics it implied.

Ang mga kidnaper ni Ronnie Lazaro (The Kidnappers of Ronnie Lazaro)

Funded through the Film Development Council's newly formed Sineng Pambansa initiative, Sigfreid Barros Sanchez's *The Kidnappers of Ronnie Lazaro* encapsulates Philippine cinema culture—the diegetic filmmakers include a former stuntman who laments the death of the Filipino action film; a Muslim pirated-DVD vendor; and a self-styled Catholic prophet, based in Quiapo. Moreover, the film positions these local, working-class directors against filmmakers deemed inadequately Filipino—the local elites catering to foreign art-cinema tastes rather than those of an imagined "Filipino viewer." As one critic describes: "*Kidnapper* further succeeds in portraying how the Filipino indie film is slowly being taken over by European cinema, as well as how some up and coming directors are obsessed in patterning their films to works of directors whose surnames end with 'nini' (or basically anyone with an Italian sounding name!). In a light and funny way, it showed how Filipino indie films are no longer being produced for the Filipino viewer."[21] Another review points to the film's class commentary, as well as the tendency of middle-class directors to seek adequately masa surroundings for their films: "In the Philippines where most independent filmmakers are the educated elite, these fictional amateurs are comparatively at the bottom of the food chain. . . . When an apartment above them was used as location by a group of well-to-do, English-speaking filmmakers, who look down on them, we grow to love them all the more. Finish your film, make us proud!"[22] The review positions the "well-to-do, English-speaking" filmmakers as "them," thus identifying with the film's working-class heroes as a national "us." The reviewer describes the film's humble filmmakers as local alternatives to both global auteurs and the local filmmakers who mimic them. Moreover, it also blurs the lines between production and reception, as the working-class filmmakers become stand-ins for the broader Filipino public: "In contrast to the pretentious filmmakers quoting Zhang Yimou, Quentin Tarantino, and other famous foreign filmmakers, the kidnappers learn a lesson from the most sought-after indie actor himself: Tell stories, as genuinely as you can, regardless of money, time and power. Make it Filipino."[23] These discussions demonstrate the film's overt commentary on the transnational circuits of prestige cinema, viewing local filmmakers who cater to those markets as inauthentically Filipino, while also endorsing an assumed authenticity tied to ideal notions of a national audience. In this vision, "genuine" stories are those made by *and for* Filipinos. This authenticity is not articulated, but is structurally marked through boundaries between "us" and "them."

The *Kidnappers* trailer also conveys the sense that independent filmmaking has become a series of aesthetic and narrative clichés. Its voice over begins with the question, "Paano nga ba gumawa ng isang indie film?" (How does one make an indie film?) It then answers with a series of conventions, all beginning with variations on the phrase "There should be" (*dapat may*). Recommended traits include a "deep" director; confusing cinematography, unclear sound, and ugly lighting; prostitutes, callboys, a "gay element," "*taong grasa*" (roughly, "vagrant"); a "squatters' area" setting; and a coterie of familiar indie stars, whom the trailer shows in quick succession, ending in Lazaro himself. The trailer ends by affirming that this laundry list of elements is how you make an indie film; the voice over then states in English, "Pinoy indie cinema is dead." This claim gives the film a sense of finality, marking it as dirt on the grave of a departed film culture. However, the positive response to *Kidnappers* suggests that the movement was not so much dead as shifting. Indeed, Sanchez noted his shock when a cinema in Davao bumped Hollywood's *The Amazing Spider-Man* from two screens to make room for his film.[24] Premised on inside jokes only domestic audiences would understand, this satirical film's success indicates a desire for a cinema reflecting local sensibilities.

Ang Babae sa Septic Tank (The Woman in the Septic Tank)

Kidnappers suggests a transition point, in which foreign film festivals were no longer a fix for a dying industry. Now these festivals had created a system in which foreign prestige audiences and the tropes they demanded had taken priority over their local counterparts. Perhaps the most overt representation of the transnational film festival's role within that transition was the 2011 self-reflexive satirical film *Ang Babae sa Septic Tank (The Woman in the Septic Tank)*. Its differences from the conventions of Philippine independents involve its aesthetics, as well as its intended audience. Rather than aiming for an international contingent of art-film cinephiles, the movie offered a series of inside jokes about national film culture, thus aiming for a local audience. Like *Kidnappers*, the primary target of its satire was filmmakers' tendency to pander to transnational festivals.

The film begins as a typically dark, "third world" film might, with establishing shots of an informal community and its residents. However, a voice-over soon reveals that this is a screenwriter's imagining of his own script. Titled *I, Who Have Nothing*, the film within a film draws from the most horrific variations of developing world, heart-of-darkness narratives, following an impoverished mother as she readies her son to deliver him to a foreign pedophile. However, this narrative is soon revealed to be the speculation of middle-class filmmakers—writer/director Rainier, producer Bong, and their production assistant Jocelyn, whose silence throughout the film is a perhaps unintentional comment on the largely male-dominated film scene. The camera follows them from their air-conditioned car to a Starbucks-like coffee shop, where they discuss their international aims.

We see varied iterations of the same scene, in different genres. The filmmakers debate whether the child in question should be a girl or a boy, with one saying a boy would be "too transgressive," to which the other replies, "Trust me, if it's a boy, that means awards." When the writer/director declares that he only wants to tell his story, Bong assures him that his story is "worth nothing if it doesn't get noticed abroad," urging him to "think about the festivals, think about the awards. Think about Oscars, Cannes! Dude, we know what they want. Let's give it to them."[25] He goes on to suggest that they should have gone for his original treatment: "That was daring! That's what the international critics want!" The film cuts to the object of international critics' desire, which is a handheld, documentary-style variation with nonactors. From off camera, a director asks a group of children what their daily diet of instant noodles is like; they reply politely, "Delicious, sir." He presses them, asking if they starve later in the day.[26]

The film's climax is a location-scouting trip to Payatas, an urban poor community in the northern Metro area, located next to a dump site (figure 5.1). The filmmakers delightedly discuss renting a crane, shout phrases like "Majestic," pose for tourist shots (thumbs up, peace signs), and gawk at their surroundings with starry-eyed grins. This celebration ends abruptly when they see the producer's car being stripped for parts by an angry, though ultimately harmless, group of residents, who warn them to stay back. The film's mockery of their middle-class, car-theft

5.1 Location scouting.

trauma comes in genre form, as the lighting darkens and the characters scream to the heavens, falling to their knees in tears. The film's critique is clear. Poverty is a boon for cinematic aesthetics; the real atrocity is the loss of their vehicle.[27]

The stand-in for the transnational festival circuit comes in the form of Arthur Poongbato, a caricature of Filipino world cinema posturing. Scouring his Facebook site on their MacBook, the film's striving, affluent antiheroes mock his English grammar errors, his posting of only good reviews ("not the bad ones in *Hollywood Reporter* and *Variety*"), his photos in front of festival backdrops. Declaring a hierarchy of international prestige, the director declares that Poongbato can have Venice; their film will go straight to the Kodak Theater for the Oscars. When he enters the café accompanied by his entourage, he dons a hodge-podge of "ethnic" regalia, commenting on his jetlag as he sits (figure 5.2). He lists the festivals he will attend that year, revealing that he does not know where some of them are located. The transnational festival circuit does not consist of individual organizations or even specific geographic locations. Rather, it becomes a generically foreign stage for the performance of a national, ethnicized, and, within the *Septic Tank*, artificial identity.

The film ends with the eponymous scene by the septic tank. Their star, the real-life actress Eugene Domingo playing a diva version of herself, holds her nose to block the smell. She expounds on the project, with increasing hysteria: "[The film] really hits you. That's very important. That's what works in festivals, I'm telling you. Mark my word, you're going to win. You're going to win, Direk. All we're going to do next year is travel. That's going to be fun. . . . I'll be flying in business class, okay? It's beautiful. We'll go to all the festivals—we'll go to Toronto, Tribeca, Venice, Berlin, I haven't been to Berlin. We'll go to New York and Cannes." As she gesticulates, she inevitably falls in. The film closes

5.2 Festival regalia.

on a low-angle medium close-up of Domingo floundering in brown water, looking shell-shocked. The director, off-screen, asks if he can roll camera. She nods. Her wild enthusiasm for the transnational festival circuit landed her in a tank of shit, which will, ostensibly, land her back into the film festival circuit, in a cycle of exploitation in exchange for transnational distribution.

Septic Tank's writer Chris Martinez describes his inspiration as derived from his own experience traveling international festivals with his prior film, *100*, a story about a middle-class woman diagnosed with a terminal illness who tries to accomplish one hundred items on her bucket list. (The film was inspired by the 2007 Hollywood film of that name.) As Martinez relates, the film's middle-class setting came as a surprise to international audiences weaned on images of what he dubs poverty:

> Ang nila sa mga pelikula natin [Their expectation of our movies] is poverty porn. That's where it all started. And then I observed some more how the whole process of selection happens. Importante kasi kung ano ang napipiling pelikula sa [It's important because if it's our movies at] film fests—it's the world's window to our country. It all boils down to what they want to see is what they don't have in their country which is, yun nga, kahirapan [just that, the poor]. So, it's not surprising if independent filmmakers do films on poverty because it's those kinds of stories that get picked up by the programmers.[28]

It is important to point out that in his emphasis on foreign viewerships, Martinez does not acknowledge the legitimate and crucial reasons to make films set amid the poverty that is a reality for the vast majority of Filipinos.[29] In counterpoising *100* to these works, Martinez uses the other films' impoverished locations to set his own affluent, globalized settings apart, thereby elevating his film. Unlike notions of authenticity in previous chapters, which draw on constructions of a usable past or on working-class cultures that sit outside global consumerism's reach, this is a version of authenticity premised on the idea of affluent, middle-class filmmakers reflecting their own experience in their work. Nonetheless, I would argue that *Septic Tank* and *Kidnappers* aim their critiques not so much at images of poverty themselves but at the alleged *intentions* of the filmmakers creating these portrayals—easy access to a cosmopolitan film culture hungry for images of "what they don't have in their country."[30] In this way, their critiques are based on the kinds of audiences the films allegedly aim for. Tellingly, *Septic Tank*'s success at the local level was groundbreaking for Filipino alternative cinema. This feat was a result of its combination of accessible aesthetics (classical form and narrative) and locally specific humor. Beyond these features however, access to industrial distribution and exhibition infrastructure also played a key role. After winning a rare distribution deal from the mainstream studio Star Cinema, the film became the highest-grossing independent feature in Philippine history, grossing P20 million in five days.[31] For the first time since international programmers had declared the birth of a new national cinema, a mass of viewers within that national setting shared the enthusiasm.

These films imagine the relationship between local filmmakers and global production as one in which local filmmakers have gone stale in their quest to be international. In discussions of global cultural homogenization, the usual target is Hollywood mass culture. In the Philippines, however, the level of institutionalization that the transnational film festival circuit achieved created another, foreign presence for the local to contend with. Moreover, it distilled a value system that lays out the parameters for what qualifies as the "correct" notion of Filipinoness. If one version of this system entails the performance of cultural identity for international markets, another version, presented in the insider satires that *Kidnappers* and *Septic Tank* present, involves making films for a Filipino audience and being "true" to class backgrounds. This model has obvious problems. Any allusions to authenticity are ideological constructs, as the chapter on Quiapo's imaginary suggests. Paradoxically, while making claims to a core, essential identity, authenticity is achieved by design, coupled with circumstances that allow that design to be taken up in particular ways (e.g., a sense of certain versions of cultural history under threat or slipping away). Authenticity is not singular; as a construct, it can manifest in various ways. For example, other filmmakers have taken different routes to making films "for" the middle-class, local audience. In the documentary *Signed, Lino Brocka* (dir. Christian Blackwood, 1987), the famed martial-law-era filmmaker describes his motivation for filming stories set in the city's urban poor areas. For him, it was crucial for those Filipinos not living in those settings to be exposed to them. The emphasis on poverty in some of his films was not motivated by international festivals but by the need to educate the *local* audience about broader social realities.

Kidnappers and *Septic Tank* take a different tack in their indictments of inauthenticity, and part of their critique stems from the idea of transnational film festivals promoting cultural and aesthetic homogeneity. Significantly, *Septic Tank* and *Kidnappers* critique not just the filmic production of authenticity but the foreign institutional infrastructures that enable it. This suggests the shifting perspective of this localized, transnational institution within Philippine contexts, from financial balm to an entrenched system of paternalism. As domestic films became increasingly embedded within circuits of exchange that crossed national borders, visions of greater state participation entered as a desired alternative, one that would enable access to broader domestic audiences. These visions of a pure, uncompromised institutional structure for national cinema would prove difficult—likely impossible—to attain.

Cinemalaya and the Speculative State

Septic Tank did make the festival rounds; for example, Maggie Lee of the *Hollywood Reporter* calls the film "a lambast of the pretensions of independent cinema in his country and his fellow filmmakers' inflated egos ... the antithesis of the rambling, 'real time' works being sent up."[32] More importantly, Lee also points out the irony that the film was a Cinemalaya Foundation project, given that "since 2005 [Cinemalaya] has supplied funds for many movies—often dealing with poverty and violence—that have dramatically raised the international profile of Filipino cinema."[33] Her comment offers an outsider's perspective on the aesthetic similarity of certain kinds of festival films; moreover, it points to the local institutional infrastructure that many of these films are associated with.

Started in 2005, Cinemalaya became the country's largest independent film festival and funding institution. In its inception, it was a collaboration among the state, via the Cultural Center of the Philippines

(CCP) and the Film Development Council (FDCP); academe, primarily the University of the Philippines Film Institute but also other schools; and the private sector, Econolink, Inc.

Cinemalaya had become tied to international prestige as the Philippines established itself as a major presence in festival circuits. But its connections to national audiences were more tenuous, and its institutional ties to the state became a touchstone for debates about the state's role in domestic film production and circulation. The controversies that erupted around Cinemalaya, the state, and the possibility of domestic publics offer a compelling view of the impasse of alternative cinema. The debates demonstrate how this impasse became tied to speculative, asymptotic visions of national culture in which the state became the primary institutional framework for supporting alternative cultural production. Here, the paradox of alternative cinema is the disjuncture between culturally specific forms of representation and alternative modes of production and dissemination, versus transnational, elite paths of circulation.

Cinemalaya was also not the only film festival that included forms of government sponsorship. Many festivals had developed through a mixture of municipal and corporate backing. The Cinemanila International Film Festival, started by the filmmaker Tikoy Aguiluz in 1999, was co-organized with then mayor of Mandaluyong City, Benhur Abalos. The Metro Manila International Film Festival discussed in chapter 3 has involved the Metropolitan Manila Development Authority, an agency created by the federal government. Cinemalaya followed in the footsteps of such festivals. Its mix of government and corporate sponsorship was also seen in later events, such as the QCinema International Film Festival. In 2013, The Quezon City Film Development Commission (QCFDC) became the first government unit to develop a commission for cinema initiatives. Headed by the Quezon City mayor and vice mayor, the QCIFF was one outcome of this ordinance, suggesting the persistent links between governance and film festivals at the municipal levels.

Initially, Cinemalaya's structure was intended to support independent and early-career filmmakers. Would-be directors submitted screenplays to the Cinemalaya organizing committee, which was headed by the veteran director Laurice Guillen until 2012; of around two hundred entries, the organizers would choose ten films, providing "seed investments" of P500,000 ($10,000).[34] Before receiving funds, filmmakers are required to submit a production plan including materials such as a listing of technical staff (director of photography, assistant director, musical director), the final draft of the script, and a shooting schedule. In addition, they must also provide details of their counterfinancing.[35] As these two entertainment journalists indicate, the festival positions itself against both the local commercial industry and global Hollywood:

> If the mainstream film industry has its annual Metro Manila Film Festival for showcasing its best and brightest, independent films have Cinemalaya, the country's most prestigious indie film festival.[36]
>
> Even as Harry Potter ruled in metro cineplexes last week, crowds also flocked to the Cultural Center of the Philippines, where the 7th Cinemalaya Film Festival went on a week-long run. Enthusiasts spent entire days on marathon screenings of Filipino independent films.[37]

Positioned against both local and global commercial industries, the institution had become synonymous with independent cinema in the country. Cinemalaya had deflected some of the multiplex's crowds to a state institution, luring them away from Hollywood blockbusters toward local alternative cinema.

Perhaps because of its affiliation with a film sector perceived as "nobler" than its globalized, commercial counterparts, Cinemalaya was held to standards of cultural value seen as lacking in other parts of the film industry. Much of this value was grounded in the notion that as a public institution, it would support arts that represented the national public. Thus, it was obliged to be culturally specific, supportive of filmmakers, and linked to an ideal vision of the state. In this instance, the state effect was rendered through the state's perceived failures—the shortcomings that highlight its absence, presenting a speculative outline of what it *should* be. Here, the speculative public enters not through its role as an aspirational audience but through its ideal function as constitutive of state institutions constructed for and representative of the people. The speculative public that the state represents formed the stakes of Cinemalaya's integrity. This section examines debates that questioned Cinemalaya's institutional legitimacy, suggesting that these public discussions—often performative and sometimes personal—became a means of problematizing Cinemalaya as a reified, symbolic institution and thus as a representative of a speculative, Filipino public, freed from the demands of commerce. The debates staged the process of institutionalization itself, using this struggle to symbolically map alternative cinema's ideal position within state infrastructure.

These controversies about its integrity were in some sense surprising, given that Cinemalaya had always been supported through corporate funding. In part, the institution was financed by the businessman Antonio "Tonyboy" Cojuangco, a member of a wealthy haciendero family and cousin of former president Corazon Aquino. Cojuangco's critics argued that at the time, Cojuangco envisioned the festival as a means of funding cinema content for the two television stations he owned, Dream TV and ABC 5. This would follow the model of ABS-CBN, which uses Regal Films and Viva Entertainment to produce works that would ultimately circulate on the studio's television networks.[38]

However, this economically oriented origin is seldom discussed in relation to Cinemalaya's institutional identity, which is couched in independence rhetoric and nationalist iconography. This rhetoric promotes the institution's role as a true representation of the Filipino public, contrasting it to the mainstream industry. When it began, the festival was only open to those who had not directed a full-length feature. As this 2005 description suggests, the idea of supporting "fresh" talent outside the studios was key to the festival's initial incarnation: "While the top production outfits—Star Cinema, Regal Films, Viva Films—continue to churn out their annual, if reduced, quota of movies, a call is being made for new filmmakers to create fresh works in the First Cinemalaya Philippine Independent Film Festival."[39] Descriptions of Cinemalaya frame the organization as a supporter of young filmmakers working outside the dominant studio system, a persona it heightens through its presentation within nationalist symbols. The festival's logo is a *balanghai*, a large boat used in precolonial Philippines, which festival organizers describe as bringing Filipinos to freedom. The organization's name itself translates to "cinema freedom," a portrayal of its autonomy.

In this way, Cinemalaya had cultivated an image that linked it to a specific version of the Filipino public, one connected to a variation of national culture filtered through high culture and fine arts. It was promoted as an avenue for aspiring filmmakers outside the mainstream industry, creating a new cinema that would represent the nation. This was a fitting connection for an arts institution representing an ideal of the state and the public that constituted it (even if in practice, Cinemalaya had always maintained corporate ties). As the organization's reputation grew however, its structure changed. Given its symbolic identity within the local film scene, these changes were controversial. In 2010 the festival opened entry to veteran filmmakers as a part of its Directors Showcase. As one entertainment journalist describes: "Independently produced movies were once relegated to small venues with limited audiences. But the success of movies like *Ang Pagdadalaga ni Maximo Oliveros*, *Tribu*, *Jay*, and *Engkwentro*, among others, in various film festivals around the world compelled everybody to pay attention. For years veteran filmmakers have approached Cinemalaya competition director Laurice Guillen asking to take part in the film festival/competition, which focuses on young directors.... The veterans have finally gotten their wish."[40] In addition to broadening the requirements to include more established directors, Cinemalaya casting decisions also began to include more actors affiliated with the mainstream studio system. In part, this was a hope for local box-office potential; however, it also had to do with the highly integrated local media system. When asked to comment on ABS-CBN, TV5, and GMA7's involvement in the festival, the screenwriter and jury member Ricky Lee described: "More and more mainstream actors are crossing over to independent movies. Hence, TV studios are supporting more indie projects, too.... Indie producers and filmmakers want more people to watch their movies, so they hire mainstream actors, whose schedules are handled by these studios. Inevitably, they get the support of the studios as well."[41] Marketing and promotion were among the most difficult challenges facing independent filmmakers in a context of highly concentrated local media ownership; the move toward mainstream casting thus reflected a practical strategy. But it is also framed as a matter of reaching broader local audiences. Here, this broad local audience is not the aim of nationalist sentiments; it addresses more practical concerns of financial sustainability. The addition of recognizable stars has also led to changes in the general atmosphere of the event. As one journalist notes, these stars' mere presence at the CCP changed the festival's high-art atmosphere: "As mainstream stars now top-bill competition entries and fans' shrieks echo in the hallowed theaters of the Cultural Center of the Philippines, the Cinemalaya Philippine Independent Film Festival reaches a crossroads—or so it seems."[42] The CCP theaters are "hallowed" because of their associations with both national history and with the state. The divide between cultured moviegoers and "fans' shrieks" presents an uneasy parallel with the good versus bad audience discourses that surrounded the mall multiplex. Cinemalaya and the CCP both differentiate themselves from the country's malls through their symbolic ties to Philippine culture and, implicitly, to the citizenry that culture represents. While the malls' revanchist cinemas are predicated on social division, the CCP and Cinemalaya are based on ideals of national unity. The image above reveals the fractures in this ideal construction.

As the organization grew, these policy changes also affected perceptions of its institutional integrity. Indeed, at the 2011 festival, the programmer and director of the CCP Media Arts Division, Ed Cabagnot, joked, "It's a game of thrones."[43] This idea of institutional politicking was most potent in the controversies that surrounded its eighth incarnation. The Cinemalaya organizing committee's disqualification of the independent film MNL 143 and the director's subsequent campaign raised questions regarding the institution's values. Significantly, much of that faded integrity had to do with its overly close affiliations with both the transnational festivals and the mainstream film industry. As we have seen, these two "institutions" of the alternative film scene had been deemed inordinately tied to the wrong kinds of audiences—elite foreign moviegoers and the bad audience of multiplex cinema. This rendered them incompatible with the ideal, speculative state that Cinemalaya and the cultural center represented.

Written and directed by newcomer Emerson Reyes, MNL 143 tells the story of an OFW (overseas foreign worker) who returns to his home country to become an FX (air-conditioned jeepney) driver and search for his lost love. The film was disqualified due to the casting of the semiretired actors Alan Paule and Joy Viado as "not suitable to the material," ostensibly because they lacked marketability.[44] While the committee had disqualified works previously, Reyes's decision to take his cause to Facebook and Twitter created an intense public debate regarding the nature of the institution. The organizing committee stood its ground, claiming its casting decisions were based on the desire for "competence, suitability to the role, and greater audience acceptability."[45] The notion of "audience acceptability" translated the ideal publics of alternative cinema into a market demographic, an association that seemed incompatible with Cinemalaya's values of autonomy, nationalism, and cultural identity.

The critic Oggs Cruz resigned from the jury.[46] An online petition circulated via Change.org also generated commentary from fans and film-

5.3 Online calls for reform target specific figures.

makers about Cinemalaya's purpose and the definition of independent film (figure 5.3). This commentary referred to the urgency of circulation and the speculative public these films should seek: "There is no essence of independent filmmaking in the policies implemented by Cinemalaya, which is weird (and wrong) since this institution should promote independent filmmaking. Reform is needed. Make Cinemalaya truly free! Freedom from oppressive and unjust policies and bring Cinemalaya movies to the mass majority!"[47] Here, "true freedom" is constituted through the ability to circulate Cinemalaya films to their publics. These speculative publics are not an elite cadre of moviegoers but the "mass majority" that would render this body of films an ideal national cinema, one that would prosper across production, circulation, and reception. In this rendering, this ideal national cinema would operate under the state.

The state thus became a measure of institutional corruption in much of this discourse. Perhaps the most vocal critic was the veteran filmmaker Erik Matti, who likened Cinemalaya to martial law:

> Everyone wanted to be a part of it just like everyone wanted to be a part of Imelda Marcos' blue ladies [female companions / personal assistants in the Marcos inner circle]. I once asked a screening committee member why filmmakers put up with [Cinemalaya's system]. She answered, in true *mata pobre* [one who looks down on the poor] fashion, "Pasalamat na nga lang sila na may Cinemalaya 'no?" [They're just thankful

that there is a Cinemalaya]. This sums up how these people organizing Cinemalaya think. Like the hacienderos [plantation owners] to their *sakadas* [seasonal workers], like *amos* [bosses] to their *katulongs* [assistants], like producers to their directors. . . . For years, they enjoyed the privileges and the perks that Cinemalaya offered them in the same way that everyone sat in [the deposed president] Erap's table guilty of downing the same expensive wine that people will impeach him for later. Cinemalaya is as guilty as the ones who supported it.[48]

This assessment mirrors those of the filmmaker Lav Diaz, who had likened the mainstream film industry to feudalism (see the introduction). Here, this metaphor is translated to an institution that was associated with independent cinema and with ideals of governance. In this heavily circulated appraisal, Cinemalaya's perceived corruption becomes aligned with the corruption of the Philippine state—a betrayal of the Filipino public. Linking institutional structure to societal stratification, festival organizers are hacienderos and amos, Imelda and Erap. Within this model, just as members of the elite forsook their countrymen for access to a privileged political cadre, filmmakers and organizers turned a blind eye to Cinemalaya's wrongdoings. The moviegoing public under Cinemalaya parallels the nation under martial law.

This metaphor is rooted in the country's long history of what Benedict Anderson calls "cacique democracy," in reference to the powerful, landowning national oligarchy.[49] Empowered through the American imposition of democracy, this mestizo ruling class created an economic base through their provincial fiefdoms, which relied on the exploitative labor of the Indio peasants who worked the land.[50] The metaphor links Cinemalaya to a corrupted version of the state, a vision forged through provincial dynasties, in which the presidential office "could sedately circulate within the charmed circle" of landowners.[51] If for some, Cinemalaya's ideal form is to be firmly located in the state, for others like Matti, the state is too corrupt a model. It exploited the people it was supposed to represent.

Like *Kidnapper* and *Septic Tank*, Matti's criticism also takes aim at the transnational festival circuit, in this instance combining the corrupted state with the desire for international fame: "Everyone went to festivals abroad carrying that banner as a product of an 'independent' film festival. '*Taga*-Cinemalaya *kami*!!!!' [We came from Cinemalaya] . . . [I am an] 'Indie filmmaker *akooooo*!!!! Ahrtiiissst!' But everyone knew what was happening since day 1 of this festival and no one took a stand."⁵² The comment connotes Cinemalaya's position as a recognizable marker of independence, both within and outside the country. It creates links between a festival industrial system and an unscrupulous local mainstream industry. Additionally, the writer places this perceived degeneracy within a long history of institutional corruption at the national level.

Matti became a primary spokesperson for anti-Cinemalaya rhetorics; in an editorial in an online magazine, he moves beyond government as metaphor to describe his fears that these institutional practices come from an organization with state ties: "And the terrifying part of it is that Cinemalaya is partnered with the Cultural Center of the Philippines, the same government agency that's supposed to look after cultivating the arts and the artist.... The arts have been corrupted just like road buildings and pork barrels."⁵³ In a more subdued assessment, the director Jade Castro views the problem as one of inappropriate fraternizing between state and private sector: "If they want to make Cinemalaya a private enterprise, it's better if the CCP isn't involved, because the CCP is for the public.... But it's their decision whether they want to make it private or if they still want to continue as a festival for the people."⁵⁴ As these discussions suggest, Cinemalaya's affiliation with the CCP becomes a critical symbol of public ambivalence toward the cinema institution and toward the state that provides its architectural home. By the time of the festival, Cinemalaya monitoring committee head Robbie Tan, CCP festival director Nes Jardin, and competition chair Laurice Guillen had resigned. As the eighth installment of Cinemalaya opened its doors to Manila audiences, Reyes premiered *MNL 143* continents away, at the Edinburgh International Film Festival.⁵⁵

On the one hand, the CCP building represents the hope of government arts and culture initiatives; this hope takes both elite and democratizing forms. As the journalist above playfully describes, screaming fans have besmirched its "hallowed theaters"; in contrast, for the director Jade Castro, the building is "for the public."

While Castro's comments point to the most utopian, democratizing aspects of the CCP's symbolism, the building is also an artifact of Marcos-era violence, having been built with public funds as the pet project of Imelda Marcos. In her plans to make Metro Manila a cosmopolitan City of Man, Marcos razed urban poor communities as she erected state arts and culture establishments, building walls to block views of the slums from international visitors. As Neferti Tadiar suggests in her analysis of martial law, "The magical aura of authoritarian modernization derives from witnessing its theatrical effects without its production and from seeing its inhuman power dynamics personified."[56] Tadiar thus contends that because this process of violent modernization is made possible by "the transcendent, universal representation of an achieved modernity," one means of protest is attention to "the immediate, experiential, and corporeal."[57]

The cause of individual filmmakers' artistic visions might seem to romanticize ideas of the independent auteur. But I would suggest that publicizing internal, organizational practices, making impassioned and perhaps performative declarations in public forums, and raising the conflicting values that inform these collaborations between filmmakers and the organizations on which they rely bring the experiential and immediate to what has come to be seen as a monolith of independent cinema production. They make the *process* of institutionalization as much a visible, legible symbol of the institution-ideal as the edifice that houses it.

In January 2014, it seemed that protesters got at least part of their wish—Cojuangco withdrew the majority of his funds from Cinemalaya, though he remained on the organizing committee.[58] He described his withdrawal as a financial decision. Thus, to fund the festival, the CCP included Cinemalaya in its annual budget, and organizers sought ways to monetize past films in order to secure the organization's financial future.[59] This was a complex goal. Cinemalaya's reputation was grounded in its reputation for freeing filmmakers from financial constraints. If Cinemalaya were to be a public institution, it would have to prioritize a domestic audience. However, given the constraints of financing, this audience would be defined as a sustainable market. Even films that promise to be box-office hits do not always fare well after the festival's end. In 2018, Kip Oebanda's *Liway*, a drama about martial-law-era prisons, broke Cinemalaya's box-office records. Some audience members were so moved by its story of a young mother in the communist guerrilla insurgency that they broke into anti-martial-law protest calls, chanting, "Makibaka! Huwag matakot!" (Fight! Don't be frightened!) as the credits rolled. Nonetheless, the film was unable to stay in theaters; cinemas pulled it after one week's run as audiences dwindled.[60] The journalist Marco Sumayao draws parallels between the film's narrative and its cinema run: "*Liway*, like its protagonist, was a film trapped within an oppressive system; and as in events past, its only way out was for audiences to act with urgency. The Filipino market needs to prove to cinemas that local movies—including indies—are in demand by watching them before they're cut. The system acts quickly, so audiences need to act faster."[61] The festival has reduced the number of venues with the hope of drawing more audiences to select theaters.[62] At the time of writing, whether this market could coexist with notions of an ideal public remained to be seen.

Circulating Cinema, Decentralizing the State

Cinema and the State Ideal

As the discussions surrounding Cinemalaya suggest, the state was an idealized form for institutionalizing local cinema culture, persisting as a speculative concept despite its historical weakness, corruption, and censorship. With Cinemalaya and the Cultural Center of the Philippines, corporate conceptions of the national audience as market were incompatible with what the institutions represented. Through their ties to the state, they were obligated to and constituted by the Filipino public—at least in their ideal form, if not in practice.

Other discourses jumped directly to the state itself rather than viewing Cinemalaya as its representative. Upon his film's screening at the CCP, *Kidnapper* director Sigfried Barros Sanchez described the need for broad-based financial support from the government: "There are still a lot of young filmmakers emerging. They need the support of our government, both local and national. Just removing the tax on indie films is of great help to the indie filmmakers. They should tax the Hollywood mainstream films and the big local productions."[63] Barros Sanchez positions Philippine independent film against both global Hollywood and local commercial cinema. However, unlike the previous commentators, in his argument, Cinemalaya is not Philippine independent cinema's organizational home. Rather, the state becomes the institution-ideal for supporting the future of local cinema.

While the ideal state functions as a representative of the people, it also serves as an infrastructural resource, circulating cinema to the people. At a Southeast Asian Film Festival Q&A in Singapore, producer Moira Lang described the independent film scene's challenges as linked to government and audience building. Marketed as a "gay zombie movie," Lang's *Zombadings* was a hit with local audiences, despite mainstream studios' attempts to block the film's exhibition:[64]

We did not have the clout of the studio or Hollywood. . . . It was also a wake-up call that it's like a party that we're not really invited to. It's like we're gatecrashers. . . . So, that's the first thing is [for filmmakers] to group together. And then the other thing is to work with government, because there's a Film Development Council of the Philippines, which is supposed to help us to develop a national cinema. . . . So we want to coordinate with them in developing this program. And we think that we should talk to each other about our goals. Big companies, Hollywood and Star Cinema, they will have their profit objective.[65]

Lang describes this national cinema building as a dialogue between filmmakers and government, united in a joint effort to reach audiences. While conceding the importance of financial sustainability, she positions the profit motive as secondary to audience building, leaving the state in the best position to realize this ideal model. She suggests lowering ticket prices to reach more viewers, as well as encouraging an audience raised on piracy to pay a small fee for media consumption: "We should be after growing an audience. Not making lots of money."[66] Again, government is opposed to global Hollywood and seen as a more noble-minded institution for alternative filmmaker partnerships. Moreover, the idea of national cinema formation is based on audiences, and one proposed means of building those audiences is doing away with a purely profit-driven model. Such a model would preclude both the foreign festival circuit, which is not invested in building local audiences, and the local, mainstream industry, which sees these audiences purely in market terms. Lang's descriptions offer a counterpoint to those above, which position Cinemalaya alongside a history of state corruption. Within these models, the state becomes a possibility for institutionalizing Philippine cinema.

While problems with governance are well documented, as scholars such as Akhil Gupta have pointed out, the tendency to view postcolonial states as failures to live up to Eurocentric expectations is problematic.[67] For example, in the Philippines, a robust civil society sector has countered state weakness since the fall of the Marcos dictatorship.[68] The country maintains the region's densest network of civil society organizations (CSOs), and numerous groups monitor state functions.[69] As is often the case in global southern countries, CSOs' provision of services becomes an alternative to government inadequacies for many communities; the groups also engage in a system of "mutual aid" that operates outside the auspices of the state or the private sector.[70] However, this system is not intended as a replacement for government but as a necessary, provisional salve for institutional shortcomings. As sociologist Randy David described in a column on the increasing politicization of CSOs, the "dead-end nature of pure advocacy" has led many organizations to try electoral politics, though this tactic has had mixed outcomes.[71] While CSOs are in part an answer to government failings, their attempts to enter public office suggest continued faith in state institutions. Thus, despite the state's troubling history within Philippine culture, it remains an elusive site of institutional desires. As the debates around the legitimacy of foreign festivals, Cinemalaya, and the Cultural Center of the Philippines demonstrate, the speculative vision of the state is intimately connected to ideals of a national public.

"Bringing Filipino Films to Filipinos"
One important part of these desires for state involvement was defining a national audience, often in relation to global Hollywood and alternative transnational circuits. The Film Development Council of the Philippines (FDCP) is the closest institutional link between cinema and the state, as Lang implies above. My discussion here refers to the FDCP as it existed during this transitional period for Philippine alternative cinema, within the period immediately following Benigno Aquino's election. Its mandate encompassed several tasks, ranging from the promotion of the Philippine movie industry's "growth and development" to cultural appreciation through film and creating "new opportunities for aspiring filmmakers."[72]

These are typical for state film councils; however, the task of "generating a bigger audience for Philippine cinema by bringing Filipino films to Filipino communities everywhere" indicates the specific problems of film circulation at the domestic level.[73] Likewise, the FDCP slogan, "Bringing Filipino films to Filipinos," suggested the importance of local distribution and exhibition.[74] The organization reiterated this idea in its objectives, which included the goal to "localize film festivals and provide a venue for Filipino filmmakers to showcase their works to the community."[75] As then FDCP chair Briccio Santos described to me in a September 2011 interview, this localization was important "because Hollywood is not us. It's something we can be entertained by, but it's not us." The speculative Filipino "us" that the FDCP's mandate entailed was diverse and separated by region, ethnicity, and social class.

At the same time, it is important to note that because funding channels would originate with the central FDCP, these ideas of a regionalist, diverse nation-state were difficult to achieve in practice. These efforts to consolidate film culture under the wing of a centralized state body were not met with universal approval, especially in relation to the film archive. For example, the Society for Filipino Archivists for Film (Sofia) has worked towards film archiving since 1993, outside the auspices of the state, in part because of concerns about state instability.[76] The FDCP's efforts to cull prints from this long-standing activist initiative were controversial.

Given filmmakers' calls for state participation in film circulation, I am interested in the inevitable tensions that emerge when state bodies take on these projects of distribution and exhibition. In theory, the FDCP's Sineng Pambansa initiative involved a process of simultaneous vertical integration and decentralization, combined with translocal associations across national borders. Santos described this process, saying, "If they can do it, so can we," in reference to the local commercial media industry.[77] However, one important aspect that differentiated the FDCP plans was that vertical integration was to be mitigated by a concurrent move toward decentralization, enacted through both cultural and administrative initiatives. These multiculturalist efforts could easily reiterate patterns of national dominance. In a Latin American context, Néstor García Canclini notes that cultural policy debates dominated by the state considered whether diverse ethnicities and regions were adequately represented in national heritage, "reducing their local specificities to politico-cultural abstractions in the interest of social control or to legitimate a certain form of nationalism."[78] Regionalization on its own does not necessarily entail a more inclusive relationship among the state, filmmakers, and audiences.

However, the FDCP's plans for administrative decentralization, combined with its attention to regionalism, was intended to create opportunities for a movement of power outside the capital branch. The organization's goal was that FDCP representatives from the regions would affiliate with their local government units (LGUs). Municipal governments operated with a relative degree of autonomy from the centralized state in the Philippines, a model put in place due to the country's history of authoritarianism.[79] This decentralization into many, locally operating film councils was intended to sustain the project beyond Santos's term. Current government structure runs through the Office of the President, and each prospective project the FDCP begins may not continue with their successor. Dispersing power across the institution was one preemptive measure to counteract this possibility. But as the debates about the archive imply, the FDCP's idea of administrative decentralization was selective, sitting in tension with counterposing efforts toward consolidation under the central government. Oscillating between the organization's utopian schemes and its efforts to materialize them, the accounts below suggest that these visions were sometimes more ideal than their outcomes, raising critical questions about the possibilities of decentralized, collaborative models originating in federal arts bodies.

De-Westernized, Translocal Practices
The FDCP framed this administrative dispersal across the nation as a non-Western structure, constructing a different version of transnationalism than that offered in the festival circuit. This version of transnational regionalization enacted a *selective* version of transnational affiliation through the FDCP's involvement with other national film commissions via the Asian Film Commissions Network (AFCNet), a regional nonprofit organization. Santos saw a major impetus of the FDCP as fighting global Hollywood, and he drew the organization's structural inspiration from other AFCNet members, who had faced similar battles:

> For instance, the ability of the Japanese and also the Koreans to engage their communities into film awareness and film production . . . The one thing that makes them successful, even in the strong influx of Hollywood in their country, is that they're highly localized. There are hundreds of FDCPs in Japan alone, because they are highly localized, like Kobe, Sapporo. Each one is able to create a film commission of their own.[80]

This version of regionalization evokes the inter-Asia cultural studies movement, which advocates examining the interconnected histories of geographically proximate states across the Cold War fiction of "Asia" (i.e., "inter-Asia"), as a means of combating Eurocentrism without falling into nativism.[81]

Eventually, Santos hoped that the localized film commissions would be largely independent of the Manila branch, operating autonomously and even producing.[82] The description presented a vision of "national cinema" as filmmaking liberated from both the Manila studios and from global Hollywood, sponsored by decentralized, fully operational state institutions. Within this instance, the transnational became a model for a highly localized institutional structure. Moreover, this transnationalism was regionally oriented, pitting diverse Asian nations against a homogenous West: "This trend, by the way, has not registered in the Western festivals. It is too local, too incomprehensible. In many such instances, a work considered too local is dismissed from global film culture. But this effort by local critics and filmmakers shows that within Asia, there is already a struggle to find equality amongst the cacophony of voices."[83] The Western festival circuit critiqued in *Septic Tank* and *Kidnappers* is deliberately excluded within this vision. Rather, it offered a specific kind of localization that translates only within the Asian region, where diverse, discordant voices can coexist on equal terms. This is not a vision of a homogenous "Asian cinema" but one in which there was a pan-Asian struggle for intranational diversity and, ostensibly, local autonomy.

Film Fiestas and Mobile Cinemas

To provide this localized counterpoint to global Hollywood and the Western festivals, the FDCP's circulation efforts via Sineng Pambansa were twofold. First, they were spatially oriented, through their emphasis on the country's furthest regions and *barangays* (neighborhoods). Second, they were concerned with temporality, through their emphasis on longevity. Paradoxically, this model frames the state as the most viable institutional structure to achieve these aims, despite its historical instability. I would suggest that one reason for this contradiction is that the project of nationhood in the Philippines is an ongoing project; as such, institutional structures remain in formation, with all the promise that an ongoing process implies. Despite all evidence to the contrary, one such promise is the ability to outlast more fragmented initiatives. The state becomes the idealized mechanism for overcoming alternative cinema's own paradox; it became a site for speculation, promising the publics that other initiatives had not quite reached.

The presence of the mobile cinema enacted the goal of state outreach, filtered through local representatives. Literally making its way into their schools, parks, and streets, the mobile cinema enacted a process of rescaling the national so that it was worked into the scale of the regional-local. This is an unusual combination of the state and the nation merging through cinema. It occurred not through policy or texts but through displayed efforts at local circulation and cultivating speculative publics, which perform an ideal of the state.

As a part of its integration into regional culture, the FDCP organized yearly Sineng Pambansa Film Festivals, scheduled to coincide with the ongoing fiestas of the provinces. The events screened a range of films, both in conventional theaters and through the Sine ng Masa (People's Cinema), a mobile cinema van with its own sound system and generators, which brought screenings to areas without electricity. In addition, screenings were sometimes selected to coincide with fiesta themes. For example, the 2011 Ilocos Norte festival focused on supernatural or horror films, in keeping with the Semana ti Ar-Aria, or "Ghost Week" festival of the province.[84] The first festival was held over the course of three days in borrowed mall multiplexes at SM City Iloilo, to coincide with the Dinagyang Festival, an annual festival held to honor Santo Niño.[85] Involving elaborate costumes and street dancing, the fiesta has been established as a major tourism event for the community. Perhaps in part because of this celebratory atmosphere, the initial Sineng Pambansa festival reportedly drew a crowd of over forty thousand people over three days.

A newspaper for the Western Visayas region reported on the mobile cinema as a welcome alternative to theatrical screenings, emphasizing the role of local government in the event:

> Mayor Jed Patrick E. Mabilog said the deployment of the mobile cinema especially in the barangays will bring entertainment to people in the community who may want to take a rest from their day to day activities. "This is truly a welcome treat to all Ilonggo movie lovers," he stated. As an innovation of the FDCP, the "Sine ng Masa" mobile cinema is deployed to remote barangays in the country and brings Filipino films closer to the masses. It uses a truck on which films are projected on back to back LCD screens, so that audiences can watch films on either side of the mobile cinema truck. . . . For those who cannot come to the movie houses to see the "Sineng Pambansa" 2nd Iloilo International Film Festival on January 19 to 21, the mobile cinema will be the best choice.[86]

While government participation is clear, this is not the prescriptive, ideologically driven picture one might expect of state-sponsored cinema. Rather, its professed goal is to "bring Filipino films to Filipinos" as a form of "entertainment," a chance to "take a rest" following the day's labor.

This is a very different perspective on the role of film in cultivating publics. In this way, the performance of state film exhibition diverges from the colonial state-sponsored mobile cinemas described in historical studies, such as those by Brian Larkin, Zoë Druick, and J. M. Burns, who examine British mobile cinemas as instruments of empire.[87] These colonial state projects focused on bringing modernity to the masses through films focusing on social guidance and technology. As Larkin argues, these mobile cinema projects offer a new means of considering modernity and cinema; rather than being guided by the "Ur-form" of modernity, the commodity, these films were guided by politics, with aims to maintain colonial order.[88]

In its emphasis on entertainment and on highly localized, postcolonial nationalism, the FDCP's mobile cinema project offered a counterpoint to such models. Rather than the presence of the state emerging through the content of the films themselves, via images of political figures, state development projects, or social guidance, the rites and rituals that Taussig would call the "magic of the state" occurred through the exhibition event itself. The impact of the films' content lie not in their explicit portrayal of state power but in their Philippine origins. This is not to suggest that these screening events were absent of power relations. As Charles Acland points out in his analysis of AV's introduction to the classroom, the technologies associated with film screenings index a "structure of authority and a vision of the future."[89] Regardless of the films' entertainment content, the presence of technology itself is an indication of power. However, my focus is not on the impact of the screenings themselves but on their stated intentions, which revealed the position of cinema institutions within public imaginaries. For instance, as with the Mogwai Film Festival in chapter 3, the screenings were worked into existing, local fiesta calendars. But in the case of the regional festivals, the films were not the focus. They became an appendage to an ongoing repertoire of other activities, thereby undercutting their role as specific forms of spectacle. Institutionalization within this ideal version of the state was again an attempt to transfer power to the local level. In these ways, mobile cinema as colonial education became mobile cinema as localized, nationalist entertainment event, a melding of state, nation, and audience. Indeed, as one newspaper reported on an Ilocos Norte installment of Sineng Pambansa, "[The FDCP] will use a 'mobile cinema' . . . to visit selected municipalities in the province starting Oct. 24 to coincide with FDCP'S mission of encouraging more Filipinos to patronize Filipino films by literally reaching out to various localities in the Philippines."[90]

Here, the state effect created through the mobile cinema was not one of moviegoing as a leisure practice, built into everyday life, but of moviegoing as a belabored project, working through the state and complying with the ongoing, preexisting calendars of the local setting. Alongside local government units, the FDCP performed the screenings as spectacle and event. The exhibition event became a display of national technological dexterity, but at the same time, it was also a display of national acquiescence to local norms—through syncing with local festival calendars, including regional filmmakers, and highlighting the participation of local governments. This was an important part of how the institution staged its symbolic meaning. Staging a government-supported cinema became staging the state's circulatory labor, its efforts at "literally reaching out" to the audiences it sought.

Cinema and Fantasies of Peace Building

In addition to traversing class boundaries, the Sineng Pambansa project also made deliberate moves to cross cultural and geographic borders, in its plans to position cinema as an instrument for peace and inclusion within the broad, fragmented nation-state that the FDCP used as its national model. One means of displaying their institutional commitment to a regionalized notion of national cinema was through seeking the provincial audiences whose connection to the central state is most tenuous. The southern, Muslim region of the Philippines has existed for centuries in complex relation to the central, Christian nation-state. Local sultanates resisted both Spanish and American colonization, leading to a culture of mistrust between Muslim minorities and the Christian majority.[91] Ongoing conflict and misdirected state policy have beset the region, which includes many of the Philippines' poorest provinces.[92] The FDCP's performative work as a proxy for a benevolent central state was particularly charged in this context, where the audience's own, ideal vision of the state is one that is separate and sovereign.

Thus, the institution wove a narrative of inclusion, portraying state arts and culture projects as an important gesture to regions left outside of national narratives:

> There are all those other areas that have relatively been untapped and totally neglected and totally unvisited, which is the Muslim area,

Tawi-tawi and Marawi. . . . In Marawi, when we arrived there, the wife of the governor came to me and said, "Why only now? All these decades we've been waiting for this." Because of the security situation. But we feel that sometimes when you are entering this place, and you bring culture and film with you, you don't have the baggage of politics, and everything opens up. Adversaries are sitting down and watching film together. And we tried it also in Zamboanga, because I told the mayor there (because you know they had a spate of bombings before), and I said that if we have the film festival here, it will give a semblance of normalcy. . . . We hope in December we're going to Cotabato, where we've been having a lot of bombings also, and I know that the mayor is not in good terms with the governor, but I talked to the mayor and I said, "Are you willing to," because there's only one theater there, which is inside the [domain of the] governor, in ARMM [Autonomous Region of Muslim Mindanao], so I said, "Would you be able to sit down with the governor, and so that we can watch things together?" Maybe we can instigate peace, among factions and everything, if they're watching films and culture. . . . Maybe that's when culture can be important in political development.[93]

This account portrays an optimistic vision of cinema's potential as a cultural tool, an optimism that may be grounded in outsider perspectives. Framing culture as a kind of gift from the center to periphery, it also suggests a precarious line between collaborative forms of state support and top-down models of altruism. Whether in the form of administration or event planning, the account insinuates how efforts at decentralization can be difficult to operationalize.

The FDCP's festival in Tawi-Tawi, one of the three poorest provinces in the country, became its initial move toward its idea of cinema as peacemaking.[94] Members of the FDCP visited the region alongside the mainstream cinema star Robin Padilla, whose presence drew a crowd of thousands by FDCP estimates. As the organization's newsletter explains, the FDCP viewed the Tawi-Tawi venture as an important part of establishing institutional commitment to its mission of national distribution: "The decision to hold a Filipino film festival in Tawi-Tawi—the first ever cultural activity of its kind to be staged in the province which in the past was considered a 'remote outpost'—underscored the commitment of the FDCP to 'bring Filipino films to Filipinos,' wherever they may be in the scattered islands of the archipelago, or in their overseas communities."[95] Santos described the reaction among local cinemagoers as one of surprise: "The first question from the people in Tawi-Tawi then was, 'Why did you choose us? *Parang* [like], there has been in the past so much cultural neglect they can't believe anyone would bother.'"[96] Again, the account implies the idea of culture as a gift, to be given to a chosen recipient. As theorists have long cautioned, such exchanges are embedded in asymmetries between giver and receiver. They can create relations of debt at odds with the idea of decentralized power structures.

The good intentions of individuals within institutions can often do little in the face of long-standing hierarchies, political conflicts, and cultural distance. The efforts in Tawi-Tawi were a brief gesture of inclusion within national narratives, but there has not been a follow-up. The short-lived project stemmed from a kind of institutional optimism about screening Filipino cinema. While accounts of the event's success suggest an enthusiastic response, it is unclear how widely this optimism was shared among the local organizers who might have sustained it. These efforts demonstrate the complexity and limits of the state as a speculative, institution-ideal.

National Cinematheques and Institutional Longevity
One reason for the FDCP's moves toward organizational decentralization was its longevity, as its staff usually turn over upon the election of each president. As such, there was a concern for creating infrastructures that might endure a potential transition. During Santos's tenure, one such move was the National Cinematheque project, which aimed to build state-sponsored, brick-and-mortar theaters in various sites across the country.

In September 2011, I joined a group of Film Development Council members on a seven-hour road trip from the nation's capital to attend the opening of the country's first National Cinematheque. Significantly, the first state-sponsored theater opened not in Manila but in Baguio, a small city in the Cordillera mountains of Luzon. Newly appointed FDCP representatives from across the archipelago met in Manila, drove to the north, and attended the inaugural screening. That evening, a small crowd of local cinephiles, students, and city officials gathered at the modest screening space opened in the building of the century-old Casa Vallejo Hotel, a newly restored building that had served as a dormitory for government workers during the American colonial period.[97] It was one of only two Baguio structures to survive the Japanese bombings of 1941, lending its restoration a particular historical significance.[98] Its contemporary incarnation housed a tastefully decorated boutique hotel with views of pine-filled mountains, a small bookstore, a restaurant, and a spa, positioning the site as a hub for localized heritage and middle-class leisure. As an art-house cinema, with a nationalist, historical bent, the National Cinematheque fit well within its walls.

As with the mobile cinema events, the inauguration was highly ceremonial, involving words from the FDCP chair Briccio Santos and Baguio City officials, introductions of the various FDCP representatives from around the region, a pop ballad from local performers, and the national anthem. The National Cinematheque opened with a screening of *Anak Dalita (The Ruins)*, a 1956 Lamberto Avellana work shot on location in Intramuros, the crumbling Spanish district of a largely destroyed, post–World War II Manila. The movie screened on a DVD made from a newly restored print, part of the FDCP's National Film Archive project, which had been established the previous year. This historical orientation was visible throughout the screening space, as posters from across Philippine film history decorated the theater's office.

The FDCP would go on to open three more cinematheques in the following year, in Iloilo, Marawi, and Davao City. At the opening of the National Cinematheque in Davao City, Santos described the modest theaters as an emblem of the Philippine government: "At first glance, this structure may not be as luxurious and imposing as the grand palaces of Philippine and world cinema, but it definitely symbolizes a lifetime commitment of the Philippine government to advance the cause of the local motion picture industry to revive and energize it, and make it as strong and robust as it used to be in years gone by."[99] The distinctly local scale of the site was evident in the comparison to both national and world cinema "grand palaces." It positions these modest, locally scaled theaters not just as exhibition sites but as symbols of institutional longevity. They index an ideal state, whose "lifetime commitment" to cinema includes audiences across the archipelago.

While the "grand palaces" of national and world cinema were not the models for the National Cinematheque spaces, the structures that did provide an aspirational blueprint for these regional theaters is decidedly more mundane—the mall multiplex. One of the more speculative aspects of the FDCP's future vision was that of complete independence from commercial infrastructures. Santos described the idea of government-owned malls built on land donated by LGUs. The state malls would focus on locally owned businesses, with cineplexes integrated into these spaces. Describing a mass utopian mixture of tradition and modernity, Santos stated that the sites would offer the cleanliness of the mall space that has become such an integral part of Philippine leisure; however, visitors would also be able to experience a holistic presentation of local culture, including food, consumer items, and cinema: "You can have things around that show its Filipino culture. I want to be Pinoy, I want to be Pilipino and I want to go to that place. I want to watch these films, I want to eat this food."[100] This construct follows a logic seen in many of the previous chapters. Like Indie Sine's proposed links among culture, identity, and the mall multiplex, Santos saw cultural consumerism as a possibility for galvanizing Filipino audience-citizens. As with the Quiapo Cinematheque imaginary, this was a vision predicated on melding putatively authentic variations of localism with the modernity of globalized infrastructures—in this instance, the modern shopping mall.

In some respects, the vision could be seen as unsettling, particularly if it were placed entirely within a centralized, national context; the capital-intensive, large-scale conceptualization of arts and culture projects certainly share parallels with the state-driven initiatives that took shape under martial law. But this vision's location within dispersed local governments, operating independently, does undercut evocations of homogenizing government power and state paternalism. Sineng Pambansa viewed national cinema formation as a project of decentralized vertical integration. In its founding years, part of its establishment included performative events that staged a version of national culture reflecting this institutional structure. Within this staging, the national is fragmented and localized, and the central state worked in service to its peripheries. Santos described this regionalist view: "[Today is] unlike before, when everything was so centralized here in Manila that to be in the film industry, you had to go to studios here. . . . There's no more monopoly of the north."[101]

The decentralized state is another institution-ideal, a relational form constructed in response to the capital city's power and to the global flows seen as implicated within that dominance. If Santos posited that "Hollywood is not us," he also argued that neither was the

Manila-centrism that had come to represent national cinema at that point. Decentralization under globalization became a project of recentering the scale of the local, not simply through production and circulation but through taking institutional measures to cultivate its longevity. This is a utopic vision in which power has no source: the national capital becomes just one of many laterally networked centers, and local government units are accountable to filmmakers and audiences from their areas. But this theoretical decentralization obscures the power dynamics that inevitably emerge in institutional practices.

In practice, the FDCP's decentralized model had its limits. In her insightful research on regional cinemas, Katrina Tan describes that when an FDCP Davao coordinator received a directive to create a film council in cooperation with local government units and private sector entities in 2013, filmmakers and other cultural workers were not consulted.[102] Tan argues that this positioning of filmmakers as workers rather than "stakeholders" suggests a more commercial future for FDCP-sponsored cinema initiatives.

For large-scale, state arts bodies like the FDCP, theory and practice are always in tension with one another. Institutional instability, politicking, and administrative transition affect which of the organization's many plans will be sustainable. Nonetheless, analyzing the *process* of envisioning a state-supported, decentralized, long-term institution can be revealing. Filmmakers seeking new systems for distribution and exhibition invoked an institutional ideal: a functioning public enterprise, subject to its citizens, working to create a long-standing circulatory infrastructure, across a dispersed archipelago. This vision overlapped with those of figures embedded in state bureaucracies. Such shared fantasies suggest the persistence of the state's "magic," as Taussig calls it, the effect that positioned it as a desired institutional possibility for film exhibition and distribution, despite its historical weakness.

Instituting Circulation

The transnational film festival circuit and Cinemalaya were among the foundational institutions of Philippine cinema's revival, and they remain important parts of independent cinema circulation within Philippine screen culture. At the same time, during the period discussed in this chapter, filmmakers began to see these institutions as lacking, and the state became a speculative goal for filling this void. Thus, the Film Development Council created the *effect* of a benign, diversified central state by creating regional circuits for national cinema. Through mobile cinemas and National Cinematheques, the institution projected a vision of Philippine cinema as both regionally specific and supported by an industrious central state. The performative process of institutionalization became a part of the state effect.

It is critical to acknowledge that such large-scale institutions are difficult to manage with limited funding and that local government outposts, operating independently, often have more pressing concerns than cinema. The progression I describe is not meant to be teleological, culminating in the state as a model institutional form. Rather, I am interested in the state in part because of how the institution and its publics were speculated—by filmmakers who sought better options for distribution and exhibition, and by state cultural institution workers who envisaged its possibilities. For the Philippines' alternative film culture, publics were not just objects of circulation. They became objects of speculative institutional formation, constituting the institution-ideals that would evolve a national cinema across production, exhibition, and reception. In their ideal variation, such institutions would be public in both practice and form, disseminating films to prospective spectators and representing those spectators' interests. Projections of the state indexed an achieved modernity, signaling the impossible end of an asymptotic trajectory. But as the account above suggests, this ideal of the state had its limits in a culturally and economically diverse archipelago.[103]

EPILOGUE

At the 2009 Cannes festival, Brillante Mendoza was awarded Best Director, alongside Alain Resnais, who received a Lifetime Achievement Award for his contributions to cinema history. Among Resnais's accomplishments is the 1959 film *Hiroshima Mon Amour*, a watershed in modernist art cinema, which explores war, memory, and representation through the narrative of an affair between a Japanese architect and a French actress. Five decades after its initial release, the film would serve as an inspiration for an article in the *Philippine Inquirer Sunday Magazine* titled "Quiapo Mon Amour," which depicted a newly vibrant, Manilenyo cinephilia brought on by works of world cinema, available in pirated form in the heart of Manila, the "crossroads" of the diverse Philippine nation. It seemed fitting, then, that this French director of a cross-cultural meditation on memory and representation would share the 2009 Cannes Film Festival stage with Mendoza, one of the Philippines' entrées into world cinema "auteurdom." Philippine cinema's emergence on this international cinema stage presented a complex image: a cinema with little circulation outside national borders, moving from the cinematic "hinterlands" to newfound international fame. The transnational circulations of cinema, which have largely been relegated to center-periphery models of global exchange, seemed poised for new models.

What does it mean to create a new film culture? The phrase suggests a flourishing wave of productions, breaking new ground in their aesthetics and production structures. That much is rather straightforward. But as the previous chapters suggest, the more complicated questions have to do with circulation—channels of distribution and exhibition, the mobilities of film texts and the paratextual discourses that orbit them, the movement of potential audiences in urban space. Mendoza's victory at Cannes offers one vision of film culture achieved. But it is only a partial picture, one that is framed in relation to production and transnational publics. As a new Philippine film culture took shape in the transitional, early-2000s period, audiences, filmmakers, and organizations worked to imagine national publics, across a range of models: the mall-going crowds; the inclusive, placid multiculturalism that belied the historic marginalization of Manila's ethnic minorities; a nostalgic, cosmopolitan subculture; a site of latent revolutionary potential; and diverse regional publics, under the wing of an idealized state. Cinema circulation played a role across all of these projected publics, acting as an aspirational vehicle for traversing intranational borders of ethnicity and class. These local systems of exchange were shaped by ambient transnationalisms—the partitions between wealth and poverty, private and public, foreign and domestic—that structured the city. The speculative routes of alternative cinemas helped create a vision of a national cinema, not just as texts or an industrial sector but as a prospective, national film culture that in its ideal form would overcome the impasse of alternative cinema. It would resolve the contradiction between alternative cultural forms' radicalism and elitism. This is likely an impossible goal, but as the projects in the previous chapters suggest, for many invested in Philippine cinema, it was one worth working toward. While neoliberal political and economic contexts have imposed ideals of progress, modernity, and futurity, this model of alternative film culture exceeds that logic. It recuperates different forms of speculation, envisioning the prospective publics that would further ideals of national unity. This version of alternative film culture foregrounds different trajectories, which can negotiate ongoing dynamics of speculation, progress, delay, and reformation. The book's chapters offer not a romantic view of volatility but a recognition of resilience— they track the persistence of exhibitors, writers, cultural institution workers, and filmmakers, trying to make sense of a film culture that was in the throes of transition.

Philippine film culture has evolved since the early, transitional period this book covers, and the trajectories of speculation traced in the previous chapters have slightly altered their course. Other, more basic questions of domestic audiences remained, as the vision of such audiences shifted from a national public to a domestic market. The current version of Philippine alternative cinema has multiplied across a diverse spectrum of film practice, from more experimental films to those that operate as a hybrid between mainstream and indie. One outcome of this diversification is a growing tendency to see certain independent films not just as an alternative to the local mainstream industry but as a *bridge* to the local, mainstream industry. Several years into the movement, works began to cross into more mainstream narratives and aesthetics, leading to a new category in entertainment journalism and production discourse: maindie, a portmanteau of "mainstream" and "independent."[1]

Reflecting on these shifts in 2012, the director Pepe Diokno described the changing scene as a move toward more variety among independents and calls for a more inclusive local film industry: "We're just one Filipino film industry, and it makes no sense for us to divide ourselves based on petty definitions."[2] Rather than dividing the industry by mode of production or aesthetics, Diokno proposed a unified, national filmmaking sector. Within this model, independent film became broader through becoming more mainstream, branching into recognizable genres. The idea that filmmakers across the independent-mainstream divide are "just one Filipino film industry" suggests another version of a national film culture. Importantly, the rise of this new category is also a move toward larger local viewerships. As one journalist describes, "Projects under the category 'maindie,' short for mainstream-indie, aim to provide a different movie experience without limiting itself to a small audience."[3]

Here, the idea of reaching beyond the "small audience" of independent films is not so much a vision of a new public culture but of an expanded market, reflecting a shift in focus from overt nationalism to greater financial sustainability. But this was not just a one-way street, as mainstream studios began experimenting with alternatives to their usual genre- and sequel-driven fare. For example, in 2012, ABS-CBN opened Skylight Films, which they described as a "laboratory" for experimenting with new techniques, actors, or narratives.[4] ABS-CBN's Enrico Santos of the company's cinema branch, Star Cinema, described

Skylight as separate from the mainstream production house: "It is the network's 'maindie' or 'mainstream-indie' film unit. It's not a label of Star Cinema. We don't do the kinds of movies that Star Cinema makes, like *yung mga* family dramas. Ours have more edge. They're not as experimental as the indie films made for Cinemalaya, but they're [still] indie *pa rin* [as well], although we do try to cater to and entertain mainstream sensibilities."[5] The idea of giving local audiences "something different" indicated the perception of changing tastes among Filipino markets. While independent directors were branching out to wider local viewerships through a turn to the mainstream, the studios countered these moves with turns toward films with "more edge."

This view of the indie audience as a potential market was supported in the unexpected box-office success of a handful of maindie films, which received wide domestic releases. In 2014, Antoinette Jadaone's Cinema One Originals romantic comedy, *That Thing Called Tadhana*, became the highest-grossing independent production in history.[6] The following year, Jerrold Tarog's historical epic *Heneral Luna* drew enthusiastic crowds. The Artikulo Uno Productions film had a much higher budget than typical independent productions but still managed to make a profit, earning ₱257 million at the box office.[7] In 2017, the independent outfit Spring Films' romantic comedy *Kita Kita*, directed by Sigrid Andrea Bernardo, broke *Heneral Luna*'s records.[8] Its production structure overlaps with the studios. Spring Films is a crossover enterprise founded by superstar Piolo Pascual, who has himself made a career in both mainstream and independent features. *Kita Kita* was distributed through Viva Entertainment, a large commercial studio. Their production practices involved test screenings at the University of the Philippines–Diliman and focus groups, which resulted in two versions of the film: one for a domestic release and a director's cut for international festivals.[9] The hybridized maindie film saw the domestic audience in marketplace terms and succeeded in winning a vast viewership.

Considered historically, this pattern of studio co-optation does present a more promising form of appropriation than that which the industry has previously engaged in. José B. Capino partly attributes the industry's 1990s decline in commercial filmmaking to features of Philippine cinema's hybridity.[10] He proposes that Filipino filmmakers lost their audiences to foreign films in part because they "failed to evolve a more dynamic relationship with them and with global culture—in other words, a complacency of sorts in tending to the strategic aspects of its hybridity."[11] Capino describes the formal and aesthetic failures of local mainstream cinema, which were soon matched with failures in box-office revenue. Perhaps an engagement with more experimental, localized forms of filmmaking could be a means of untethering mainstream cinema from its history of Hollywood mimicry, providing new models of aesthetic innovation and greater latitude for the filmmakers who choose to work within this system.[12]

As the teens drew to a close, new exhibition cultures emerged to reflect this diverse range of filmmaking. On one end of the spectrum, more avant-garde, experimental works found a home in community-based production/exhibition projects, such as Los Otros, a "film lab" and exhibition space based in the studio/home of artists Shireen Seno and John Torres.[13] In addition, several microcinemas catering to a wide range of alternative productions sprouted across Metro Manila during the latter half of the teens, marking a new era in Philippine film circulation.

These smaller venues framed their interventions into circulation as an intervention into the temporalities of industrial film distribution, creating a kind of exhibition safety net for films that might have short runs in larger venues. In 2017, the filmmaker Hector Barretto Calma co-founded Cinema Centenario in the bustling area of Maginhawa, near several universities. Calma describes his reason for opening the theater as based on a desire for audiences, which may grow over time. Referencing multiplex policies to remove films that fail to perform before they are given time to develop an audience, Calma describes, "As much as possible, we want to showcase local films. As a filmmaker, I know the feeling that you have a movie and then you cannot bring it to the audience you like because you have no venue. These are movies that have no chance at a big cinema, or they are given an opportunity to screen, but will be removed immediately on the first day."[14]

Similar logic drives San Juan City's Cinema '76 Film Society. The cinema has been very successful, partnering with local film festivals and establishing an additional location in Quezon City, which includes a 70-seat MP4 theater and a 130-seat DCP cinema. One cofounder, Vincent Nebrida, is the president of TBA, the parent company of Artikulo Uno Productions, the outfit behind *Heneral Luna*. Like Calma, Nebrida describes Cinema '76 as a means of extending independent films' short runs in mainstream theaters. As he says, "It takes a while for a film to find its audience. We at TBA really wanted to create an avenue for studios to screen their films after it gets a theatrical release."[15] Other microcinemas that have emerged share a similar aim to extend the public, circulatory lives of local films. Noting the distribution challenges that smaller productions face, the filmmaker Carl E. Balita founded the 250-seat CBRC Dream Theater in Sampoloc, Manila, near the area's universities.[16] Balita describes the theater as a means of prolonging these films' potential to draw audiences: "Many times, films lose their reach. They're easily pulled out from commercial cinemas and they are shelved for a long period of time."[17] The CBRC Dream Theater targets not just students but teachers; Balita sees the screenings as an opportunity to influence curriculums. The siblings Angelo and Patricia Santos cofounded the 40-seat Black Maria Cinema in the former screening space of their grandparents' production company, SQ Film Productions, which made features during the 1970s.[18] Black Maria has been successful in drawing what Santos described as the "ABC," or middle to upper classes; he also expressed a desire to someday bring in the "CDE," or lower classes, to enable them to have a different kind of moviegoing experience.[19]

This wave of microcinemas signals a new period of Philippine film circulation, in which alternative cinema's speculative publics have become the niche audiences of microcinemas, spaces defined precisely by their small scale and limited reach; but at the same time, their proprietors see these spaces as a means of intervening into the commercial temporalities of larger multiplex outlets. Established near schools, they see their potential publics as part of an educational community.

Ten years following the publication of Alexis Tioseco's "Wishful Thinking for Philippine Cinema," it would seem that many of his "wishes" had been fulfilled—and indeed, many of them have. At the same time, this subjunctive, would-be temporality is still visible in much of the discourse surrounding alternative cinema culture. A decade after Tioseco's essay, a producer posted a similar wish list on social media: "Welcome to the future. Time to adapt. Or die. But YES, WE NEED HELP! Here's a wish list . . . : 100% tax holiday for all local films. Cut ticket prices by half. Or at least implement student-price tickets to local films. Support microcinemas. Build microcinemas all over the country. (Attention: entrepreneurs) Include film history and appreciation in the K-12 curriculum."[20] This 2019 wish list was a response to a widely circulated post by the director Erik Matti, which lamented the continued absence of national audiences: "The film industry is at its busiest the past three years but no one gets to see the movies we make except for the sporadic mega hits.... What happened to our local audience?"[21]

The establishment of microcinemas offers one measure of Philippine cinema's proliferation, presenting a powerful extension of film-circulation temporalities, grounded in local spaces. But as these calls to action suggest, the work of film culture continues, with ideals of state policy (tax holidays, school curriculums) and hopes for a wider audience. These exchanges encapsulate the ongoing negotiation of Philippine cinema's futures; speculation about its publics continues, alongside the ongoing labor of those invested in its trajectories.

Another vision of Philippine cinema futures took shape in 2016, with the election of Rodrigo Duterte as president in an overwhelming victory.[22] Years after his Cannes success, Brillante Mendoza became a staunch ally of the new head of state, who had campaigned on a populist, nationalist platform that promised social change at the cost of state violence. An alliance formed. On one side was a politician steeped in populist rhetoric and hypermasculine posturing. On the other was an internationally canonized filmmaker, whose work had been at the center of debates around representations of poverty and Philippine art films' elite, transnational audiences. Despite the documented human rights abuses that marked Duterte's tenure, Mendoza remained a staunch ally.[23] He filmed the 2016 State of the Nation Address (SONA) using extreme close-ups, double exposures, and low angles, leading media and other observers to remark on the broadcast's "indie" aesthetics.[24] This was an unexpected turn in the union of the state and cinema; rather than tax holidays and state-sponsored distribution infrastructures, it offered a different, darker projection of alternative cinema's potential role in public life. When questioned about his loyalties to the authoritarian leader, Mendoza framed his stance in his hopes for Philippine futures: "The Philippines must change.... I am hopeful things will change for the better. That's my goal, that's why I do these kinds of films. He [Duterte] will do whatever he has to do as the new president and I will do what I do as an artist."[25] With his 2009 Cannes victory, Mendoza had helped secure a place for Philippine cinema within a transnational public sphere. Seven years later, he framed his commitment to domestic publics as doing whatever necessary—even supporting an administration that had carried out thousands of extrajudicial killings in its "war on drugs."[26] Mendoza's hopefulness is predicated on a temporality of immediacy. It is a form of film-cultural speculation that differs, in obvious ways, from the slow work of building circulation initiatives and audiences, and in this case, its outcome was the support of unspeakable violence.

As the previous chapters suggest, the speculative publics addressed through many local circulation spaces were *ideal* objects of desire, tied to visions of national and/or democratic culture. As is often the case with utopian projects, their paths have not been linear or smooth. This is the pattern of many art projects, whose moves from obscurity to renown are met with equal measures of trepidation and excitement. As with most discussions of mainstreaming, its outcomes are mixed.

These contradictions have become a condition of working toward a film culture within conditions of infrastructural instability: state cinematheques and state violence, flourishing microcinemas and low box-office, thriving film production and stalled circulation. Unevenly distributed across class and geography, this instability has become a routine, systemic condition for the viewers and makers of alternative films. To siphon films into the channels guaranteed to welcome them (festivals, classrooms, and microcinemas) is one means of contending with these conditions. Certainly, this might be the case for alternative cinema in any setting. But when alternative film is so closely tethered to ideals of national cinema and to the possibility of new publics, striving for the impossible becomes another, necessary means of dealing with conditions of ongoing instability, conditions that observers such as Rolando Tolentino and Walden Bello have described as the country's perpetual crisis.[27]

I would suggest that both the pragmatic use of existing institutions *and* the optimistic intervention into prevailing systems are necessary parts of a film culture in formation. Accounting for this negotiation between pragmatism and idealism—between the here and now and the perhaps possible—becomes a means of assessing alternative film movements as neither celebrations of transgressive resistance nor cynical ploys for cultural capital. The object of analysis becomes the interminable process of their formation, across production, exhibition, and reception.

Crucially, that formation is as much a product of discourse and speculation as the establishment of systems. The project of an alternative national cinema is one of obstacles, contradictions, and frictions rather than a smooth progression toward an espoused ideal. Alternative film cultures are often short-lived, their more principled variations sometimes fading or taking different form in their inevitable move toward existing institutions (the state, the commercial studio system, foreign festivals). However, I would not like to posit this move as a transition from prelapsarian authenticity to some corrupted phoniness. Rather, if we see these alternative film cultures as relational, then as a current crop of films and their makers move to the middle, new cultural formations will emerge to take their place on the peripheries, even if their claims to marginality take a different shape.

This is one model to describe contemporary film cultures in Manila, and I suspect it could apply in many settings where the dull ache of ongoing crisis and the dogged optimism of cultural initiatives exist in constant tension with one another. Infrastructural instability, a lack of resources, and profound social divisions are among the crises that structure Manilenyo film culture. But at the same time, filmmakers, cultural institution workers, organizations, and audiences work against these circumstances, struggling to move closer to that ever-receding curve. This process in itself has value as a means of imagining alternative futures for local cinema. As Raymond Williams describes, emergent and preemergent structures of feeling are "changes of presence," "social experiences in solution."[28] While articulate and explicit social forms are more recognizable when fixed, "the strongest barrier to the recognition of human cultural activity is the immediate and regular conversion of experience into finished products."[29]

Thus, attention to the ongoing, unfinished, and "failed" projects of particular film cultures could provide a fresh means of considering alternative cinemas not as calcified bodies of work, classified into independent and mainstream, but as ongoing efforts to work within particular modes of production and aesthetics, as well as to link films and their prospective publics. This occurs both through discourses that establish new taxonomies and through new systems of distribution and exhibition that aim to traverse various intra- and transnational borders. Film studies scholars have long argued that both independent and art cinema are categories created through cultural institutions' systems of exchange. As we have seen, these systems create a film culture that is both oppositional and elite, forming the core tension of nonmainstream cultural production. This elitism is a fair assessment, and it is common in burgeoning film cultures in many settings. I would also suggest that attention to alternative film cultures' often unmet, sometimes paradoxical aspirations to work against those innate hierarchies would help to position them as alternative cinemas "in solution," working within an asymptotic, speculative imaginary that has particular power in the global south, where discussions of alternative films frequently contend with ideals of cinema and nation.

Circulation plays a crucial role here, and there is more work to be done on the social experience of exhibition and distribution in settings outside the United States and Europe.[30] In their essay in a special issue of *Public Culture* dedicated to circulation, coeditors Dilip Gaonkar and Elizabeth A. Povinelli describe the project as dedicated to transnationally charting the emergence of publics under global modernity, often using "thickly descriptive case studies" to depict "the circulatory matrix, both national and global, through which new discursive forms, practices, and artifacts carry out their routine ideological labor of constituting subjects who can be summoned in the name of a public or a people."[31] They call for scholarship that can move between the "seductive sparkle of the 'thing' and the quiet work of the generative matrix," work that "can be carried out only within a set of circulatory fields populated by myriad forms, sometimes hierarchically arranged and laminated but mostly undulating as an ensemble, as a mélange."[32]

Within early-2000s Manila, films and their modes of circulation were not so easily parsed into "seductive sparkle" and "quiet work." As this book suggests, the feature films themselves were not always widely seen. Thus, their circulation took on a preeminent role, producing a localized film culture, founded on imagining routes that cross intra- and transnational borders. Circulation itself, reified into a dense web of patterns connoting particular class associations, national identities, and cosmopolitan markers, constituted the film culture, which gave off its own seductive luster. Circulation initiatives are not simply transparent practices that disseminate meanings but are "constitutive acts," generating meaning themselves.[33] In the case of alternative cinema in Manila, what these circulation projects constituted were the contested speculations of a national film culture and its publics: always imminent, always receding, always worth working toward.

NOTES

Introduction

1. Tioseco, "Wishful Thinking for Philippine Cinema," *Criticine*, March 15, 2009, https://alexistioseco.wordpress.com/2009/03/15/wishful-thinking-for-philippine-cinema/.
2. Tioseco, "Wishful Thinking."
3. Comment by Misha, April 11, 2009. Tioseco, "Wishful Thinking."
4. *Criticine*, home page, accessed July 20, 2014, http://criticine.com/main.php.
5. Even on the post itself, one commenter was skeptical of this earnest call to arms. Writing in Taglish, they offered their own wish that Alexis would be less "elitist" ("wish ko lang maging less elitist *si* alexis Tioseco"), reflecting competing bids for Philippine cinema's futures. Comment by pokwang, April 11, 2009. Tioseco, "Wishful Thinking."
6. Dudley Andrew has noted the speed with which new Philippine films became a known quantity in international film festivals, in comparison to new Taiwanese cinema of the 1980s, which took years to develop. See Andrew, "Forward," *Global Art Cinema*, vii.
7. Ruben V. Nepales, "Redd Ochoa Is Hopeful about RP's Indie Scene," *Philippine Daily Inquirer*, August 24, 2007, http://showbizandstyle.inquirer.net/entertainment/entertainment/view/20070824-84554/Redd_Ochoa_is_hopeful_about_RP%92s_indie_scene.
8. Nepales, "Redd Ochoa Is Hopeful."
9. Armes, "Context of the African"; Robinson, *Satyajit Ray*.

10 The terms "north" and "south" are admittedly imperfect shorthand. I use them to describe the divides between wealthy, industrialized nations (the G8, members of the UN Security Council) and the rest of the world. However, I realize that there are areas of poverty and deindustrialization within northern countries, as well as areas of extreme wealth in the global south. In those instances, the demographic majority/minority dynamic becomes a defining factor. See also Walter Mignolo's historical analysis of the concept in "The Global South and World Dis/Order." Mignolo argues that the metaphor north/south works in that the global south provides resources for the north, while also being the locus for the emergent political society that will eventually liberate even those wealthier countries.
11 Ross, "Film Festival as Producer"; Shackleton, "Indian Film's Tender Shoots"; Peranson, "First You Get," 42.
12 De Valck, *Film Festivals*; de Valck, Kredell, and Loist, *Film Festivals*; Wong, *Film Festivals*.
13 See Choi, "National Cinema"; Hjort, "On the Plurality of Cinematic Transnationalisms."
14 Harbord, *Film Cultures*, 14.
15 Harbord, *Film Cultures*; M. Newman, *Indie*.
16 Robbins, *Phantom Public Sphere*.
17 See Joel David's collection of essays, *The National Pastime: Contemporary Philippine Cinema*.
18 Tiongson, "Audiences," 99–100.
19 See Tiongson, "Best of Times."
20 Fair Trade Alliance, "Clipped Wings Prevent Philippine Cinema from Soaring," FairTrade Web, June 20, 2007, http://fairtradeweb.wordpress.com/2007/06/20/clipped-wings-prevent-philippine-cinema-from-soaring/.
21 Philippine Information Agency, "Philippine Film and Video," Philippine Culture and Information, May 21, 1998, http://www.pia.gov.ph/philinfo/phfilm.html.
22 Tiongson, "Best of Times," 9.
23 Tiongson, 427.
24 Bello, "Neoliberalism."
25 Flores makes similar claims, without the ethnic markers.
26 Tiongson, "Best of Times," 8.
27 Tiongson, 8.
28 Flores, "Philippine Cinema and Society," 427.
29 Tiongson, "Audiences," 99–100.
30 Caroline S. Hau points out that the Chinese presence in mercantilism was due to the American colonial state imposing the Chinese Exclusion Act in the Philippines, which pushed the minority into a niche trade. See Hau, *Chinese Question*, 149.
31 Hau, 147.
32 The following chapters touch on this topic. See the conclusion of chapter 1, for example.
33 Fair Trade Alliance, "From Reel to Real," FairTrade Web, June 21, 2007, http://fairtradeweb.wordpress.com/2007/06/21/from-reel-to-real/.

34 "Movie Spending Contributes 0.06% to GDP-NSCB," *Rappler*, February 13, 2012, http://www.rappler.com/business/1505-movie-spending-contribute-0-06-to-gdp-%E2%80%93-nscb.
35 For more on Cinemalaya and debates about what constitutes "independent cinema" in the Philippines, see Patrick Campos's chapter on the festival and congress, "Cinemalaya and the Politics of Naming a Movement," in Campos, *End of National Cinema*, 217–76.
36 I discuss Cinemalaya further in chapter 5.
37 Don Jaucian, "Why All the TV Stars Are Going Indie," CNN *Philippines*, August 9, 2016, http://cnnphilippines.com/life/entertainment/film/2016/08/09/benjamin-alves-janine-gutierrez-dagsin.html.
38 Elizabeth Kerr, "Imburnal—Film Review," *Hollywood Reporter*, March 24, 2009, http://www.hollywoodreporter.com/review/imburnal-film-review-92993.
39 Romulo A. Virola, "Now Showing: Panday nag-shake, Rattle and Roll," Philippine Statistics Authority, National Statistical Coordination Board, 2012, accessed July 20, 2014, http://www.nscb.gov.ph/headlines/StatsSpeak/2012/021312_rav_mpg.asp.
40 *Oxford English Dictionary*, s.v., "speculative," accessed July 23, 2020, https://www.oed.com/view/Entry/186115?redirectedFrom=speculative&.
41 Uncertain Commons, *Speculate This!*, n.p.
42 Uncertain Commons, *Speculate This!*, n.p.
43 Uncertain Commons, *Speculate This!*, n.p.
44 See Shatkin, "City and the Bottom Line."
45 Bello, *Anti-Development State*.
46 Harvey, *Brief History of Neoliberalism*.
47 Bliss Cua Lim writes about the effects of the late-1990s crisis on the commercial film industry in "Gambling on Life and Death: Neoliberal Rationality and the Films of Jeffrey Jeturian."
48 Brown, *Undoing the Demos*, 279n43.
49 *Oxford English Dictionary*, s.v., "asymptote," accessed November 19, 2019, https://www.oed.com/oed2/00013928;jsessionid=0EBADC8A9226996DCFB520259599FD59. While the mathematical definition describes movement toward a fixed curve, rather than receding one, I am using the term more generally, as an illustrative metaphor. I am grateful to Mette Hjort for suggesting this term.
50 Buck-Morss, "Democracy: An Unfinished Project."
51 Mouffe, "Democratic Citizenship."
52 Larkin, *Signal and Noise*, 78–80. One recent collection that problematizes the metro-centrism of much early cinema scholarship is Kathryn H. Fuller-Seeley's *Hollywood in the Neighborhood*, which focuses on rural and small-town moviegoing.
53 Neves and Sarkar, *Asian Video Cultures*, "Introduction," 2.
54 Neves and Sarkar, 5.
55 Buck-Morss, "Democracy: An Unfinished Project," 46.
56 Tolentino, "Nations, Nationalisms," 122–23.

57 Writing on the United States and United Kingdom, respectively, Michael Z. Newman and David Hesmondhalgh each observe that categories like "indie" carry a fundamental tension between their democratic and elitist tendencies. As Newman argues, this contradiction is difficult to overcome. Popularity threatens independent artists' credibility, their works' status as outsider art, and, most crucially, their consumers' sense of being separate from the dominant culture. Similarly, Janet Harbord has described the paradox of art cinema as a conflict between its political potential and its place within circuits of value. Harbord's *Film Cultures* is particularly useful because it shifts emphasis from film texts to spaces and networks of exhibition. Harbord describes film cultures as "social practices, materially rooted and connected to larger networks of exchange and flow" (56). Harbord's analysis of the mutually defining arthouse-multiplex binary draws from James Clifford's art-culture system. Culture refers to all routine and symbolic activities in its widest application; it is "collective, material, reproduced." Its ubiquity leads to a devalued meaning in relation to art, which is premised on "individual production, originality, transcendence." Hence its contradiction. As Harbord writes, "The discourses through which oppositional identity is produced reinvade the *social status of art as distinct*, in contrast to its *political remit to invoke a more pluralist agenda* for filmmaking" (emphasis added). Like Newman and Hesmondhalgh, Harbord identifies this incongruity as the core that underlies notions of independent film, art cinema, and other labels that claim distance from a discursively constituted mainstream. See Thornton, *Club Cultures*, for more on the subcultural production of the idea of "mainstream."

58 Ingawanij and McKay, *Glimpses of Freedom*.

59 Dennison and Lim, *Remapping World Cinema*; Grant and Kuhn, *Screening World Cinema*; Ezra and Rowden, *Transnational Cinema*.

60 Galt and Schoonover, "The Impurity of Art Cinema," 7.

61 Galt and Schoonover, 7. See also Steve Neale's classic essay, "Art Cinema as Institution."

62 Nagib, "Towards a Positive Definition of World Cinema," 31.

63 Edgar O. Cruz, "French Connection," Stir: Showbiz Talk, May 14, 2009, accessed May 29, 2009, http://www.stir.ph/LM/articles~level2/id-1242267214271_4/ai-null/French_connection.html.

64 Similar concerns arise in the context of Latin American filmmaking, as noted in Ross, "Film Festival as Producer."

65 De la Cruz, *Philippine New Wave*, 111.

66 "Fonds Sud Cinema," Films from the South, accessed May 12, 2012, http://www.filmfrasor.no/en/program/Fondsud. Interestingly, the funding body changed its name to Aides aux Cinemas du Monde, in early 2012, placing less emphasis on its developing country focus. On public funding for film and audiovisual works in Europe, see "Fonds Sud Cinema," Korda: Database, accessed June 1, 2015, http://korda.obs.coe.int/korda.php/organisation/indexType1/id/49.

67 Edgar O. Cruz, "Cannes 'Formula' Exposed," Stir, accessed May 15, 2009, http://www.stir.ph/LM/articles~level2/id-1242267214271_4/ai-null/French

_connection.html. These are long-standing debates. See also Nicanor Tiongson's history of the filmmaker Manuel Conde's *Gengis Kahn*. Tiongson quotes Conde saying, "I went out of the Philippines like a country bumpkin eager to know more about the art of motion pictures. I found out that the Philippines was a wealthy country in [terms of] culture and traditions. . . . I resolved never to make a movie of foreign origin [again]." Tiongson, *Cinema of Manuel Conde*, 83.

68 Charlie Samuya Veric, "Who's Afraid of Philippine Cinema?," *Philippine Star*, June 18, 2001, http://www.philstar.com/arts-and- culture/85938/who%C3%A3%C2%A2%C3%A2%E2%80%9A%C2%AC%C3%A2%E2%80%9E%C2%A2s- afraid-philippine-cinema.

69 This is not a situation specific to the Philippines. Bangkok-based filmmaker Aditya Assarat has noted, "For us [independent] filmmakers in Thailand, a theatrical release is more for the heart than for revenue—our market is Europe with other bits here and there." Quoted in Shackleton, "How Independent Filmmakers in Southeast Asia Are on the Rise."

70 For an analysis of how filmmakers use terms like "feudalism" and "revolution" to discuss independent cinema, see Campos, *End of National Cinema*, 225–26.

71 R. S. David, *Nation, Self and Citizenship*, 266.

72 David surmises, "Our collective representations beyond the family are blurred, and we do not see the nation-state as possessing any moral authority over us." R. S. David, *Nation, Self, and Citizenship*, 281. Similarly, in an essay titled, "Toward a Community Broader than the Kin," the sociologist Fernando Nakpil Zialcita poses analogous questions regarding the nature of community in Philippine culture: "The kindred too, has constituted the moral universe of many Filipinos, whether in the lowlands or in the uplands." Zialcita, *Authentic though Not Exotic*, 40. Zialcita contends that the notion of a broader community called the Philippines was created as a reaction to and as an outcome of Spanish imposition, though this product of colonization was inevitably localized and transformed. The historian Mina Roces parallels this contention, arguing that *politica de familia*, or values of family solidarity, underpin structures of factionalism and patron-client ties. Roces, *Kinship Politics*, 185. The word "family" does not necessarily mean "household," the demographic definition; nor does it mean kinship per se, as ethnographers generally use the term; rather, to describe the political role of the family, Alfred McCoy offers the phrase "kinship network," described as "a working coalition drawn from a larger group related by blood, marriage, and ritual." McCoy, *Anarchy of Families*, 10. These ideas of kinship and national community are divisive subjects within Philippine studies scholarship, and while it is outside the scope of this introduction to discuss the extensive debates surrounding them at length, they merit mention here. Historians who emerged out of the martial-law-era Left, such as Zeus Salazar and Reynaldo Ileto, critiqued works by U.S. authors that blamed the failure of the Philippine state on Filipino values. (Salazar founded the Pantayong Pananaw school of indigenous historiography.) For example, in his provocative 1999 essay on Orientalism in American Philippine studies, Ileto contends

that these works frame Filipinos as doomed to failure, due to being ruled by passion and personal loyalties. His piece generated a range of responses, both supportive and critical. Ileto, "Orientalism and the Study of Philippine Politics." Priscelina Patajo-Legasto uses Ileto's critique as a framework for defining Philippine studies: see Patajo-Legasto, "Introduction." Critiques include Curaming, "Beyond Orientalism?"; Sidel, "Response to Ileto"; Claudio, "Postcolonial Fissures."

73 Halberstam, *Queer Art of Failure*; Muñoz, *Disidentificaitons*.
74 Halberstam, *Queer Art of Failure*, 88.
75 Halberstam, 88.
76 J. Scott, *Seeing Like a State*, quoted in Halberstam, 9–10.
77 Macdonald, "Filipino as Libertarian," 430.
78 See also Azurin, *Reinventing the Filipino*, 99; Garrido, "Civil and Uncivil Society," 459; Pinches, "Working Class Experience," 186.
79 Tadiar, *Things Fall Away*, 265.
80 Hau, *Necessary Fictions*, 100.
81 Hau, 100. In this context, Hau is discussing the idea of the "Great Divide" in Philippine history, marked by Teodoro Agoncillo's watershed 1948 book, *Revolt of the Masses: The Story of Bonifacio and the Katipunan*. This was the beginning of a historiography of the Philippines that constructed Filipino society in both Marxist terms (as economically and socially divided into elites and masses) as well as nationalist orientation (as unified through national identity). It argues for the idea of nation as an ideal, if not realized, possibility, with nationalist discourse as a means to heal this rift.
82 Hau, 125–26. This nationalist imaginary is a stabilizing force, and this has won the argument some criticism. Charlie Samuya Veric particularly takes issue with what he sees as Hau's conflation of elite and underground literatures. See Veric, "Fiction of Necessity."
83 While Habermas himself later acknowledged the model's limitations, subsequent revisions have noted an underlying nostalgia for the public sphere as a forum for cultural debate, rather than cultural consumption. See the collections Robbins, *Phantom Public Sphere*; Calhoun, *Habermas*. For Habermas, the latter condition was brought about through the advent of mass media. But as film historian Dana Polan argues in an essay published in the initial wave of revisions, the capitalist public sphere has never been rational—rather, it is far more often grounded in spectacle and affect. In addition, as Polan points out, this condition is not necessarily antidemocratic. As this wide range of scholarship suggests, the public sphere's original formulation has long been established as an ideal type rather than a historical artifact. See Polan, "Public's Fear." See also Miriam Hansen's discussion of Kluge in her discussion of early cinema as an alternative public sphere in *Babel and Babylon*.
84 Crisp, *Film Distribution*; Lobato, *Shadow Economies* and *Netflix Nations*; Perren, "Rethinking Distribution"; M. Lim, *Philippine Cinema*.
85 Fraser, "Rethinking the Public Sphere."
86 Warner, *Publics and Counterpublics*.

87 These scholars' works oppose Habermas's original view of circulation as circular and tightly bound. For example, Janet Newman describes "the mobile, elusive, and problematic character of publicness." J. Newman, "Going Public."
88 Barnett, "Convening Publics."
89 Gray, *Show Sold Separately*.
90 Gray, *Show Sold Separately*.
91 The films I am speaking of here are the independent films that circulate primarily in international festivals. Other nonmainstream films like political news documentaries and activist works have much more successful dissemination within their own, localized networks. Tolentino, "Cinema and the State." These kinds of works do come into discussion in my examination of censorship in chapter 4.
92 Massey, *For Space*, 153
93 Massey, 168.
94 Online distribution is a possibility that filmmakers sometimes point to in lamenting the state of theatrical exhibition; experiments have been mixed. In 2014, controversy emerged when Cinemalaya film festival entries were surreptitiously uploaded to YouTube. See "Cinemalaya Films Uploaded to YouTube without Authorization," GMA *News Online*, August 10, 2014, https://www.gmanetwork.com/news/lifestyle/artandculture/374186/cinemalaya-films-uploaded-to-youtube-without-authorization/story/; Marga Deona, "Cinemalaya Movies Uploaded Online, Filmmakers Livid," *Rappler*, August 10, 2014, https://www.rappler.com/entertainment/news/65756-cinemalaya-online-angry-filmmakers. NETPAC, the Network for the Promotion of Asia Pacific Cinema, also tried digital delivery with AsiaPacificFilms.com, a website launched in 2010. The collection has since been integrated into the online, ProQuest-affiliated streaming service, Alexander Street. The Singapore-based Viddsee platform has taken up the mantel since 2013, exhibiting Asian short films in partnership with film festivals. Adapting festival language, the company held the Viddsee Juree Awards in the Philippines at the Film Development Council Cinematheque in Manila in 2018.
95 Quoted in de la Cruz, *Philippine New Wave*, 71–72.
96 Quoted in de la Cruz, 30.
97 Quoted in de la Cruz, 30. Bautista's more working-class background may explain his consciousness about these questions. His father was a policeman and his mother worked in catering. Bautista grew up in Cavite, a province outside Manila. See also Alexis A. Tioseco, "A Conversation with Ato Bautista." *Criticine*, January 30, 2006, http://criticine.com/interview_article.php?id=20.
98 The film was produced with a budget of less than $40,000 and shot in thirteen days.
99 The term itself is a portmanteau of the Tagalog words for woman (*babae*) and man (*lalake*). Manalansan, *Global Divas*, 25.
100 Oggs Cruz, "Ang Pagdadalaga ni Maximo Oliveros (2005)," *Lessons from the School of Inattention*, September 25, 2006, http://oggsmoggs.blogspot.com/2006/09/ang-pagdadalaga-ni-maximo-oliveros.html.

101 Jay Weissberg, "A Short Film about the Indio Nacional (or The Prolonged Sorrow Of Filipinos)," *Variety*, March 19, 2006, https://variety.com/2006/film/reviews/a-short-film-about-the-indio-nacional-or-the-prolonged-sorrow-of-filipinos-1200517616/.
102 Quoted in de la Cruz, *Philippine New Wave*, 102.
103 This desire for international visibility can sometimes outweigh the desire to censor critical filmic representations. For example, the Singapore state initially censored and then approved Royston Tan's depiction of youth gangs, 15, in a bid to seem tolerant to foreign eyes. See O. Khoo, "Slang Images."
104 Chow, *Primitive Passions*, 176.
105 Here, ethnicity plays a significant role, as Muhammed is Indian Malaysian, while the independent filmmakers are often, though not exclusively, from the Chinese Malaysian minority who have been pushed out of mainstream filmmaking by postcolonial government policy favoring the Malays, who were economically marginalized under colonization. Khoo sees the indie films' transnational appeal as a part of the films' deep humanism. G. C. Khoo, "Just-Do-It-(Yourself)."
106 Ethnicity is also a factor here, as Anderson points out that most of the Bangkok population is of Chinese Thai descent. Anderson, "The Strange Story of a Strange Beast."
107 Blanco, *Frontier Constitutions*.
108 In his analysis of media cultures in India, Rajagopal has described the Hindu public sphere as fractured along a split between electronic and print media, as well as English-language and Hindi-language print media. Rajagopal, *Politics after Television*, 208. The model he presents is, of course, very specific to the conditions of publicity within Indian media history. The split public marks a moment in which the "spectre of . . . unity remained as a politically potent weapon, even though it came to be acknowledged as an unrealizable goal" (151).
109 Chatterjee, "Beyond the Nation?," 169.
110 Ileto, "Towards a Nonlinear Employment," 101.
111 Ileto, "Towards a Nonlinear Employment."
112 Campos, *End of National Cinema*, 261.
113 When passages I quote come from people whose professional identities tie them with the public culture of film, I name them. Other passages emanate from more casual commenters, many of whose posts are no longer available. To offer them some anonymity, I put their usernames in the end notes but not in text.
114 Grainge, *Ephemeral Media*.
115 See Patajo-Legasto, "Discourses of 'Worlding.'" The most widely read critique of Orientalism in American work on the Philippines is Rey Ileto's "Orientalism and the Study of Philippine Politics." For responses to this work, see Sidel, "Response to Ileto"; Azurin, "Orientalism?"; Curaming, "Beyond Orientalism?"; Hau, "Privileging Roots and Routes."
116 Behar, *Vulnerable Observer*.

117 See, for example, Caroline Hau's critique of the Filipina American author Jessica Hagedorn's much lauded novel, *Dogeaters*. For Hau, the novel works from a position of exteriority, trading depth for surfaces. Hau, "Dogeaters."
118 In some ways, this mixture of critical distance and emotional proximity resonates with the "aca-fan" discourse introduced by Henry Jenkins and developed by scholars like Alexander Doty, Abigail De Kosnik, and Jason Mittell. The aca-fan combines academic intellectualism and emotional engagements, but the engagement is primarily around fictional media worlds, and the main form of affective engagement is pleasure, though Mittell has recently countered this with the idea of the "anti-fan." See Jenkins, "Acafandom and Beyond: Confessions of an Aca-Fan," September 30, 2011, http://henryjenkins.org/2011/09/acafandom_and_beyond_alex_doty_1.html.
119 Abu-Lughod, "Writing against Culture," 466.
120 Teddy Co, interview by the author, May 2010.
121 The U.S.-based International Intellectual Property Alliance removed the Philippines from the USTR piracy watch list in 2013. Ben Arnold O. De Vera, "US Anti-Piracy Lobby Wants Philippines Stricken Off Washington's Watch List," *InterAksyon*, February 11, 2013, http://www.interaksyon.com/business/54764/us-anti-piracy-lobby-wants-philippines-stricken-off-washingtons-watch-list.
122 They were murdered in a botched robbery. Author Laurel Fantauzzo wrote a nonfiction book about them, *The First Impulse*. The title of this book is from Alexis's open letter to Nika, in which he wrote, "The first impulse of a good critic must be of love." Titled "The Letter I Would Love to Read to You in Person," the letter was published in *Rogue* magazine's July 2008 issue. The Asian film magazine *Nang* published a special online issue dedicated to the couple on the tenth anniversary of their deaths. See Ben Slater, "2009–2019," accessed May 10, 2020, *Nang*, https://www.nangmagazine.com/ten-years-after/.
123 No arrests have been made.

Chapter One. Revanchist Cinemas and Bad Audiences

Epigraph: Elvin Valerio, "An Interview with Brillante Mendoza," *ASEF culture 360*, November 30, 2011, http://culture360.asef.org/film/an-interview-with-brillante-mendoza-part-1/.

1 Special economic zones (SEZs) are free-trade zones and free ports that operate under different laws than the rest of the country. For a perspective on gendered labor and the SEZ status, see Gonzalez, "Military Bases."
2 Mendoza's films are among those most associated with the "poverty porn" label. See Gonzaga, "The Cinematographic Unconscious of Slum Voyeurism." Mendoza became the cinematic mouthpiece for Rodrigo Duterte upon the authoritarian president's 2016 election, shooting the State of the Union address in a strange mix of extreme angles and close-ups.

3 For example, statements from industry members, film journalism, political punditry, and newspaper articles.
4 The IFC was founded in 2006. As their website describes, "Our vision is to have an empowered and ethical cooperative of committed, united, independent filmmakers, artists and workers, bound by common dreams and advocacies, trust amidst diversity; managed with passion, determination and creativity; sharing resources and nurturing skills, towards the propagation and sustainability of Philippine independent Cinema." The founding chair was the filmmaker Emmanuel de la Cruz. See "About," Indiecine, accessed April 24, 2020, https://ifcpilipinas.wordpress.com/about/. Indie Sine was not the first screen of its kind. Shangri-La Plaza designated a screen for art cinema in the 1990s, screening Miramax films. Louie's THX cinema, in a Makati shopping complex, screened Hollywood prestige pictures, as well as foreign films. Indie Sine's focus on local art cinema is what sets it apart.
5 Michel, "Going Global"; Shatkin, "City and the Bottom Line"; Smith, *New Urban Frontier*.
6 Tadiar, "Life-Times of Disposability," 22.
7 Tadiar, "Life-Times of Disposability."
8 See Park, Hill, and Saito, *Locating Neoliberalism*; Springer, "Neoliberalism in Southeast Asia."
9 Shatkin, "City and the Bottom Line," 397. More recently, ride-sharing services like Grab and Uber have become widespread. In addition, the Department of Transportation initiated a "PUV (public utility vehicle) Modernization campaign" in June 2017, intended to overhaul transportation infrastructure. Jeepney drivers responded with a two-day strike in October of that year. See Julia Nebrija, *CNN*, "Philippines' Brightly Decorated Jeepneys Face an Uncertain Future," November 12, 2017, https://www.cnn.com/style/article/jeepney-philippines-cultural-icon/index.html; Heather Chen, "Philippines Strike: Filipinos Rally around Iconic Jeepney Drivers," *BBC*, October 16, 2017, https://www.bbc.com/news/world-asia-41632035.
10 Lico, *Arkitekturang Filipino*, 466.
11 "SM City North Edsa's New Annex Makes It World's Third-Largest Mall," *GMA News*, December 11, 2008, http://www.gmanetwork.com/news/story/138821/economy/companies/sm-city-north-edsa-s-new-annex-makes-it-world-s-third-largest-mall.
12 The land Trinoma occupies was already contested space. The mall sits on a plot of land that was formerly the site of People's Park, a project by the former Quezon City mayor Brigido R. Simon Jr. People's Park was a flea market that was built as a livelihood project for the large informal settlement nearby. This may sound like a noble venture, but the settlement already had its own economy. In 1990 they received notice from the city's Integrated Hawkers Management Council that their existing stalls, *sari-sari* (variety) stores, and *carinderia* (open-air eatery) would face demolition to give way to the People's Park project, and the North EDSA Vendors Association began a lawsuit with the help of the Commission on Human Rights. The settlement was demolished in 1995.

See G.R. No. 100150, January 5, 1994, Brigido R. Simon Jr., Carlos Quimpo, Carlito Abelardo, and Generoso Ocampo, Petitioners, vs. Commission On Human Rights, Roque Fermo, and Others as John Does, Respondents, http://www.lawphil.net/judjuris/juri1994/jan1994/gr_100150_1994.html.

13 See Lalu-Santos, "Kambal na Disyerto."
14 Del Mundo, "Film Industry Is Alive," 2.
15 The Cultural Center of the Philippines' Cinemalaya involved corporate funding through the media tycoon Antonio Cojuangco of TV5 and ABC5. ABS-CBN sponsored the Cinema One Originals film festival; the Film Development Council worked with SM for Sineng Pambansa festivals.
16 *Bagong Agos: The Current Wave of Philippine Digital Cinema*, festival program, January 16–24, 2007.
17 Mall multiplexes play a mixture of Hollywood and domestic commercial cinema. I am focusing only on the art-house version of domestic cinema, which was then juxtaposed with the commercial space of the mall, both local and foreign.
18 Dick and Rimmer, "Beyond the Third World City."
19 Smith, *New Urban Frontier*. "Revanchist" means "revenge" in France, referring to the period following the fall of the Paris Commune, in which bourgeois nationalists sought to rid the country of the working class. Smith, *New Urban Frontier*, 45.
20 Smith, *New Urban Frontier*.
21 Whitehead, "Rent Gaps"; Jou, Clark, and Chen, "Gentrification and Revanchist Urbanism."
22 Swanson, "Revanchist Urbanism Heads South," 709.
23 Swanson, 709.
24 Michel, "Going Global"; Shatkin, "City and the Bottom Line," 390.
25 Hansen, *Babel and Babylon*, 13.
26 Hansen, 14.
27 Rafael, "Cellphone and the Crowd."
28 Mitchell, "Annihilation of Space."
29 I intend the demarcation of "good" and "bad" more as organizing labels rather than as heavily theorized terms. But I do feel that they get at the patterns of audience infantilization and monitoring occurring on all sides of these interactions.
30 Seki, "Difference and Alliance."
31 Garrido, "Civil and Uncivil Society."
32 Lopez and Weinstein, *Making of the Middle*.
33 Ileto, "On Sidel's Response." See also Caroline Sy Hau, "Privileging Roots and Routes"; Rivera, "Middle Class Politics."
34 Bryant, *Nongovernmental Organizations*; Silliman and Noble, *Organizing for Democracy*.
35 I will discuss Cubao further in the next chapter.
36 This turn to outdoor space is seen in other, more affluent shopping centers, such as the Ayala Corporation's Greenbelt, located in the business district of

Makati. Strollers may walk through Greenbelt's outdoor space, designed to vaguely resemble a Zen garden, in order to reach other wings of the mall.
37 Hebdige, "Fax to the Future." See also José Capino's discussion of Philippine films' representation of mundane cosmopolitanism in *Dream Factories*, xvii.
38 Nina, "Blessed Cubao," Manila Metblogs, August 2, 2005, http://manila.metblogs.com/2005/08/02/blessed-cubao/.
39 Michel, "Going Global"; Shatkin, "City and the Bottom Line."
40 Shatkin, "City and the Bottom Line," 384. Shatkin points out that although the Philippines has the region's densest network of NGOs, civil society organizations, and people's organizations and the urban poor compose the most crucial electorate, it is still difficult to challenge government measures.
41 "The Illustrated Prophecies," *Asiaweek*, January 27, 1995, 8.
42 For example, in April 2012, a crowd of ten thousand informal settlers and market vendors blocked roads to the Silverio Compound, an informal settlement in the Parañaque City area of the Metro scheduled for demolition. Four people were killed and thirty-six injured. Voltaire Tupaz, "Bloody Demolition: For Socialized Housing or Business?," *Rappler*, April 26, 2012, http://www.rappler.com/move-ph/4338-silver-homes-to-rise-from-rubble-of-demolished-silverio-compound.
43 Tolentino, *Kulturang Mall*, 3.
44 Tolentino, 4.
45 For example, a common employer practice is to hire "end-of-contract workers," who are hired and fired every five months to avoid adhering to the labor code, which requires that they become regular employees after six months. The director Jade Castro reflected this practice to audiences in his 2007 Cinemalaya film, *Endo*. See Marya Salamat, "Workers Turn 'Endo' into Demand to End Contractualization," *Bulatlat*, May 2, 2014, http://bulatlat.com/main/2014/05/02/workers-turn-endo-into-a-demand-to-end-contractualization/#sthash.QmiJ4XZZ.dpuf; Kirsten Birnabe, Penelope P. Endozo, and Sara Isabelle Pacia, "Worker Hired, Fired Every 5 Months," *Philippine Daily Inquirer*, May 1, 2014, http://newsinfo.inquirer.net/598582/worker-hired-fired-every-5-months.
46 Bello, *Anti-Development State*.
47 Connell, "Beyond Manila."
48 M. Pinches, "Consumers Discover New Place for Worship as Malls Transform Cities," *The Australian*, December 16, 1995.
49 Dick and Rimmer, "Beyond the Third World City," 2313.
50 See Bobby Benedicto's *Under Bright Lights* for further discussion of this kind of urbanism in The Fort and Eastwood areas of the city.
51 Jennifer Robinson contends that the image of the global city differs from its formulation as an actual center for global control, working more as a "regulating fiction," which "offers an authorized image of city success (so people can buy into it) that establishes an end point of development for ambitious cities." Robinson, *Ordinary Cities*, 111.
52 "Henry Sy & Family," *Forbes*, May 25, 2017, http://www.forbes.com/profile/henry-sy/.

53 SM Prime Holdings, Annual Report, 2011.
54 Donald, *Imagining the Modern City*, 168.
55 Doreen Massey describes how urban theorists have made disorder and instability the site of political hope: Ernst Laclau argues that the "field of the political" is made possible through antagonism, Richard Sennett advocates the usefulness of disorder, and Jacques Derrida argues that chaos is both risk and opportunity. Massey, *For Space*, 151–53.
56 Walzer, "Pleasures and Costs," 470.
57 Walzer, 471.
58 Fraser, "Rethinking the Public Sphere."
59 Macleod and Ward, "Spaces of Utopia," 163.
60 This trend parallels declining theatrical attendance elsewhere. For example, in 2014, attendance numbers in North America were the lowest they had been in two decades. See Pamela McClintock, "Box Office 2014: Moviegoing Hits Two-Decade Low," *Hollywood Reporter*, December 31, 2014, http://www.hollywoodreporter.com/news/box-office-2014-moviegoing-hits-760766?.
61 While "megaplexes" encompassing twelve or more screens and offering more than cinema for amusement have become the norm in the United States, perhaps because of multiplexes' presence primarily inside urban malls, which already offer other alternatives to cinema, moviegoing in Manila does not reflect these trends. For example, Robinsons Galleria houses ten screens. The amusements available in the cinemas usually do not extend outside movies, though of course, the malls themselves offer a range of entertainments.
62 "Exporters Advised to Extend ASEAN Market Penetration," *Korea Herald*, November 29, 2007.
63 Jennee Grace U. Rubrico, "'Traditional' Media Still Relevant, Says Nielsen Media Research," *Business World*, July 31, 2006, S1/7.
64 Carlos H. Conde, "Filipino Movie Business Fading Out? Piracy, Hollywood Competition and Low Incomes Take Their Toll," *International Herald Tribune*, February 12, 2007, 11.
65 Conde, "Filipino Movie Business."
66 Anna Barbara L. Lorenzo, "Filmmakers Plan Road Map for Revival of Industry," *Business World*, June 22, 2007, S2/20.
67 The Motion Picture Anti-Film Piracy Council (MPAFPC), the Philippine Motion Pictures Producers Association (PMPPA), the Movie Producers and Distributors Association of the Philippines, and large theater operators created a series of videos featuring stars fighting camcorder pirates as recently as 2015, when the "cam copies" were already far fewer than they were in their pretorrents heyday. The ads received some mockery in parody videos posted online. While most featured mainstream stars (e.g., British Filipino heartthrob Derek Ramsay), one featured actors known for independent films. See Edwin P. Sallan, "WATCH | New Anti-Piracy Infomercial to Hit PH Theaters This Month," *Interaksyon*, June 1, 2015, http://www.interaksyon.com/entertainment/watch-new-anti-piracy-infomercial-to-hit-ph-theaters-this-month/.

68 Camaligan, quoted in Reyma Buan-Deveza, "Film Industry Stakeholders Commit to Anti-Piracy Drive," ABS-CBN News, July 19, 2008, http://news.abs-cbn.com/entertainment/06/19/08/film-industry-stakeholders-commit-anti-piracy-drive.
69 Buan-Deveza, "Film Industry Stakeholders Commit."
70 As a way to ask whether an idea will hold up with the people, former president Ramon Magsaysay famously said, "Can we defend it in Plaza Miranda?"
71 The major freeway that cuts through the center of Manila, Epifanio de los Santos Avenue, known by its acronym EDSA, has been the site of three "EDSA Revolutions." The first, February 22–25 1986, was the "People Power" revolution that led to the ousting of Marcos. The second, in 2001, was popularly called "EDSA II," and took place January 17–20, 2001. It ended with the removal of Joseph Estrada from the presidential office and installed his vice president, Gloria Macapagal-Arroyo. This is known as a middle- and upper-class protest, as Estrada, a former action film star, was popularly known as the hero of the masses. See Tolentino, "Capital Infrastructuring," 47. Four months after the protest, "EDSA III" took place in April to protest the ousting. The protest's aim was to storm the Malacañang Palace, the presidential residence, though it was stopped before it could reach it.
72 JOSEPH E. ESTRADA, petitioner, vs. GLORIA MACAPAGAL-ARROYO, respondent, G.R. Nos. 146710–15, March 2, 2001, http://sc.judiciary.gov.ph/jurisprudence/2001/mar2001/146710_15.htm
73 Rafael, "Cellphone and the Crowd."
74 Rafael, 417.
75 Rafael, 418.
76 Rafael, 418.
77 Rafael, 414.
78 Andrew Higson discusses this distinction in "Concept of National Cinema."
79 Rafael, "Cellphone and the Crowd," 422.
80 Rafael, 414.
81 Aries B. Espinosa, "IPO, OMB to Movie Pirates: We'll Catch You with Night Vision Goggles," *Philippine Daily Inquirer*, April 29, 2013, http://entertainment.inquirer.net/91727/ipo-omb-to-movie-pirates-well-catch-you-with-night-vision-goggles#ixzz3FIph2dVY.
82 Toby Miller argues that piracy cultivates audiences for and familiarity with Hollywood films among people who would otherwise be outside its reach. Miller, "Global Hollywood 2010."
83 "Costly Cinema Tickets Criticized," *Manila Standard*, December 3, 2007.
84 "Costly Cinema Tickets Criticized."
85 Rafael, "Cellphone and the Crowd," 117.
86 Rafael, *Promise of the Foreign*, 116.
87 Sennett, *Fall of Public Man*, 206.
88 Miller et al., *Global Hollywood 2*.
89 Connie Veneracion, "The Shang Cinema Example," *Manila Standard*, May 3, 2007.
90 Veneracion, "Shang Cinema Example."

91 Veneracion, "Shang Cinema Example."
92 De Guzman, *Si Nora Aunor*.
93 Dexter Osorio, "Dex in the City," *Manila Times*, May 8, 2005.
94 Lorente, "Grip of English"; Tupas, "Bourdieu."
95 Hansen, *Babel and Babylon*; Rafael, *Promise of the Foreign*, 116.
96 "The Rich Share Similar Tastes with the Masa," *Business World*, October 11, 2007, S1/1.
97 "The Rich Share Similar Tastes with the Masa."
98 "The Rich Share Similar Tastes with the Masa."
99 While I have not found official data regarding how the wealthy consume DVDs, my own encounters with wealthier friends demonstrated the ubiquity of piracy, which falls into its own class-based hierarchies, with wealthier patrons shopping (or sending household help to shop) for DVDs in places like Makati Cinema Square or Metrowalk rather than the lower-income neighborhood of Quiapo or sending domestic helpers for palengke DVD shopping.
100 For boundary-crossing stars, see B. Lim, "Sharon's Noranian Turn."
101 Nonoy L. Lauzon, "MMFF 2013: A defining event for Filipino Cinema," *Philippine Daily Inquirer*, January 8, 2014, http://entertainment.inquirer.net/128545/mmff-2013-a-defining-event-for-filipino-cinema#ixzz3FJMIHln7. The critic Dodo Dayao describes the MMFF as "everybody's favorite horse to flog after it went from a legitimate platform for studios to showcase their prestige films into a protectionist comfort zone for their cash-cow franchises. The way it seals off the last two weeks of every year, and declares an embargo on foreign films, does seem designed to optimize the conditions for riskier domestic films to have not only an audience they wouldn't normally have any other time of the year but a legitimate stab at significant revenue. In many ways, sure, it was a protectionist gambit, too, albeit with a slightly nobler bent." Dodo Dayao, "When Did the MMFF Become a Venue for Cash-Cow Franchises?," *Esquire*, January 1, 2017, https://www.esquiremag.ph/culture/arts-and-entertainment/when-did-the-mmff-become-a-venue-for-cash-cow-franchises-a1714-20170101-lfrm.
102 Fel V. Maragay, "Tax Break for Cinema," *Manila Standard*, June 21, 2008.
103 Maricel E. Estavillo, "Digital Technology Tagged as Philippine Film Industry's Available Hope for Survival," *Business World*, September 25, 2006, S1/2.
104 Carlos H. Conde. "Filipino Movie Business Fading Out? Piracy, Hollywood Competition and Low Incomes Take Their toll," *International Herald Tribune*, February 12, 2007, 11.
105 Conde, "Filipino Movie Business Fading Out?"
106 Conde, "Filipino Movie Business Fading Out?"
107 Conde, "Filipino Movie Business Fading Out?"
108 "Turnaround for Local Cinema?," *Business World*, April 2, 2007, S1/1.
109 "RP's Film Industry Grows 40%," *BusinessWorld*, March 19, 2007, S1/6.
110 Anna Barbara L. Lorenzo with Maricel E. Estavillo, "Movie Industry Hoping to Regain Luster," *Business World*, September 26, 2006, S1/1.
111 Lorenzo with Estavillo, "Movie Industry Hoping to Regain Luster."

112 For more historical context on exhibition, see Tofighian, *Blurring the Colonial Binary*. Nick Deocampo's historical tomes on Filipino film history also provide valuable examples. While not primarily focused on exhibition, they are so voluminous in their coverage that exhibition and distribution receive ample attention. Decampo, *Cine*; Decampo, *Film*.
113 Athique and Hill, "Multiplex Cinemas," 115.
114 Athique and Hill, 116.
115 Athique and Hill, 116.
116 India is referred to as among the fast growing and influential "BRIC" countries (Brazil, Russia, India and China), while the Philippines has been named as one of the newly rising "PINE" economies (Philippines, Indonesia, Nigeria, and Ethiopia). See Michael Schuman "Forget the BRICs; Meet the PINEs," *Time*, March 13, 2014, http://time.com/22779/forget-the-brics-meet-the-pines/. These discourses of economic development have been heavily critiqued. In relation to the Philippines, see Cielito F. Habito, "A Strengthened Economy?," *Philippine Daily Inquirer*, September 16, 2014, http://opinion.inquirer.net/78525/a-strengthened-economy; Jillian Keenan, "The Grim Reality behind the Philippines' Economic Growth," *The Atlantic*, May 7, 2013, http://www.theatlantic.com/international/archive/2013/05/the-grim-reality-behind-the-philippines-economic-growth/275597/.
117 Ganti, *Producing Bollywood*, 17. Of course, one of the biggest differences between the Philippine and Indian mainstream film industries is the latter's continued health and wide range versus the former's smaller scale.
118 Shatkin, "City and the Bottom Line," 384.
119 Acland, *Screen Traffic*, 207–10.
120 Acland, 207.
121 Acland, 210–11.
122 Anna Tsing proposes distinguishing between globalization (the ideology of globalism) and transnationalism (a practice comprised of "transborder" projects on the ground). Tsing, "Global Situation."
123 That these patterns can be seen in different ways across multiple settings in the urban south suggests the possibility of what Françoise Lionnet and Shu-mei Shih term "minor transnationalism." It thus questions the notion of transnationalism as either convergent (as in the global urbanism discourses cited above) or binary (as in local-global interactions), allowing for novel, perhaps unexpected points of "lateral" contact. Lionnet and Shih, *Minor Transnationalism*.
124 Higson, "Concept of National Cinema."
125 See Higson, 38.
126 Festivals are common in malls. (For example, embassies hold festivals of their countries' cinemas in more upscale malls.) Perhaps the closest recent predecessor to the Bagong Agos model would be Nick Deocampo's Pelikula at Lipunan (cinema and society) series, organized through the Mowelfund Institute as a means of celebrating the Philippines' cinematic heritage. See "Two Lost Films to Be Screened at Pelikula at Lipunan Fest," *Manila Times*, February 9, 2004,

http://www.aenet.org/family/zambonews1.htm. Tikoy Aguiluz's Cinemanila festival is also mall based, though it focuses both on local and foreign films.

127 Warner, *Publics and Counterpublics*.
128 Warner, *Publics and Counterpublics*.
129 Emmanuel Dela Cruz, "IndieSine: The Home of Brave New Works," *Bagong Agos: The Current Wave of Philippine Digital Cinema*, festival program, January 16–24, 2007. The other "well-known cinema franchise" in question is SM, who only show "family friendly" fare in their cinemas.
130 Lang, quoted in Rosenberg, "Plex Drive."
131 Jeffrey O. Valisno, "Independent Cinema Finds a Home," *Business World*, January 19, 2007, S3/3.
132 Valisno, "Independent Cinema Finds a Home."
133 The 1986 Constitution states: "The State recognizes the sanctity of family life and shall protect and strengthen the family as a basic autonomous social institution." Protection of the family is thus a national principle. Quoted in McCoy, *An Anarchy of Families*.
134 McCoy, *Anarchy of Families*.
135 Acland, *Screen Traffic*, 47.
136 See Torres, "Piracy Boom Boom."
137 Acland, *Screen Traffic*.
138 Acland, *Screen Traffic*.
139 "Daluyan Awards," *Bagong Agos: The Current Wave of Philippine Digital Cinema*, festival program, January 16–24, 2007.
140 "Daluyan Awards."
141 Chatterjee, "Beyond the Nation?," 31. See also Srinivas, "Is There a Public."
142 Chatterjee, "Beyond the Nation?"
143 Fapweb, "FAP Officials Attend Indie Film Summit," FDCP, November 10, 2008, http://filmacademyphil.org/?p=1127.
144 Morales, quoted in Bayani San Diego Jr., "State of IndieSine," *Philippine Daily Inquirer*, March 15, 2010, https://www.pressreader.com/philippines/philippine-daily-inquirer-1109/20100315/285224484069264.
145 Alix, quoted in San Diego, "State of IndieSine."
146 Biglang-awa, quoted in San Diego, "State of IndieSine."
147 The banishment of R-rated work from the cinemas led to the end of independent works that specialized in more "adult" content. See Tolentino, "Bomba Queens"; Flores, "Bodies of Work." In addition, SM managed to skirt its own restrictions by working with the MTRCB to create the R-16 classification. See Marinel R. Cruz, "MTRCB Reviews Classification System to Include R-16 Rating," *Philippine Daily Inquirer*, May 19, 2012, http://entertainment.inquirer.net/41567/mtrcb-reviews-classification-system-to-include-r-16-rating.
148 Jose Javier Reyes, quoted in Edwin P. Sallan and Enrique V. Ramos, "Forum: Would an R-16 Rating Benefit the Film Industry and the Audience?," *Interaksyon*, June 16, 2012, http://www.interaksyon.com/entertainment/forum-would-an-r-16-rating-benefit-the-film-industry-and-the-audience-2/.

149 Jim Libiran, quoted in Sallan and Ramos, "Forum: Would an R-16 Rating Benefit the Film Industry and the Audience?"
150 Hau, *Chinese Question*, 7.
151 Rafael, *White Love*, 187. For more on the hyphen, see Hau, *Chinese Question*, 12–13.

Chapter Two. The Quiapo Cinematheque

Epigraph: Sandwich, "DVD X," *Five on the Floor*, compact disc, EMI Philippines, 2006.

1 Ramon Lobato examines the implications of the term "piracy" in "The Paradoxes of Piracy."
2 Warner, *Publics and Counterpublics*; Fraser, "Rethinking the Public Sphere."
3 Fraser, "Rethinking the Public Sphere."
4 Eickelman and Anderson, "Redefining Muslim Publics," 5; Lahiri, "Rhetorical 'Indios.'"
5 R. Reyes, *Love, Passion, and Patriotism*. During the Spanish colonial period, *ilustrados* were nationalist intellectuals.
6 R. Reyes, *Love, Passion, and Patriotism*, quoted in Cruz, *Transpacific Femininities*, 78.
7 Cruz, *Transpacific Femininities*, 78.
8 Cruz, 78.
9 Hau, "Dogeaters."
10 Obusan, "Multireligious Filipino Pilgrimage," 150–51.
11 Silvestre, "Chronicle of Music," 293.
12 Andrade, "Quiapo in the History," 66.
13 Tolentino, "Piracy and Its Regulation;" San Juan, "Ethnic Identity."
14 "Optical Media Board Law Signed by GMA Yesterday," *Manila Bulletin*, February 11, 2004; "USTR Decision Recognizes RP's Anti-Piracy Efforts," Intellectual Property Office of the Philippines, press release, accessed July 2, 2016, http://www.ipophil.gov.ph/htm_doc/pressrelease02212006.htm.
15 It is important to note that the OMB also made efforts to nuance this dichotomy. For instance, Edu Manzano received media attention for convincing some Muslim traders to cooperate with the OMB, specifically regarding locally produced 2007 Metro Manila Film Festival (MMFF) movies, which played during an annual two-week blackout of foreign films in Manila multiplexes. Creating the idea of "good" versus "bad" Muslim traders, Manzano stated, "If not for the help of our Muslim brothers, the local movie industry, especially the producers who joined the film festival, could have lost millions in projected revenues." See Isah V. Red, "Traders of Pirated DVD Now OMB Informants," *Manila Standard Today*, January 15, 2008, http://www.manilastandardtoday.com/?page=goodLife4_jan15_2008.
16 While pornography is arguably the most common media form, its presence in public space is still out of the ordinary.
17 Baumgärtel, "Culture of Piracy."

18 Wilinsky, "A Thinly Disguised Art Veneer."
19 San Juan, "Paradox of Multiculturalism."
20 San Juan, "Paradox of Multiculturalism."
21 As an example of how this has been mythologized in film, Brillante Mendoza's independent film *Tirador* (2007) takes place in Quiapo, depicting the lives of residents who eke out a hand-to-mouth living through petty crime. Laurice Guillen offers a more mainstream variation in her 2004 religious melodrama, *Santa Santita (Magdalena, the Unholy Saint)* (2004), which depicts a Quiapo Church amulet vendor who finds herself gifted with healing powers. The film is not from a mainstream studio but from Unitel, which produces and distributes both mainstream films and art-house fare with high production values and wider aesthetic and narrative accessibility. Quiapo thus appears in a wide range of depictions.
22 Benjamin, "Work of Art."
23 Peterson, *Creating Country Music*; Halbwachs, *On Collective Memory*.
24 Halbwachs, *On Collective Memory*.
25 Joaquin, *Almanac for Manileños*, 16.
26 Zialcita, "Revitalizing the City," 10.
27 Joaquin, *Almanac for Manileños*; Zialcita, *Quiapo*.
28 Fraser, "Rethinking the Public Sphere," 60.
29 See chapter 4 for more on censorship.
30 The proportion of the population who consider themselves "poor" is 70 percent. Tolentino, "Cinema and the State in Crisis." In his ethnographic study of media ethics and representations of suffering in the Philippines, Jonathan Ong writes that certain television shows, such as *Wowowee*, even take on the role of governance by providing social services. Ultimately, Ong argues that such representations fail to create a united public, as more affluent classes turn a blind eye to suffering. Ong, *Poverty of Television*.
31 Ingawanij, "Dialectics of Independence."
32 Gertjan Zuilhof, "A Programmer's Chronicles," Rotterdam International Film Festival, April 2006, accessed September 19, 2008, http://professionals.filmfestivalrotterdam.com/eng/blogs/gertjan_zuilhof/a_programmers_chronicles_april_2006.aspx.
33 Eric S. Caruncho, "The Quiapo Cinematheque," *Philippine Daily Inquirer*, June 24, 2007, 9, 12.
34 Mighty, "How Piracy Helps the Movie Industry," *Penstalker's Movie Blog*, August 6, 2008, http://www.penstalker.com/2008/how-piracy-helps-the-movie-industry.
35 Rain Contreras, "Microsoft to Mass-Produce Single-Play DVDs," *Pinoy Tech Blog*, October 3, 2005, accessed September 19, 2008, http://www.pinoytechblog.com/archives/microsoft-and-single-p . . . .
36 Angel, "Trip to Quiapo," *The Coffeehouse*, July 23, 2007, http://thecoffeehouse-angel.blogspot.com/2008/07/trip-to-quiapo.html.
37 Thea Alberto, "Pirated Goods Seized at Ortigas, Greenhills Malls," *INQ7.net*, August 29, 2006. Quoted in "Video Piracy," baratillo@cubao, August 30, 2006, http://baratillo.net/?p=502.

38 Jules, "DVD Pirates, Quiapo and Art films Gone Loco!," *Idiot Board*, July 21, 2004, accessed September 18, 2008, http://idiotboard.blogspot.com/2004/07/dvd-pirates-quiapo-and- . . . .
39 For an overview of this discussion, see Lobato, "Six Faces of Piracy," in *Shadow Economies*.
40 Lobato, *Shadow Economies*, 3.
41 "How Pirated DVDs Make the World a Better Place," *Atlas(t): The Galleon Trade Edition*, August 1, 2007, http://clairelight.typepad.com/atlast_galleon_trade/2007/08/how-pirated-dvd.html.
42 "How Quiapo's DVDS Promote Peace," *The Q*, November 26, 2007, http://quiapo-dvd.blogspot.com/2007/11/youtube-documentary-on-quiapos-dvd.html.
43 Stephanie Dychiu, "Pax DVD in Quiapo," *GMA News Online*, September 20, 2009, http://www.gmanetwork.com/news/story/172742/news/nation/pax-dvd-in-quiapo.
44 Amaya, *Citizenship Excess*, 42–44.
45 Ghertner, "Why Gentrification Theory Fails."
46 Zukin, "Consuming Authenticity,"
47 Zukin, 729.
48 Duncombe, *Notes from Underground*, 148–82.
49 Goyitarca, comment, August 24, "Quiapo! Quiapo! Quiapo!," *Decide. Commit. Succeed*, August 24, 2008, accessed September 18, 2008, http://goyitarca.multiply.com/photos/album/16/quiapo_quiapo_ . . . .
50 sharongil, "The Thing about Quiapo . . . ," *Gecko Crossings*, March 13, 2007, http://sharongil.multiply.com/journal/item/28.
51 Jules, "Quiapo Underground: A Repost," *The Idiot Board*, February 6, 2005, http://idiotboard.blogspot.com/2005_02_01_archive.html.
52 Adler, "Travel"; Pratt, *Imperial Eyes*.
53 San Juan, "Ethnic Identity," 398.
54 San Juan, 401.
55 San Juan, 401.
56 Tolentino, "Piracy Regulation," 10.
57 mojacko, "Latest DVDs You Bought," QPDVD, September 8, 2008, http://qpdv.freeforums.org/latest-dvds-you-bought-t7-60.html.
58 See Klinger, *Beyond the Multiplex*, 34–36.
59 Isadora, comment, 4:00 P.M., February 25, 2008, comment on ajay, "Lasang Pinoy 3: Quiapo Street Food," *Ajay's Writings on the Wall*, October 24, 2005, http://www.annalyn.net/2005/10/24/lasang-pinoy-3-quiapo-street-food/.
60 "How Pirated DVDs Make the World a Better Place," *Atlas(t): The Galleon Trade Edition*, August 1, 2007, http://clairelight.typepad.com/atlast_galleon_trade/2007/08/how-pirated-dvd.html.
61 Sidney, Snoeck, "Quiapo," *My Sari-Sari Store*, October 15, 2007, http://my_sarisari_store.typepad.com/my_sarisari_store/quiapo/.
62 Angel, "Trip to Quiapo," *The Coffeehouse*, July 23, 2007, http://thecoffeehouse-angel.blogspot.com/2008/07/trip-to-quiapo.html.

63 "Downtown," *Ka-Blog!*, January 8, 2007, http://bukaneg.blog.friendster.com/2007/01/downtown/.
64 sharongil, "The Thing about Quiapo . . . ," *Gecko Crossings*, March 13, 2007, http://sharongil.multiply.com/journal/item/28.
65 sharongil, "The Thing about Quiapo . . ."
66 sharongil, "The Thing about Quiapo . . ."
67 ajay, "Lasang Pinoy 3: Quiapo Street Food," *Ajay's Writings on the Wall*, October 24, 2005, http://www.annalyn.net/2005/10/24/lasang-pinoy-3-quiapo-street-food.
68 chinita, "City on Foot: Pinaywife Venturing to Quiapo, Manila," *Pinaywife Atbp.*, February 18, 2008, http://pinaywifeatbp.blogspot.com/2008/02/city-on-foot-pinaywife-venturing-to.html.
69 The term "coño" is a Spanish curse word meaning "vagina"; it was an insult used toward inferiors. In a clever play of linguistic transference, the Filipino use of the term now refers to wealthy mestizos of Spanish descent. The historian Ambeth Ocampo wrote a piece for the *Inquirer* about the sometimes humorous shifts in meanings as words move from dialect to dialect or from Spanish to Tagalog. See Ambeth Ocampo, "El coño de Tondo," *Philippine Daily Inquirer*, August 12, 2009, http://opinion.inquirer.net/inquireropinion/columns/view/20090812-219864/El-coo-de-Tondo.
70 misterq, "Nasunog ang Good Earth!," QPDVD, August 4, 2008, http://qpdv.freeforums.org/nasunog-ang-good-earth-t29.html.
71 Zukin, "Changing Landscapes of Power," 546.
72 "Pirated Discs Worth P10M Seized in Quiapo Raid," *GMA News Online*, July 2, 2011, http://www.gmanetwork.com/news/story/225072/news/nation/pirated-discs-worth-p10m-seized-in-quiapo-raid.

Chapter Three. Alternative Exhibition

Epigraphs: "Mag:net News," Mag:net Galleries, September 2007, accessed July 3, 2008, http://magnet.com.ph/news/2007-09.htm; "Cubao X," *Cubao-X* (blog), July 29, 2006, http://cubao-x.blogspot.com/search?q=+a+sense+of+place/.

1 The establishment was named for the creatures in the film *Gremlins* (dir. Joe Dante, 1984).
2 Acland, *Screen Traffic*; Cubitt, "Distribution and Media Flows"; Himpele, *Circuits of Culture*; Lobato, "Subcinema"; Verhoeven, "Film Distribution."
3 These differential distribution patterns can sometimes lead to unexpected cultural connections. For example, the distribution of low-cost, Hong Kong kung fu movies to second-run theaters and video stores in African American neighborhoods led to a popular culture fusion of Asian and black culture. See Gateward, "Wong Fei Hong"; Marchetti, "Jackie Chan"; Prashad, *Everybody Was Kung Fu Fighting*.
4 In her piece "Rethinking Distribution," Alisa Perren asks, "How does one draw distinctions between production and distribution or distribution and

exhibition or retailing? Do such distinctions matter, and if so, to whom?" (170). Viewing distribution from the receiving end of the channel, distribution and exhibition are especially linked in these sites of semi-industrial circulation, where filmmakers often circulate their work through social interactions rather than industrial means.

5 Acland, *Screen Traffic*.
6 The full quote: "It's cosmopolitan but definitely not a fadmonger. Call it the local Greenwich Village if you must, but its character makes it uniquely Filipino." See Askmogs, "An Art Space Called Cubao X," *Think Philippines*, May 14, 2008, http://www.thinkphilippines.com/life/an-art-space-called-cubao-x .html, 80. There are distinct differences in scale between these two sites—Greenwich Village in the 1960s is a far cry from Katipunan Avenue, Cubao, or Remedios Circle in the early twenty-first century, which are much smaller outposts of alternative culture, with a much more moderated degree of subcultural identity. However, the New York City neighborhood has become easy shorthand to describe the kind of bohemian communities Bane describes, and what they share is an urban turn to folk, ritual, and subcultural styles.
7 Banes, *Greenwich Village 1963*, 9.
8 Banes, 80.
9 Tadiar, "Life-Times of Disposability," 22.
10 Tadiar, 22.
11 Tadiar, 22. Tadiar elaborates the conflicts between neoliberalism's time of financialization and the temporalities of "disposable lives." This explanation sets the stage for her argument. The piece's larger argument is interested in the kinds of subjectivities that are illegible to neoliberal models, existing outside such models' borders while playing a critical role in upholding them: "Beyond the moment of simple reproduction, within which the 'free' work of slaves, colonial peoples, and subordinate women served to augment the surplus labor-time expropriated from labor through formal processes of capitalist exchange, I am also speaking of the arena of not only this kind of hidden *labor-time* in the reproduction of the worker but also forms of remaindered *life-times*, the time of social reproduction that lies beyond contemporary modes of exploitation of life as living labor."
12 See Gaonkar, "On Alternative Modernities."
13 This subject merits more research by someone inside this community. Such theaters are often former single-screen cinemas, evoking a moviegoing past. Several are in the former downtown cinemagoing hub of Quiapo (see chapter 2). For a descriptive account of how such cruising worked in the mid-2000s, see the blog post "Theater Cruising," *Pinoy Gay Guy Confidential*, June 30, 2009, http://pinoygayguyconfidential.blogspot.com/2009/06/theater-cruising.html. More mainstream, multiplex theaters have become cruising sites at later shows, including Robinsons Galleria, which was especially known because of showing gay indie films. See jimmusan, "Kabaklaan Pasok!!!," *Missology: The Science of Beauty*, January 14, 2013, 4:34 A.M., http://missosology.info/forum/viewtopic.php?f=1&t=176825. For more on Manila's

gay cultural spaces and their intersections with class, see Benedicto, *Under Bright Lights*.
14 Baudelaire, *Painter of Modern Life*, 13.
15 Himpele, *Circuits of Culture*, 23–24.
16 Verhoeven, "Film Distribution," 45.
17 Acland, *Screen Traffic*.
18 Acland, 244.
19 Acland, 237. Unlike Henry Jenkins's idea of "pop cosmopolitanism" as an outcome of convergence culture, Acland accounts for the discrepant rates of transnational flows. Jenkins, "Pop Cosmopolitanism."
20 Highmore, *Cityscapes*, 9; Massey, *Space, Place, and Gender*.
21 Mike Crang discusses this notion of subjunctive, future perfect space in "Rhythms of the City," 197.
22 Lefebvre, *Writings on Cities*, 16.
23 Tadiar, "Manila's New Metropolitan Form."
24 Tolentino, "The Capital Infrastructuring," 160.
25 Virilio, "Third Window," 188; see also Friedberg, "Urban Mobility."
26 Benedicto, *Under Bright Lights*, 60.
27 Benedicto, 60.
28 A. Scott, "Shoe Industry of Marikina," 76.
29 Ronald James Panis, "Cubao Goes Vintage and Funky," GMA News TV, OFW Station, January 8, 2008, http;//www.gmanews.tv/story/75769/Cubao-goes-vintage-and-funky.
30 Clone at Cubao X, "Acid42 Is the Soft Asian Enemy," May 1, 2005, http://acid42.bluechronicles.net/blog/?p=160.
31 Pj, "Cubao X or Formerly Known as Marikina Shoe Expo," *FilTrip*, February 7, 2008, http://filtrip.com/2008/02/07/Cubao-x-or-formerly-known-as-marikina-shoe-expo.
32 Jesse Hernandez, "Cubao Daytrip and a Tenuous Metaphor about Haunting," *Jesse Liwag Cuts His Finger, Really, Here Look*, October 16, 2005, http://jesseliwag.blogspot.com/2005/10/cubao-daytrip-and-tenuous-metaphor.html.
33 Boyer, *City of Collective Memory*, 4.
34 Naficy, "Poetics and Practice."
35 Deener, "Commerce as the Structure."
36 Gallaga's World War II film, *Oro, Plata, Mata* (1982), circulated in international festivals, but he has also directed commercial work, such as Regal's horror anthology franchise, *Shake, Rattle, and Roll*.
37 Matti's action thriller *On the Job* (2013) was a coproduction between Reality and Star Cinema. The film played in the Directors' Fortnight of the 2013 Cannes Film Festival, while also being picked up for an American remake. In 2014, Reality created the Reality Film Lab, a month-long workshop for up-and-coming filmmakers. See "XYZ Confirms *On the Job* Remake," *Film Business Asia*, June 26, 2013, http://www.filmbiz.asia/news/xyz-confirms-on-the-job-remake.

38 "Mogwai," *Mogwai Cinematheque*, accessed June 4, 2008, http://mogwaifilm.multiply.com.
39 Philbert Ortiz Dy, "Mogwai," *Click the City*, December 11, 2007, http://guides.clickthecity.com/metro/?p=2484.
40 Wilinsky, *Sure Seaters*; Huffer, "Popcorn-Free Zone"; Wasson, *Museum Movies*.
41 Ronald James Panis, "Cubao Goes Vintage and Funky," GMA News TV, OFW Station, January 8, 2008, http://www.gmanews.tv/story/75769/Cubao-goes-vintage-and-funky.
42 Tannock, "Nostalgia Critique," 454.
43 Davison, "Heritage," 32.
44 Himpele, *Circuits of Culture*, 63–64.
45 Marketing professor Raymond Allan G. Vergara argues that Mag:net's combination of the art gallery with a bar and restaurant makes it more democratic than some art spaces. In Vergara's assessment, this is an effort to educate what he terms "the common folk" about art: "The bar gallery is a down-to-earth art gallery that aims to bring art to the masses. The idea is to take out the reserve and staidness that may be found in a traditional art exhibit to encourage the common folk to look at and appreciate art." Because he is interested in the space as a sustainable business model, he commends Mag:net's later move to the affluent Fort Bonifacio area. Vergara, "Art of Mag:net," n.p.
46 A common joke delineating the reputations of the city's universities is that one goes to U. P. if one has a lot of brains and no money, to Ateneo if one has a little brains and some money, and De La Salle, a university in the City of Manila, if one has no brains and a lot of money. Many alternative filmmakers are associated with one of these institutions, called, alongside the University of Santo Tomas, the "Big Four" schools.
47 Yelle, "Sinekalikasan@Cinekatipunan," *Blogging Miles around the Metro*, April 12, 2007. http://www.bloggingmiles.com/events/sinekalikasancinekatipunan/.
48 Dolan, *Utopia in Performance*, 25–26.
49 Dolan, 26.
50 "Cinekatipunan: Screening against All Odds," Mag:net News, September 2007, accessed June 6, 2008, http://magnet.com.ph/news/2007-09.htm.
51 "Cinekatipunan: Screening against All Odds."
52 "Cinekatipunan: Screening against All Odds."
53 "Cinekatipunan: Screening against All Odds." Jonas Burgos was a farmer and activist who was abducted from a Quezon City mall by armed men on April 28, 2007. He was a member of leftist organizations the Philippine military deemed "enemies of the state." For more on the Jonas Burgos campaign, please see Free Jonas Burgos Movement, "Sa Lahat ng Sulok—a Photo Essay," *Free Jonas Burgos*, August 31, 2008, http://freejonasburgosmovement.blogspot.com/.
54 Stewart, *On Longing*, 13.

55 Bernardo later become a well-known director of features. Her "maindie" romantic comedy, *Kita Kita*, produced through film industry star Piolo Pascual's studio, Spring Films, became the highest-grossing "independent" film in 2017. See "'Kita Kita' passes 'Heneral Luna' as PH's top grossing indie movie," ABS-CBN News, August 10, 2017, https://news.abs-cbn.com/entertainment/08/09/17/kita-kita-passes-heneral-luna-as-phs-top-grossing-indie-movie.
56 Warner, *Publics and Counterpublics*, 95.
57 Warner, 96.
58 Warner, 66.
59 I do not want to suggest that there is no sense of an industry here, but that it is a microscale, nonprofit, disaggregated "scene" more than an institutionalized industry.
60 In 1975, local film producers initiated a presidential proclamation that required all first-run theaters in Metro Manila to solely exhibit Filipino films for ten days, beginning Christmas day. See Lumbera, "Problems in Philippine Film," 266. Since 1978, the Philippine Motion Picture Producers Association, the Movie Workers' Welfare Fund, and the Cultural Center of the Philippines choose ten new films from the end-of-year production to highlight during the festival.
61 Isah V. Red, "Manila Film Festival: A Hundred Percent Tax Rebate," *Manila Standard*, June 24, 1999, C8–9, https://news.google.com/newspapers?nid=1370&dat=19990624&id=UZQVAAAAIBAJ&sjid=NAsEAAAAIBAJ&pg=6484,2807699&hl=en.
62 Red, "Manila Film Festival."
63 More recently, the 2016 iteration of the festival sparked controversy for featuring primarily independent films. Nonetheless, it was voted the favorite Manila film festival in *Pinoy Rebyu*, an online film blog. The independent film producer Moira Lang posted in response on Facebook, "From most reviled not so long ago to this. Not bad. May magandang naitanim ang #reelvolution. (There is a beautiful reelvolution being planted)." See Nicki Wang, "MMFF 2016 Goes Indie, Snubs Big Films," *Manila Standard*, November 22, 2016, http://manilastandard.net/showbitz/222088/mmff-2016-goes-indie-snubs-big-films.html; "Erik Matti Defends Indie Films, MMFF 2016 Lineup," *Rappler*, November 24, 2016, http://www.rappler.com/entertainment/news/153447-erik-matti-defends-mmff-2016-lineup; Nathalie Tomada, "2016 MMFF Line-Up Is 'Final and Unanimous,'" *PhilStar*, November 24, 2016, http://www.philstar.com/entertainment/2016/11/24/1644797/2016-mmff-line-final-and-unanimous#z6e5qDeWOAVdMmtR.99. The subsequent iterations have returned to mainstream fare. The critic Philbert Dy, who had defended the MMFF's possibilities, admitted defeat in December 2018. He posted a Twitter thread that went viral, saying, "And now we have this year. I look at this lineup, and I just feel defeated. That's it, really. My skipping the MMFF isn't an act of defiance. It's an admission of defeat. They won, I lost. I just don't think it's going to get any better anymore. There's nothing else to do." See "Film Critic Philbert Dy Says He's Skipping This Year's Metro

Manila Film Festival," *Coconuts Manila*, December 26, 2018, https://coconuts.co/manila/lifestyle/film-critic-philbert-dy-says-hes-skipping-years-metro-manila-film-festival/.

64 Jessica Zafra, "Metro Manila Film Festival 2012 Moviethon," *Interaksyon*, January 2, 2013, http://www.interaksyon.com/article/51785/jessica-zafra—metro-manila-film-festival-2012-moviethon-day-6-the-battle-for-dingdongs-dingdong.

65 Since 2017, the Film Development Council of the Philippines has partnered with the Cinema Exhibitors Association of the Philippines to create a similar event, the Pista ng Pelikulang Pilipino (Festival of Filipino Films), held annually for one week in August. The festival screens "new quality genre Filipino films" during a one-week blackout on foreign film exhibition. See "Pista ng Pelikulang Pilipino," Film Development Council of the Philippines, accessed June 10, 2020, http://pistangpelikulangpilipino.ph/.

66 Sarah Brown, "The Philippines Shows the World How to Celebrate Christmas," *CNN*, December 5, 2012, http://www.cnn.com/2012/12/05/world/asia/irpt-xmas-philippines-traditions/.

67 Devotees attend mass in the earliest hours of the morning (between 3:00 and 5:00 A.M.), with completion of all nine masses resulting in an answered prayer.

68 See chapter 2. For a more detailed overview, see Norma I. Alcaron, "Role of the Plaza," 87–106.

69 Acland, *Screen Traffic*, 239–40.

70 Alexis Tioseco, "One 'M' Is Better Than Two," *Concentrated Nonsense*, December 30, 2007, http;//alexistioseco.wordpress.com/2007/12/30/mmff-mff/.

71 Tioseco, "One 'M' Is Better Than Two."

72 Alexis Tioseco, "The First Unofficial MFF (Mogwai Film Festival)," *Criticine*, December 27, 2007, http://www.criticine.com.

73 Tioseco, "The First Unofficial MFF."

74 Czach, "Film Festivals"; Ross, "Film Festival as Producer."

75 "Mag:net News," Mag:net Galleries, News Archives, September 2007, accessed July 3, 2008, http://magnet.com.ph/news/2007-09.htm.

76 Sharma, *In the Meantime*.

77 Sharma, 12.

78 Sharma, *In the Meantime*.

79 Turner, *Anthropology of Performance*.

80 Turner, "Are There Universals," 12.

81 Harbord, *Film Cultures*, 40.

82 Harbord, 44–45.

83 Collins, "Identity, Mobility."

84 Garcia, *Philippine Gay Culture*, 231.

85 Connell, *Rise and Fall*.

86 Connell. While the district has most recently become the home of many Korean-owned shops and restaurants, this was not the case in 2008.

87 Van Beers, "Plea."

88 Van Beers.
89 Andrew, "Public Rituals," 169.
90 Bonifacio Global City: Home of Passionate Minds, home page, accessed December 12, 2015, http://bgc.com.ph/.
91 The series was organized by Alexis Tioseco.
92 "Cubao Things to Do," Virtual Tourist, February 20, 2007, http://www.virtualtourist.com/travel/Asia/Philippines/Quezon_City; metrosuburban, "Marikina Shoe Expo," *Skyscraper City*, January 29, 2007, http://www.skyscrapercity.com/showthread.php?t=436213.
93 Clarissa Chikiamco, "Death of an Independent Art Space?," *Philippine Star*, January 29, 2007, https://www.philstar.com/lifestyle/arts-and-culture/2007/01/29/382338/death-independent-art-space.
94 See, for example, Ackbar Abbas's work on Hong Kong as a "space of disappearance." Abbas, *Hong Kong*.
95 Dmib, "Automatic Center Cubao," Sulit, July 28, 2008, http://www.sulit.com.ph/index.php/search+results/q/automatic+center+cubao; "Welcome Head of the Family," Manhattan Garden City at Araneta Center (website), 2007, accessed September 3, 2008, http://www.themanhattangardencity.com/manhattan/home.php?profile=family.
96 "Memories of Mogwai: Super Says Goodbye to a Great Cubao X Hangout," *Philippine Daily Inquirer*, August 20, 2011.
97 "Memories of Mogwai."
98 Quoted in "Memories of Mogwai."
99 Quoted in "Mogwai: Our Collective Memories," accessed July 2, 2012, http://storify.com/hitorisetsunai/mogwai-our-collective-memories.
100 Quoted in "Memories of Mogwai."
101 Dyer, "In Defence of Disco," 23.
102 Muñoz, *Cruising Utopia*, 97.

Chapter Four. "Not for Public Exhibition"

Epigraph: Raul Pangalangan, "Human Rights Film Was Initially Rated X?," *Philippine Daily Inquirer*, October 5, 2007.

1 Barker, Arthurs, and Harindranath, *"Crash" Controversy*; Cather, "'I Know It'"; Grieveson, *Policing Cinema*; Kuhn, *Cinema, Censorship, and Sexuality*; Mehta, *Censorship and Sexuality in Bombay Cinema* and "Reframing Film Censorship"; Staiger, *Bad Women*; E. Scott, "Censorship and Regulation."
2 Rosalinda L. Orosa, "P-Noy Reappoints Grace Poe as MTRCB Chief," *Philippine Star*, October 25, 2011, https://www.philstar.com/entertainment/2011/10/25/740634/p-noy-reappoints-grace-poe-mtrcb-chief.
3 "New MTRCB Chief Vows No Censorship," *Rappler*, December 6, 2012, https://www.rappler.com/nation/17457-new-mtrcb-chief-vows-no-censorship.
4 Pio Ranada, "Rachel Arenas Is New MTRCB Chairperson," *Rappler*, January 30, 2017, https://www.rappler.com/nation/159990-rachel-arenas-mtrcb-chairperson.

5   Rajagopal, *Politics after Television*.
6   Rolando Tolentino, "Indie Cinema bilang Kultural na Kapital," *Bulatlat*, August 2, 2008, http://bulatlat.com/main/2008/08/02/indie-cinema-bilang-kultural-na-kapital/.
7   Lumbera, "Introduction," 1.
8   "FDCP, CCP Hold Philippine Independent Film Summit," *Manila Bulletin*, November 14, 2008. However, as the filmmaker and writer Clodualdo del Mundo pointed out, their profits were still miniscule compared to "mainstream standards."
9   Arroyo's administration was plagued with corruption scandals and violence. See San Juan, "Ethnic Identity"; Abinales, "Philippines in 2009"; Aguilar, Mendoza, and Candelaria, "Keeping the State."
10 J. David, "Phantom Limbs." The state has actively produced the OFW economy, transitioning into what Robyn Magalit Rodriguez terms a "labor brokerage state." See *Migrants for Export*.
11 J. David, "Phantom Limbs," 106.
12 Raslan, "Framing the Body Politic," quoted in McKay, "Politics of Mirrored Metaphors."
13 McKay, "Politics of Mirrored Metaphors," 471.
14 Scholars of affect theory differentiate between affect as prelinguistic and emotion as existing within language. See Gould, *Moving Politics*. These distinctions are not relevant here. In Philippine cinema, emotionality has been associated with the melodramatic form. For example, Katrina Macapagal's discussion of melodrama draws from Nicanor Tiongson's discussion of the *sinakulo*, or reenactments of the passion of the Christ, and Nick Deocampo's work on melodrama. Both emphasize emotionality as integral to Philippine film history, with Deocampo claiming melodrama as "the Filipino's common universal film experience." See Macapagal, "Slum Chronotope"; Tiongson, "From Stage to Screen"; Deocampo, *Film*.
15 Tolentino, "Macho Dancing," 87.
16 Tolentino, 79–81.
17 Tolentino, 81.
18 Tolentino, 81.
19 Fel V. Maragay, "Infighting at the Censors Board," *Manila Standard Today*, May 3, 2008, http://www.manilastandardtoday.com/?page=felMaragay_may3_2008.
20 To give one, highly publicized example, though the country boasts a free press, the Center for Media Freedom and Responsibility (CMFR) reported in December 2008, amid these MTRCB debates, that sixty-two journalists had been murdered over the course of Arroyo's rise to power. Prime Sarmiento, "Philippines: Killing of Journalists Continue," *Asia Media Forum*, December 17, 2008, http://www.theasiamediaforum.org/node/958.
21 The divides between affect, emotion, and reason have a long, charged history in social movement theory. Social movements' emotionality and volatility were first pathologized as rejections of policy and due process, while then

being recuperated as an alternative form of reason. See Jasper, "Emotions and Social Movements"; Gould, *Moving Politics*.
22 Ramussen and Brown, "Body Politic"; Grosz, "Bodies/Cities."
23 Grosz, "Bodies/Cities," 246–47. Elizabeth Grosz questions this isomorphism, interrogating the "metaphoric function of the genitals" in the body politic and pointing to the unspoken phallocentrism of the model. As we have seen above, this works somewhat differently in the Philippines, where the figure of the OFW has constructed a national image of the "Madonna-martyr," as McKay describes.
24 Boutros and Straw, *Circulation and the City*; Lury and Massey, "Making Connections." See also Giuliana Bruno's theories of mobility and cinema, *Atlas of Emotion*.
25 LiPuma and Koelble, "Cultures of Circulation," 154.
26 Edward LiPuma and Thomas Koelble, for example, conceptualize the urban imaginary as a "culturally imaginary space that is created in and through the relationship between these forms of circulation and the practices of stabilization that seek to objectify the city as a totality." LiPuma and Koelble, "Cultures of Circulation and the Urban Imaginary," 154. Deleuze and Guattari likewise argue for mobility as the defining aspect of urban spaces; they argue, "The town is a correlate of the road. The town exists only as a function of circulation and of circuits; it is a singular point on the circuits which create it and which it creates." Deleuze and Guattari, "City/State," 297.
27 As discussed in previous chapters, Plaza Miranda was the site of political campaign rallies during the martial-law era, and EDSA was the site of the 1986 People Power revolution that precipitated the end of martial law.
28 The Marcoses had a complex relationship with Philippine cinema. On the one hand, the regime supported the medium based on its ability to garner international prestige and acclaim. On the other, the dictatorship suppressed—often violently—works critical of its rule. Under the Marcoses' two-decade tenure, the country had seen the emergence of several cinema-related projects: the rise of the failed Metro Manila International Film Festival, the First Lady's attempt to put her metropolitan "City of Man" on the international cultural map; the formation of the Experimental Cinema of the Philippines; and the creation of the Movie and Television Review and Classification Board (MTRCB).
29 "PGMA Reappoints Laguardia as MTRCB Chairman," Philippine News Agency (PNA), November 22, 2007.
30 Chita Jimenez, opening remarks, Kontra-Agos Film Festival, Manila, December 5, 2007.
31 *A Day in the Life of Gloria* is available to view at YouTube: http://www.youtube.com/view_play_list?p=43594A6123654C5C&search_query=a+day+in+the+life+of+gloria+1; *Holy Bingo* is available to view at YouTube: http://www.youtube.com/watch?v=9BurxVins7U&feature=related
32 Filmless Films statement, quoted in "TO 'X' OR NOT TO 'X': 'Three Days of Darkness' Confuses Censors of Confusion," oracafe@rocketmail.com mailing list, December 12, 2007, http://lists.topica.com/lists/disturbances/read/message.html?sort=a&mid=812959848.

33 Anderson, *Imagined Communities*; San Juan, "Ethnic Identity."
34 Quimpo, *Contested Democracy*.
35 Bienvenido Lumbera, quoted in Noel Sales Barcelona, "National Artist Condemns Censorship, 'State Fascism,'" Antonio Zumel Center for Press Freedom, December 3, 2007, http://zumel.com/index.php?Itemid=2&id=389&option=com_content&task=view; Karapatan and Selda, quoted in Julie Javellana-Santos, "Philippine Activists Rally against 'Undeclared Martial Law,'" *Arab News: The Middle East's Leading English Language Daily*, September 22, 2007, http://www.arabnews.com/?page=4&section=0&article=101510&d=22&m=9&y=2007.
36 Auslander, *Liveness*; Kumar, "Unbearable Liveness"; White, "Television Liveness."
37 Anna Isabelle Matutina, "Short Film 'Rights' Marked X by the MTCRB," *Philippine Daily Inquirer*, September 26, 2007, http://globalnation.inquirer.net/mailbag/mailbag/view_article.php?article_id=90854.
38 Oliver Teves, "Censors Lift Ban on Collection of Human Rights Films," Associated Press, September 28, 2007.
39 Emily Vital, "MTRCB Bans Indie Film Critical of Arroyo," *Pinoy Press*, December 3, 2007, http://www.pinoypress.net/2007/12/03/mtrcb-bans-indie-film-critical-of-arroyo/.
40 Jeanette Andrade, "Filmmakers Slam Review Board's X-Rating for 'Rights' film. Media Group Joins Condemnation of 'censorship,'" *Philippine Daily Inquirer*, September 21, 2007.
41 Andrade, "Filmmakers Slam Review Board's X-Rating for 'Rights' Film."
42 See Kenway and Youdell, "Emotional Geographies of Education."
43 J. David, "Phantom Limbs," 123.
44 Boy Villasanta, "'Imburnal' to Be Shown Uncut at UP," ABS-CBN News, November 19, 2009, http://www.abs-cbnnews.com/entertainment/11/19/08%E2%80%98imburnal%E2%80%99-be-shown-uncut.
45 Sherad Anthony Sanchez, quoted in "Imburnal Only Gets One Screening in Cinema One," *Mindanao Times*, posted on dinabaw, December 4, 2008, http://www.skyscrapercity.com/showthread.php?t=712920&page=48.
46 Joycelyn Dimaculangan, "Mainstream Stars Support Fourth Edition of Cinema One Originals Digital Film Fest," *Telebisyon*, November 19, 2008, http://telebisyon.net/balita/Mainstream-stars-support-fourth-edition-of-Cinema-One-Originals-digital-film-fest/artikulo/38954/.
47 Ronald Arguelles, quoted in Boy Villasanta, "'Imburnal to Be Shown Uncut at UP," ABS-CBN News, November 19, 2008, http://www.abs-cbnnews.com/entertainment/11/19/08/%E2%80%98imburnal%E2%80%99-be-shown-uncut.
48 Rebecca Zlotowski, quoted in Bayani San Diego Jr., "'X' Rating Too Harsh," *Philippine Daily Inquirer*, October 27, 2008, http://showbizandstyle.inquirer.net/entertainment/entertainment/view/20081027-168601/X-rating-too-harsh.
49 Rebecca Zlotowski, quoted in San Diego Jr., "'X' Rating Too Harsh."
50 It is important to acknowledge that this dynamic is not ideologically simple. These festival networks' ties to what James English calls the transnational

"prestige economy" complicate these transnational routes. See English, *Economy of Prestige*.

51 "PEP: Encantos Rated X by MTRCB, Show Canceled," *GMA News*, October 13, 2008, http://www.gmanews.tv/story/126703/PEP-Encantos-rated-X-by-MTRCB-show-canceled.
52 J. P. Carpio, "Lav Diaz Prays for the End of Censorship at Cinemanila 2008," October 16, 2008, http://momentaries.multiply.com/journal/item/68.
53 Quoted in Carpio, "Lav Diaz Prays for the End of Censorship at Cinemanila 2008."
54 Armida Siguion-Reyna, "Regardless of the Motive," *The Tribune*, October 14, 2008, http://www.tribune.net.ph/commentary/20081014com5.html.
55 Siguion-Reyna, "Regardless of the Motive."
56 Siguion-Reyna, "Regardless of the Motive."
57 Siguion-Reyna, "Regardless of the Motive."
58 "PEP: Encantos Rated X by MTRCB, Show Canceled."
59 Siguion-Reyna, "Regardless of the Motive."
60 J. P. Carpio, "MTRCB Gives X Rating to Lav Diaz's 'Death in the Land of the Encantos' (or When Dumb Just Got Dumber)," *Momentaries*, October 6, 2008, http://momentaries.multiply.com/journal/item/62/62.
61 Desai, *Beyond Bollywood*, 39.
62 Bayani San Diego Jr., "A Summit against All Odds," *Philippine Daily Inquirer*, November 17, 2008.
63 Bayani San Diego Jr., "Search for Solutions," *Philippine Daily Inquirer*, November 18, 2008.
64 Ross, "Film Festival as Producer."
65 Blackshama, "Are Films Shown in UP Exempt from the MTRCB?," *Filipino Voices*, March 18, 2009, http://filipinovoices.com/are-films-shown-in-up-exempt-from-the-mtrcb.
66 Mario E. Bautista, "UP No Place for Gay Porno," *Philippine Journal*, February 9, 2009, http://www.journal.com.ph.
67 Bautista, "UP No Place for Gay Porno."
68 Marichu Lambino, "(2nd Update) Overriding Jurisdictional Questions: The Censors (MTRCB) to 'Monitor' U. P. Film Institute Screenings," *Notes of Marichu C. Lambino*, February 19, 2009, http://marichulambino.wordpress.com/2009/02/19/the-censors-mtrcb-to-monitor-up-film-institute-screenings/.
69 Lambino, "(2nd Update) Overriding Jurisdictional Questions."
70 The awards included (1) *Serbis*, Centerstage Productions, Swift Productions (France), dir. Brillante Mendoza: official selection for the Palme d'Or, 2008 Festival de Cannes; winner, Best Director, Best Actor for Gina Pareño, Vladivostok International Film Fest of Asian Pacific Countries, Best Southeast Asian Film, 2008 Bangkok International Film Festival; official selection, 2008 New York International Film Festival; (2) *Masahista*, Gee Entertainment Presentation of a Centerstage Production, dir. Brillante Mendoza: Grand Prize, Golden Leopard-Video, 2005 Locarno International Film Festival; winner, Audience Prize, 2006 Torino International Gay and Lesbian Film

Fest; winner, Interfaith Prize, 2006 Brisbane International Film Festival; (3) *Sikil* (Unspoken passion), New Life Cinema, dir. Ronaldo Bertubin: official selection, 2007 Valencia Film Festival, 2008 Cancun International Film Festival, 2008 Palm Springs International Film Festival, 2008 Frameline Film Festival, 2008 San Diego Asian Film Festival.

71 Lambino, "(2nd Update) Overriding Jurisdictional Questions."
72 The word *bakla* has a different connotation in the Filipino than the word "gay" in U.S. English. For more on this, see Manalansan, *Global Divas*.
73 "Should U. P. Ban 'Gay Porno'?," *The Bakla Review: Queer Eye for Queer Things in the Philippines*, March 3, 2009, http://thebaklareview.blogspot.com/2009/03/should-up-ban-gay-porno.html.
74 "Should U. P. Ban 'Gay Porno'?"
75 "Should U. P. Ban 'Gay Porno'?"
76 "Should U. P. Ban 'Gay Porno'?"
77 Translated from Filipino text. Anonymous, comment, March 2, 2009, 8:11 P.M., "How Was It Again?," *Hot Men in the Philippines*, February 28, 2009, http://www.rddantes.com/2009/02/how-was-it-again.html?zx=54c2ac81ac528ela.
78 Anonymous, comment, March 15, 2009, 2:54 P.M., "How Was It Again?," *Hot Men in the Philippines*, February 28, 2009, http://www.rddantes.com/2009/02/how-was-it-again.html?zx=54c2ac81ac528ela.
79 Anonymous, comment, March 16, 2009, 11:54 P.M., "How Was It Again?," *Hot Men in the Philippines*, February 28, 2009, http://www.rddantes.com/2009/02/how-was-it-again.html?zx=54c2ac81ac528ela.
80 Anonymous, comment, March 16, 2009, 11:58 A.M., "How Was It Again?," *Hot Men in the Philippines*, February 28, 2009, http://www.rddantes.com/2009/02/how-was-it-again.html?zx=54c2ac81ac528ela.
81 Diaz, "*Biyuti* from Below," 404.
82 Diaz, 419.
83 "Cinemanila '08 Winners Feted at Malcañang," *GMA News*, October 21, 2008, http://www.gmanews.tv/story/128364/Cinemanila-08-winners-feted-at-Maca&ntildeang.
84 Benedict Anderson uses the notion of political love to describe the affective relation between the nation and its people; this love creates a "profound emotional legitimacy" to the idea of the nation. Anderson, *Imagined Communities*, 4.
85 Vitali and Willemen, "Introduction."
86 Vitali and Willemen.

Chapter Five. "Hollywood Is Not Us"

1 Karl Malakunas, "Aquino Set for Landslide Win in Presidential Race," *Philippine Daily Inquirer*, May 11, 2010, http://newsinfo.inquirer.net/breakingnews/nation/view/20100511-269297/Aquino-set-for-landslide-win-in-presidential-race.

2. Agence France-Presse, "Imelda Marcos Wins Big," *Philippine Daily Inquirer*, May 11, 2010, http://newsinfo.inquirer.net/breakingnews/nation/view/20100511-269426/Imelda-Marcos-wins-big.
3. J. David, *National Pastime*, 14–16.
4. Abinales and Amoroso, *State and Society*, 2–3.
5. Abinales and Amoroso, 125.
6. "Philippine Poll Body Says Voter Turnout at 75 pct," Reuters, May 10, 2010, http://www.reuters.com/article/2010/05/10/philippines-elections-result-idUSMNA00274120100510.
7. Taussig, *Magic of the State*; Steinmetz, *State/Culture*.
8. Taussig, *Nervous System*.
9. Taussig, 111.
10. Rafael, *Contracting Colonialism*.
11. Rafael. See also McCoy, "Baylan."
12. Mitchell, "Society, Economy."
13. Mitchell, 170.
14. Mitchell, 179–80.
15. Mitchell, 180.
16. Some activists also view the state as a site of potential. Walden Bello sees the rise of neoliberalism as in part a product of middle-class perceptions that blame state corruption for halted economic growth rather than neoliberalism's exacerbation of market-driven inequalities. Bello, "Neoliberalism as Hegemonic Ideology," 17.
17. Rolando Tolentino, "Kris Aquino at ang Politika ng Showbiz at Showbiz ng Politika," *Philippine Center for Investigative Journalism*, accessed December 12, 2015, http://pcij.org/blog/wp-docs/tolentino_excerpt.pdf.
18. See Patrick Campos's chapter "Cinemalaya and the Politics of Naming a Movement" in *End of National Cinema*, 216–74.
19. De Valck, *Film Festivals*.
20. Ross, "Film Festival as Producer," 262.
21. Camille Bianca E. Lopez, "How to Make a Filipino Indie Film for the World," *Manila Times*, August 3, 2012, http://www.manilatimes.net/index.php/life-and-times/showtime/28214-how-to-make-a-filipino-indie-film-for-the-world.
22. Alina R. Co, "'Mga Kidnaper ni Ronnie Lazaro'—an Indie Film within an Indie Film," *GMA News*, September 13, 2012, http://www.gmanetwork.com/news/story/273831/lifestyle/reviews/movie-review-mga-kidnaper-ni-ronnie-lazaro-an-indie-film-within-an-indie-film.
23. Co, "'Mga Kidnaper ni Ronnie Lazaro.'"
24. Camille Bianca E. Lopez, "How to Make a Filipino Indie Film for the World," *Manila Times*, August 3, 2012, http://www.manilatimes.net/index.php/life-and-times/showtime/28214-how-to-make-a-filipino-indie-film-for-the-world.
25. These quotes are from the English subtitles. The characters switch back and forth between English and Taglish, a combination of Tagalog and English and a marker of class.

26 Though it is outside the purview of this chapter, the production of this meta-film itself merits further scrutiny. A couple of images satirizing the exploitation of the poor come very close to being exploitative themselves. When I asked activist friends their thoughts on the film, they said that they couldn't make it through the opening parody sequence, due to its imagery.

27 Miriam Ross notes similar critiques of what have been termed "porno-miseria" (porno misery) films in Latin America. See Ross, "Film Festival as Producer."

28 Pam Pastor, "Why You Should Watch 'Ang Babae Sa Septic Tank,'" *Philippine Daily Inquirer*, July 30, 2011, http://lifestyle.inquirer.net/7513/why-you-should-watch-%E2%80%98ang-babae-sa-septic-tank%E2%80%99.

29 As of 2010, 32 percent of Filipinos live in informal settlements (17 percent in urban metros), and that percentage is increasing at a rate of 3.4 percent annually. See Ballesteros, "Linking Poverty." As Tolentino writes, in 2006, 27.6 million people lived below the poverty level; in a 2009 survey, 71.4 percent of Filipinos self-identified as "poor." Tolentino, "Cinema and the State," 188–89.

30 These films are not the first to critique this kind of work. Mike de Leon's 1993 short film, *Aliwan Paradise* (Paradise entertainment), includes a sequence that sends up social-realist depictions of urban poor communities in films like those of Lino Brocka.

31 Allan Sancon, "*Ang Babae sa Septic Tank* Grosses P20 Million in Five Days," *Philippine Entertainment Portal*, August 9, 2011, http://www.pep.ph/guide/guide/8677/ang-babae-sa-septic-tank-grosses-p20-million-in-five-days.

32 Maggie Lee, "*The Woman in a Septic Tank*: Film Review," July 7, 2011, *Hollywood Reporter*, http://www.hollywoodreporter.com/review/woman-a-septic-tank-film-271138.

33 Maggie Lee, "*The Woman in a Septic Tank*."

34 Cinemalaya, home page, accessed July 2, 2012, http://www.cinemalaya.org/.

35 Euden Valdez, "'Full Force' for Cinemalaya," *Manila Times*, June 29, 2012, http://www.manilatimes.net/index.php/life-and-times/showtime/25782-full-force-for-cinemalaya.

36 Ricardo Saludo, "Can Indie Films Save Philippine Cinema?," *Manila Times*, August 27, 2012, http://www.manilatimes.net/~manilati/index.php/opinion/columnist1/29779-can-indie-films-save-philippine-cinema.

37 Jose Javier Reyes, "Philippine Cinema Reborn," *Philippine Daily Inquirer*, July 24, 2011, http://entertainment.inquirer.net/6727/philippine-cinema-reborn.

38 Cinema One Originals began the same year, and like Cinemalaya, it offered funding and festival distribution to independently made films. It was associated with a television network, the Cinema One cable channel of the media conglomerate ABS-CBN, known primarily for its "mainstream" film studio, ABS-CBN Film Productions Inc., better known as Star Cinema.

39 Leah Salterio, "Cinemalaya: Discover, Honor, Encourage New Filmmakers," *Philippine Inquirer*, August 2004, accessed July 2, 2012, http://web.archive.org/web/20051013124109/http://www.inq7.net/globalnation/secsho/2004/aug/09-03.htm.

40 Jeffrey O. Valisno, "Old Hands Join Newbies in Cinemalaya," *Business World*, July 8, 2011, http://www.bworldonline.com/weekender/content.php?id=13910.
41 Marinel R. Cruz, "Mainstream Crosses over to Indies," *Philippine Daily Inquirer*, July 28, 2012, http://entertainment.inquirer.net/52017/mainstream-crosses-over-to-indies.
42 Bayani San Diego Jr., "Cinemalaya: State of the Nation," *Philippine Daily Inquirer*, July 26, 2012, http://entertainment.inquirer.net/51709/cinemalaya-state-of-the-nation.
43 Philip Cheah, "Filipino Indie Faith," NETPAC: *Network for the Promotion of Asian Cinema*, August 3, 2011, http://www.netpacasia.org/blogs.aspx?id=2&rid=48.
44 Abby Mendoza and Jocelyn Dimaculangan, "PEP Exclusive: Robbie Tan Explains Why MNL 143 Was Disqualified from Cinemalaya 2012," *Philippine Entertainment Portal*, February 28, 2012, http://www.pep.ph/news/33177/PEP-EXCLUSIVE:-Robbie-Tan-explains-why-MNL-143-was-disqualified-from-Cinemalaya-2012).
45 Mendoza and Dimaculangan, "PEP Exclusive: Robbie Tan Explains Why MNL 143 Was Disqualified from Cinemalaya 2012."
46 Oggs Cruz, "Cinemalaya Resignation Letter," *Lessons from the School of Inattention*, March 2, 2012, http://oggsmoggs.blogspot.sg/2012/03/cinemalaya-resignation-letter.html.
47 "Comment, Cinemalaya Foundation: Reform Cinemalaya Independent Film Festival Now!," Change.org, accessed September 4, 2012, http://www.change.org/petitions/cinemalaya-foundation-reform-cinemalaya-independent-film-festival-now#. Translation from the original: "Nawawala ang esensya ng independent filmmaking sa mismong polisiya na ipinatutupad ng Cinemalaya, which is weird (and wrong) since dapat ang institusyong ito ang nagtataguyod ng malayang paggawa ng pelikula. Kailangan na ng reporma. Gawing tunay na malaya ang Cinemalaya! Malaya sa mapanupil at hindi makatarungang polisiya at ilapit sa kalakhan ng masa ang mga pelikulang Cinemalaya!"
48 Zig Marasigan, "Direk Erik Matti Speaks Up: 'No, I Don't Want to Reform Cinemalaya. I Want to Take It Out,'" *Lagarista*, March 7, 2012, http://lagarista.com/site/entry/direk_erik_matti_speaks_up_no_i_dont_want_to_reform_cinemalaya._i_want_to_t.
49 Anderson, "Cacique Democracy."
50 In accounts of Hacienda Luisita, the plantation of Corazon Aquino's Cojuangco family, workers received poverty-level wages and poorer food than the hacienda's horses. See Anderson, "Cacique Democracy."
51 Anderson, 18.
52 Marasigan, "Direk Erik Matti Speaks Up."
53 Erik Matti, "Cinemalaya: Then and Now," *Rappler*, June 15, 2012, http://www.rappler.com/entertainment/2714-cinemalaya-then-and-now.
54 Abby Mendoza, "Director Jade Castro Calls on Reassessment of Cinemalaya Organizing Committee; Recognizes Emerson Reyes's Commitment," *Philippine Entertainment Portal*, March 13, 2012, http://www.pep.ph/news/33356

/director-jade-castro-calls-on-reassessment-of-cinemalaya-organizing-committee-recognizes-emerson-reyes39s-predicament/1/4. Original: "Nag-agree ako sa isang sinabi na . . . kung gusto nilang gawing private enterprise ang Cinemalaya, mas maganda kung wala sa CCP kasi CCP is for the public . . . Pero desisyon nila yun kung gusto nila gawing private or gusto pa rin nilang ipagpatuloy . . . [as a] festival for the people."

55 Marinel R. Cruz, "Robbie Tan Set to Quit Cinemalaya," *Philippine Daily Inquirer*, July 24, 2012, http://entertainment.inquirer.net/51535/robbie-tan-set-to-quit-cinemalaya; Marinel R. Cruz, "Cinemalaya Director Resigns," *Philippine Daily Inquirer*, March 13, 2012, http://entertainment.inquirer.net/33299/cinemalaya-director-resigns.
56 Tadiar, *Things Fall Away*, 154.
57 Tadiar, 154.
58 Jocelyn Dimaculangan, "Cinemalaya Pushes Through Even without Funding from Tonyboy Cojuangco," *Philippine Entertainment Portal*, February 6, 2014, http://www.pep.ph/guide/indie/13346/cinemalaya-pushes-through-even-without-funding-from-tonyboy-cojuangco; Bayani San Diego Jr., "Cinemalaya 'Loses' Cojuangco," *Philippine Daily Inquirer*, January 25, 2014, http://entertainment.inquirer.net/131455/cinemalaya-loses-cojuangco.
59 Jocelyn Dimaculangan, "Cinemalaya Pushes Through Even without Funding from Tonyboy Cojuangco," *Philippine Entertainment Portal*, February 6, 2014, http://www.pep.ph/guide/indie/13346/cinemalaya-pushes-through-even-without-funding-from-tonyboy-cojuangco; Bayani San Diego Jr., "Cinemalaya 'Loses' Cojuangco," *Philippine Daily Inquirer*, January 25, 2014, http://entertainment.inquirer.net/131455/cinemalaya-loses-cojuangco.
60 Marco Sumayao, "How the Mainstream Cinemas Are Killing Indie Films Like 'Liway,'" *Esquire*, October 17, 2018, https://www.esquiremag.ph/culture/arts-and-entertainment/highest-grossing-cinemalaya-liway-a2239-20181017-lfrm.
61 Marco Sumayao, "How the Mainstream Cinemas Are Killing Indie Films Like 'Liway.'"
62 Totel V. de Jesus, "Lesser Venues for Cinemalaya 2017, but Hopefully More Viewers," *Philippine Daily Inquirer*, August 4, 2017, https://entertainment.inquirer.net/237370/lesser-venues-for-cinemalaya-2017-but-hopefully-more-viewers#ixzz5mz7Qbpv8. As of 2017, twenty-four Cinemalaya films have achieved a theatrical run. These include *Ang Babae sa Septic Tank* (dir. Marlon Rivera, 2011), *Bwakaw* (dir. Jun Robles Lana, 2012), *Pamilya Ordinaryo* (dir. Eduardo Roy Jr., 2016), and *Kusina* (dir. David R. Corpuz and Cenon O. Palomares, 2016). The conglomerate ABS-CBN's cinema branch, Star Cinema, released Cinemalaya awardees, such as *Ekstra* (dir. Jeffrey Jeturian, 2013) and *Sta. Niña* (dir. Emmanuel Quindo Palo, 2012), because of the filmmakers' history with the network and the films' well-known leads (*Ekstra*'s Vilma Santos and *Sta. Niña*'s Coco Martin). See Bayani San Diego Jr., "Film Fest Fever or Fatigue?," *Philippine Daily Inquirer*, August 5, 2017, http://entertainment.inquirer.net/237443/film-fest-fever-fatigue#ixzz4r9tBevIk.

63 Edwin P. Sallan, "'Ang Mga Kidnaper ni Ronnie Lazaro' Spoofs Indie Filmmaking," *Interaksyon*, July 26, 2011, http://www.interaksyon.com/entertainment/ang-mga-kidnaper-ni-ronnie-lazaro-spoofs-indie-filmmaking/.
64 *Zombadings* earned a respectable $741,838 at the 2011 annual box office in the Philippines. It ranked forty-seventh of films released in the country that year. *Ang Babae sa Septic Tank* ranked forty-ninth. See "Philippines Yearly Box Office," Box Office Mojo, accessed July 5, 2018, https://www.boxofficemojo.com/intl/philippines/yearly/?yr=2011&p=.htm.
65 Moira Lang, Q&A, *Zombadings* screening, Southeast Asian Film Festival, Singapore Art Museum, March 10, 2012. See "[Post-Screening Discussion] Remington and the Curse of the Zombadings (2nd Screening)," Singapore Art Museum, September 6, 2012, https://www.youtube.com/watch?v=j5j1i-F4IoU.
66 Lee, Q&A, *Zombadings* screening, Southeast Asian Film Festival, March 10, 2012.
67 Abinales and Amoroso, *State and Society*; Kraft, "Philippines"; Gupta, "Blurred Boundaries."
68 Silliman and Noble, *Organizing for Democracy*, cited in Dressel, "Philippines."
69 Silliman and Noble, *Organizing for Democracy*, cited in Dressel, "Philippines."
70 Mathews, "Power Shift"; Abao, "Mapping and Analyzing."
71 Randy David, "When Civil Society Becomes Political," *Philippine Daily Inquirer*, October 11, 2008, http://opinion.inquirer.net/inquireropinion/columns/view/20081011-165850/When-civil-society-becomes-political.
72 Sineng Pambansa National Film Competition, "FDCP Sineng Pambansa Launches National Film Competition," Facebook, accessed July 4, 2012, https://www.facebook.com/pages/Sineng-Pambansa-National-Film-Competition/264370110242257?sk=info.
73 Sineng Pambansa National Film Competition, "FDCP Sineng Pambansa Launches National Film Competition."
74 "Sineng Pambansa," Film Development Council of the Philippines, accessed July 4, 2012, http://www.fdcp.ph/contents/view?id=Sineng%20Pambansa.
75 "Sineng Pambansa," Film Development Council of the Philippines.
76 Bliss Cua Lim has written about the history of film archives in "Archival Fragility: Philippine Cinema and the Challenge of Sustainable Preservation."
77 Briccio Santos, interview, September 18, 2011.
78 Canclini, "Cultural Policy Options," 303.
79 Guevara, "Fiscal Decentralization Process"; Ishii, et al. "Participation in Decentralized Local."
80 Briccio Santos, interview, September 18, 2011.
81 Chen and Chua, *Inter-Asia Cultural Studies*.
82 At the time of writing, the FDCP outposts have not moved into production.
83 Philip Cheah, "My Travels in the Post-Colonial Film Festival World," *Asia Pacific Films Blog*, 2011, accessed March 4, 2012, http://asiapacificfilms.tv/host-philip-cheah-blog-my-travels-in-the-post-colonial-film-festival-world/.

84 "7th Sineng Pambansa Film Festival Reels off in Ilocos Norte," *Film Development Council National Cinema Newsletter* 3, no. 4 (2011): 1.
85 "The History of Dinagyang Festival," Dinagyang Festival 2013, accessed January 20, 2013, http://dinagyangsailoilo.com/about-dinagyang/the-history-of-dinagyang-festival/.
86 "Mobile Cinema Hits City Villages, Schools," *Daily Guardian*, accessed January 20, 2013, http://thedailyguardian.net/index.php/uncle-toms-ad/114-community-news-cat/6840-mobile-cinema-hits-city-villages-schools/.
87 Burns, *Flickering Shadows*; Larkin, *Signal and Noise*; Druick, "At the Margins."
88 Larkin, *Signal and Noise*, 80.
89 Acland, "Curtains, Carts," 166.
90 "Norte to Dish Out Second Semana ti Ar-Aria Halloween Fest," *Malaya: Business Insight*, October 24, 2012, http://www.malaya.com.ph/index.php/living/16061-norte-to-dish-out-second-semana-ti-ar-aria-halloween-fest.
91 Majul, *Muslims in the Philippines*.
92 Gutierrez and Saturnino, *Moro Conflict*.
93 Briccio Santos, interview, September 18, 2011.
94 Schelzig, *Poverty in the Philippines*.
95 "Tawi-Tawi Film Festival a Resounding Success," *Film Development Council, National Cinema Newsletter* 3, no. 4 (2011): 1, 4.
96 Briccio Santos, quoted in Bibsy M. Carballo, "Briccio Santos: Let Film Be an Agent for Peace," *Philippine Star*, October 31, 2011, http://www.philstar.com/entertainment/742700/briccio-santos-let-film-be-agent-peace.
97 Vincent Cabreza, "Baguio's Casa Vallejo Restored," *Philippine Inquirer*, December 25, 2009. http://newsinfo.inquirer.net/inquirerheadlines/regions/view/20091225-243974/Baguios-Casa-Vallejo-restored.
98 Cabreza, "Baguio's Casa Vallejo Restored."
99 Briccio Santos, quoted in Marinel R. Cruz, "FDCP Gets 35-mm Projector for Cinematheque," *Philippine Daily Inquirer*, July 14, 2012, http://entertainment.inquirer.net/49909/fdcp-gets-35-mm-projector-for-cinematheque.
100 Briccio Santos, interview, September 18, 2011. The sentiments expressed mirror those of the 1935 National Economic Protectionism Association, which encouraged Filipino consumers to buy locally made products from national retailers. See Pante, "Quezon's City."
101 Briccio Santos, interview, September 18, 2011.
102 See Tan, "Constituting Philippine Filmic and Linguistic Heritage," 155.
103 The project that has offered the most sustained support for regional filmmaking is Cinema Rehiyon, founded in 2009 by Teddy Co through the National Commission on Culture and the Arts. Marketed as "Films from the Other Philippines," the festival takes place in different parts of the country and showcases films from around the Philippines, usually shot on location by filmmakers from the region, in languages other than Tagalog. As Katrina Tan has written, the filmmaking scenes remain precarious, with uncertain fund-

ing measures and no distribution system. See Tan, "Constituting Philippine Filmic and Linguistic Heritage." For a history of cinema from Cebu, see Anissimov and Grant, *Lilas*.

Epilogue

1. Nestor U. Torre, "From Indie to 'Maindie,'" *Philippine Daily Inquirer*, February 13, 2012, http://entertainment.inquirer.net/30179/from-indie-to-%E2%80%98maindie%E2%80%99.
2. Pepe Diokno, quoted in Ricardo Saludo, "Can Indie Films Save Philippine Cinema?," *Manila Times*, August 27, 2012, http://www.manilatimes.net/index.php/opinion/columnist1/2977.
3. "'Maindie' Movies Combine Edge, Relevance," *ABS-CBN News*, August 22, 2012 http://rp3.abs-cbnnews.com/lifestyle/08/22/12/%E2%80%98maindie%E2%80%99-movies-combine-edge-relevance.
4. ABS-CBN, "Skylight Films Presents New Horror 'Maindie' Movie 'Amorosa: The Revenge,'" *Starometer*, August 22, 2012, http://www.starmometer.com/2012/08/22/skylight-films-presents-new-horror-maindie-movie-amorosa-the-revenge/.
5. ABS-CBN, "Skylight Films Presents New Horror 'Maindie' Movie 'Amorosa: The Revenge.'"
6. "'Tadhana' Is Top Grossing Local Indie Film of all Time," *ABS-CBN News*, March 15, 2015, https://news.abs-cbn.com/entertainment/03/15/15/tadhana-top-grossing-local-indie-film-all-time.
7. "'Kita Kita' Passes 'Heneral Luna' as PH's Top Grossing Indie Movie," *ABS-CBN News*, August 10, 2017, https://news.abs-cbn.com/entertainment/08/09/17/kita-kita-passes-heneral-luna-as-phs-top-grossing-indie-movie.
8. Mixkaela Villalon, "How Kita Kita Became the Biggest Filipino Film of the Year," *Rouge*, December 2017–January 2018, accessed December 1, 2018, http://rogue.ph/kita-kita-biggest-filipino-film-year/.
9. Villalon, "How Kita Kita Became the Biggest Filipino Film of the Year."
10. Capino, "Philippines."
11. Capino, "Philippines," 43–44.
12. This is not to suggest that local independents are not imitative; like any creative work, they do not occur in a vacuum, and many of these films also fall into transnational patterns of influence, even if they draw from art- or indie-cinema trajectories.
13. See Los Otros, http://www.los-otros.com/.
14. Translation. Original available at Aimee Dacamay, "This Cinema Is the Newest Home of Pinoy Indie Films in Maginhawa," *Spot.PH*, December 1, 2017, https://www.spot.ph/entertainment/movies-music-tv/72218/cinema-centenario-maginhawa-a00001-20171201-lfrm.
15. Aimee Dacanay, "This New Cinema Is Perfect for Pinoy Indie Movie Fans," *Spot.PH*, July 8, 2016, https://www.spot.ph/entertainment/movies-music-tv/66970/cinema-76-pasig-city-a00001-20160708.

16 Nikki Wang, "Microcinema Indie Films' New Lease on Life," *Manila Standard*, June 27, 2018, http://manilastandard.net/showbitz/tv-movies/269089/microcinema-indie-films-new-lease-on-life.html.
17 "Japanese Actress Named Phl Tourism Fun Envoy," *The Freeman*, July 6, 2018, https://www.pressreader.com/philippines/the-freeman/20180706/281517931874021.
18 Anna Bueno, "This Little Cinema Is Mandaluyong's Newest Hidden Gem," *CNN Philippines*, December 13, 2017, http://nine.cnnphilippines.com/life/entertainment/film/2017/12/07/black-maria-pictures-filipino-films.html.
19 Bueno, "This Little Cinema Is Mandaluyong's Newest Hidden Gem."
20 Facebook, February 7, 2019.
21 Erik Matti, Facebook, February 6, 2019.
22 He won 16,601,997 votes, 6.6 million more than the administration candidate Mar Roxas.
23 Duterte has supported extrajudicial killings and critiqued media outlets. See Untalan, "Curious Case."
24 Josh Bianc, "Brillante Mendoza Explains 'Indie' Broadcast of Duterte's SONA," *Philippine News*, July 26, 2016, https://philnews.ph/2016/07/26/brillante-mendoza-indie-duterte-sona/; "Brillante Mendoza Explains 'Indie' SONA Broadcast," *ABS-CBN News*, July 26, 2016, https://news.abs-cbn.com/entertainment/07/26/16/brillante-mendoza-explains-indie-sona-broadcast.
25 Agence France-Presse, "Director Brillante Mendoza Urges Duterte to 'Change' Philippines," *Rappler*, May 19, 2016, https://www.rappler.com/entertainment/news/133582-brillante-mendoza-duterte-change-philippines-ma-rosa-cannes-film-festival.
26 By some estimates, Duterte's administration has overseen the extrajudicial killings of twenty thousand drug dealers and addicts, a narrative that Mendoza dramatized in his controversial Netflix series, *Amo*. Ted Regencia, "Senator: Rodrigo Duterte's Drug War Has Killed 20,000," *Al Jazeera*, February 21, 2018, https://www.aljazeera.com/news/2018/02/senator-rodrigo-duterte-drug-war-killed-20000-180221134139202.html; Agence France-Presse, "Brillante Mendoza: Netflix Series Shows 'Necessary' PH Drug War," *Rappler*, April 5, 2018, https://www.rappler.com/entertainment/news/199605-netflix-series-director-amo-war-on-drugs-philippines.
27 Tolentino, "Cinema and the State," 187; Bello, *Anti-Development State*.
28 Williams, *Marxism and Literature*, 132.
29 Williams, 128.
30 As I discuss in chapter 1, there has been a prolific body of work on India, though focused primarily on mainstream Bollywood cinema and multiplexes rather than alternatives to those commercial models.
31 Gaonkar and Povinelli, "Technologies of Public Forms."
32 Gaonkar and Povinelli, 391–92.
33 Lee and LiPuma, "Cultures of Circulation," 192.

BIBLIOGRAPHY

Abao, Carmel Veloso. "Mapping and Analyzing Philippine Civil Society Organizations (CSOs)." In *Civil Society Organizations in the Philippines: A Mapping and Strategic Assessment*, edited by Lydia N. Yu Jose, 1–8. Quezon City: Civil Society Resource Institute, 2011.

Abbas, Ackbar. *Hong Kong: Culture and the Politics of Disappearance*. Minneapolis: University of Minnesota Press, 1997.

Abinales, Patricio N. "The Philippines in 2009: The Blustery Days of August." *Asian Survey* 50, no. 1 (2010): 218–27.

Abinales, Patricio N., and Donna J. Amoroso. *State and Society in the Philippines*. Lanham, New York, and Oxford: Rowman and Littlefield, 2005.

Abu-Lughod, Lila. "Writing against Culture." In *Recapturing Anthropology: Working in the Present*, edited by Richard G. Fox, 137–54. Santa Fe, NM: School of American Research Press, 1991.

Acland, Charles. *Screen Traffic: Movies, Multiplexes, and Global Culture*. Durham, NC: Duke University Press, 2003.

Acland, Charles. "Residual Media." In *Residual Media*, edited by Charles Acland, xiii–xxvi. Minneapolis: University of Minnesota Press, 2007.

Acland, Charles. "Curtains, Carts and the Mobile Screen." *Screen* 50, no. 1 (2009): 148–66.

Adler, Judith. "Travel as a Performed Art." *American Journal of Sociology* 94, no. 6 (1989): 1366–91.

Aguilar, Filomeno V., Jr., Meynardo P. Mendoza, and Anne Lan K. Candelaria. "Keeping the State at Bay: The Killing of Journalists in the Philippines, 1998–2012." *Critical Asian Studies* 46, no. 4 (2014): 649–77.

Ahmed, Sarah. *The Cultural Politics of Emotion.* Abingdon, UK: Routledge, 2004.

Alcaron, Norma I. "The Role of the Plaza in the Philippine Experience." In *Public Places in Asia Pacific Cities: Current Issues and Strategies*, edited by Pu Miao, 87–106. Berlin: Springer Science and Business Media, 2001.

Amaya, Hector. *Citizenship Excess: Latino/as, Media, and the Nation.* New York: New York University Press, 2013.

Anderson, Benedict. "Cacique Democracy and the Philippines: Origins and Dreams." *New Left Review* 169 (May–June 1988): 3–33.

Anderson, Benedict. *Imagined Communities: Reflections on the Origin and Spread of Nationalism.* New York: Verso, 1991.

Anderson, Benedict. "The Strange Story of a Strange Beast: Receptions in Thailand of Apichatpong Weerasethakul's *Sat pralaat*." In *Glimpses of Freedom: Independent Cinema in Southeast Asia*, edited by May Adadol Ingawanij and Benjamin McKay, 149–64. Ithaca, NY: Cornell University Southeast Asia Program, 2012.

Andrade, Pio, Jr. "Quiapo in the History of the Nation." In *Quiapo: Heart of Manila*, edited by Fernando Nakpil Zialcita, 40–69. Quezon City: Cultural Heritage Studies Program, Ateneo de Manila University, 2006.

Andrew, Dudley. "Public Rituals and Private Space." In *Exhibition: The Film Reader*, edited by Ina Rae Hark, 161–72. London: Routledge, 2001.

Anissimov, Misha Boris, and Paul Douglas Grant. *Lilas: An Illustrated History of the Golden Ages of Cebuano Cinema.* Cebu City, Philippines: University of San Carlos Press, 2016.

Armes, Roy. "The Context of the African filmmaker." In *A Call to Action: the Films of Ousmane Sembene*, edited by Sheila Petty, 11–26. Westport, CT: Praeger, 1996.

Athique, Adrian, and Douglas Hill. "Multiplex Cinemas and Urban Redevelopment in India." *Media International Australia* 124 (2007): 108–18.

Athique, Adrian, and Douglas Hill. *The Multiplex in India: A Cultural Economy of Urban Leisure.* New York: Routledge, 2010.

Auslander, Philip. *Liveness: Performance in a Mediatized Culture.* New York: Routledge, 1999.

Azurin, Arnold Molina. *Reinventing the Filipino Sense of Being & Becoming.* Quezon City: University of the Philippines Press, 1995.

Azurin, Arnold Molina. "Orientalism? Privileged Vista Most Probably." *Philippine Political Science Journal* 23, no. 46 (2002): 139–50.

Baker, Houston A., Jr. "Critical Memory and the Black Public Sphere." *Public Culture* 7, no. 1 (1994): 3–33.

Ballesteros, Marife M. "Linking Poverty and the Environment: Evidence from Slums in Philippine Cities." *Philippine Institute for Development Studies, Discussion Paper Series* 33 (2010): 1–32.

Banes, Sally. *Greenwich Village 1963: Avant-Garde Performance and the Effervescent Body.* Durham, NC: Duke University Press, 1993.

Barker, Martin, Jane Arthurs, and Ramaswami Harindranath, *The "Crash" Controversy: Censorship Campaigns and Film Reception*. London: Wallflower, 2001.
Barnett, Clive. "Convening Publics: The Parasitical Spaces of Public Action." In *The SAGE Handbook of Political Geography*, edited by Kevin Cox, Murray Low, and Jennifer Robinson, 403–17. London: Sage, 2008.
Baudelaire, Charles. *The Painter of Modern Life and Other Essays*. Translated by Jonathan Mayne. London: Phaidon, 1964.
Baumgärtel, Tilman. "The Culture of Piracy in the Philippines." Paper presented at the Asian Edition: A Conference on Media Piracy and Intellectual Property in Southeast Asia, University of the Philippines Film Institute, Manila, November 24, 2006. Accessed October 1, 2008. http://www.asian-edition.org/.
Behar, Ruth. *The Vulnerable Observer: Anthropology That Breaks Your Heart*. Boston: Beacon, 1996.
Bello, Walden. *The Anti-Development State: The Political Economy of Permanent Crisis in the Philippines*. London: Zed Books, 2005.
Bello, Walden. *Deglobalization: Ideas for a New World Economy*, Philippine ed. Quezon City: Ateneo de Manila University Press, 2006.
Bello, Walden. "Neoliberalism as Hegemonic Ideology in the Philippines: Rise, Apogee, and Crisis." Paper presented at the National Conference of the Philippine Sociological Society, Focus on the Global South, Quezon City, October 16, 2009.
Benedicto, Bobby. *Under Bright Lights: Gay Manila and the Global Scene*. Minneapolis: University of Minnesota Press, 2014.
Benjamin, Walter. "The Work of Art in the Age of Mechanical Reproduction." In *Illuminations*, edited by Hannah Arendt, 217–51. New York: Schocken Books, 1968.
Berlant, Lauren. *Cruel Optimism*. Durham, NC: Duke University Press, 2011.
Berner, Erhard. "The Metropolitan Dilemma: Global Society, Localities and the Struggle for Urban Land in Manila." In *Space, Culture and Power: New Identities in Globalizing Cities*, edited by Ayşe Öncü and Petra Weyland, 98–116. London: Zed Books, 1997.
Berry, Chris. "From National Cinema to Cinema and the National: Chinese-Language Cinema and Hou Hsiao-hsien's 'Taiwan Trilogy.'" In *Theorising National Cinema*, edited by Valentina Vitali and Paul Willemen, 148–57. London: British Film Institute, 2006.
Berry, Chris. "What Is Transnational Cinema? Thinking from the Chinese Situation." *Transnational Cinemas* 1, no. 2 (2010): 111–27.
Blanco, John D. *Frontier Constitutions: Christianity and Colonial Empire in the Nineteenth-Century Philippines*. Berkeley: University of California Press, 2009.
Bourdieu, Pierre. *The Field of Cultural Production*. Cambridge: Polity, 1993.
Boutros, Alexandra, and Will Straw, eds. *Circulation and the City: Essays on Urban Culture*. Montreal: McGill-Queen's University Press, 2010.
Boyer, M. Christine. *The City of Collective Memory: Its Historical Imagery and Architectural Entertainments*. Cambridge, MA: MIT Press, 1996.

Brown, Wendy. *Undoing the Demos: Neoliberalism's Stealth Revolution*. Cambridge, MA: MIT Press, 2015.

Bruno, Giuliana. *Atlas of Emotion: Journeys in Art, Architecture, and Film*. London: Verso, 2002.

Bryant, Raymond L. *Nongovernmental Organizations in Environmental Struggles: Politics and the Making of Moral Capital in the Philippines*. New Haven, CT: Yale University Press, 2005.

Buck-Morss, Susan. "Democracy: An Unfinished Project." *boundary 2* 41, no. 2 (2014): 71–98.

Burns, J. M. *Flickering Shadows: Cinema and Identity in Colonial Zimbabwe*. Athens: Ohio University Press, 2002.

Butsch, Richard, and Sonia Livingstone. "'Translating' Audiences, Provincializing Europe." In *Meanings of Audiences: Comparative Discourses*, edited by Richard Butsch and Sonia Livingstone, 1–19. London: Routledge, 2013.

Caldwell, John Thornton. "Corporate and Worker Ephemera: The Industrial Promotional Surround, Paratexts and Worker Blowback." In *Ephemeral Media: Transitory Screen Culture from Television to YouTube*, edited by Paul Grainge, 175–94. New York: Palgrave Macmillan, 2011.

Calhoun, Craig. *Habermas and the Public Sphere*. Cambridge, MA: MIT Press, 1992.

Campos, Patrick. *The End of National Cinema: Filipino Film at the Turn of the Century*. Quezon City: University of the Philippines Press, 2016.

Canclini, Néstor García. "Cultural Policy Options in the Context of Globalization." In *The Politics of Culture: Policy Perspectives for Individuals, Institutions, and Communities*, edited by Gigi Bradford, Michael Gary, and Glenn Wallach, 302–26. New York: New Press, 2000.

Caoili, Manuel A. *The Origins of Metropolitan Manila: A Political and Social Analysis*. Quezon City: University of the Philippines Press, 1999.

Capino, José B. "Philippines: Cinema and Its Hybridity." In *Contemporary Asian Cinema*, edited by Anne Tereska Ciecko, 32–44. New York: Berg, 2006.

Capino, José B. *Dream Factories of a Former Colony: American Fantasies, Philippine Cinema*. Minneapolis: University of Minnesota Press, 2010.

Cather, Kirsten. "'I Know It When I Hear It: The Case of the Blind Film Censor." *Velvet Light Trap* 63 (Spring 2009): 60–62.

Chatterjee, Partha. "Beyond the Nation? Or Within?" *Economic and Political Weekly* 32, nos. 1–2 (1997): 30–34.

Chen, Kuan-Hsing, and Chua Beng Huat. *The Inter-Asia Cultural Studies Reader*. Abingdon, UK: Routledge, 2007.

Choi, JungBong. "National Cinema: An Anachronistic Delirium?" *Journal of Korean Studies* 16, no. 2 (2011): 173–91.

Chow, Rey. *Primitive Passions: Visuality, Sexuality, Ethnography, and Contemporary Chinese Cinema*. New York: Columbia University Press, 1996.

Claudio, Lisandro E. "Postcolonial Fissures and the Contingent Nation: An Antinationalist Critique of Philippine Historiography." *Philippine Studies: Historical and Ethnographic Viewpoints* 61, no. 1 (2013): 45–75.

Co, Teddy. "In Search of Philippine Regional Cinema." *Movement* 2, no. 1 (1987): 17–20.

Collins, Dana. "Identity, Mobility, and Urban Place-Making: Exploring Gay Life in Manila." *Gender and Society* 19, no. 2 (2005): 180–98.

Connell, Jon. "Beyond Manila: Malls, Walls, and Private Spaces." *Environment and Planning A* 31, no. 3 (1999): 417–39.

Connell, Jon. *The Rise and Fall of an Urban Sexual Community: Malate (Dis)placed*. London: Palgrave-Macmillan, 2016.

Crang, M. "Rhythms of the City: Temporalised Space and Motion." In *Timespace: Geographies of Temporality*, edited by John May and Nigel Thrift, 187–207. London: Routledge, 2001.

Crisp, Virginia. *Film Distribution in the Digital Age: Pirates and Professionals*. London: Palgrave-Macmillan, 2015.

Crofts, Stephen, "Reconceptualising National Cinema/s." In *Theorising National Cinema*, edited by Valentina Vitali and Paul Willemen, 44–58. London: British Film Institute, 2006.

Cruz, Denise. *Transpacific Femininities: The Making of the Modern Filipina*. Durham, NC: Duke University Press, 2012.

Cubitt, Sean. "Distribution and Media Flows." *Cultural Politics: An International Journal* 1, no. 2 (2005): 193–214.

Curaming, Rommel A. "Beyond Orientalism? Another Look at Orientalism in Indonesian and Philippine Studies." *Kyoto Review of Southeast Asia* 11 (2011): 1–10.

Czach, Liz. "Film Festivals, Programming, and the Building of a National Cinema." *Moving Image* 4, no. 1 (Spring 2004): 76–88.

David, Joel. *The National Pastime: Contemporary Philippine Cinema*. Manila: Anvil Publishing, 1990.

David, Joel. "Philippine History as Postcolonial Discourse." In *Geopolitics of the Visible: Essays on Philippine Film Cultures*, edited by Rolando B. Tolentino, 3–12. Quezon City: Ateneo de Manila University Press, 2000.

David, Joel. "Review: *Glimpses of Freedom: Independent Cinema in Southeast Asia*." *Southeast Asian Studies* 1, no. 3 (2012): 529–33.

David, Joel. "Phantom Limbs in the Body Politic: Filipinos in Foreign Cinema." *Plaridel* 11, no. 1 (2014): 102–27.

David, Randolf S. *Nation, Self and Citizenship: An Invitation to Philippine Sociology*. Mandaluyong, Philippines: Anvil Publishing, 2004.

Davison, Graeme. "Heritage: From Patrimony to Pastiche." In *The Heritage Reader*, edited by Graham Fairclough, Rodney Harrison, John Schofield, and John H. Jameson, 31–41. New York: Routledge, 2008.

Deener, Andrew. "Commerce as the Structure and Symbol of Neighborhood Life: Reshaping the Meaning of Community in Venice, California." *City and Community* 6, no. 4 (2007): 291–314.

de Guzman, Nestor. *Si Nora Aunor Sa Mga Noraian: Mga Paggunita at Pagtatapat*. Quezon City: Milflores Publishing, 2005.

de la Cruz, Khavn. *Philippine New Wave: This Is Not a Film Movement.* Quezon City: MovFest, 2010.

Deleuze, Gille, and Félix Guattari. "City/State." In *Rethinking Architecture: A Reader in Cultural Theory,* edited by Neal Leach, 292–99. London: Routledge, 1997.

del Mundo, Clodualdo. "The Film Industry Is Alive, Filipino Cinema Is Dead." In *The Urian Anthology 1980–1989,* edited by Nicanor G. Tiongson, 2–7. Manila: Antonio P. Tuviera and Manunuri ng Pelikulang Pilipino, 2001.

del Mundo, Clodualdo. "Philippine Movies in 2001: The Film Industry Is Dead! Long Live Philippine Cinema!" *Asian Cinema* 14, no. 1 (2003): 167–74.

De Mesa, Karl R. "Street Magic." In *Quiapo: Heart of Manila,* edited by Fernando Nakpil Zialcita, 125–47. Quezon City: Ateneo de Manila University, 2006.

Dennison, Stephanie, and Song Hwee Lim, eds. *Remapping World Cinema: Identity, Culture and Politics in Film.* London: Wallflower Press, 2006.

Deocampo, Nick. "Alternative Cinema." In *CCP Encyclopedia of Philippine Art,* Vol. 7, edited by Nicanor G. Tiongson and Joi Barrios, 58–67. Manila: Cultural Center of the Philippines, 1994.

Deocampo, Nick. *Cine: Spanish Influences on Early Cinema in the Philippines.* Quezon City: National Commission for Culture and the Arts, 2003.

Deocampo, Nick. *Films from a "Lost" Cinema: A Brief History of Cebuano Films.* Quezon City: Center for New Cinema, 2005.

Deocampo, Nick. *Film: American Influences on Philippine Cinema.* Quezon City: Anvil Publishing, 2011.

Desai, Jigna. *Beyond Bollywood: The Cultural Politics of South Asian Diasporic Film.* New York: Routledge, 2004.

de Valck, Marijke. *Film Festivals: From European Geopolitics to Global Cinephilia.* Amsterdam: Amsterdam University Press, 2007.

de Valck, Marijke, Brendan Kredell, and Skadi Loist, eds. *Film Festivals: History, Theory, Method, Practice.* London: Routledge, 2016.

Diaz, Robert. "*Biyuti* from Below: Contemporary Philippine Cinema and the Transing of *Kabaklaan.*" *TSQ: Transgender Studies Quarterly* 5, no. 3 (2018): 404–24.

Dick, Howard, and Peter Rimmer. "Beyond the Third World City: The New Urban Geography of South-east Asia." *Urban Studies* 35, no. 12 (1998): 2304–21.

Dolan, Jill. *Utopia in Performance: Finding Hope at the Theater.* Ann Arbor: University of Michigan Press, 2005.

Donald, James. *Imagining the Modern City.* Minneapolis: University of Minnesota Press, 1999.

Dressel, Björn. "The Philippines: How Much Real Democracy?" *International Political Science Review* 32, no. 5 (2011): 529–45.

Druick, Zoë. "At the Margins of Cinema History: Mobile Cinema in the British Empire." *Public* 40 (2009): 118–25.

Duncombe, Stephen. *Notes from Underground: Zines and the Politics of Alternative Culture.* New York: Verso Books, 1997.

Dyer, Richard. "In Defence of Disco." *Gay Left* 8 (1979): 20–23.

Eickelman, Dale F., and John W. Anderson. "Redefining Muslim Publics." In *New Media in the Muslim World: The Emerging Public Sphere*, edited by Dale F. Eickelman and John W. Anderson, 1–18. Bloomington: Indiana University Press, 1999.

Ellis, Paul. "Interstitials: How the 'Bits in Between' Define the Programmes." In *Ephemeral Media: Transitory Screen Culture from Television to YouTube*, edited by Paul Grainge, 59–69. New York: Palgrave Macmillan, 2011.

England, Marcia R., and Stephanie Simon. "Scary Cities: Urban Geographies of Fear, Difference and Belonging." *Social and Cultural Geography* 11, no. 3 (2010): 201–7.

English, James. *The Economy of Prestige: Prizes, Awards, and the Circulation of Cultural Value*. Cambridge, MA: Harvard University Press, 2005.

Ezra, Elizabeth, and Terry Rowden, eds. *Transnational Cinema: The Film Reader*. New York: Routledge, 2006.

Fantauzzo, Laurel. *The First Impulse*. Mandaluyong City, Philippines: Anvil Publishing, 2017.

Flores, Patrick D. "Philippine Cinema and Society." In *Filipiniana Reader*, edited by Priscelina Patajo-Legasto, 420–29. Quezon City: University of the Philippines Open University, 1998.

Flores, Patrick D. "Bodies of Work: Sexual Circulations in Philippine Cinema." *Humanities Diliman* 1, no. 1 (2000): 54–68.

Fraser, Nancy. "Rethinking the Public Sphere: A Contribution to the Critique of Actually Existing Democracy." *Social Text* 25/26 (1990): 56–80.

Friedberg, Anne. "Urban Mobility and Cinematic Visuality: The Screens of Los Angeles—Endless Cinema or Private Telematics." *Journal of Visual Culture* 1, no. 2 (2002): 183–204.

Galt, Rosalind, and Karl Schoonover, eds. *Global Art Cinema: New Theories and Histories*. Oxford: Oxford University Press, 2010.

Galt, Rosalind, and Karl Schoonover. "Introduction: The Impurity of Art Cinema." In *Global Art Cinema: New Theories and Histories*, edited by Rosalind Galt and Karl Schoonover, 3–30. Oxford: Oxford University Press, 2010.

Ganti, Tejaswini. *Producing Bollywood*. Durham, NC: Duke University Press, 2012.

Gaonkar, Dilip Parameshwar. "On Alternative Modernities." *Public Culture* 11, no. 1 (1999): 1–18.

Gaonkar, Dilip Parameshwar, and Elizabeth A. Povinelli. "Technologies of Public Forms: Circulation, Transfiguration, Recognition." *Public Culture* 15, no. 3 (2003): 385–97.

Garcia, Neil J. *Philippine Gay Culture: Binabae to Bakla, Silahis to MSM*. Quezon City: University of the Philippines Press, 2008.

Garrido, Marco. "Civil and Uncivil Society: Symbolic Boundaries and Civic Exclusion in Metro Manila." *Philippine Studies: Historical and Ethnographic Viewpoints* 56, no. 4 (2008): 443–65.

Gateward, Frances. "Wong Fei Hung in da House: Kung Fu Cinema and Hip Hop Culture." In *Chinese Connections: Critical Perspectives on Film, Identity, and*

Diaspora, edited by Gina Marchetti, Peter Feng, and Tan See-Kam, 51–67. Philadelphia: Temple University Press, 2010.

Genette, Gérard. *Paratexts: Thresholds of Interpretation*. Cambridge: Cambridge University Press, 2007.

Ghertner, D. Asher. "Why Gentrification Theory Fails in 'Much of the World.'" *City* 19, no. 4 (2015): 552–63.

Gonzaga, Elmo. "The Cinematographic Unconscious of Slum Voyeurism." *Cinema Journal* 56, no. 4 (2017): 102–25.

Gonzalez, Vernadette V. "Military Bases, 'Royalty Trips,' and Imperial Modernities: Gendered and Racialized Labor in the Postcolonial Philippines." *Frontiers: A Journal of Women Studies* 28, no. 3 (2007): 28–59.

Gould, Deborah. *Moving Politics Emotion and ACT UP's Fight Against AIDS*. Chicago: University of Chicago Press, 2009.

Grant, Catherine, and Annette Kuhn, eds. *Screening World Cinema: A Screen Reader*. Oxford: Routledge, 2006.

Gray, Jonathan. *Show Sold Separately: Promos, Spoilers, and Other Media Paratexts*. New York: New York University Press, 2010.

Grieveson, Lee. *Policing Cinema: Movies and Censorship in Early Twentieth-Century America*. Berkeley: University of California Press, 2004.

Grosz, Elizabeth. "Bodies/Cities." In *The Blackwell City Reader*, edited by Gary Bridge and Sophie Watson, 297–303. Malden, MA: Blackwell, 2002.

Guerrero, Rafael Ma. *Readings in Philippine Cinema*. Manila: Experimental Cinema of the Philippines, 1983.

Gupta, Akhil. "Blurred Boundaries: The Discourse of Corruption, the Culture of Politics, and the Imagined State." *American Ethnologist* 22, no. 2 (1995): 375–402.

Gutierrez, Eric, and Borras Saturnino Jr. *Moro Conflict: Landlessness and Misdirected State Policies*. Washington, DC: East-West Center Washington, 2004.

Habermas, Jürgen. *The Structural Transformation of the Public Sphere: An Inquiry into a Category of Bourgeois Society*. Cambridge, MA: MIT Press, 2009.

Halberstam, Jack. *The Queer Art of Failure*. Durham, NC: Duke University Press, 2011.

Halbwachs, Maurice. *On Collective Memory*. Translated by Lewis Coser. Chicago: University of Chicago Press, 1992.

Hansen, Miriam Bratu. *Babel and Babylon: Spectatorship and American Silent Film*. Cambridge, MA: Harvard University Press, 1994.

Harbord, Janet. *Film Cultures*. London: Sage, 2002.

Harvey, David. *Spaces of Hope*. Berkeley: University of California Press, 2000.

Harvey, David. *A Brief History of Neoliberalism*. Oxford: Oxford University Press, 2007.

Hau, Caroline S. "Dogeaters, Postmodernism, and the 'Worlding' of the Philippines." In *Philippine Post-Colonial Studies: Essays on Language and Literature*, edited by Christina Pantoja Hidalgo and Priscelina Patajo-Legasto, 113–27. Manila: University of the Philippines Press, 1993.

Hau, Caroline S. *Necessary Fictions: Philippine Literature and the Nation, 1946–1980*. Quezon City: Ateneo de Manila University Press, 2000.
Hau, Caroline S. *The Chinese Question: Ethnicity, Nation, and Region in and beyond the Philippines*. Singapore: National University of Singapore Press, 2014.
Hau, Caroline S. "Privileging Roots and Routes: Filipino Intellectuals and the Contest over Epistemic Power and Authority." *Philippine Studies: Historical and Ethnographic Viewpoints* 62, no. 1 (2014): 29–65.
Hebdige, Dick. "Fax to the Future." *Marxism Today*, January 1990, 18–23.
Hesmondhalgh, David. "Subcultures, Scenes or Tribes? None of the Above." *Journal of Youth Studies* 8, no. 1 (2005): 21–40.
Highmore, Ben. *Cityscapes*. London: Palgrave-Macmillan, 2005.
Higson, Andrew. "The Concept of National Cinema." *Screen* 30, no. 4 (1989): 36–46.
Higson, Andrew. "The Limiting Imagination of National Cinema." In *Cinema and Nation*, edited by Mette Hjort and Scott Mackenzie, 63–74. Abingdon, UK: Routledge, 2000.
Himpele, Jeff D. "Film Distribution as Media: Mapping Difference in the Bolivian Cinemascape." *Visual Anthropology Review* 12, no. 1 (1996): 47–66.
Himpele, Jeff D. *Circuits of Culture: Media, Politics and Indigenous Identity in the Andes*. Visible Evidence Series, vol. 20. Minneapolis: University of Minnesota Press, 2008.
Hjort, Mette. *Small Nation, Global Cinema: The New Danish Cinema*. Minneapolis: University of Minnesota Press, 2005.
Hjort, Mette. "On the Plurality of Cinematic Transnationalisms." In *World Cinemas, Transnational Perspectives*, edited by Natasa Durovicova, 12–33. London: Taylor & Francis, 2011.
Huffer, Ian. "'A Popcorn-Free Zone': Distinctions in Independent Film Exhibition in Wellington, New Zealand." In *Watching Films: New Perspectives in Movie-going, Exhibition and Reception*, edited by Albert Moran and Karina Aveyard, 279–94. Bristol, UK: Intellect, 2013.
Ileto, Reynaldo. "Towards a Nonlinear Employment of Philippine History." In *The Politics of Culture in the Shadow of Capital*, edited by Lisa Lowe and David Lloyd, 98–126. Durham, NC: Duke University Press, 1997.
Ileto, Reynaldo. "Orientalism and the Study of Philippine Politics." In *Knowing America's Colony: A Hundred Years from the Philippine War*, 41–65. Honolulu: Centre for Philippine Studies, 1999.
Ileto, Reynaldo. "On Sidel's Response and Bossism in the Philippines." *Philippine Political Science Journal* 23, no. 46 (2002): 151–74.
Ingawanij, May Adadol. "Dialectics of Independence." In *Glimpses of Freedom: Independent Cinema in Southeast Asia*, edited by May Adadol Ingawanij and Benjamin Kay, 1–14. Ithaca, NY: Cornell University Southeast Asia Program, 2012.
Ingawanij, May Adadol, and Benjamin McKay, eds. *Glimpses of Freedom: Independent Cinema in Southeast Asia*. Ithaca, NY: Cornell University Southeast Asia Program, 2012.

Jancovich, Mark, Lucy Faire, and Sarah Stubbings. *The Place of the Audience: Cultural Geographies of Film Consumption*. London: British Film Institute, 2003.

Jasper, James M. "Emotions and Social Movements: Twenty Years of Theory and Research." *Annual Review of Sociology* 37 (2011): 285–303.

Jenkins, Henry. "Pop Cosmopolitanism: Mapping Cultural Flows in an Age of Media Convergence." In *Globalization: Culture and Education in the New Millennium*, edited by Marcelo M. Suárez-Orozco and Desirée Baolian Qin-Hilliard, 114–40. Berkeley: University of California Press, 2004.

Joaquin, Nick. *Almanac for Manileños*. Manila: Mr and Ms, 1979.

Joaquin, Nick. *Manila, My Manila*. Makati City, Philippines: Bookmark, 1990.

Jou, Sue-Ching, Eric Clark, and Hsiao-Wei Chen. "Gentrification and Revanchist Urbanism in Taipei?" *Urban Studies* 53, no. 3 (2014): 560–76.

Kenway, Jane, and Deborah Youdell. "The Emotional Geographies of Education: Beginning a Conversation." *Emotion, Space and Society* 4, no. 3 (2011): 131–36.

Khoo, Gaik Cheng. "Just-Do-It-(Yourself): Independent Filmmaking in Malaysia." *Inter-Asia Cultural Studies* 8, no. 2 (2007): 227–47.

Khoo, Olivia. "Slang Images: On the 'Foreignness' of Contemporary Singaporean Films." *Inter-Asia Cultural Studies* 7, no. 1 (2006): 81–98.

Klinger, Barbara. *Beyond the Multiplex: Cinema, New Technologies, and the Home*. Berkeley: University of California Press, 2006.

Kraft, Herman Joseph S. "The Philippines: The Weak State and the Global War on Terror." *Kasarinlan: Philippine Journal of Third World Studies* 18, nos. 1–2 (2003): 133–52.

Kuhn, Annette. *Cinema, Censorship, and Sexuality, 1909–1925*. London: Routledge, 1988.

Kumar, Akshaya. "The Unbearable Liveness of News Television in India." *Television & New Media* 16, no. 6 (2015): 538–56.

Lahiri, Smita. "Rhetorical 'Indios': Propagandists and Their Publics in the Spanish Philippines." *Comparative Studies in Society and History* 49, no. 2 (2007): 243–75.

Lalu-Santos, Corazon. "Kambal na Disyerto: Ang Kolonyal na Kanon at Komersyalismo at ang Panimulang Pagpapaagos ng Mga Agos sa Disyerto" [Twin deserts: colonial canon and commercialism and the first streams of Mga Agos sa Disyerto]. *Kritika Kultura* 21/22 (2013/2014): 281–98.

Larkin, Brian. *Signal and Noise: Media, Infrastructure, and Urban Culture in Nigeria*. Durham, NC: Duke University Press, 2008.

Lee, Benjamin, and Edward Lipuma. "Cultures of Circulation: The Imaginations of Modernity." *Public Culture* 14, no. 1 (2002): 191–213.

Lico, Gerard. *Edifice Complex: Power, Myth and Marcos State Architecture*. Quezon City: Ateneo de Manila University Press, 2003.

Lico, Gerard. *Arkitekturang Filipino: A History of Architecture and Urbanism in the Philippines*. Quezon City: University of the Philippines Press, 2010.

Lim, Bliss Cua. "Sharon's Noranian Turn: Stardom, Embodiment, and Language in Philippine Cinema." *Discourse* 31, no. 3 (2009): 318–58.

Lim, Bliss Cua. *Translating Time: Cinema, the Fantastic, and Temporal Critique.* Durham, NC: Duke University Press, 2009.

Lim, Bliss Cua. "Gambling on Life and Death: Neoliberal Rationality and the Films of Jeffrey Jeturian." In *Neoliberalism and Global Cinema: Capital, Culture, and Marxist Critique*, edited by Jyotsna Kapur and Keith B. Wagner, 279–305. New York: Routledge, 2011.

Lim, Bliss Cua. "Archival Fragility: Philippine Cinema and the Challenge of Sustainable Preservation." *Kyoto Center for Southeast Asian Studies Newsletter* 67 (2013): 18–21.

Lim, Michael Kho. *Philippine Cinema and the Cultural Economy of Distribution.* London: Palgrave-Macmillan, 2019.

Lionnet, Françoise. "Thinking Through the Minor, Transnationally." In *Minor Transnationalism*, edited by Françoise Lionnet and Shu-mei Shih, 1–26. Durham, NC: Duke University Press, 2005.

Lionnet, Françoise, and Shu-mei Shih, eds. *Minor Transnationalism.* Durham, NC: Duke University Press, 2005.

LiPuma, Edward, and Thomas Koelble. "Cultures of Circulation and the Urban Imaginary: Miami as Example and Exemplar." *Public Culture* 17, no. 1 (2005): 153–79.

Lefebvre, Henri. *Writings on Cities.* Translated by Eleonore Kofman and Elizabeth Lebas. Oxford: Blackwell, 2000.

Lobato, Ramon. "Subcinema: Theorizing Marginal Film Distribution." *Limina* 13 (2007): 113–20.

Lobato, Ramon. *Shadow Economies of Cinema: Mapping Informal Film Distribution.* London: British Film Institute, 2012.

Lobato, Ramon. *Netflix Nations: The Geography of Digital Distribution.* New York: New York University Press, 2019.

Lobato, Ramon, and Michael Ryan. "Rethinking Genre Studies through Distribution Analysis: Issues in International Horror Movie Circuits." *New Review of Film and Television Studies* 9, no. 2 (2011): 188–203.

López, A. Ricardo, and Barbara Weinstein, eds. *The Making of the Middle Class: Toward a Transnational History.* Durham, NC: Duke University Press, 2012.

Lorente, Bea. "The Grip of English and Philippine Language Policy." In *The Politics of English in Asia: Language Policy and Cultural Expression in South and Southeast Asia*, edited by Lionel Wee, Robbie B. H. Goh, and Lisa Lim, 187–203. Amsterdam: John Benjamin, 2013.

Lumbera, Bienvenido. "Problems in Philippine Film History." In *Readings in Philippine Cinema*, edited by Rafael Ma Guerrero, 67–82. Manila: Experimental Cinema of the Philippines, 1983.

Lumbera, Bienvenido. "Introduction." In *Philippine New Wave: This Is Not a Film Movement*, edited by Khavn de la Cruz, 1–2. Quezon City: MovFest, 2010.

Lury, Karen, and Doreen Massey. "Making Connections." *Screen* 40, no. 3 (1999): 229–38.

Macapagal, Katrina. "The Slum Chronotope and Imaginaries of Spatial Justice in Philippine Urban Cinema." PhD diss., Queen Margaret University, 2017.

Macdonald, Charles J-H. "The Filipino as Libertarian Contemporary Implications of Anarchism." *Philippine Studies* 61, no. 4 (2013): 413–36.

Macleod, Gordon, and Kevin Ward. "Spaces of Utopia and Dystopia." *Geografiska Annaler* 84, nos. 3–4 (2002): 153–70.

Majul, C. A. *Muslims in the Philippines*. Manila: University of the Philippines Press, 1999.

Maltby, Richard, Daniël Biltereyst, and Philippe Meers, eds. *Explorations in New Cinema History: Approaches and Case Studies*. Malden, MA: Wiley-Blackwell, 2011.

Maltby, Richard, Melvyn Stokes, and Robert C. Allen, eds. *Going to the Movies: Hollywood and the Social Experience of Moviegoing*. Exeter, UK: University of Exeter Press, 2008.

Manalansan, Martin F. *Global Divas: Filipino Gay Men in the Diaspora*. Durham, NC: Duke University Press, 2003.

Marchetti, Gina. "Jackie Chan and the Black Connection." In *Keyframes: Popular Cinema and Cultural Studies*, edited by Matthew Tinkom and Amy Villarejo, 137–58. London: Routledge, 2001.

Massey, Doreen. *Space, Place and Gender*. Minneapolis: University of Minnesota Press, 1994.

Massey, Doreen. *For Space*. London: Sage, 2005.

Mathews, Jessica T. "Power Shift." *Foreign Affairs* 76 (January/February 1997): 50–66.

Matilac, Justino Dormiendo, and Nicanor G. Tiongson. "Audiences." In *CCP Encyclopedia of Philippine Art*, edited by Nicanor G. Tiongson and Joi Barrios, 99–100. Manila: Cultural Center of the Philippines, 1994.

McCoy, Alfred W. "Baylan: Animist Religion and Philippine Peasant Ideology." *Philippine Quarterly of Society and Culture* 10 (1982): 141–94.

McCoy, Alfred W., ed. *An Anarchy of Families: State and Family in the Philippines*. Madison: University of Wisconsin Center for Southeast Asian Studies in cooperation with Ateneo de Manila University Press, 1993.

McKay, Benjamin. "The Politics of Mirrored Metaphors: Flor Contemplacion and *The Maid*." *positions* 19, no. 2 (2011): 463–98.

Mehta, Monika. "Reframing Film Censorship." *Velvet Light Trap* 63 (Spring 2009): 66–69.

Mehta, Monika. *Censorship and Sexuality in Bombay Cinema*. Austin: University of Texas Press, 2011.

Michel, Boris. "Going Global, Veiling the Poor Global City Imaginaries in Metro Manila." *Philippine Studies* 58, no. 3 (2010): 383–406.

Mignolo, Walter D. "The Global South and World Dis/Order." *Journal of Anthropological Research* 67, no. 2 (2011): 165–88.

Miller, Toby. "Global Hollywood 2010." *International Journal of Communication* 1 (2007): 1–4.

Miller, Toby, Nitin Govil, John McMurria, Ting Wang, and Richard Maxwell. *Global Hollywood 2*. London: British Film Institute, 2005.

Mitchell, David. "The Annihilation of Space by Law." *Antipode* 29, no. 3 (1997): 303–35.

Mitchell, Timothy. "Society, Economy, and the State Effect." In *State/Culture: State Formation after the Cultural Turn*, edited by George Steinmetz, 76–97. Ithaca, NY: Cornell University Press, 1999.

Mouffe, Chantal. "Democratic Citizenship and the Political Community." In *Community at Loose Ends*, edited by Miami Theory Collective, 70–82. Minneapolis: University of Minnesota Press, 1991.

Muñoz, José Esteban. *Disidentifications: Queers of Color and the Performance of Politics*. Minneapolis: University of Minnesota Press, 1999.

Muñoz, José Esteban. *Cruising Utopia: The Then and There of Queer Futurity*. New York: New York University Press, 2009.

Naficy, Hamid. "Poetics and Practice of Iranian Nostalgia in Exile." *Diaspora: A Journal of Transnational Studies* 1, no. 3 (1991): 285–302.

Nagib, Lúcia. "Towards a Positive Definition of World Cinema." In *Remapping World Cinema: Identity, Culture and Politics in Film*, edited by Stephanie Dennison and Song Hwee Lim, 30–37. London: Wallflower Press, 2006.

Naremore, James. "Authorship." In *A Companion to Film Theory*, edited by Toby Miller and Robert Stam, 9–24. Oxford: Blackwell, 1999.

Neale, Steve. "Art Cinema as Institution." *Screen* 22, no. 1 (1981): 11–40.

Newman, Janet. "Going Public: People, Policy, and Politics." Inaugural lecture, Open University, May 18, 2005. https://www.youtube.com/watch?v=Ii9xp7In69U.

Newman, Michael Z. *Indie: An American Film Culture*. New York: Columbia University Press, 2011.

Obusan, Teresita. "A Multireligious Filipino Pilgrimage." In *Quiapo: Heart of Manila*, edited by Fernando Nakpil Zialcita, 148–71. Quezon City: Cultural Heritage Studies Program, Ateneo de Manila University, 2006.

Ong, Jonathan Corpus. *The Poverty of Television: The Mediation of Suffering in Class-Divided Philippines*. London: Anthem Press, 2015.

Pante, Michael D. "Quezon's City: Corruption and Contradiction in Manila's Prewar Suburbia, 1935–1941." *Journal of Southeast Asian Studies* 48, no. 1 (2017): 91–112.

Park, Bae-Gyoon, Richard Child Hill, and Asato Saito, eds. *Locating Neoliberalism in East Asia: Neoliberalizing Spaces in Developmental States*. Chichester, UK: Wiley-Blackwell, 2012.

Patajo-Legasto, Priscelina. "Discourses of 'Worlding' and Philippine Postcolonial Studies." In *Philippine Postcolonial Studies*, edited by Priscelina Patajo-Legasto, 3–17. Quezon City: University of the Philippines Press, 2007.

Patajo-Legasto, Priscelina. "Introduction." In *Philippine Studies: Have We Gone beyond St. Louis?*, edited by Priscelina Patajo-Legasto, ix–xiv. Quezon City: University of the Philippines Press, 2008.

Peranson, Mark. "First You Get the Power, Then You Get the Money: Two Models of Film Festivals." *Cinéaste* 33, no. 3 (2008): 37–43.

Perren, Alisa. "Rethinking Distribution for the Future of Media Industry Studies." *Cinema Journal* 52, no. 3 (2013): 165–71.

Peterson, Richard A. *Creating Country Music: Fabricating Authenticity*. Chicago: University of Chicago Press, 1999.

Pinches, Michael D. "The Working Class Experience of Shame, Inequality and People Power in Tatalon, Manila." In *From Marcos to Aquino: Local Perspectives on Political Transition in the Philippines*, edited by B. Kerkvliet and R. Mojares, 166–86. Honolulu: University of Hawai'i Press, 1991.

Polan, Dana. "The Public's Fear: Media as Monster in Habermas, Negt, and Kluge." In *The Phantom Public Sphere*, edited by Bruce Robbins, 33–41. Minneapolis: University of Minnesota Press, 1993.

Prashad, Vijay. *Everybody Was Kung Fu Fighting: Afro-Asian Connections and the Myth of Cultural Purity*. Boston: Beacon Press, 2001.

Pratt, Mary Louise. *Imperial Eyes: Travel Writing and Transculturation*. New York: Routledge, 2007.

Quimpo, Nathan Gilbert. *Contested Democracy and the Left in the Philippines after Marcos*. Yale Southeast Asian Studies Monograph no. 58. New Haven, CT: Yale University Southeast Asian Studies, 2008.

Rafael, Vicente. *Contracting Colonialism: Translation and Christian Conversion in Tagalog Society under Early Spanish Rule*. Durham, NC: Duke University Press, 1992.

Rafael, Vicente. *White Love and Other Events in Filipino History*. Quezon City: Ateneo de Manila University Press, 2000.

Rafael, Vicente. "The Cellphone and the Crowd: Messianic Politics in the Contemporary Philippines." *Public Culture* 15, no. 3 (2003): 399–425.

Rafael, Vicente. *The Promise of the Foreign: Nationalism and the Technics of Translation in the Spanish Philippines*. Durham, NC: Duke University Press, 2005.

Rajagopal, Arvind. *Politics after Television: Hindu Nationalism and the Reshaping of the Public in India*. Cambridge: Cambridge University Press, 2001.

Rajagopal, Arvind. "A 'Split Public' in the Making and Unmaking of the Ram Janmabhumi Campaign." In *The Indian Public Sphere: Readings in Media History*, edited by Arvind Rajagopal, 207–27. New Delhi: Oxford University Press, 2009.

Ramussen, Claire, and Michael Brown. "The Body Politic as Spatial Metaphor." *Citizenship Studies* 9, no. 5 (2005): 469–84.

Reyes, Emmanuel A. "The Truth out There: Short Films and Alternative Filmmaking in the '90s." In *The Urian Anthology, 1990–1999*, edited by Nicanor G. Tiongson, 84–89. Honolulu: University of Hawai'i Press, 2011.

Reyes, Raquel A. G. *Love, Passion and Patriotism: Sexuality and the Philippine Propaganda Movement, 1882–1892*. Seattle: University of Washington Press, 2008.

Rivera, Temario C. "Middle Class Politics and Views on Society and Government." In *Exploration of the Middle Classes in Southeast Asia*, edited by Hsin-Huang Michael Hsiao, 363–75. Taipei: Academia Sinica, 2001.

Robbins, Bruce. *The Phantom Public Sphere*. Minneapolis: University of Minnesota Press, 1993.

Robinson, Andrew. *Satyajit Ray: The Inner Eye; The Biography of a Master Film-Maker*. London: I. B. Tauris, 2004.

Robinson, Jennifer. *Ordinary Cities: Between Modernity and Development*. Abingdon, UK: Routledge, 2006.

Roces, Mina. *Kinship Politics in Postwar Philippines: The Lopez Family, 1946–2000*. Manila: De La Salle University Press, 2001.

Rosenberg, Scott. "Plex Drive." *Film Journal International* 110, no. 12 (December 2007).

Ross, Miriam. "The Film Festival as Producer: Latin American Films and Rotterdam's Hubert Bals Fund." *Screen* 52, no. 2 (2011): 261–67.

San Juan, E., Jr. "The Paradox of Multiculturalism: Ethnicity and Identity in the Philippines." Department of Comparative American Cultures, Washington State University, Pullman, April 18, 1999. https://www.univie.ac.at/Voelkerkunde/apsis/aufi/ethno/paradox.htm.

San Juan, E., Jr. "Ethnic Identity and Popular Sovereignty: Notes on the Moro Struggle in the Philippines." *Ethnicities* 6, no. 3 (2006): 391–422.

Sarkar, Baskar, and Joshua Neves, eds. *Asian Video Cultures: In the Penumbra of the Global*. Durham, NC: Duke University Press, 2017.

Schelzig, Karin. *Poverty in the Philippines: Income, Assets, and Access*. Asian Development Bank, 2005.

Scott, Allen. "The Shoe Industry of Marikina City, Philippines: A Developing Country Cluster in Crisis." Urban/Regional, University Library of Munich, Germany, 2005. EconPapers (website). Accessed April 23, 2020. http://EconPapers.repec.org/RePEc:wpa:wuwpur:0511003.

Scott, Ellen. "Censorship and Regulation." *Feminist Media Histories* 4, no. 2 (2018): 44–50.

Scott, James C. *Seeing Like a State: How Certain Schemes to Improve the Human Condition Have Failed*. New Haven, CT: Yale University Press, 1999.

Seki, Koki. "Difference and Alliance in Transnational Social Fields: Identity of the Filipino Middle Class." *Philippine Studies: Historical and Ethnographic Viewpoints* 60, no. 2 (2012): 187–222.

Sennett, Richard. *The Fall of Public Man*. New York: Random House, 1978.

Shackleton, Liz. "Indian Film's Tender Shoots." *Screen Daily*, July 1, 2010. https://www.screendaily.com/indian-films-tender-shoots/5015235.article.

Shackleton, Liz. "How Independent Filmmakers in Southeast Asia Are on the Rise." *Screen Daily*, September 11, 2019. https://www.screendaily.com/features/how-independent-filmmakers-in-southeast-asia-are-on-the-rise/5142223.article.

Sharma, Sarah. *In the Meantime: Temporality and Cultural Politics*. Durham, NC: Duke University Press, 2014.

Shatkin, Gavin. "The City and the Bottom Line: Urban Megaprojects and the Privatization of Planning in Southeast Asia." *Environment and Planning A* 40, no. 2 (2008): 383–401.

Shohat, Ella, and Robert Stam. *Unthinking Eurocentrism: Multiculturalism and the Media*. London: Routledge, 1994.

Sidel, John. "Response to Ileto: or, Why I Am Not an Orientalist." *Philippine Political Science Journal* 23, no. 1 (2001): 109–22.

Silliman, Sidney G., and Garner Lela Noble, eds. *Organizing for Democracy: NGOs, Civil Society and the Philippine State*. Honolulu: University of Hawai'i Press, 1998.

Silvestre, Patricia Brillantes. "Chronicle of Music in the Heart of Manila." In *Quiapo: Heart of Manila*, edited by Fernando Nakpil Zialcita, 148–71. Quezon City: Cultural Heritage Studies Program, Ateneo de Manila University, 2006.

Smith, Neil. *The New Urban Frontier: Gentrification and the Revanchist City*. Abingdon, UK: Routledge, 1996.

Springer, Simon. "Neoliberalism in Southeast Asia." In *Routledge Handbook of Southeast Asian Development*, edited by Andrew McGregor, Lisa Law, and Fiona Miller, 27–38. New York: Routledge, 2018.

Srinivas, S.V. "Is There a Public in the Cinema Hall?" *Framework: The Journal of Cinema and Media* 42 (2000b). Accessed June 20, 2020. https://www.frameworknow.com/vol-42.

Staiger, Janet. *Bad Women: Regulating Sexuality in Early American Cinema*. Minneapolis: University of Minnesota Press, 1995.

Steinmetz, George. *State/Culture: State Formation after the Cultural Turn*. Ithaca, NY: Cornell University Press, 1999.

Stewart, Susan. *On Longing: Narratives of the Miniature, the Gigantic, the Souvenir, the Collection*. Durham, NC: Duke University Press, 1993.

Swanson, Kate. "Revanchist Urbanism Heads South: The Regulation of Indigenous Beggars and Street Vendors in Ecuador." *Antipode* 39, no. 4 (2007): 708–28.

Tadiar, Neferti Xina. "Manila's New Metropolitan Form." *Differences: A Journal of Feminist Cultural Studies* 5, no. 3 (1993): 154–78.

Tadiar, Neferti Xina M. *Fantasy Production: Sexual Economies and Other Philippine Consequences for the New World Order*. Quezon City: Ateneo de Manila University Press, 2004.

Tadiar, Neferti Xina M. *Things Fall Away: Philippine Historical Experience and the Makings of Globalization*. Durham, NC: Duke University Press, 2009.

Tadiar, Neferti Xina M. "Life-Times of Disposability within Global Neoliberalism." *Social Text (115)* 31, no. 2 (2013): 19–48.

Tan, Katrina Ross A. "Constituting Philippine Filmic and Linguistic Heritage: The Case of Filipino Regional Films." In *Citizens, Civil Society and Heritage-Making in Asia*, edited by Hsin-Huang Michael Hsiao, Yew-Foong Hui, and Philippe Peycam, 137–63. Singapore: ISEAS–Yusof Ishak Institute, 2017.

Tannock, Stuart. "Nostalgia Critique." *Cultural Studies* 9, no. 3 (1995): 453–64.

Taussig, Michael. *The Nervous System*. Abingdon, UK: Routledge, 1991.

Taussig, Michael. *The Magic of the State*. Abingdon, UK: Routledge 1997.

Thornton, Sarah. *Club Cultures: Music, Media, and Subcultural Capital*. Middletown, CT: Wesleyan University Press, 1996.

Tiongson, Nicanor. "From Stage to Screen." *Philippines: International Popular Culture* 1 (1980): 60–67.

Tiongson, Nicanor. *The Cinema of Manuel Conde*. Manila: University of Santo Tomas Publishing House, 2008.

Tiongson, Nicanor. "The Best of Times, the Worst of Times: The Filipino Cinema in 1990–1999." In *The Urian Anthology, 1990–1999*, edited by Nicanor G. Tiongson, 2–43. Manila: Antonio P. Tuviera and Manunuri ng Pelikulang Pilipino, 2010.

Tolentino, Rolando. "Nations, Nationalisms, and *Los últimos de Filipinas*: An Imperialist Desire for Colonialist Nostalgia." In *Refiguring Spain: Cinema/Media/Representation*, edited by Marsha Kinder, 133–54. Durham, NC: Duke University Press, 1997.

Tolentino, Rolando. *Richard Gomez at ang Mito ng Pagkalalake, Sharon Cuneta at ang Perpetwal na Birhen at iba pang sanaysay hinggil sa bida sa pelikula bilang kultural na texto* [Richard Gomez and the masculine myth, Sharon Cuneta and the perpetual virgin and other essays on film stars as cultural texts]. Manila: Anvil Publishing, 2000.

Tolentino, Rolando. "Bomba Queens and National Development: A Genealogy of the Filipina Cinematic Body." *Review of Women's Studies* 11, nos. 1–2 (2001): 236–49.

Tolentino, Rolando. "The Capital Infrastructuring and Technologization of Manila." In *Cinema and the City: Film and Urban Societies in a Global Context*, edited by Mark Shiel and Tony Fitzmaurice, 158–70. London: Blackwell, 2001.

Tolentino, Rolando. *Kulturang Mall*. Manila: Anvil Publishing, 2004.

Tolentino, Rolando. "Piracy and Its Regulation: The Filipino's Historic Response to Globalization." Paper presented at the Asian Edition: A Conference on Media Piracy and Intellectual Property in Southeast Asia, University of the Philippines Film Institute, Manila, November 24, 2006. Accessed October 1, 2008. http://www.asian-edition.org/.

Tolentino, Rolando. "Macho Dancing, the Feminization of Labor, and Neoliberalism in the Philippines." *TDR: The Drama Review* 53, no. 2 (2009): 77–89.

Tolentino, Rolando. "Piracy Regulation and the Filipino's Historical Response to Globalization." *Social Science Diliman* 5, nos. 1–2 (2009): 1–25.

Tolentino, Rolando. "Cinema and the State in Crisis: Political Film Collectives and People's Struggle in the Philippines." In *Film in Contemporary Southeast Asia*, edited by David C. L. Lim and Hiroyuki Yamamoto, 199–216. Abingdon, UK: Routledge, 2012.

Torres, John. "Piracy Boom Boom." In *Glimpses of Freedom: Independent Cinema in Southeast Asia*, edited by May Adadol Ingawanij and Benjamin McKay, 63–72. Ithaca, NY: Cornell University Southeast Asia Program, 2012.

Tsing, Anna. "The Global Situation." *Cultural Anthropology* 15, no. 3 (2000): 327–60.

Tupas, Ruanni. "Bourdieu, Historical Forgetting, and the Problem of English in the Philippines." *Philippine Studies* 56, no. 1 (2008): 47–67.

Turner, Victor. *The Anthropology of Performance*. New York: PAJ Publications, 1986.

Turner, Victor. "Are There Universals of Performance in Myth, Ritual, and Drama?" In *By Means of Performance: Intercultural Studies of Theatre and Ritual*, edited by Richard Schechner and Willa Appel, 8–18. Cambridge: Cambridge University Press, 1990.

Uncertain Commons. *Speculate This!* Durham, NC: Duke University Press, 2013.

Van Beers, Henk. "A Plea for a Child-Centred Approach in Research with Street Children." *Childhood* 3, no. 2 (1996): 195–201.

Vergara, Raymond Allan G. "The Art of Mag:net." Paper presented at the Third De La Salle University Arts Congress, Manila, 2010. Accessed

June 20, 2020. https://scholar.google.com/scholar?oi=bibs&cluster=8180896201588420294&btnI=1&hl=lv.

Verhoeven, Deb. "Film Distribution in the Diaspora: Temporality, Community and National Cinema." In *Explorations in New Cinema History: Approaches and Case Studies*, edited by Richard Maltby, Daniel Biltereyst, and Philippe Meers, 243–60. Malden, MA: Wiley-Blackwell, 2011.

Veric, Charlie Sumaya. "The Fictions of Necessity." *Kritika Kultura* 1 (2002): 101–4.

Virilio, Paul. "The Third Window: An Interview with Paul Virilio." In *Global Television*, edited by Cynthia Schneider and Brian Wallis, 185–97. Translated by Yvonne Shafir. Cambridge, MA: MIT Press, 1981.

Vitali, Valentina, and Paul Willemen. "Introduction." In *Theorising National Cinema*, edited by Valentina Vitali and Paul Willemen, 1–16. London: BFI Publishing, 2006.

Walzer, Michael. "Pleasures and Costs of Urbanity." *Dissent* 33 (1986): 470–75.

Warner, Michael. *Publics and Counterpublics*. Cambridge: Zone Books, 2005.

Wasson, Haidee. *Museum Movies: The Museum of Modern Art and the Birth of Art Cinema*. Berkeley: University of California Press, 2005.

White, Mimi. "Television Liveness: History, Banality, Attractions." *Spectator* 20 (1999): 38–56.

Whitehead, Judy. "Rent Gaps, Revanchism and Regimes of Accumulation in Mumbai." *Anthropologica* 50, no. 2 (2008): 269–82.

Wilinsky, Barbara. "'A Thinly Disguised Art Veneer Covering a Filthy Sex Picture': Discourses on Art Houses in the 1950s." *Film History* 8, no. 2 (1996): 143–58.

Wilinsky, Barbara. *Sure Seaters: The Emergence of Art House Cinema*. Minneapolis: University of Minnesota Press, 2001.

Williams, Raymond. *Marxism and Literature*. Oxford: Oxford University Press, 1976.

Wong, Cindy Hing-Yuk. *Film Festivals: Culture, People, and Power on the Global Screen*. New Brunswick, NJ: Rutgers University Press, 2011.

Zialcita, Fernando Nakpil. *Authentic though Not Exotic: Essays on Filipino Identity*. Quezon City: Ateneo de Manila University, 2005.

Zialcita, Fernando Nakpil. *Quiapo: Heart of Manila*. Manila: Cultural Heritage Studies Program, Department of Sociology and Anthropology, Ateneo de Manila University, 2006.

Zialcita, Fernando Nakpil. "Revitalizing the City through Heritage." In *Quiapo: Heart of Manila*, edited by Fernando Nakpil Zialcita, 15–39. Quezon City: Cultural Heritage Studies Program, Ateneo de Manila University, 2006.

Zukin, Sharon. "Consuming Authenticity: From Outposts of Difference to Means of Exclusion." *Cultural Studies* 22, no. 5 (2008): 724–48.

Zukin, Sharon. "Changing Landscapes of Power: Opulence and the Urge for Authenticity." *International Journal of Urban and Regional Research* 33, no. 2 (2009): 543–53.

INDEX

Page numbers in italics refer to figures.

Abinales, Particio N., 194
ABS-CBN, 8, 26, 208, 209, 251n15, 274n38; Skylight Films, 232–33
Abu-Lughod, Lila, 31
Abu-suki, term usage, 106–7
aca-fan discourse, 249n118
access, fantasies of, 34, 74, 128, 170; Quiapo's, 83, 96–102, 111, 115
Acland, Charles, 67–68, 73, 116, 120, 140, 222, 263n19
activist films, 135–37, 157, 165–68, 169–71
aestheticization, 91, 102, 106
agency, 10, 126, 137
agos, term usage, 43
Alix, Adolf, 15, 76, 181
alterity, 86–87, 90–91, 96, 102
alternative film movements, 10, 237
alternative films, term usage, 9
Amoroso, Donna J., 194
Anak Dalita (The Ruins) (1956), 226

Anderson, Benedict, 28, 212, 248n106, 272n84
Anderson, John W., 81
Andrew, Dudley, 148, 241n6
Ang Babae sa Septic Tank (2011), 36, 193, 198, 200–205, 215, 220, 277n64
Angeles City, 39–40
Ang mga kidnaper ni Ronnie Lazaro (2012), 36, 193, 198–200, 204–5, 220
Ang Nawawala (What Isn't There) (2012), 88
animated films, 144, 167
anticensorship discourses, 163, 164, 174, 182, 187
anti-obscenity bills, 176
Aquino, Benigno, III, 155–56, 189–90, 194, 196, 217
Aquino, Corazon, 161, 168, 180, 208
Aquino, Kris, 190, 196
Arguelles, Ronald, 173, 176

Arroyo, Gloria Macapagal, 161–62, 166, 186, 189, 254n71
Arroyo administration, 87; censorship and, 35, 154, 167–68; instability and decline, 156, 159, 162–63, 186–87, 189–90; presidential election (2004), 155–56; violence and corruption, 136, 161–62, 189, 268n9, 268n20
art-culture system, 244n57
art galleries, 126, 145, 150, 264n45. *See also* Mag:net Galleries and Café
art-house cinema, 5, 104, 145, 178, 179, 226, 238; absent audiences, 3; aesthetics, 91, 127, 129, 264n45; class dimension, 129–30; films, 6, 15; homogeneity, 36; modernist, 94, 230; nostalgia and, 130; paradox of, 244n57; politics of location, 14. *See also* Indie Sine; Mogwai Cinematheque
Artikulo Uno Productions, 233, 234
artistic merit, 176, 181–85
Asian Film Commissions Network (AFCNet), 219
Asian Video Cultures (Sarkar/Neves), 12
Asiaweek, 49, 50
Assarat, Aditya, 245n69
asymptomatic film culture, 6, 11, 12, 18, 21, 41
asymptote model, 11, 243n49
Athique, Adrian, 67
audiences: acceptability, 210; alternative film, 80, 121, 156, 160; behavior, 61–63; as citizens, 55–56, 194, 227; filmmakers and, 16, 23, 76–77; gay, 36, 159, 163, 179–86; global, 178–79; good vs. bad, 54, 59, 63–64, 210; homogenization of, 148; infantilized, 55, 77–78, 174, 251n29; "maindie," 232–33; Malaysian independent film, 28; mall multiplex, 40–41, 54; middle-class, 41, 60–61, 64; niche, 159, 182, 235; prospective, 153, 160, 170, 184, 234; rationality of, 162, 163, 173, 187; repetition and, 134; social hierarchies and, 115, 120, 175; specialist, 76, 257n147; texts and, 145, 155; Thai, 28; Western metropolitan, 16–17; youth, 157–58. *See also* cinemagoing; local audiences; mass audiences
authenticity: alternative film cultures and, 80, 82–83, 91; consumer, 95–96; cultural, 15, 16, 92, 111, 193; filmic production of, 200, 204–5; insider-outsider relations, 106; nationalist, 78; problem of, 98; Quiapo's urban-cinematic, 33–34, 82–84, 86, 92–94, 109, 112; travel and, 104; of urban space, 33, 103
autonomy, 82, 96, 103, 208, 210; local, 218, 220; from the mainstream, 98, 102
Ayala Corporation, 48, 251n36

"bad audiences," 40, 47, 59, 60, 210, 251n29; alternative film's notion of, 77–78; of revanchist cinema, 41, 45, 53, 69, 154
Bagong Agos Film Festival, 74–75, 166; inaugural festival, 43–44, 69–70; programming, 70, 71, 73–74
Bagong Lipunan (New Society) Improvement of Sites and Services (BLISS), 42
Baguio Casa Vallejo Hotel, 225–26
bakal (metal) boys, 124
bakla, term usage, 25, 186, 272n72
Bakla Review, 182–84
Balita, Carl E., 235
Banes, Sally, 117, 262n6
banning of films: for political content, 35, 157, 165–68; for sex and nudity, 172–77, 182, 184
Barnett, Clive, 22
Barros Sanchez, Sigfried, 198, 199–200, 215
Baudelaire, Charles, 119
Baumgärtel, Tilman, 90–91
Bautista, Ato, 24, 247n97
Bautista, Mario E., 180–81

Behar, Ruth, 31
Bello, Walden, 51, 237, 273n16
belonging, class, 106
Benedicto, Bobby, 124
Benjamin, Walter, 93
Bernardo, Sigrid Andrea, 136, 233, 265n55
Biglang-awa, Pablo, 76
Black Maria Cinema, 235
Blanco, Jose, 28
blogs, 49, 125, 133, 166, 177; on "gay films," 182, 184–85; on Quiapo DVD market, 98–99, 101, 108–9; Tioseco's, 1
Blossoming of Maximo Oliveros, The (2005), 24–27, 209, 247n98
body politic: alternative film scene and, 162; the city as, 163–64; metaphoric function of, 160, 163, 269n23; national, 188; Philippine and Singaporean, 158, 160–61, 163; speculative publics and, 35, 160
bohemians, 35, 117, 123–26, 130, 145–46, 262n6
Bohinc, Nika, 37–38, 249n122
Bollywood, 67, 108, 280n30
Bonifacio Global City, 149
Bourdieu, Pierre, 95
bourgeois publics, 53, 81, 82, 84, 91, 95
box-office revenues, 64–66, 214, 233–34, 277n64
Boyer, Christine, 126
Brocka, Lino, 15, 74, 172, 180, 274n30
Brown, Wendy, 10
Buck-Morss, Susan, 13
Burgos, Jonas, 135, 136, 165, 170, 264n53

Cabagnot, Ed, 73, 75, 210
Calma, Hector Barretto, 234
Camaligan, Ric, 55–56, 60, 66
Campos, Patrick, 30
Cannes Film Festival, 14–15, 16, 97, 173–74, 263n37; *Chacun son cinéma*, 128; Mendoza's victories, 230–31; Palme d'Or prize, 181, 271n70

Capino, José B., 233–34
capitalism, 10, 18, 94, 120, 126
Caruncho, Eric S., 98
Castro, Jade, 213, 252n45
CBRC Dream Theater, 235
cell phones, 25, 57, 61
censorship, 128, 152, 193; of activist films, 165–68, 169–71; circulation and, 157–58, 171–72; free zones, 36, 114, 159, 179, 186; of "gay films," 179–86; of local feature-length films, 157, 171–78; MTRCB and the state, 155–56, 186–87; Singapore state, 248n103; spatial dimensions of, 155, 157, 163, 171, 184; strategic rationality and, 36, 158
Center for Media Freedom and Responsibility (CMFR), 268n20
chance and contingency, 33, 52–53, 56, 58, 71, 145
Chatterjee, Partha, 29, 75
children, 132, 146, 148, 201
Chinese businessmen, 7–8, 77–78, 242n30
Chinese Exclusion Act, 242n30
Chow, Rey, 27
Christmas, 117, 139, 265n60, 266n67
Cinekatipunan, 35, 113, 127, 148–49, 152; regularity and ritual and, 34, 131; screenings, 117, 132–38, 134, 142, 165
Cinema '76 Film Society, 234
Cinema Centenario, 234
cinemagoing, 2, 34–35, 109, 129, 223, 243n52; admission fees, 48, 59, 61, 135, 181, 216, 235; in Cubao Expo, 124, 126; decline in, 54–55, 59–60, 253n60; ephemerality of, 131; mall multiplex, 40, 47, 48, 66; protocols and behavior, 60–64, 146; ritual of, 121, 131, 141; surveillance and, 59
Cinemalaya, 4, 192–93, 196, 233, 247n94; casting decisions, 209, 210; criticism, 210–13, *211*; Cultural Center of the Philippines and, 8, 36, 213, 251n15;

Cinemalaya (*continued*)
 funding, 8, 208, 214, 251n15; Philippine Independent Film Festival, 36, 127, 193, 208, 209; screenings, 24, 37; structure and institutional identity, 205–9; theatrical runs, 276n62
Cinemanila International Film Festival, 172, 173, 175, 186–87, 206
Cinema One Originals, 4, 8, 173, 233, 251n15, 274n38
Cinema Rehiyon, 278n103
cinema studies, 11, 12, 20, 30–31, 33, 129, 154, 243n52
circulation: censorship and, 157–58, 171–72, 178; city as a space of, 164, 170; domestic cinema, 191, 192, 217; imaginaries, 112; informal, 1, 82; initiatives, 12, 21, 34, 35, 120, 160, 193, 239; institutionalization of, 191–92; local, 3, 151, 179, 221, 237; media, 4, 12, 22–23, 46, 111–12; problems, 5, 11, 16, 19, 20, 152; Quiapo as a site of, 91, 95, 98, 104; role in alternative film culture, 84, 95, 158, 231, 239; space, 32, 35, 103, 154, 165, 237; temporalities, 22, 117, 137, 140, 234; of texts, 22–23, 46; transnational, 3, 171–72, 174, 177, 198, 230; world cinema as, 27
civil society, 29, 48, 75, 216–17; micro, 134, 138
class. *See* elitism; social divisions
Co, Teddy, 31, 278n103
Cojuangco, Antonio, 8, 208, 214, 251n15
collective memory, 93, 118, 120–21; nostalgia and, 116, 126, 130–31, 145, 150–51
collective reception, 3, 45–46, 52
collectivity, 18, 19, 142–43, 245n72
colonization, 18, 19, 26, 87, 223, 245n72, 248n105; feudalism and, 175; mobile cinema and, 222; state formation and, 194–95; treatment of Moro people, 104, 106
commercialism, 64, 72, 73, 139, 141

community: alternative film, 131, 159; artistic, 176; bohemian, 117, 262n6; building, 114, 142; gated, 51; gay, 182, 185–86; clubs, 146; geographic proximity and, 140; national, 18–19, 245n72; of sentiment, 152
Conception, K. C., 123
Conde, Manuel, 245n67
condominiums, 10, 51, 149–50
coños, term usage, 108, 261n69
consumer culture, 115–16, 123–24, 126, 131, 227; global, 44, 56
consumers: of alternative cinema, 98; audiences as, 64, 77; authenticity and, 95–96; autonomy of, 102; DVD vendors and, 82, 86, 98–99, 106–9; mall multiplex, 33, 47, 49–52; mass, 115–16, 134; middle-class, 40, 47, 51, 54–55, 61, 66, 82–83, 90; power, 53; solidarity, 112; wealthy, 63, 255n99
corporate funding, 8, 206, 208, 251n15
cosmopolitanism, 48, 50, 67, 69, 80, 88, 90, 103; alternative film culture, 92, 98, 99, 100–101, 117; compulsory or obligatory, 172, 178, 182; of Cubao Expo, 150; of Mag:net Galleries and Café, 132; popular, 82, 120, 126, 130, 263n19; Quiapo's, 84, 94, 98; taste cultures, 83
counterpublics: competing, 53; Quiapo and, 81–82, 84, 86, 94, 116; solidarity, 112; speculative, 34, 82–83, 88, 95, 112, 131, 146
crime, 108–9, 259n21
Criticine, 1, 2, 37
crowd, the, 56–59, 62, 68, 72, 77, 115; control of, 49–50, 53. *See also* masses, the
Cruz, Denise, 81
Cruz, Edgar O., 14–16
Cruz, Oggs, 25, 210
Cubao Expo ("Cubao X"): appeal and magnetism of, 130; closure, 149–50; description of, 113, 117, 145; location

and maps, 48, 121, *122*; spatial timeline and nostalgia of, 116, 123, 124–26, 131; theaters, 12
cult cinema, 88, 89
Cultural Center of the Philippines (CCP), 119, 158–59, 178, 179, 209–10; Cabagnot of, 73, 210; connection to Cinemalaya, 8, 36, 205, 213, 251n15

Dalena, Kiri, 133, 135, 170
daluyan, term usage, 75
David, Joel, 160, 172
David, Randy, 18, 217, 245n72
Dayao, Dodo, 255n101
Day in the Life of Gloria Arroyo, A (Southern Tagalog Exposure), 167, 170–71
Death in the Land of Encantos (2007), 157, 171, 174–78
decentralization, 218–19, 224–25, 227–28
Dela Cruz, Emmanuel, 71–72
de la Cruz, Khavn, 2, 23, 26–27, 179
Deleuze, Gilles, 164, 269n26
del Mundo, Clodualdo, 43, 169, 178, 268n8
democracy, 11, 13, 18, 75, 212; censorship and, 184, 185; elitist tendencies and, 13, 95, 101, 110, 244n57; open spaces and, 23; political society and, 75–76; post-martial-law, 166, 168, 189
Deocampo, Nick, 74–75, 159, 169, 256n112, 256n126, 268n14
Desai, Jigna, 178
Diaz, Lav, 15, 23–24, 29, 44, 179, 212; *Death in the Land of Encantos,* 157, 171, 174–78
Diaz, Robert, 186
Dick, Howard, 51
difference: authenticity and, 80; class and ethnic, 84–85, 90, 102, 103, 106–9; cultural, 81, 84; familiarity and, 25; Filipino, 73; "indie," 78; spatial and temporal, 12
digital technologies, 8, 17, 74

Diokno, Pepe, 232
disorder, usefulness of, 52, 253n55
distances, 83, 86, 90, 102–3, 112, 127–28
distribution: audience social hierarchies and, 115, 120; challenges, 28, 235; channels, 26, 69, 100, 231; control of, 7–8; industrial film, 120, 204, 234; informal media, 87; institutional ideal for, 228; local, 3, 178–79, 191, 217; networks, 2, 35, 120, 140; online, 23, 30, 247n94; and production distinction, 261n4; Quiapo's role in, 83, 84, 90; scholars, 115; state involvement, 217–18; temporality of, 34, 115, 261n3
Dogeaters (Hagedorn), 249n117
Dolan, Jill, 133–34
domestic audiences. *See* local audiences
Domingo, Eugene, 202–3
Donald, James, 52
Du, Dominic, 65
Duncombe, Stephen, 103
Duterte, Rodrigo, 40, 156, 236, 249n2, 280n23, 280n26
DVD trade: access and choice, 98–99; cinemagoing decline and, 55, 60; government-sponsored releases, 1; international networks, 90–91; Quiapo vendors, 33, 84–85, *85,* 97, 97–98, 101, 106–9, 112; raids and shutdown, 37, 87–90, 106, 111; wealth and, 63, 255n99
"DVD X" (video), 79, 88, 89
Dy, Philbert, 265n63
Dychiu, Stephanie, 101
Dyer, Richard, 151

economic policy, 10
economy, 67, 256n116; global, 7, 98; market, 18; political, 51, 102; preliberalization, 125, 130
EDSA (Epifanio de los Santos Avenue), 42, 75, 123, 164, 250n12; revolutions, 44, 57, 254n71, 269n27

INDEX   303

education, 23–24, 132, 142–43; of audiences, 1, 36, 153, 159, 205, 235; censorship and, 179–81, 184; cinema pedagogy, 74–76; film access and, 89, 157–58; spaces, 170–71
egalitarianism, 13
Eickelman, Dale F., 81
elitism, 63, 90, 160, 199, 238, 241n5; democratic tendencies and, 13, 95, 101, 110, 213, 244n57; in India, 67; international, 14, 157; nationalists, 81–82; political society and, 28–29, 75; radicalism and, 5, 29, 110, 131, 231
embodiment discourses, 158, 161–62
emotionality, 158, 161–62, 171, 268n14, 272n84
English, James, 270n50
ephemerality, 30, 58, 119, 131, 149, 188
Estrada, Joseph "Erap," 57, 58, 144, 168, 190, 212, 254n71
ethnicity, 8, 77–78, 248nn106–7; and markers of difference, 84–85, 90, 102, 103, 106–9
ethnic minorities, 33, 45, 116, 231; elite nationalists and, 81–82; Muslim communities, 80, 81–82, 86–87, 92, 223–24; working-class, 83, 96
exhibition space: alternative, 112, 114–15, 118, 142–43; art-house, 129–30, 264n45; censorship-free, 179–86; economic sustainability of, 159; ephemerality and utopianism of, 148–51; for independent films, 2, 3, 169–71, 234–37; labor and, 142–43; lack of, 157–58; multiplex, 33, 40; regional theaters, 225–26; spatial timelines and, 121, 123–26; state-funded, 119; texts and paratexts, 22–23. *See also* mobile cinema; public exhibition; street exhibitions
exhibitors, 59–60; Chinese businessmen, 7–8, 77–78; largest cinema, 51–52; vision of multiplex audiences, 54, 55

Experimental Cinema of the Philippines (ECP), 192, 269n28

failures, 18–19, 238
family, 18, 73, 245n72, 257n133
Farmers Plaza, 48–49
Festival of Filipino Films, 266n65
feudalism, 19; mainstream film industry and, 17, 23, 212; MTRCB and, 174–75, 177
Film Academy of the Philippines, 65–66
Film Development Council of the Philippines (FDCP), 65–66, 192, 196–97, 206, 216, 266n65; decentralization model, 218–19, 224–25, 228; future vision, 227; localization goal, 217; National Cinematheque project, 225–26; Sineng Pambansa project, 37, 193, 199, 218, 220–23, 227; Tawi-Tawi festival, 223–25
film festivals: funding, 4, 14, 191, 197–98, 206, 214, 274n38; international, 1–3, 171, 179, 197–98, 241n6; Malaysian, 28; online streaming services and, 247n94; regional, 221–23, 278n103. *See also name of festival*
financial crisis (1997), 10, 65, 125, 243n47
Fonds Sud Cinema, 15, 244n66
foreign films: audiences, 193, 200, 233; blacking out, 138–40, 266n65; festival circuits, 192–93, 197–99, 200; imports, 7, 77; middle-class patrons, 64; revenues, 64–66. *See also* mainstream film industry
form and content, 24–26
For the First Time (2008), 123
Fort McKinley, 149
Fraser, Nancy, 21, 53, 81, 95
freedom, 185, 208, 211
French New Wave, 94, 98–99

Gallaga, Peque, 74, 127, 263n36
Galt, Rosalind, 14
Ganti, Tejaswini, 67

Gaonkar, Dilip, 239
García Canclini, Néstor, 218
Garrido, Marco, 47
Gateway Mall, 49–50
"gay films," 36, 76, 159, 179–86, 215, 262n13
gentrification, 13, 45, 67, 102
Ghertner, D. Asher, 102
global cinema. *See* world cinema
globalization, 69, 91, 110, 120, 126, 256n122; decentralization under, 228; urbanization within, 67
global south, 5, 12, 69, 102, 179, 239; films and filmmakers from, 3, 15, 193, 198; incomplete modernities of, 13, 28, 157; mass audience in, 16; term usage, 242n10
"good audiences," 54, 63, 64, 80, 210; traits of, 40, 59, 61
government sponsorship, 206, 215, 221–22, 225
Grainge, Paul, 30
Greater Manila Theaters Association, 7
Greenwich Village, 117, 262n6
Grosz, Elizabeth, 269n23
Guattari, Félix, 164, 269n26
Guillen, Laurice, 206, 209, 213, 259n21
Gupta, Akhil, 216

Habermas, Jürgen, 20, 246n83, 247n87
hacienderos, 23, 208, 212
Halberstam, Jack, 18
Hansen, Miriam, 45–46, 52, 63
Harbord, Janet, 145, 244n57
Hau, Caroline S., 19–20, 78, 85, 242n30, 246nn81–82, 249n117
Henares, Quark, 37–38, *114*
Heneral Luna (2015), 233, 234
Hesmondhalgh, David, 244n57
Hill, Adrian, 67
Himpele, Jeff, 12, 120, 131, 134
Hiroshima Mon Amour (1959), 94, 230
historiography, Philippine, 17–20, 29, 246n81

Hollywood films, 64, 77, 128, 191, 219–20; blockbusters, 9, 116, 207; distribution, 7, 140; independent films and, 71, 72, 215–16, 234; mall multiplexes for, 44, 48, 251n17; piracy and, 27, 99–100; saturation of, 65, 66; translation of, 63
Holy Bingo (2007), 167–68
home, notion of, 70–71; for independent cinema, 43, 71–73, 75
human rights. *See Rights* (2007)

ideal publics, 4–5, 44, 131, 154, 165, 172; alternative cinema's, 47, 180, 210; IFC's construction of, 41, 45, 51; Indie Sine's vision of, 53, 57, 70, 75–76, 79; for national cinema, 153, 192, 215
identity: Cinemalaya's, 208–9, 210; class, 47; collective, 18, 80, 93, 120, 134; cosmopolitan, 102; Cubao Expo's, 125–26; cultural, 15, 92, 161, 172, 204, 210, 262n6; ethnic, 81; Indie Sine's, 69; institutional, 145; Mogwai Cinematheque's, 121, 128, 131; national, 14–15, 18, 31, 81, 86, 94, 187, 246n81
Ileto, Reynaldo, 29, 47, 245n72
Ilocos Norte festival, 221–22
imaginaries: audience, 40, 56, 143; cinema, 7, 159, 160, 180; ethnicized, 8; film culture, 158; global city, 47, 51–52, 252n51; national, 19–20, 161, 246n82; political, 163–64; public, 30, 53, 160–61, 193, 222; Quiapo's new, 33, 80, 83, 98, 100–101, 110, 112; urban cultural, 164, 269n26
Imahe Nasyon (2006), 44, 75
Imburnal (Sewer) (2008), 8–9, 157, 171, 172–73, 176, 186–87
Independencia (2009), 15
Independent Filmmakers' Multipurpose Cooperative (IFC), 59, 76, 78, 166–67; Daluyan Awards, 73, 75; founding, 250n4; Indie Sine project, 33, 41, 43, 46, 79

independent films: aesthetics and clichés, 200, 236, 279n12; audiences, 71–72, 76, 232; casting of mainstream actors for, 209; censorship and ratings, 163, 167–70, 172–80; Cinemalaya's practices and, 207–13; economic sustainability, 159; highest-grossing, 9, 204, 233, 265n55; international circulation of, 13–15; local filmmakers, 74, 199–204; production and venues, 8–10, 232–35; Southeast Asian, 28; state support and, 215–16. *See also* Indie Sine; "maindie"

India, 67, 68, 256nn116–17, 280n30

Indie Sine, 134, 143; activist events, 157, 165, 169; cinema pedagogy and, 74; closure, 76; founding, 33, 41, 56, 124; idea behind, 34, 35, 115, 250n4; ideal publics and, 57, 70, 75–76; and ideas of home, 43–44, 70–73; MTRCB and, 169–70. *See also* Bagong Agos Film Festival

informal settlements, 42, 45, 50, 250n12, 252n42, 274n29

infrastructures: circulation, 26, 151; distribution and exhibition, 27, 90, 153, 157–58, 204, 236; globalized, 227; instability, 237, 238; institutional, 14, 205; media, 9; Quiapo's, 86; shortcomings, 2, 6; state, 194, 208, 215; urban, 57, 164

Ingawanij, May Adadol, 96

institution-ideal, 193–94, 214, 215, 225; decentralization and, 227–28

Intellectual Property Office (IPO), 59

inter-Asia cultural studies movement, 219

International Film Festival Rotterdam (IFFR), 98, 179

internet, 30. *See also* online streaming

Jamora, Marie, 88
Jardin, Nestor O., 178, 213
jeepney, 42, 103, 108, 210, 250n9; cinema-home routes, 71–72
Jenkins, Henry, 249n118, 263n19
Jimenez, Chitz, 166–67
Joaquin, Nick, 93, 103
journalism, 21, 30, 137, 166–67, 171; entertainment, 14, 175, 207, 209, 232

kabaklaan, definition, 186
Katipunan Avenue, 132, 262n6
Khoo, Gaik Cheng, 28, 248n105
Kidnappers of Ronnie Lazaro, The. See *Ang mga kidnaper ni Ronnie Lazaro* (2012)
Kinatay (2009), 15
kinship, 18, 245n72
Kita Kita (2017), 233
knowledge dissemination, 165, 167, 168–70, 180, 187
Koelble, Thomas, 164, 269n26
Kontra-Agos Film Festival, 35, 157, 166, 166–68, 169, 187

labor: child, 148; conditions, 51, 252n45; exhibition spaces and, 142–43; exploitation, 212, 275n50; overseas Filipino workers (OFWs), 160–61, 210; time, 262n11
Laguardia, Consoliza, 162, 165, 175
Lambino, Marichu C., 181–82
Lang, Moira, 72, 215–17, 265n63
Lapoirie, Jeanne, 15
Larkin, Brian, 12, 222
Last Temptation of Christ, The (1988), 180
Lauzon, Nonoy, 64
League of Filipino Students, 136
Lee, Maggie, 205
Lee, Ricky, 209
leisure, 145, 148, 223, 226, 227; time, 119, 142, 143; urban, 67, 124, 129–30
Leon, Mike de, 74, 75, 88, 274n30
Lim, Alfredo, 37, 49, 50, 111
LiPuma, Edward, 164, 269n26
liveness, notion of, 157, 168–69
Liway (2018), 214
Lobato, Ramon, 100

local audiences, 2, 6, 9, 14, 25, 158; absent, 24; economic sustainability and, 159, 198, 209, 214, 216; educating, 205; local films for, 141, 142, 200, 201, 205; for maindie films, 232–33; middle-class patrons, 64; mobile cinema for, 220–23; urgency and, 214–15

local film industry: censorship and, 171–77; distribution and exhibition, 3, 171, 174, 178–79, 191, 217, 225–26; elite interest in, 63; filmmakers, 198–204; financial strain, 6–7; funding for, 179; ideal state and, 215–17; inclusive vs. divided, 232; regionalization, 219–20; revenues and growth, 64–66, 159; role in Philippine culture, 156; seasonal film festivities and, 139–40, 265n60; venues, 234–35. *See also* local audiences

local government units (LGUs), 218, 221, 223, 227–29

Locarno International Film Festival, 182, 271n70

location, politics of, 14

Los Otros, 234

Lost and Found (Bernardo), 136–37

LSBYTTHS (Lady Sitting behind You Talking to Her Seatmate), 62–63

Lumbera, Bienvenido, 157–58

Macdonald, Charles J-H, 18

MacLeod, Gordon, 54

Maddin, Guy, 26

Mag:net Galleries and Café, 34, 113, 132–35, 142, 149, 264n45

"maindie," 4, 190, 232–33, 265n55

mainstream film industry: alternative cinema vs., 140–42, 210; Chinese importers, 77–78; Cinemalaya's contrast to, 207, 208; commercialism, 64; decline, 8; as feudal, 17, 23, 212; financial strain, 6–7, 9; local, 232–34; mass audiences and, 138; overdeveloped, 123–24; piracy and, 100; shared values and, 3; the state and, 86, 90; ticket sales, 65. *See also* Hollywood films

mainstream media industries, 87, 97, 100, 123–24, 127–28

Malate, 144–46, 266n86

Malaysian independent films, 28, 248n105

mall multiplexes: amusements, 253n61; Bagong Agos events, 43–44; class hierarchies and, 13, 48–49, 51, 60–64; closures, 66; competing visions of, 32–33; development in Manila, 39, 41–43, 49–50, 50, 66, 250n12; festivals held at, 221, 256n126; as home, 70, 75; Indian, 67; for information dissemination, 168; for political demonstrations, 56–59, 163; for potential audiences, 40, 74, 76; private/public spaces of, 52–53, 56; revanchism and, 54, 56, 130; speculative publics and, 46; state malls compared to, 227; as a streetscape, 71, 72; themed space of, 67–68

Manalansan, Martin, 25

Manhattan Garden City, 149–50

Manzano, Edu, 87, 88–89, 89, 258n15

Marasigan, Raymund, 89

Marcos, Ferdinand, 139, 161, 165, 168, 269n28

Marcos, Imee, 190, 192

Marcos, Imelda, 8, 42, 190, 211–12, 213, 269n28

marginalization, 84, 231; community, 18, 179, 185–86; economic, 27, 248n105

Marikina Shoe Expo, 113, 125, 126, 150

markets: consumer, 44, 51, 54; elite, 63; gray, 88–89, 90, 100; local or domestic, 65, 125; multiplex, 66; piracy, 74; speculation and, 11

martial law, 6, 44, 87, 165–66, 180, 192, 245n72; Cinemalaya compared to, 211–12; end of, 74, 163; revolutions, 57, 269n27

Martin, Raya, 15, 25, 97, 179
Martinez, Chris, 203
mass audiences, 7, 27, 77, 138, 139, 160, 163; absent, 12, 16, 23; histories of political revolution and, 11, 12, 13, 17, 21–22; nation building and, 16, 19
masses, the, 19, 159, 186, 222; educating, 23, 157, 264n45; mall multiplexes and, 62, 63, 68, 69; middle class and, 48, 57
Massey, Doreen, 23, 52–53, 143, 253n55
mass medium, 46–47, 69, 117
Matti, Erik, 114, 127, 144, 211–13, 235, 263n37
Maynila (2009), 15
McCoy, Alfred, 245n72
McKay, Benjamin, 160–61
McLuhan, Marshall, 117
media studies, 11, 12, 20, 22, 30–31, 154
megaprojects, 49–50
melodrama, 268n14
Mendiola (Sine Patriyotiko), 167, 170–71
Mendoza, Brillante, 3, 39, 249n2, 259n21; alliance with Duterte, 236, 280n26; festival awards, 15, 181–82, 230–31, 271n70
Metro Manila: City Hall, 140; gay district, 146; mainstream media in, 123–24; mall development, 41–43, 48–51, 250n12; neoliberal policies, 39; as a revanchist city, 32–33, 41; social divisions, 13; urban development, 47, 53, 56–57, 82, 123, 146
Metro Manila Film Festival (MMFF), 64, 117, 138–42, 206–7, 255n101, 258n15, 265n63
Metro Manila Theater Association (MMTA), 7
Mga Agos sa Disyerto (short-story collection), 43
microcinemas, 34, 123, 127, 196, 234–37
middle class, 69, 81; audiences, 28, 41, 64, 67, 146, 157; cinemagoers, 129–30; consumers, 40, 47, 51, 54–55, 66, 82–83, 90; the crowd and, 57, 59; filmmakers, 29, 193, 199, 201, 204; global, 54, 94; growth in, 54; ideas of childhood, 146, 148; intellectuals, 13, 82, 124; optimism, 190; in Quiapo, 33, 86, 103, 104, 108; term usage, 47–48
Mignolo, Walter, 242n10
Milby, Sam, 123
Miller, Toby, 254n82
Mindanao, 87, 91
Mitchell, Timothy, 195
MNL 143 (2012), 210, 213
mobile cinema, 144, 188, 220–23, 226, 229
mobility, 46, 103, 108, 144, 164; culture of, 196
modernity, 5, 11, 12, 18, 81, 142, 188; achieved, 214, 229; colonial projects of, 222; cosmopolitan, 129; global, 52, 68, 95, 106, 239; historical, 131; incomplete, 13, 22, 28, 29, 157; India, 67; malls and, 51–52, 227; Manila, 43; middle-class, 61; multisided, 119; non-Western, 75; pirated cinema trade and, 91, 106; Quiapo and, 92; travel and, 104; urban, 119
Mogwai Cinematheque, 34, 114; closure, 149–51; Film Festival, 117, 138, 140–42, 222; identity, 121, 131, 261n1; location, 121; opening, 125; programming and decor, 127, 127–31
Morales, Paul, 76
Morato, Manoling, 180
Moros, 81, 104. *See also* Muslim community
Mouffe, Chantal, 11
Movie and Television Review and Classification Board (MTRCB), 114, 127–28, 136, 150, 169, 269n28; classification system, 76–77, 257n147; conflicts with alternative film scene, 35, 135, 159, 160; employee protests, 162–63; regulations and censorship, 165–70, 171–85; speculative publics

and, 154, 158; state relations, 155–56; UPFI and, 36, 179–86
moviegoing. *See* cinemagoing
movie palaces, 129, 226
Movie Producers Distributors Association of the Philippines (MPDAP), 6, 253n67
Mowelfund, 144, 256n126
Muhammad, Amir, 28, 248n105
multiculturalism, 92, 231; Quiapo's, 33–34, 80, 81–84, 104, 106, 111
music scene, 88, 133
Muslim community: DVD vendors, 2, 33–34, 79–80, 98, 101, 106–9, 112, 258n15; elite nationalists and, 81–82; national cinema and inclusion and, 223–25; population in Quiapo, 79–80, 86–87; violence and oppression, 34, 85, 104, 106
mythologizing, 26, 93, 94, 259n21

Naficy, Hamid, 126
Nagib, Lúcia, 14
national audience, 19, 78, 142, 154, 177, 200; absent, 3, 18, 23, 235; state institutions and, 206, 215–16, 217
national cinema, 2, 13–14, 58, 76, 187–88, 231; aspirational, 3, 27; as a cultural tool, 223–25; failure of, 78; formation, 191–92, 216, 227; ideal of, 211, 237; publics for, 41, 51, 77, 79, 153, 211; regional circuits for, 223, 229, 278n103; role of state in, 192, 196–97
National Commission for Culture and the Arts (NCCA), 31, 144, 278n103
national culture, 4, 58, 154, 179, 196, 206, 208; importance of circulation in, 19–20; peace building and inclusion, 223–25
nationalism, 31, 120, 194, 218, 232, 246n81; as affective attachment, 187; elite, 81–82; *ilustrado*, 81; Quiapo and, 93–94, 99; revolutionary, 17–20

national publics, 86, 112, 117, 231, 232; formation of, 46; ideals of, 41, 51, 77, 79, 153, 211; rationality of, 126, 187; the state's vision of, 193, 195, 217
National Union of Journalists of the Philippines (NUJP), 170
nation building, 16, 19
Nebrida, Vincent, 234
neoliberalism, 4, 9, 10, 18, 33, 273n16; policy, 39, 57, 70, 231; sex trade and, 40; temporality and, 41, 118–19, 121, 262n11; urbanism or cityscapes and, 45–47, 69, 71, 151
Network for the Promotion of Asia Pacific Cinema (NETPAC), 247n94
networks: of affinity, 34; alternative film, 46, 83; circulation, 27; distribution, 2, 35, 74, 120, 140; exhibition, 164, 244n57; industrial, 120; local, 247n91; magazine, 132; piracy, 90; transnational, 87, 90, 156; urban, 3, 4, 12; virtual, 30
Neves, Joshua, 12
Newman, Michael Z., 95, 244n57
Noel, Florencio, 59–60
No Other Woman (2011), 9
nostalgia: aesthetics of, 152; of Cubao Expo, 116, 123, 124–26; heterogeneity of, 130; of Mogwai Cinematheque, 129, 131, 150; of Sinemusikalye, 145; symbolic ownership through, 126
Now Showing (2008), 97, 97–98, 179
nudity, 172, 175–77, 180–81, 185

Ocampo, Ambeth, 261n69
Ochoa, Redd, 3, 16
100 (2008), 203
Ong, Jonathan, 259n30
online streaming, 4, 23, 37, 165, 169, 247n94
Optical Media Board (OMB), 106, 258n15; Quiapo raids, 37, 87–89, 89, 109, 111; surveillance strategy, 59
otherness. *See* alterity

Padilla, Robin, 224
Padilla, Rustom, 72
Pag-Asa, 42
pang-masa (of the masses), 62–63, 68, 72
paradox of alternative cinemas, 5, 17, 28, 29, 116, 206; overcoming, 11, 121, 146, 196, 220
paratexts. *See* texts and paratexts
Paris Cinema Festival, 178
Pascual, Piolo, 233, 265n55
passionate observation, 30–32
People's Park, 250n12
Perfumed Nightmare (1977), 16–17, 72
Perren, Alisa, 261n4
Philippine Motion Picture Producers Association (PMPPA), 6, 253n67
Philippine New Wave (de la Cruz), 23, 26–27
piracy: anti-piracy strategies, 59, 253n67; "cam copies," 89–90, 253n67; danger and criminality of, 109; film access and, 89, 99; of Hollywood films, 27, 254n82; markets, 74; moviehouse decline and, 55; networks, 90–91; Quiapo DVD market, 2, 37, 98–102, 106–10, 154; state regulation and, 87–89; USTR watch list, 249n121
Plaza Miranda, 55–56, 59, 93, 140, 269n27
Poe, Fernando, Jr., 155–56
Poe-Llamanzares, Grace, 155–56
Polan, Dana, 246n83
political revolutions, 19–20, 22, 56–58, 254n71. *See also* activist films; social movements
political society, 28–29, 75, 242n10
pornography, 90, 124, 176, 184, 258n16; gay, 180–81, 182; "poverty," 193, 203, 249n2
poverty, 10, 42, 213, 275n50; global north/south differences, 242n10; rates, 274n29; representations in film, 193, 201–5, 236, 249n2, 274n26, 274n30

Povinelli, Elizabeth A., 239
power relations, 21, 104, 179, 222
privatization, 32, 41, 47, 49, 59
producers, 6–8, 65
property development, 49–51, 149–50
public culture, 3, 13, 16, 35, 82, 232; cinema as a site of, 45–46; ideals of, 80, 84, 231; spaces of circulation and, 22–23
public exhibition, 187; for gay cinema, 183–84; liveness and urgency of, 168–70; prohibiting, 155, 165–66, 168
publics: alternative cinema's, 3, 6, 38, 117, 191, 192, 193; circulation and, 20–21, 24, 46, 239; creating or building, 131, 132, 157; as divided, 28–29, 157; domestic, 36, 172, 191, 196, 206, 236; egalitarian, 33, 40; mall multiplex, 32–33, 56–57, 67; mass, 56, 68, 112, 159, 161, 162, 163, 164; as necessary and impossible, 5; as paradoxical, 22; prospective or potential, 34, 36, 120, 163, 182, 231, 235, 238; the state's view of, 35, 177. *See also* counterpublics; ideal publics; national publics; speculative publics
public sphere, 20, 21, 28, 45, 137, 187, 246n83; bourgeois, 53, 81, 95; globalized, 13; Hindu, 248n108; phantom, 5
purity and danger, 103, 110
pusong babae (female heart), 25, 247n99

quality films, 179, 181–186, 196
Quezon City, 2, 37, 113, 132, 183, 264n53; theaters, 66, 124; Trinoma mall, 31, 42, 250n12
Quezon City Film Development Commission (QCFD), 206
Quiapo: alterity, 86–87, 90–91, 96, 102; alternative culture's contradictions and, 95; Cinematheque, 94, 97, 99–100, 109, 111–12; cultural representations, 93–94, 230; DVD vendors and buyers, 2, 33, 85, 97, 101, 106–9;

experiences of ethnic difference, 84–85, 102, 103, 106–9; films set in, 97, 199, 259n21; Muslim population, 79–80, 86–87, 101; OMB raids, 37, 87–88, 109, 111; as a site of media access, 96–102; travel and map of, 104, 105; urban-cinematic authenticity, 33–34, 82–84, 92–94, 109–10. *See also* Plaza Miranda

Quiapo Pirated DVD (QPDVD) website, 109, *110*

Rafael, Vicente, 46, 57–59, 60, 63, 68, 195
Rajagopal, Arvind, 28–29, 248n108
Rakenrol (2011), 37–38, *114*
Ramos administration, 7, 10, 161, 168
ratings system: PG-13, 77, 167, 171; R-rating, 76–77, 173, 183, 257n147; X-rating, 163, 167–68, 170, 172–77, 182, 183
Reality Entertainment, 127, 263n37
Regal Films, 23, 127, 208, 263n36
regionalization, 218–23, 229, 278n103
regularity, 34, 131, 133–34, 137, 142
Remedios Circle, 117, 144, 146, 262n6
repetition, 35, 132, 134, 136, 142, 148
Resnais, Alain, 84, 230
revanchist cinema, 32, 47, 56, 66, 68, 71; bad audiences of, 41, 45, 53, 69, 154
revanchist city, 119, 121; concept, 45, 54, 251n19; control and, 56; Manila as, 32, 33, 41, 130; neoliberal, 46, 69, 118
Reyes, Emerson, 210, 213
Reyes, Raquel A. G., 81
Ricketts, Ronnie, 111
Rights (2007), 35, 157, 165–67, 170–71
Rimmer, Peter, 51
ritual: film festivals and, 138–42; moviegoing, 39, 40, 117, 121, 131, 142; time and seasonal, 118, 119, 120–21, 148
Rivera, Temario, 48
Roadmap for Philippine Film Development, 59

Robbins, Bruce, 5
Robinson, Jennifer, 252n51
Robinsons Galleria, 43, 44, 56–57, 58, 72, 173, 253n61, 262n13
Roces, Mina, 245n72

Sacris, Lyle, 144
Salazar, Zeus, 245n72
Sanchez, Sherad Anthony, 8, 157, 171, 172–73, 186–87
San Diego Asian Film Festival, 182, 272n70
Sandwich (band), 79, 88–89, *89*, 133
San Juan, E., Jr., 16, 92, 104
Santa Santita (2004), 259n21
Santos, Angelo and Patricia, 235
Santos, Briccio, 217–19, 225–27
Santos, Enrico, 232–33
Sarkar, Bhaskar, 12
Schoonover, Karl, 14
Seki, Koki, 47
Service (Serbis) (2008), 39–40, 181, 271n70
sex trade, 39–40, 146
Shangri-La Plaza cinemas, 61, 63, 250n4
shared values, 3
Sharma, Sarah, 143
Shatkin, Gavin, 49, 252n40
shoe industry, 125
shopping history, 124–26
Short Film about the Indio Nacional, A (2005), 25–27
Signed, Lino Brocka (1987), 205
Siguion-Reyna, Armida, 175–77
Siguion-Reyna, Carlitos, 170–71
silent cinema, 26, 45, 63
Sinemusikalye, 35, 143–46, *147*, 148
Sineng Pambansa (National Cinema), 37, 188, 192–93, 199, 218, 220–23, 227
Singapore, 160–61, 247n94, 248n103
Smith, Neil, 41, 45, 251n19
SM Prime Holdings, 51–52, 66

social divisions, 19, 27, 32, 46, 210, 238, 246n81; among audiences and, 60–64, 67, 115, 120; the crowd and, 58; DVD consumers and, 63, 255n99; global south, 5, 242n10; mall multiplexes and, 47–51, 68; in Manila, 13, 41

social movements, 132, 135, 154, 155, 171, 268n21; Free Jonas Burgos Movement, 165, 170, 264n53; "People Power" revolutions, 58, 163, 190, 254n71, 269n27; spaces for, 164

solidarity, 110, 112, 169

Solito, Auraeus, 24, 180

Southern Tagalog Exposure, 132, 133, 135, 167, 170

space: censorship and, 155, 159; circulation, 6, 23, 95, 164, 269n26; consumer, 39, 41, 50; education, 170–71; Lefebvre on, 121; liminal, 145; mall multiplex, 50–51, 67, 71, 73–74, 168; material, 91–92, 95; media and, 144; memory and, 131; national, 99; and passage of time, 126; public, 46, 51, 52–53, 56, 57, 59, 70, 148; separation and, 124, 184; single-minded and open-minded, 52–53, 58; state regulation of, 164; surveillance, 59; themed, 67–68; transnational, 13, 24. *See also* exhibition space; urban space

special economic zones (SEZs), 40, 52, 249n1

speculation, concepts, 9–11, 41, 46, 118

speculative fiction, 9

speculative publics: alternative cinema's, 11–12, 37, 79, 115, 165, 235; circulation initiatives and, 21, 24, 160, 211; concept of, 9, 29; construction of, 32, 35, 71, 131; emergence of, 8, 163; gay community and, 186; locality and, 69, 118; mall multiplexes and, 32–33, 46, 51, 54, 68; MTRCB and, 154, 158; national film culture's, 96, 154, 237; Quiapo and, 80, 82, 83, 98, 110; the state and, 35–36, 207, 229

Spring Films, 233, 265n55

stand-alone theaters, 39–40, 119, 124, 225–26, 262n13

Star Cinema, 43, 69, 204, 216, 232–33, 276n62; film production, 9, 123, 127, 208, 263n37

state, the: activist films and, 136–37; alternative film scene and, 154–56, 159–60, 196–97; Cinemalaya and, 206–13; cinephiles and, 88–89, 128; in the city, 163–64; corruption, 174, 180, 188, 211–12, 273n16; ideal of, 195–97, 207, 215, 220–22, 226, 229; irrationality of, 157, 160–62, 164, 168, 171, 187; magic of, 195, 222, 228; MTRCB and, 155–56, 162–63, 186–87; Muslims and, 86, 87, 106, 154, 223, 258n15; national cinema formation and, 192–94, 223–25, 236; parochialism of, 172, 177; power, 112, 187, 194, 195, 196, 222; retreat of, 57; role in film circulation, 36–37, 164, 166, 170, 174; speculative publics and, 35–36, 207, 229

state formation: Philippines' transition (2010), 189–91; postcolonial contexts, 194–95

state institutions, 86, 177, 191–95, 207, 217, 220

Stewart, Susan, 136

strategic rationality, 35–36, 158, 161–62, 165, 169, 179, 182

streaming services. *See* online streaming

street exhibitions, 143–46, 147, 148

subcultures, 88, 116, 117, 124, 126, 151, 184, 231. *See also* bohemians

subjunctive mood, 116, 117, 144, 145

Sumayao, Marco, 214

Sundance Film Festival, 25

surveillance, 32, 49, 59, 69, 114, 154

Swanson, Kate, 45, 53

Sy, Henry, 42, 51

synchronicity, 142; of film release dates, 34, 115, 116; global, 119–20, 140, 148

Tadiar, Neferti, 19–20, 41, 118, 123, 213–14, 262n11
Tahimik, Kidlat, 16–17, 71–72, 74
Tan, Katrina, 228, 278n103
Tannock, Stuart, 130
taste cultures, 5, 83, 100, 102, 129
Taussig, Michael, 195, 222, 228
Tawi-Tawi, 224–25
tax, 6–7, 55, 59–60, 215
television shows, 88, 259n30
temporality: collective memory and, 116; of everyday life, 136, 137; exhibition sites and, 114, 121, 131, 142, 148; of film circulation, 22, 34, 115, 119–20, 131–38, 140, 234–36, 261n3; of immediacy, 237; of labor, 146; localized, 140, 152; neoliberalism and, 41, 118–19, 121, 262n11; speculative publics and, 29, 35; subjunctive, 20; uneven politics of, 143; urban, 117
texts and paratexts, 22–23, 152, 155, 231; cinematic or filmic, 30, 40, 73, 96, 145; circulation of, 46, 71; urgency and, 169
Thai films, 28
That Thing Called Tadhana (2014), 233
theater owners, 7, 55, 234–35
Three Days of Darkness (2007), 167
Tiongson, Nicanor, 7, 245n67, 268n14
Tioseco, Alexis, 138, 140–41; Criticine magazine and blogs, 1, 2, 37, 235, 241n5; death, 37–38, 249n122
Tirador (2007), 259n21
Tolentino, Rolando, 13, 50, 106, 157, 161, 196, 237
transnational festival circuit, 3, 36, 154, 164, 210, 212, 228; constructions of authenticity and, 204–5; institutionalization and, 191–93; local filmmakers and, 197–99, 200–203
transnationalism, 177, 191, 231; minor, 256n123; obligatory, 171–72, 197; regionalization, 219–20
transportation, 42, 48, 103, 123, 250n9. *See also* jeepney
travel and travel writing, 104, 108–9, 112, 123
Trinoma mall, 31, 42, 250n12
Tropical Malady (2004), 28
Tsing, Anna, 256n122
Turner, Victor, 117, 144, 145

Uncertain Commons manifesto (2013), 9–10
Unitel, 25, 259n21
universalism, 24–25
universities, 132, 137, 163, 264n46
University of the Philippines Film Institute (UPFI), 36, 158–59, 173, 178, 179–86, 187
Unkabogable Praybeyt Benjamin, The (2011), 9
urban development, 47, 49–50, 53, 56–57, 82, 94, 123. *See also* revanchist city
urbanism, 80, 114; global, 92, 96; Manila's, 46, 112; neoliberal, 45, 47, 69, 71
urban space, 4, 41, 99, 149; authenticity of, 33, 103; circulation and, 111, 115, 164, 170, 269n26; collective memory and, 126; histories, 116, 120–21, 150; Manila's, 13, 46–47; mobility and, 164; revitalization, 42, 45, 112, 146
U.S. Office of the Trade Representative (USTR), 37, 87–88, 90, 154, 249n121
utopian visions, 11, 14, 112, 192, 228; of alternative exhibition sites, 145, 148–49, 151; aspirations, 116, 188, 195; of the crowd, 58–59; FDCP's, 219; of local film culture, 139–40; performance and, 133; of Quiapo's DVD market, 84, 86, 98

Variety, 176, 202
VCDs, 1, 4, 55, 100, 107
Venice International Film Festival, 177–78

Vergara, Raymond Allan G., 264n45
Verhoeven, Deb, 120
Veric, Charlie Samuya, 16–17, 246n82
Viddsee platform, 247n94
Villaluna, Paolo, 43, 74
Villegas, Antonio, 139
violence: of Arroyo administration, 136, 162, 187, 268n9; of Duterte administration, 236–37, 280n26; interethnic, 34, 84; of Marcos regime, 168; murder, 37–38, 249n122
Virilio, Paul, 123
visibility, global, 27, 248n103
Vitali, Valentina, 188
Viva Entertainment, 208, 233
vulnerable observer, 31

Walzer, Michael, 52
Ward, Kevin, 54
Warner, Michael, 22, 53, 71, 81, 137
Wave Festival, 74
wealth, 63, 67, 108, 255n99
Western privilege, 104
Willemen, Paul, 187–88
Williams, Raymond, 238
Woman in the Septic Tank, The. See *Ang Babae sa Septic Tank* (2011)
working-class filmmakers, 199
world cinema, 2–3, 14, 15, 226, 230; access to, 83, 99; circulation of, 27, 110; festival circuit's role, 198, 202
writing culture, 31

Zafra, Jessica, 139
Zialcita, Fernando Nakpil, 93, 245n72
Zlotowski, Rebecca, 173–74
Zombadings (2011), 215, 277n64
Zuilhof, Gertjan, 98
Zukin, Sharon, 103, 104, 109

www.ingramcontent.com/pod-product-compliance
Lightning Source LLC
Chambersburg PA
CBHW051048230426
43666CB00012B/2612